Business and Bureaucracy in a Chinese City

CHINA RESEARCH MONOGRAPH 43

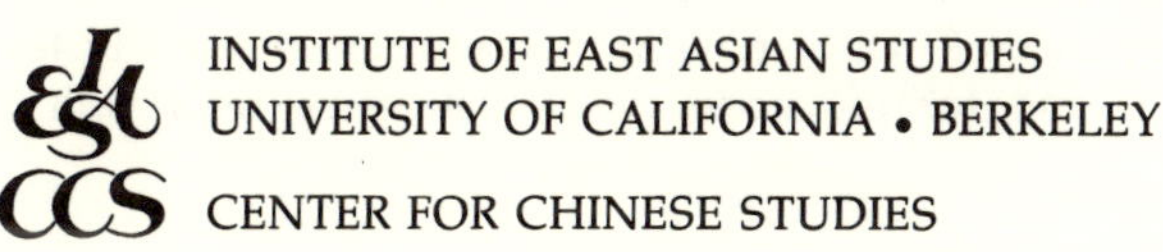

Business and Bureaucracy in a Chinese City

An Ethnography of Private Business Households in Contemporary China

OLE BRUUN

A publication of the Institute of East Asian Studies, University of California, Berkeley. Although the Institute of East Asian Studies is responsible for the selection and acceptance of manuscripts in this series, responsibility for the opinions expressed and for the accuracy of statements rests with their authors.

Correspondence may be sent to:
Joanne Sandstrom, Managing Editor
Institute of East Asian Studies
University of California
Berkeley, California 94720

The China Research Monograph series, whose first title appeared in 1967, is one of several publications series sponsored by the Institute of East Asian Studies in conjunction with its constituent units. The others include the Japan Research Monograph series, the Korea Research Monograph series, the Indochina Research Monograph series, and the Research Papers and Policy Studies series. A list of recent publications appears at the back of the book.

Library of Congress Cataloging-in-Publication Data

Bruun, Ole.
Business and bureaucracy in a Chinese city : an ethnography of private business households in contemporary China / Ole Bruun.
p. cm. — (China research monograph : 43)
Revision of the author's thesis (doctoral)—Copenhagen, 1990.
Includes bibliographical references and index.
ISBN 1-55729-042-3
1. Business anthropolog—China—Ch'eng-tu. 2. Urban anthropology—China—Ch'eng-tu. 3. Family-owned business enterprises—China—Ch'eng-tu—Management. 4. Bureaucracy—China—Ch'eng-tu. 5. Ch'eng-tu (China)—Economic conditions. 6. Ch'eng-tu (China)—Social conditions. I. Title. II. Series: China research monographs ; no. 43.
GN635.C5B83 1993
302.3'5'095138—dc20 93-31927
CIP

Printed in the United States of America

Contents

Acknowledgments

The present study was made possible by a generous scholarship from the Research Council of the Danish International Development Agency (DANIDA) for the 35-month period from January 15, 1987, to December 15, 1989. The Cristian and Ottilia Brorson's Travel Foundation supported a short stint of fieldwork performed in 1991. The research included a development study combined with an anthropological investigation of a contemporary urban Chinese community. The outcome of the research was submitted to the Department of Anthropology, University of Copenhagen, as a Ph.D. thesis in 1990. I am grateful to supervisory committee members Susan Whyte, Søren Clausen, and Steven Sampson for valuable criticism. I am also indebted to Professor Thomas B. Gold for his constructive comments on the final manuscript and to Managing Editor Joanne Sandstrom for her conscientious work.

The data were collected during three months of fieldwork in the spring of 1987 and another three months in the autumn of 1987. A series of follow-up interviews was conducted in May 1988 and an additional three months of fieldwork in the spring of 1989, specifically aimed at interviewing the young people in the area. In 1991 the overall situation was investigated. Thanks are due to the Sichuanese authorities for issuing all pertinent permits for accomplishing this fieldwork.

The practical arrangements for fieldwork in Chengdu — interviewing owners and employees of private businesses as well as officials responsible for controlling the individual economy, meeting with Chinese scholars, and investigating all possible sources of information — were made in cooperation with the Sichuan Academy of Social Science, which also provided excellent assistance in conducting the interviews. In addition, a number of people from the University of Sichuan, also in the provincial capital of Chengdu, have helped out and provided inspiration in certain stages or aspects of the research.

I would like to extend very special thanks to my Chinese assistants Liu Jinshi, Zhang Xiangrong, and Chen Beimin for their painstaking work and tolerant attitude toward the many arduous tasks involved in our research.

Note

Transliteration: Chinese *pinyin* romanization is used throughout, except when such disturbs the reading of names and concepts for which other spellings have been established in Western languages. Quotations are kept in their original form. Quotes of local speech and proverbs are shown in the common language, *kouyu*.

Names: All personal names have been changed to protect the identities of the local people and other interviewees.

Dr. Ole Bruun is a researcher at the Nordic Institute of Asian Studies, 84 Njalsgade, DK-2300, Denmark. The title of his latest monograph is *Fengshui and the Chinese Nature* (Forthcoming).

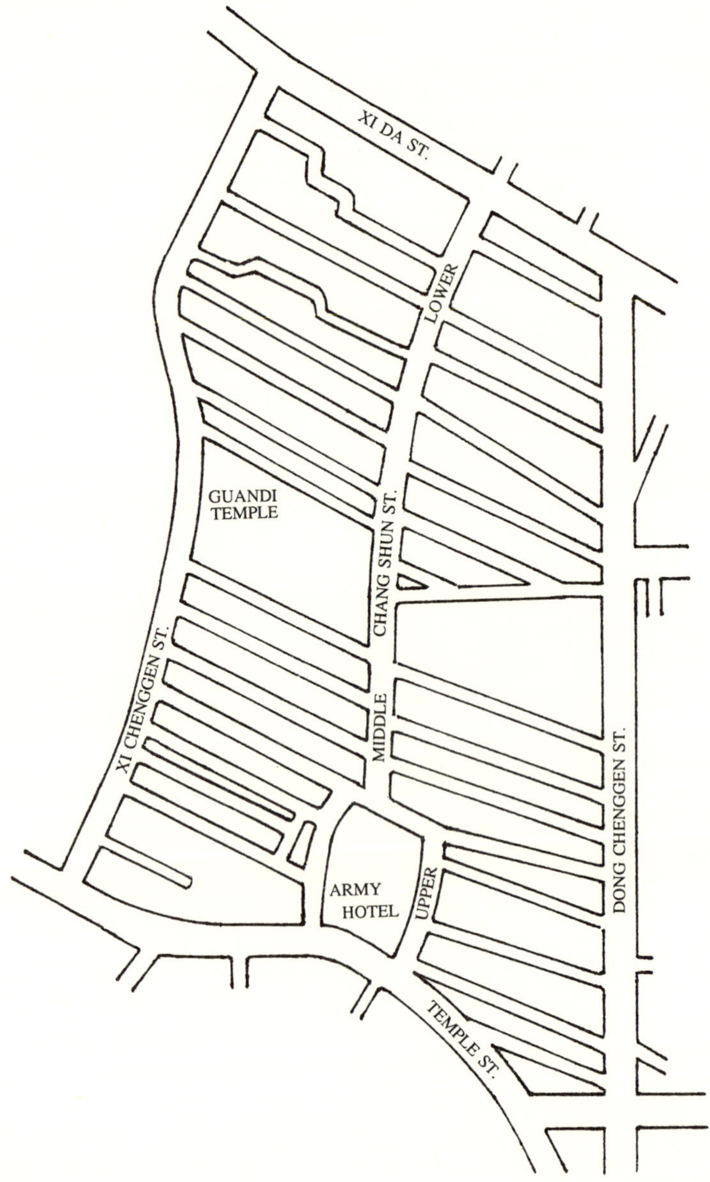

FIGURE 1. Bin Shen Area. The map shows the entire area of the former walled Manchu city (*shaocheng*), of which only the lower half (below the Guandi Temple) belongs to Bin Shen (*Bin shen xiaqu*).

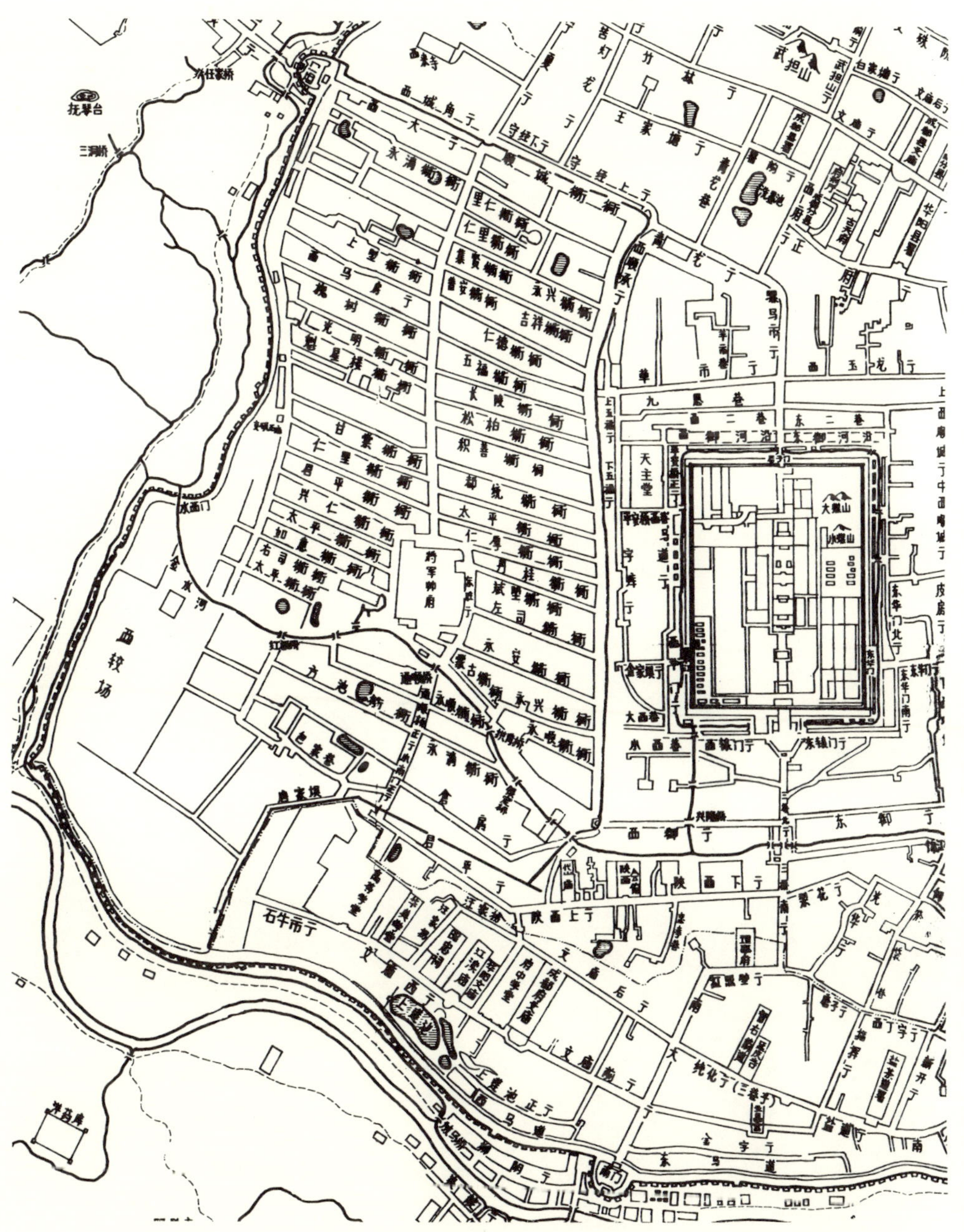

FIGURE 2. Map of Chengdu from the thirtieth year of Emperor Guangxu's rule (1905), showing the palace and the Manchu quarters.

CHAPTER ONE

Methodology and Fieldwork

This is an account of the people, their private businesses, and their relationship with bureaucracy in a small neighborhood within a contemporary Chinese urban area. The study follows a community of private business households (*geti hu*) in Chengdu, Sichuan, the People's Republic of China, during the five-year period 1987–91. The fieldwork area coincides with the smallest unit of urban administration (*xiaqu*) and comprises about 270 businesses, some thousands of ordinary households, a free market, and various bureaus of public authorities. Though limited in size, the area is fairly representative for the private business environment in a large number of contemporary Chinese cities.

The study deals with a new aspect of modern Chinese society. With the Open Door Policy and economic reforms after 1978, private business was allowed to rise and become a vital social and economic factor. Such business was, however, already known to a vast number of urban Chinese households, for whom it was their primary economic activity up until the Liberation in 1949 and even for a number of years after until the new regime branded them the tails of capitalism and destroyed their businesses. The study is exploratory in its approach: it employs anthropological methods to the study of private business, placing it firmly in the social context of Chinese household organization, local community interaction, and state ideology. While portraying a contemporary Chinese urban community, the study deals with some fundamental Chinese values and ideologies as expressed in the fieldwork area.

Why business? In the first decade of the Open Door Policy, Chinese society was thrown into a surge of modernization with unprecedented force. To leave the social security and dignity of state employment in China during this phase of reform was generally an irreversible act.

It was a step that implied both great risk and a certain social marginalization. No housing, no health care, no kindergartens, no pensions were guaranteed for households that ventured into private business. The changes in the general conditions of life were in this way dramatic and permanent: from the secure but tedious and undemanding routine of state units to the new world of keen competition where one may make a fortune or lose everything. Nor could stable government policies be guaranteed under a regime that had repeatedly pushed aside economic imperatives to favor the political issues of class struggle. In this process, new groups articulated themselves, new interpretations of common values arose, and new hierarchies emerged. Viewed in the domestic group perspective, private enterprise now plays a significant role in Chinese urban life by being the alternative to state and collective employment. It offers more choice of work, more freedom of lifestyle, and for a wide range of people far more opportunity in life.

Why bureaucracy? Decades of Communist rule changed the appearance of society radically: the organization of production, patterns of habitation, and principles for social life. In another dimension, however, the strictly hierarchical power structure was by and large preserved as the means to penetrate and control every institution in society. But bureaucracy constitutes an opportunity in itself. At the local level Chinese bureaucracy still embraces a whole range of fairly independent authorities, several of which include extensions into the masses of ordinary citizens, who are assigned semiofficial duties and responsibilities. Bureaucratic organization is a vital aspect of Chinese tradition: the long presence of state power and bureaucracy bears heavily on local society since the relevant institutions are mirrored in social structures and absorbed in social values.

The overall argumentation in regard to business and bureaucracy is developed along the exposition of their structural significance: a key to the comprehension of how Chinese local communities function may be found in the complex interconnection between these separate, clearly demarcated sectors of society. The modernization process has seriously challenged the established social ideals through the displacement of such ethically well-defined sectors. While social esteem continues to be acquired through connection with the state and its bureaucracy, the present economic circumstances have compelled people to direct their pursuit of material wealth toward another area, centered on private business. In this way values are drawn from separate sources. The collective mindset is affected by the mores of two very different influences, the competition of which generates a highly charged field in which households have to maneuver in order to fulfill their common ambition of the good life.

As the study touches upon both a number of manifestations of Chinese culture and some universal characteristics of business and bureaucracy, its domain of inquiry must be very particular. To avoid oscillations between several fields, it concentrates on suggestions of the impact that Chinese culture has on business and bureaucracy — not the effect of business and bureaucracy on Chinese culture.

A natural distinction exists between those who started up a private business of their own free will and those who were more or less victims of circumstance. On one hand, relatively stable policies during the 1980s made private enterprise increasingly tempting; on the other, it became an imperative to a steadily growing number of households squeezed out of employment in the reforming of Chinese society. Private enterprise has hitherto provided an opportunity only for marginal groups. Yet from the end of the 1980s increasing numbers of people representing mainstream Chinese society have chosen to transfer from the public to the private sector. Private enterprise reflects the rapidly growing disparity of living standards in Chinese society since the reforms as it comprises the extremes: the impoverished and the nouveaux riches. The continuous growth of the private sector and the substantial social change that this growth has affected in the local community have aroused the vigilance of the established society and the public media. Standard of living, however, does not indispensably indicate social status, which seems to be rooted in long-established values, marked by education and position in the hierarchy of formal employment.

By implication, this study addresses the issues of oppression and exploitation in the context of local society. Being commoners by status, businesspeople feel their interests constrained by the Chinese state and their material means exploited by the bureaucracy. In contrast to Western public opinion concerning China, which focuses on democratic ideals, the common view of oppression in the fieldwork area relates to concrete experiences of economic exploitation. Voices of democracy were inarticulate and far between. When "democracy" was referred to, it was linked to economic freedom: the freedom to establish and run family business without infiltration from above and the freedom to manage available profits independently. Controversy over taxes, charges, and fees is intense in contemporary Chinese society, in which more and more state units are faced with demands from above that they be self-reliant. The solution sought is entirely traditional. A tremendous flow of both legal and illegal taxation indicates who is in power and who is not, demonstrates the relative positions of the old and new sectors of the economy, and symbolizes the superiority of intellectual over manual labor.

As the study shows, however, a wide range of people across the strata of Chinese society take advantage of people in structurally weaker positions. Businesspeople, although claiming to be an overlooked and even politically stigmatized group, apparently do not refrain from taking advantage of those in even lower positions in urban Chinese society: the invisible group of rural young, who are everywhere used as a cheap and convenient labor resource. Thus, this investigation intends to display social structures favoring exploitation rather than to point out oppressors and oppressed in a moral order.

Doing Fieldwork in China

Any attempt at anthropological fieldwork in a section of Chinese society raises special issues that demand special solutions. The decisive factor for a researcher aiming at a systematic investigation of ordinary households is to establish fruitful relations, which enable the researcher to overcome the all too frequent bureaucratic obstacles. Any attempt to bypass the problem via informal channels is bound to failure because bureaucratic control maintains too fast a hold to allow any unauthorized intruder to reach any depth of local society.[1] Equally important is the interconnectedness between local bureaucracy and common households in urban areas. Despite being structurally oppositional they are like an organism; approval from local bureaucracy actually assured that people would bother to answer our questions; it placed the investigation within an intelligible frame of reference to the local inhabitants, who had never before been studied, let alone met a foreigner face to face.

It is an old Chinese custom to treat strangers strictly according to rank, and for this reason the stranger may in turn wish to present himself as favorably as possible. At that time, I possessed an obscure

Scandinavian university degree not fully recognized as a Ph.D. As a consequence I ranked below the level of foreign researchers unreservedly received by a Chinese counterpart. I was, however, equipped with documents from the DANIDA, which supports several development programs in Sichuan province, as well as a letter of introduction from the Danish embassy. I knew of no reason not to turn directly to my intended institution of collaboration, the Sichuan Academy of Social Sciences (SASS) in Chengdu. I simply went to the foreign affairs office at the SASS to introduce my plans, and in this way I attempted to avoid the central Chinese Academy of Social Sciences in Beijing and prolonged correspondence with it and other institutions.

An unannounced visit to a Chinese work unit is hardly fruitful, but it may be instructive nonetheless. The academy, which is situated in the Western outskirts of Chengdu near the Qingyanggong public park, is a four-story concrete building covered in yellow tiles. It is not easy to reach. There are signs at only one of the entrances, and few people know of its existence despite its more than 500 employees. In entering the office building one passes the elderly doorman, who, wrapped in layers of thick quilting and cotton and with a cap on his head and a thermos in front of him, commonly throws a few remarks in the Sichuan dialect. Once inside I asked passersby the way further around the atrium, where a highly relaxed atmosphere prevailed. A scholarly looking gentleman carrying a stack of books hesitated slightly after being addressed and then asked me to follow him. He took me along plain concrete corridors and past rows of empty or sparsely staffed offices, and indeed, there was not much furniture or equipment in the offices to detain the employees. He pointed to a green-walled office behind steel-framed glass. Here, on the second floor, was the foreign affairs department, consisting of three desks and a typewriter. One secretary was present. She dabbled with a letter from abroad even though we were approaching the lunch and midday resting hours. She excused the absence of her boss and recommended that I return in the late afternoon, or better, make an appointment with her boss the following day.

My unorthodox approach proved fertile. In 1987 Sichuan province was in the process of strengthening its independent relations with Europe, and the head of the office, Mr. Ao, had already traveled several times to Germany and felt positive about the further development of connections with Europe. My project required that the SASS deliberate the matter, but by directly addressing the academy I had avoided much paperwork and uncertainty. What threatened the project, however, was my inappropriate choice of transportation. That I arrived at the SASS on a bicycle instead of in a limousine was judged to be incompatible with representing a government research body and thus aroused serious skepticism.[2] After I had made several courtesy visits to the office during the next few weeks, the SASS agreed to receive me on my return to China some months later. During the deliberations the fact that Danish authorities supported my stay was considered positive; it may even have weighed decisively in my favor. What kept puzzling the SASS, however, was my interest in a "backward" sector of the economy, engaged in by individuals of low status who occupied old-fashioned premises in the Chengdu City area. A similar project had never been carried out by any one of the approximately 350 research staff at the academy. Several times I had to explain my interest both in private business and in households who were in every sense ordinary.

As I had merely an outline of the research project when I arrived in Chengdu, a number of factors needed to be determined: the exact locality for my initial survey, the number of households involved, and the exact questions. I quickly learned that Chinese authorities demand such exactness before they will approve any such activities; I heard from my hosts, and later confirmed for myself, that Party authorities especially require details and predictability of research programs. Moreover, questions put to the households had first to be presented in written form to provincial government authorities. My plan for this initial investigation was really a development study of private households particularly in small workshop manufacturing, and this plan had already received approval from the DANIDA. While the first phase of the research project was set aside for this purpose,[3] the second phase consisted of an anthropological study of the entire business community. A set of fairly uncontroversial questions concerning shopkeepers, their businesses, and the organization of their households facilitated a smooth provisional approval. Because I followed this procedure to the letter, I received much more freedom later, when the authorities became familiar with me and my research.

The exact location for the investigation required a rigorous selection procedure. To make certain that an elected area was "ordinary," and not just a prearranged development exhibition center, I cycled through much of Chengdu and searched in every street and neighborhood for private businesses. With the intervention of a Chinese acquaintance, Ran Xiao Hong, a female schoolteacher with most afternoons off, I was able to speak with a large number of businesspeople, who were otherwise indisposed to answer question put forward by me alone. Older people, especially, were very reserved when asked to combine, as they were, two highly controversial issues: private business and foreigners. Our rounds in the old quarters of Chengdu where most private business took place also served as a pilot investigation into the number and types of private businesses in the city. While the number of businesses certainly was astonishing (80,000 in 1988[4]), it was equally remarkable that the businesses were merely clones from street to street. Restaurants, groceries, tailor shops, and tin smithies followed the same patterns in their interior arrangements, decoration, and, apparently, distribution of labor. I searched for a spot with a high concentration of private businesses and a comparatively large variety of businesses in operation including small workshops, and I discovered the Bin Shen area. Its main street, Chang Shun, also contained a market where denizens of the city and the country would naturally meet, and its always busy atmosphere convinced me that this was the perfect choice.

I chose to carry out fieldwork in Chengdu, a provincial capital with a metropolitan population of three million people, for several reasons. The reputation for pragmatism that the Sichuanese have preserved over the centuries shone through when their province led the way to become a national example of reform in the late 1970s. By dissolving communes and lessening bureaucratic control over people's lives, the provincial government cleared the way for private enterprise, which in turn was believed capable of contributing substantially to economic development by filling in vital gaps. The Sichuanese' comparatively pragmatic outlook was important in yet another respect: this type of fieldwork would hardly have been possible in cities nearer the Chinese center. The history of Chengdu also counted. Because a small production culture based on family enterprise was dominant until the 1950s, the households in business could be expected to resume this pattern of organization fairly smoothly, or at least benefit from the experience of the elder generation. Therefore, the contradiction between the public and private sectors was intensified, both in the economy and in the related social institutions, and the clashes involved in the general modernization process were clearly depicted.

When I returned to Chengdu some months later, I found everything nicely arranged: accommodation, limousine to take me to and from Chang Shun Street every day, an assistant, and all the permits pertinent to working in an area that had never before been visited officially by foreigners. Permits from the local authorities had caused some trouble, since they regarded Bin Shen as a "closed area" in the sense that it had not been specifically declared "open" for research purposes. The permit issued by the Sichuan provincial government, however, opened many doors that otherwise might have remained closed. I kindly refused the limousine on the grounds that it created too great a distance between me and the interviewee. The concept of "social distance" made sense to the office in charge of my research. "So you want the true answers," was their comment. I was introduced to my first assistant, Liu Jinshi, at the academy. Since he had a degree in the social sciences and knew two foreign languages, he was introduced as the very best the academy could produce. I was later to learn that he did not rank highest among the assistants at the academy, but he was very bright and pleasant to work with, and he had other qualities that made him a perfect companion when visiting private businesses. His highly relaxed appearance and open preference for going abroad rather than ascending in the Party-dominated hierarchy at the academy seemed to inspire trust among the households we were interviewing.

So our interviews started with the best possible stamps of approval and support. The powerful letter of introduction from a provincial government office, which my assistant carried permanently, was often produced when the local public security inquired about our activities or when local bureaus refused to receive us. Interviewing the private business households, however, was the main objective. A predominantly socioeconomic questionnaire was used as an entrance to the field; it generally satisfied the natural wonder about our undertakings of local authorities and the households. All households were willing to answer questions that were matters of common knowledge: everyone knew the others' social backgrounds, just as the business figures presented to the local tax bureau could, in principle, be presented to anyone. The first series of interviews involved sixty business households, out of which thirty were engaged in small manufacturing and crafts. A single interview usually lasted a full morning or afternoon with every household. Only after carefully building up relations of confidence did we gradually introduce questions on more controversial matters and make casual visits to certain households. It immediately became obvious that some households were more prone to speak out than others. As we had expected, really close relations could be attained with only a few households, but our frequent return visits were invaluable; any kind of information gathered in the neighborhood could be discussed with these people. In this way the entrance into the local community was two-dimensional: through simple initial questions, we covered everyone of interest; and by establishing intimate relations with a few, we reached some depth. As it turned out, our staying in the area for long periods made this "strategic" approach unnecessary. Both of us actually became good friends with several families, who were always ready for an unannounced visitor. Although the actual figures we received from the initial investigation could hardly be expected to hold, we were amazed by the openness with which many of the local inhabitants received us — a few to a degree that we both thought was rash, considering the circumstances. It was revealed much later to be quite intentional. Particularly during the fieldwork period in 1989, the conflict between a large segment of business households and local officials had become aggravated by ruthless taxation, and many households seemed to hope for some tenuous connection between me and a vaguely perceived sense of justice in the outside world. "We have no one to speak for us" became an increasingly common remark. This kind of response gave nourishment to my own reflections on the anthropologist's role. Instead of relaying an account of an environment unaffected by his or her presence, the anthropologist becomes a conspicuous figure.

The study builds on twelve months of anthropological fieldwork, distributed over five periods. The humid climate in the Chengdu area and the extreme temperatures (ranging from about zero in the winter to above 35° Celsius in the summer) leave only spring and autumn for valuable fieldwork. Summer in Chengdu, especially, is a period in which all activity gradually slows down to meet only the basic requirements; everyone is exhausted from struggling through the stifling days and nights. In 1987 both the spring and autumn periods were covered, but only the latter involved cooperation with the SASS. In 1988 a series of interviews was conducted in the winter and early spring, and in 1989 a longer period of fieldwork was carried out, also in the spring, ending at the time of the tragic June 4 events, which greatly affected Chengdu. Because of uncertainties after June 1989 no fieldwork was performed in 1990. In the early summer of 1991 fieldwork was resumed. At this time, however, the political turmoil resulting from "June 4" had conspicuously changed the climate for doing research. Because of my previously good cooperation, permission was granted; but Party-aligned characters stood stronger at the academy, and stricter discipline and study classes were reintroduced for the employees. Before the 1989 fieldwork period, my assistant had finally managed to arrange a period of studying abroad, and another assistant was introduced to me. This time the academy made good on its promise to supply the highest ranking among their assistants. As vice-director of the foreign affairs office, however, he was often busy with other duties. After some time I found a young woman working as a librarian in the foreign library of the SASS who was eager to try her luck as my assistent. As she eventually lived in the Bin Shen area herself, the arrangement was very convenient for both of us. In the end, she surpassed both her male counterparts as a superior assistant. When I returned in 1991, the foreign affairs office announced that she was unable to work with me; the vice-director resumed his position as my assistant. The librarian, however, was very helpful in her spare time since she still lived in Bin Shen and knew the area so well.

Data were collected primarily during unannounced visits to the businesses; only when shopkeepers were repeatedly out were appointments made. After a short time only a few were surprised to see us, since the news had spread. Our use of packets of foreign cigarettes as a small compensation for the inconvenience caused was also widely known. All households were visited several times as our inquiries extended, and most households were followed during successive periods of fieldwork from 1987 to 1991. After the initial investigation of sixty households had been accomplished, more households were drawn in either at random or when found to be in a structurally important position regarding type of business, participation in local "social work," or contradictory relations to bureaucracy. By the conclusion of the last session of fieldwork, virtually all businesses in the area had been visited. In addition, a considerable number of market vendors, itinerants, ordinary people in state employment, and young people, found in billiard saloons, restaurants, or simply encountered in the street, had been interviewed. Over the sessions of fieldwork an estimated five hundred interviews were performed, excluding various types of occasional small talk, teahouse conversation, and dinner chat.

With the exception of the police station, all local bureaus were visited and many officials interviewed. For reasons to be explained, however, a thorough examination of the organizational set-up of local bureaucracy had to be abandoned. Repeated contradictory statements made it impossible to penetrate the total structure, and the nationwide process of restructuring local administrations apparently left many officials equally perplexed about their own roles. It had nevertheless always been my aim to view local society through the daily life and happenings in ordinary households.

As regards language, I soon realized that the Sichuanese dialect of Mandarin slipped too often beyond my level of proficiency, gained from a year's studying in Beijing and a few additional courses at home and in Chengdu. My first period in Chengdu also included a language course at Sichuan University, which, as one of China's key universities frequently visited by foreign scholars in all fields, provided a valuable forum for reflections on modern Chinese society. While people with literary education spoke fairly comprehensible Mandarin, others, and especially elderly people, communicated in a tongue with little or no resemblance to my standard Chinese. They usually understood my questions, but I often failed to follow their answers; my assistant had to interpret the details. Still, my Chinese was valuable during the interviews, not to mention my spare time, which I most often spent with Chinese friends in Chengdu.

Composition of the Study

Chapter two of the study familiarizes the reader with the fieldwork area and outlines briefly the impact of major political events on the local population, while chapter three introduces its private business households. I shall report here on the results of participant observation and the contents of the numerous interviews with the business-people of the local community, mainly during fieldwork in 1987. Since it is confined to a small area of an urban community, the study attempts to present the typical, rather than the strictly average, private business households. Of specific interest is how the households express their economic and social pursuits with respect to the changing conditions of society: how business ideologies reflect a society in transition. The internal organization and composition of the domestic group are presented, as they provide an important perspective on the occurrences of public life, including the delicate relations between private business households and local authorities.

All businesses involved in this research belong to the Chinese category *geti hu* — individual households, legalized as private entrepreneurs by the policy of the Third Plenary Session of the Eleventh Central Committee of the Communist Party, December 1978, and implemented from 1979 onward. A new distinction between businesses in the private sector was decided upon in 1987, dividing these into *geti hu* with up to seven employees and *siying qiye* — private enterprises with more than seven employees. It had not been realized in May 1989.

In analyzing the ideologies of business in the local community, I emphasize the household rather than the individual as a basic unit. Since the business ideology commonly represents the household in its entirety and often embraces the household's total relations with the outside world, it is seen as a complex formation involving both purely economic and entirely social aims. For this reason, basic economic concepts concerning businesses are used, while economic theories are avoided: they are found to be largely incapable of capturing the rationale of the Chinese household. Nor are theoretical frameworks involving class struggle applied, since the major poles of interest in the present situation are voiced by business and bureaucracy or by family and state, rather than by clearly articulated classes. An anthropological approach will be followed: an analysis of the individual economy through its actual participants and their primary organizations.

Chapter four, which mainly refers to fieldwork conducted in 1988, presents the household strategies in their cultural setting. The reappearance of private business established an alternative to state-controlled employment. When profits from the new individual sector quickly rose to exceed state wages, and even produced millionaires, Chinese society was again faced with the undercurrents of its history. Private business filled important gaps in the economy as intended by the ruling Party. It rewarded many of the new entrepreneurs financially, but after decades of centrally guided "class struggle," the notion of social rank as a predominant factor turned out to be largely intact. Uncertainty toward the stability of the Open Door Policy left private business with little social prestige, and the prevailing search for quick profits of the private entrepreneurs further contributed to this low standing. Even continued reassurance of stable policies by central government and the media's proclaiming private entrepreneurs "development heroes" had been in vain: the urban population still held private business in low esteem. The predominant social orientations toward center, social competition, and formal authority remained. What private business could not offer in terms of social status, however, it has abundantly compensated for in material wealth for its successful entrepreneurs.

It can therefore be argued that a "dual flow" or dual hierarchical system emerged, presumably resembling the pre-Liberation social structure. Where a formal hierarchy of position and rank in state employment is in focus for extracting social prestige, material wealth is more easily acquired in the newly developed informal sector, or informal hierarchy, of competitive private business. Without being fully developed into a hierarchical structure, private business nevertheless developed conspicuous stratification both in its internal organization between owners and employees and among businesses. In a more abstract sense, the formal and informal sectors of society represent separate strategies of households. As asserted to be the case in the old society, such dual hierarchies are generally overlapping. A number of individuals have connections to both, and households frequently let them merge into a unified strategy. Their importance as concepts, however, lies in the conscious balancing act that households characteristically perform in their relations with the outside world and in the fact that prestige and material wealth are now usually sought in highly different areas of society and even in conflicting activities.

An important aspect of this hypothetical duality is the value transformation between its two sides: formal position is converted into wealth, and wealth gained from activities of little esteem is employed in seeking social acceptance. Because both wealth and social prestige are equally desired and tend to be mutually legitimizing and justifying in the Chinese ethos, they appear as complementary forces in the household's collective statement of purpose. Whenever possible, preponderance of one is sought to be redressed by emphasis on the other. In real life activities, transformation of formal position into wealth is the most obvious and simple form. Privileges or actual cash benefits are common gains from holding office; they may even be the essence of it, as such accrual rests on a high degree of consensus. The exploiting of material wealth in the process of elevating the household's reputation and status is the more complex of the two, and it frequently fails altogether. Doing social work (*shehui gongzuo*) in the neighborhood and engaging in the countless semiofficial duties at local level supply the actors accordingly with a semibureaucratic status, and the entire household may benefit from this "rubbing shoulders" with bureaucracy. This approach to bureaucracy nevertheless seldom entails offers of regular employment, and engaging in this lowest level of officialdom rarely confers any importance in terms of prestige, apart from local reputation. In terms of political security, however, such strategy may be logical.

Chapter five deals with local bureaucracy, which constitutes the main counterpart to private business within the local community; examination of the clashing interests of the two sides provides further perspective on the previous discussion regarding the dual character of local society. The intricate web of personalized relations and the competition for authority and privileges available in bureaucracies are, of course, crucial to the power structure of local society. Moreover, private businesses are totally dependent on their ability to maneuver within the various local bureaus representing central government as well as local Party-dominated authorities. As already indicated, however, a certain degree of continuity exists between bureaucrats and businesspeople. Furthermore, since wealth and prestige are generated in separate sectors of society, the character of exchange relations is of crucial importance. The material for this chapter was collected in 1987–88.

Chapter six presents the fieldwork conducted in the spring of 1989 with special attention to the younger generation's approach to private business. Two pertinent topics in this respect are the young's opposition to established values and their conditions of education and job searching in contemporary China. When traditional strategies prove unfeasible, they are replaced by new, and corresponding aims and values are gradually transformed. In the young people's strong desire for freedom, both inside and outside the family, private business may be an emancipating force. Advocating modernity in social organization, the young are commonly opposed to the elder generations of their households; yet in another respect previous status positions tend to be maintained among the young. Social stratification is equally conspicuous among the younger and the older age groups. Competition for the few educational opportunities and the elitist drive in educational reforms have contributed to the division of the young into two categories: those badly needed by the developing society and the rest, for whom private business may be the only alternative.

A nationwide economic setback in 1989 called for closer investigation, as it coincided with social change accelerating to the edge of a general transition of society. This chapter also reflects on developments in the balance between the state and the private sectors. Serious setbacks in especially the state sector influenced virtually everyone, and they manifested themselves in aggravated contradiction between local bureaucracy and private businesses. Not only were the established authorities threatened directly, but the entire power structure of society was seriously challenged in this period.

Chapter seven follows up on the entire private business community after two years' absence. While previous chapters are oriented toward specific issues and social groups, this chapter evaluates the impact of time and events on the entire community since the project was initiated in 1987. The aftermath of the June 4 events, the renewed political study hours at all state work units, and the resumed use of ideological campaigns are naturally in focus. After a short interval private business in Bin Shen had continued to develop, both in terms of total numbers and individual expansion, although the generation of young evidently was in a harder squeeze than before. In 1991 a few private enterprises claiming years of registration as *siying qiye* had suddenly sprung up. This seeming mystery is explained in continuation of the methodological problem relating to the locals' sense of history (discussed in chapter two). This chapter also contains an evaluation of a full "cycle of business" as an enterprise begins with the household and passes through various stages of enthusiasm, expansion, rising complications, desire for innovation, and retreat.

Chapter eight temporarily leaves the fieldwork area to discuss some broader, more generalized issues with respect to social values in a Chinese community. Instead of merely ascribing present values to determinants such as "tradition" and "convention," I present them in a historical process. As the Chinese themselves often point to an unspecified "tradition" as a frame of reference for social thought, tradition will here be treated as a body of abstract thought, denoting essential Chinese ideals. Social practice, however, is exclusively conceived as expressive of the present society. The local community is placed within the framework of a dialectical inquiry, and comparisons with other community studies are made. Discussion centers on three basic pairs of opposing factors that appear to have the most bearing on the formation of household strategies in local society: state versus family, formal versus informal hierarchies, and ideal versus social practice. By developing the analysis through such dialectical steps from state level toward local community life, a coherent approach is suggested.

CHAPTER TWO

Chang Shun Street and Market Area

Chang Shun Street lies on the western outskirts of the Chengdu City area. It opens onto Temple Street, which is the continuation of the huge People's West Boulevard, and from there runs fairly straight north. It is narrow and unimpressive, lined with old wooden houses mostly of pre-Liberation origin or, as far as their inhabitants can recall, constructed right after Liberation. Although seemingly insignificant, Chang Shun Street is well known to shoppers as it contains one of Chengdu's newly reopened free markets[1] and, in addition, countless private businesses. They are placed side by side in every possible house or stall that can provide even the minimal facilities, generally simply shelter and electric power for lighting — and an occasional television set. The street bustles with activity from dawn to dusk, the free market being the main attraction, while the remaining businesses draw their customers from the constant flow of people making their way on foot or bicycle down the street. Always crowded with people of a great variety of professions and purposes, Chang Shun Street in many ways represents Chengdu as a city or any premodern street in a Chinese urban area. Farmers on tricycles carrying huge loads of vegetables, poultry, or sides of pork for the market zigzag their way up the street to the persistent but largely ineffectual ringing of their bells. Traveling salespeople with large baskets suspended from bamboo carrier poles contribute with their boisterous calls to the noisy and busy atmosphere of the street. Unceasingly, there are people on their way to and from work, children playing under the supervision of grandparents, schoolchildren walking arm in arm, and a few jobless adolescents strolling along just to pass time. Chang Shun Street has it all.

Chang Shun,[2] meaning "long smooth," is divided into Upper, Middle, and Lower Street and stretches almost a kilometer in length.

Most attractive to private business is the Upper Street, which connects Temple Street to the market in Middle Street. Some of the most profitable businesses are on Upper Street. Middle and Lower streets gradually quiet as one approaches the northern end of the street, and businesses become farther apart. Although the street is paved and has narrow sidewalks on either side, very few automobiles venture down the length of it. Only a neighboring army unit[3] regularly sends its vehicles through Chang Shun Street, but not even the large sedans carrying uniformed army officers can maintain their privileged status when struggling along.

Flanking the street on either side are the one- or two-story wooden houses that have just recently regained their original function. Shops facing onto the street that some thirty years ago were boarded up and converted into living quarters have now been reopened as restaurants, workshops, and businesses, while their inhabitants have either moved their living quarters back into the recesses of the house or upstairs when possible. They are relatively simple structures. With two rows of poles supporting the tiled roof and plastered walls, they give an impression of timelessness. Not much has been devoted to paint or decoration of the old houses, which display a kind of crass materialism in a continuation of their original purpose. The woodwork is painted dark red or green, and the plastered walls are only sparsely adorned with posters and magazine clippings. The facades, which are only ten to fifteen feet on most of the houses, consist of a long row of shutter boards that have been carefully preserved by the inhabitants. They are easily removed and give full access to the shop in the daytime. At night they are slid back into their grooves. Most houses are two rooms deep on the ground level, although a few have three or only one. Some houses contain an additional story, but the low pitch of the roof necessitated by the loose-laid tiles barely offers standing height. Thus in the smallest of premises the ground floor serves as a shop and a living room combined, while the second floor serves as sleeping quarters. The larger premises have separate living quarters on both floors, enabling the family to occupy more than a single room with their bedding. What the houses lack by their simplicity and limited size, they possess fully in the flexibility of the interior arrangement. The simple walls and partitions are easily rearranged, allowing businesses to be launched and abandoned, families to multiply and shrink, or if necessary, several households to join under a single roof. They express the dynamics of the Chinese family very accurately.

When the reforms were instituted, these premises became coveted by future entrepreneurs, as they offered all the basic requirements. They were close to customers, fairly inexpensive, and flexible in interior arrangement, thus allowing business premises and living quarters to overlap. Most are privately owned, purchased by their occupants from disenfranchised landlords and Guomindang officers at prices negotiated by the new authorities. Demand for such premises has increased steadily, and their high prices are testimony to their value. Today their proprietors are among the privileged, whether they run businesses themselves or just collect the rent. Access to suitable lots has become essential to the success of private family business. Nonetheless, premises for family business are steadily decreasing in number as the ongoing city reconstruction program eliminates the old wooden houses all over Chengdu and replaces them with expensive concrete constructions with shop space beyond the means of private persons. The army unit next to Chang Shun Street has constructed a new hotel for army personnel that, by rising to seventeen stories, stands in odd contrast to the low houses surrounding it. As the hotel is already short of space for its facilities, however, a section of Chang Shun Upper Street is threatened by expropriation.[4]

Businesses in the street offer the entire range of goods and services necessary for the local community to which they cater. Private restaurants were welcomed when reintroduced, and they abound. Because of their high profitability, they frequently occupy the largest premises. Retail trading of various groceries is also popular, but the increasing number of shops has led to decreasing profits. Numerous tailors with their young apprentices operate in the street, and although their craft demands greater effort, their income is still comparatively high. Various other crafts can be found: a saddlemaker who now produces handbags, a tinsmith, producers of kitchen chopboards, a glazier, purveyors of knitwear, and various bakers. A traditional doctor also practices his trade alongside bicycle and television repair shops. Barbers offer their services. There are a dry cleaner and a film-processing shop, both of which work on contracts for larger units, as the equipment is too costly for these families to afford. There are retailers of plastic goods, porcelain, children's clothing, textiles, and spices. A secondhand bookstore circulates the books and magazines in the neighborhood, and a traditional Sichuan-style teahouse, run by a couple as ancient as the fragile building that shelters it, provides boiling hot jasmine tea throughout the day. Contributing to the private enterprise milieu of the area are the businesses and workshops of some adjacent streets. Besides repeating the businesses in Chang Shun Street they also include blacksmiths, locksmiths, woodworkers, manufacturers of signboards and plastic containers, private kindergartens, and a noodlemaker.

In Chang Shun Street lies one of Chengdu's newly reopened free markets, where any kind of meat, poultry, vegetable, or fruit of the season can be purchased. Offering the opportunity to buy and sell fresh foodstuffs all the year round at negotiated prices, the free markets quickly became the single most important element of the liberalization for ordinary city people. The location of Chang Shun market, right where Chang Shun Upper Street bends and widens before leading into Chang Shun Middle Street, coincides with a pre-Revolution marketplace of uncertain origin. Its history goes beyond the memory of even the oldest generation in the street: "It has always been there," they say, a statement probably not far off the mark. Even during the throes of the Cultural Revolution, vegetables were traded on this spot. Several hundred vendors of every imaginable sort of vegetable, root, mushroom, and fruit, every kind of meat from the tiniest insect to poultry and pigs gather here every morning to sell their wares. Although originally intended to be restricted to peasants selling their own produce, much of the trade has now been taken over by secondary dealers. These are marginalized peasants and rural youth who buy a load of goods in the nearby countryside and resell it at the market for a small profit. As peasants and vendors alike are country folk, they are not easily distinguishable.

The liberalization of the 1980s also brought the itinerant peddlers back into business. They travel enormous distances on foot or bicycle to reach every corner of the country, carrying a pair of baskets filled with whatever might earn them a living. This pattern — except for the bicycle of course — penetrates Sichuan in both time and space.[5] Fruit is especially prized these days by itinerant peddlers. Its high value allows them to spend more than a single day trading a load at the market. They sit silently behind their baskets, their large round hats protecting them from sun and rain, with the old steelyard, ready to serve customers. The physical setting of the market is simply the street itself. Although many of the vendors return to the same location from day to day, there are no permanent stalls. The relationship of reliability and mutual trust built up between vendors and customers is still essential and has tended even to increase in importance along with the development of private business. In order to secure fair trade, customers prefer the familiar to the tempting. The vendors in turn tend to give better rates to steady customers, luring them back time after time.

The elderly people in the street, some of whom are well into their eighties and nineties, all agree that the social life of Chang Shun Street has returned to normal. After several decades of people secluding themselves from public life in the bitter struggle for social as well as physical survival, a more relaxed atmosphere obviously prevails now. Although few of these people are wealthy, most can easily get by, and just as the economic surplus has brought an improved diet and new consumer goods, so the easing of mental strain allows for involvement in the rapidly growing social life. When the weather of Chengdu permits, most activities are carried on outdoors. Retired men can spend hours over games of *chang pai* (long cards) or *zhong zhi* (Chinese chess) around tables in the open air, relaxing in the teahouse, or chatting with neighbors. Socializing, however, is no longer a luxury to be enjoyed only by children and the retired. Private enterprise has removed the barriers between the work place and family life, as well as those between the public and private spheres. The shop is the center of all activity. Every family member lends a hand in running it, and within its confines children are nursed, aging family members are tended to, friends and neighbors pay visits, and meals are prepared. The open facades of the tiny shops reveal that the physical distinction between shop and dwelling is merely a matter of definition. Some comprise both within the same room, and shuttering up the shop at night literally means going to bed, as the limited indoor space permits few other activities.

Lao bai xing, "old hundred names," is how the locals often refer to themselves, designating commoners with no significant measure of wealth or power. They represent the average citizen as far as material wealth is concerned. They may occupy the lower echelon in the context of social status, however, because of the common disregard for private business that still prevails. The people of Chang Shun Street are, with a few exceptions,[6] Han Chinese of Sichuan province and invariably speak the Sichuanese dialect of Mandarin. Most were born in Chengdu, and some in this very street; but because of the tumultuous history of twentieth-century China, the latter are but a minority. The Japanese bombing of the area in the early 1940s left the street almost deserted; its former inhabitants scattered all over the province in search of protection and a means of livelihood. Many inhabitants come from villages in the surrounding countryside, some from villages in remote corners of the province. A small number come from other provinces, mainly Shanxi and Henan. Strong ties between family and native village can still be found among the inhabitants of the street. Some ascribe the native village of their parents, or even grandparents, as their primary affiliation, but add that they themselves were born in Chengdu. This attests to the fact that, even in the process of modernization, the Chinese family is more often than not an organic unit — the ideals of which are centered on respect and reverence for age, individual subjugation, and convention.

The household, a basic unit in individual business as well as in society at large, is recognized as the unit of enterprise in the Chinese expression *geti hu,* which means "individual household."[7] This term corresponds accurately with reality, even though Chinese authorities tend to apply it to responsible individuals rather than to families. Households in the street comprise one to several generations, the smallest constituted by the recently married and still childless couples or by the elderly couples whose children have all been married off. The largest family units consist of three and in a single case four generations, with members ranging from sixteen to ninety-four years of age. Three generations under one roof is the most common. Families follow the patrilocal pattern according to which daughters leave when married and the eldest son, and if possible also younger ones, continue the family line. The power structure within the family, where decision making and authority over others is the privilege of the eldest male, also applies to business. All business affairs, plans for future investments, and the day-to-day organization of labor are determined according to this structure, apart from the cases where a business is run solely by a woman to supplement the income of the household. The fundamentally patriarchal social order has its irregularities or informal practices: family finances are customarily controlled by the eldest female. According to a Chinese proverb, women are better with money.[8] Private business is generally identical to household business. Private business evolved out of the embattled Chinese family organization and, after decades of political campaigns and social unrest, it was the activity that gave it substance and new life. The Chinese family passed through a generation of withdrawal and confinement to a unit of social organization, but it merely needed the signal of legalization through political reform to re-emerge as an economic unit. The incorporation of economic activity into the pattern of social organization is indeed what the locals call Chinese tradition. In Chang Shun Street as elsewhere, this molded the countless numbers of small businesses and handicrafts that dominated production up until the Revolution in 1949.

The nuclear family is on the rise in modern China. Young couples often desire a home of their own, free from the authority of parents. Although this trend is much debated in public[9] and has become the model especially for city life, the stem family still prevails in most households. The atomizing of social structure is counteracted by numerous circumstances. The extremely limited space in all Chinese cities, difficulties with childcare, and the economic advantages of large households are the most important. In the case of individual enterprises, their marginal position in relation to public service and social security must be added.

Marginality is still the characteristic of individual business households. In a pronounced status-conscious society, they still occupy an inferior social position, even when this is compensated for by a much higher income than available in state jobs. Individual businesses may be run by anyone from the very rich to the very poor. This includes the new privileged class and the pauperized, the handicapped and chronically ill, retired people, former criminals, and social outcasts. These people seek more than state employment can offer; many lack the capacity to hold a state job. They all have in common a marginality to the established society. They lack the permanent connection to a *danwei,*[10] the basic unit of work, which provides the individual with material as well as social security. It implies not only social marginalization but also great risks to leave the *danwei.* No public services are available for households who choose to stand alone, which means that any service must be purchased. Traversing the demarcation causes permanent and dramatic changes, although making a living from private business is usually easy.

The businesses in Chang Shun Street make up a full spectrum. Little variation is detected, however, in the appearance of the shops themselves, where nonfunctional objects are kept to an absolute minimum. The entire street gives the impression that aesthetics are of very little interest to the inhabitants. Despite the conventional appearance of the businesses, closer investigation reveals a more than fiftyfold difference in profit in the street. From Mr. Wang's restaurant — which, with its fine location near Temple Street, specializes in banquets for work units and family gatherings, yielding a profit that has long since turned his household into a *wan yuan hu* (10,000-yuan household) — it is but a short walk to Madame Dong's porcelain store, where three generations support themselves on less than 100 yuan a month. Whereas in Mr. Wang's household two sons and their wives live an easy life from the business profits, the Dong household cannot even afford to let the eldest son marry.

A hierarchy among private businesses is evidently developing. This development reflects the capacity for further investment as well as the crucial cooperation with legal authorities. Here lies the basis for what is developing into a parallel to the state-controlled, formal hierarchy: an informal structure of private enterprise. This is both internally hierarchical in terms of distribution of labor and privileges and hierarchical in external social relations in terms of size of business, amount of ready capital to invest in both own and others' businesses, network of connections, and number of hired manual laborers.

Success in business is measured by a single parameter: the quick return on investment. Chinese business mentality is clearly depicted in the model of a successful businessman: a substantial profit produced in a fashion that enables the entrepreneur to benefit from it immediately. The endeavor is definitely of this world, a satisfaction inextricably bound to the divorce from physical labor. The hunt for compensatory values is pronounced among the new entrepreneurs. The lack of social dignity and affiliation to a group that enjoys formal recognition may be counterbalanced by attaining quick profit and material wealth. Still, in the eyes of common people, a person in private business may earn respect for accomplishment but can never rank equal to an educated person in formal office.

Although there are numerous craftspeople and workshops of small-scale production in Chang Shun Street, the majority of businesses resell goods produced elsewhere or provide services to the local population.[11] These businesses combine to cover almost every need for services and consumer goods necessary for city life. The distribution of investments between goods-producing and service sectors does not merely point to profitability; it also indicates the delicate balance between profit and social prestige. High profits are not sought at any cost, as the achievement of the final aim — the good life — is closely related to traditional values. The small production enterprises of the area originate typically in preindustrial crafts, acquired and passed on through the master craftsman–apprentice relationship. As this system was interrupted from the mid-1950s until recently, many of today's masters are obviously of the older generation, often in their late sixties. Only a little capital is invested in these businesses. Their proprietors do not entertain great aspirations for future development and expansion of business, unless they have sons or daughters who are willing to give up the security of state employment to run a business of low social prestige and an uncertain future.

To substitute for the tight organization in which the member of a *danwei* is naturally positioned, the businessperson attempts to build up his or her own. *Guanxi* — the network of informal personal relations[12] — is a determining factor in private business, but its significance extends far beyond the interplay of individuals in various trades, businesses, and offices in the local community. Some of these relations are naturally more important than others for the businessperson, and the success of the business largely depends on the person's ability to "play his cards right" in the game of personalizing impersonal relations. The task is to pin persons and names to a structure that only in official rhetoric allows the open interchange of goods and services.

Bin Shen

The numerous small lanes that branch off Chang Shun Street in both directions lead to quiet neighborhoods.[13] The contrast to the busy atmosphere of Chang Shun is striking, as are the closed facades of most of the low compounds, which turn the narrow lanes into a canal-like network. Unbroken walls too high for passersby to peer over separate the lanes from the compounds. Even where the wall also constitutes the gable of a house, a window is seldom seen. Only the traditional gateways closed by heavy timber gates break the smooth, gray walls. This is Bin Shen area (which Chang Shun Street also belongs to), a former residential area of the Chengdu elite. In a bygone era it contained the Sichuan headquarters of the Guomindang and police forces. Now, the paint on the previously colorful gateways has peeled off, and the engraved family names on the stone slabs above have been chiseled away, although many gateways still have the engraved pillars and elaborately carved woodwork that support the small, symbolic roof sheltering the gate. Most compounds that were formerly the homes of single families now contain several: some just a few, typically six to eight, and occasionally as many as fifteen. Some of the gates draw the passerby's attention. They are in better repair and have been recently painted in the original colors; they also sport the conspicuous signposts of public authorities. These are the offices of the Street Committee, Tax Bureau, Industrial and Commercial Administration Bureau, and the Self-employed Laborers Association. The district Public Security also has a large compound in the area. Inside the compounds are fine courtyards with ample bicycle parking space for the employees. Flowers beds, potted plants, and trees keep the air pleasantly cool. A budgerigar or singing bird in a cage is occasionally suspended from a tree. Encircling the courtyard are low buildings with windows traversed by sash bars forming rectangular patterns. Only the interior arrangement reveals that the place is now occupied by employees of public authorities who still hold the modesty of the Proletarian Revolution as a guiding principle. The cheerless colors on walls and furnishings contrast with the refinement in the outer appearance of the buildings. The quiet and pleasant atmosphere, however, is preserved in the compounds, which effectively seclude themselves from the outside world. Although wages are moderate, it is regarded as a privilege to be a staff member of a local bureau. The spatial distinction between street and bureau forms an analogy to the social distinction between the petty entrepreneurs and the members of a privileged *danwei*.

Business and bureaucracy represent the extreme poles in the local community. While bureaucracy offers its employee maximum security, private enterprise offers none. Whereas the state employee generally has the highest education and social prestige, the entrepreneur usually has the lowest.[14] While bureaucracy represents the virtues of formal society, private business is associated with deviation. In spite of their polarity, however, bureaucracy and private business are linked together in a system of mutual dependency. That the entrepreneur depends on the local bureaus for legalization is evident in a society that still frowns upon all spontaneous social and economic development. The supply of such services, however, is often arranged as an interchange that allows officials to acquire a share in society's economic development — from which they would otherwise be excluded. The interchange follows an unwritten code. For the businessperson to integrate representatives of authority into his or her *guanxi* network has abstract as well as material importance. Stable relations with the authority secure the smooth flow of business and facilitate long-term planning. This is essential, especially to those individuals who represent the economic impetus of local society, since the highly departmentalized local bureaus often refer decisions and the issue of permits to other authorities. The abstract content of such relations is equally important to the entrepreneur, however, and can only be understood in a value system centered on social status and household reputation. This value system bears little connection to material wealth; the economic reforms notwithstanding, social prestige and material wealth are incompatible for large groups of society. For some entrepreneurs, then, intercourse with local officials is an aim as much as a means, however costly it might be; it calls the attention of the neighborhood and implicitly identifies the household with good *guanxi*.

Another type of interchange involving the bureaucracy is essential to the functioning of local society. This concerns the countless semiofficial tasks that individuals of the general populace perform for local bureaucracy and that constitute the extension of public administration below the local bureaus. The Street Committee has the most extensive network as it is the core of administration at the local level. All bureaus, however, assign duties to households or individuals. The tasks of supervising the smallest units of administration, which contain from a dozen to a few hundred households, are organized by the Street Committee: specified areas such as security, health, and environment are all attended to by small groups responsible to the officials above. The Tax Bureau has commissioned tax collection in private businesses to a number of their managers who, in this way, collect taxes among themselves. The Industrial and Commercial Administration Bureau has, through the Self-employed Laborers Association, developed a large network of responsibilities that tie individual businesspeople to the bureau. Its division into branches and subdivision into groups (all with group heads and deputy group heads), may integrate as many as one-third of all shopkeepers in these public charges. Accordingly, the total number of citizens engaged in these types of semiofficial duties may represent one-third of all households. As all jobs at levels below the local bureaus are unpaid or yield merely small monetary benefits, incentives and rewards are likely to be found elsewhere. Security is of course a matter of great concern to any household, but in the present context, social rather than material security must be considered. Performing legal duties secures stable ties to bureaucracy, which is the one and only source of formal authority in local society; it maintains the household's legal status and its connection to power.

This petty officialdom constitutes an extension of the formal hierarchy concurrent with the extension of the administrative network. Prestige can be drawn from affiliation with the formal hierarchy. Since such connection is associated with official rank, it heightens status in relation to those who have no connection to authority at all. Thus, an interchange between bureaucracy and civilians involving voluntary labor and social prestige is an integral part of the hierarchical structure of local society. This is especially so for the older generation, whose members still follow the old ideal of doing social work as an expression of wealth and surplus in the household. Many of the individuals who perform voluntary labor are retirees, seldom experienced in administration. Others are still active in labor that gives them some free time during the day to carry out their legal duties.

The inhabitants and officials of Bin Shen area are mostly agreed that their neighborhood is fairly average for Chengdu City. Ordinary citizens here have a home with a reasonably central location, good shopping facilities, and a lively environment. Shopkeepers and market vendors are satisfied with the number of customers the street provides, although some of the more dynamic may desire shops in the downtown area. The local bureaucracy has a reputation of being comparatively fair, and stories about their malpractices are nothing out of the ordinary for the local ear.

Household Business in Modern Bin Shen History

Individual household businesses have repeatedly been the focus of major events in Chinese history under socialism.[15] In turn, individual households consider the ideological trend of their time in adopting economic strategies. As we shall see, history in the abstract sense carries little significance to the inhabitants of Bin Shen, and little is mentioned in everyday conversation or otherwise commemorated. Although some inescapable experiences were inevitably shared by all, people gathered their picture on the basis of the history of individuals and their family, rather than through history as interpreted in the public media. What is noted with particular gravity and sentiment are the conditions of the family organization. In the course of the turbulent history of modern China, serious blows have been inflicted on the family, and Bin Shen certainly had its share of the turmoil.

In pre-Liberation times, what is now the police station housed the Guomindang Sichuan headquarters. Most of the fine courtyarded and walled-off houses in the surrounding narrow lanes were owned by army officers, and the houses in Chang Shun Street by either army officers or wealthy landlords. The old people remember how these people mercilessly extorted rents from the inhabitants and chased out those unable to pay. Correspondingly, and with some grudge, stories about their extravagance in expensive consumption and entertainment with horses, monkeys, and "nurses" still abound; the elderly women especially will frown whenever conversation turns in that direction. During the war with the Japanese, the presence of Guomindang was particularly felt. Systematic bombing of the area in 1941–42 took a heavy toll, according to survivors. The sight of the Japanese planes was harmfully new for a population that was not even familiar with motorcars. Hundreds of people were killed as, stunned with amazement, they watched the planes drop their bombs. A number of houses in Chang Shun Street and the neighboring alleys were destroyed, including the Guomindang headquarters. Heavy and continuous bombardments of Chengdu scattered the population; some died from illnesses in the remote villages and mountain areas to which they fled; others for various reasons never returned to the city. Later, during the civil war through the 1940s when Chengdu was relatively unaffected, refugees from northern provinces ravaged by violent fighting appeared, and some settled in Bin Shen. Among them were a number of Guomindang officers who had fled the advancing Communist forces.

Apart from the centers of foreign trade and influence, Sichuan, along with the rest of China, had practically no modern industry at the time of the Revolution in 1949.[16] In Chengdu, native Chinese industry fell exclusively into the categories of individual handicrafts and larger production or contracting units that employed the same traditional technology. The handicraft factories marked the most advanced stage of native industry. The small workshops run by a master and his family, and occasionally employing a few laborers and apprentices, formed everywhere the common and characteristic unit of production. Their counterparts in commerce were the individual shopkeepers with permanent stalls or the itinerants, who penetrated into every street and alley. Since the Liberation, the size of China's individual economy has fluctuated dramatically, in a constant state of insecurity and change. From periods of near-extinction, private economy has again risen and gained a foothold, always in strict accordance with the policy of central government and its commitment to orthodox doctrine or occasional resurgence of pragmatism and adjustments (Bruun 1990:251).

In Bin Shen, the Liberation in 1949 brought only a short respite to the inhabitants, who were for the most part "ordinary people": most were self-employed in small local businesses and workshops or as porters in town or were poor laborers in private businesses; only very few were employed in some large textile factories in Chengdu. The persecution of landlords, which included execution for some, and the sale of their property by the new regime created a stable environment for the population. Houses in Chang Shun Street were purchased at prices tolerable to their inhabitants, typically 1,000–2,000 *jin* (500–1,000 kilos) of rice. But the acceleration of centralized socialist construction brought new bureaucratic measures toward which the inhabitants were as impotent as before.

The forced collectivization of family businesses and workshops in 1952–53 mark a dreaded point in history for most inhabitants of Bin Shen. While it was beneficial to the very poor, it was far less so to the larger and better established families as they lost all their means of production. For the largest businesses, frequently coinciding with the largest households, it was an economic disaster. Many new collectives were established in previously well off family businesses with convenient premises; thus collectivization for these businesses simply meant that a large number of less fortunate artisans moved in, to be supported on the same business. In regard to technology, nothing was gained, as their sets of tools frequently just duplicated each other, and any equipment not strictly in common use was seized by the new authorities to prevent private ownership of the means of production. A local bicycle repair shop went from supporting four to twelve adults, a noodle shop from three to eight, a restaurant from five to twenty, and so on. Socially, the atmosphere in this type of collective was tense from the outset; the new conditions were only reluctantly accepted. Businesses gradually deteriorated economically. A large number of former workers in private businesses were placed in the new large collective factories set up by the regime and remained in life-long employment. By contrast, a few of the poorest households with no specific professions escaped the restructuring of society as no units would accept them; likewise a few crippled and chronically ill were left outside the public economy and allowed to do some minor business, but were forced to keep to a subsistence level.

The period from 1957 onward, in which the Great Leap Forward from socialism to communism was declared in 1958–60, saw great fluctuations in the general economy all of which affected the conditions of individual business. Abortive development strategies resulted in the catastrophic famine in 1960–62, which in Bin Shen as elsewhere brought indescribable suffering. The monthly rations of food barely covered a week's demand, and people were forced to roam the areas outside the city walls in search of edible leaves, plants, and roots. Children were sent out daily to supplement their diet with whatever could be found. Many families lost both their eldest and youngest members, and the dramatically increased mortality among all age groups forced others to leave the city in search of alternative means of survival.

In Bin Shen, the major political events of the Cultural Revolution from 1966, which caused long periods of civil war–like fighting in the main streets of Chengdu, were only indirectly felt. As the streets were too small to be politically significant, armed patrols were only occasionally seen in Chang Shun Street. Yet the ideological witch hunting that resulted from reestablished central authority under Mao Zedong affected the entire city. In Bin Shen the doctor, who barely survived, was given hard manual labor, restaurant owners became coal porters in the streets, and a lawyer was put to work as a street sweeper. Private businesspeople were publicly beaten, humiliated, and imprisoned, and their homes were raided. Even those with only small operations were persecuted and their belongings seized. As everywhere, all private homes were emptied of antiques, ancestor tablets, books, photographs, old furniture, and anything else bearing witness to a time before. Belongings were either burned at bonfires in the streets or seized by police forces for purposes never revealed.

Economic life in Bin Shen was cut back to a subsistence level. Private businesses were abandoned and their owners and employees placed in state and collective units after punishment. A few minor businesses were allowed to continue: a shoe repair shop, a kiosk, a secondhand clothes shop, and a woman selling spices in the streets.

Seen from the perspective of local social life, the Cultural Revolution also gave rise to the most forceful and direct attacks on the Chinese family. Forced social fragmentation was added to the economic disintegration the family had already suffered; homes were destroyed, households were split up, and the family businesses that had revived shortly before were criminalized and torn to pieces. Most households had members who were sent to the countryside. Many families were divided when both parents were sent away to work in rural communes, and even small children were left to care for themselves; three children, for instance, were left behind under the responsibility of an eleven-year-old girl in one household. The education of schoolchildren and young people was suspended for years, and those who were to receive their basic schooling in those years received none. A large number of adolescents were, in spite of only having passed primary school, sent out as "educated youths." When things slowly returned to normal after 1976, most households gradually reunited; many, however, were not united until the mid 1980s. Private business was for many people the means to leave distant job assignments for the sake of family reunion. Others, however, never had the opportunity to leave their assigned units in the countryside or in towns. A large number of families simply grew apart during these years, and some of the incomplete families in Bin Shen left to live with relatives elsewhere.

Thus, for historical reasons the social organization and social composition of Bin Shen are obviously very far removed from a Chinese village–type settlement dominated by a single or by a few family groups. Present-day inhabitants come from a variety of places and professions, and the state-controlled job assignment system has contributed to the further scattering of individuals.

The Sense of History: Instrumentalization or Distortion?

My long presence in Bin Shen and the process of gathering information about the area by all possible means quite naturally raised as many questions as were answered. But time and again, I was puzzled by the sense of history expressed by ordinary Bin Sheners. For instance, my frequent inquiries about the age and history of private houses, the former layout and appearance of streets, the history of Bin Shen and that of Chengdu at large were met either with an astonishing uncertainty or with simple ignorance. Given the background of a culture that claims unparalleled historical thought and awareness, one could only conclude that the Bin Sheners' familiarity with the history of their immediate surroundings was indeed limited.

Very few knew that their own area not long ago was the walled Manchu city within the city (*shaocheng*), from which the names of several streets in Bin Shen were derived: Dong Chenggen (East Wall) Street, Xi Chenggen (West Wall) Street, Shaocheng (Little City) Street, and so on. Only the elderly were aware that a number of Manchu households still lived in the area. Even among the families that had lived in the area for several generations, little historical knowledge was passed on. Apart from baker Fu, whose own father built his house, not a single incident was recorded of anyone knowing the exact age of the house the family occupied or even a brief outline of its history. They were similarly ignorant regarding the immediate physical surroundings, including streets, markets, and neighborhoods. Apparently "things" such as streets, houses, furniture, and belongings are not attributed histories of their own and do not carry intrinsic value separated from the value of use. All recorded knowledge of the cityscape was intimately entangled in peoples' own family histories, and even those were sparse. So if a house was built by someone who did not belong to one's own family line, its "history" would not be known; if any history was recorded, it was that from the time when the present occupant family moved in. In a wider perspective, knowledge of the cityscape could hardly be expected to be distributed among the populace with any degree of evenness, particularly when taking into account the tumultuous history of Chinese cities. However, our inquiries revealed no amateur historians or other local specialists who took an interest in local history in abstract and general terms.

Knowledge of local history arises from knowledge of one's own family history. The question is whether historical knowledge is a "luxury" afforded by material welfare or if people have other motives for pursuing it. Experience showed that outsiders, meaning people from elsewhere in Chengdu, often knew considerably more about Bin Shen than insiders. Members of the old elite in particular had a basic knowledge of Bin Shen's former position and of former Bin Shen residents such as Liu Wenhui,[17] the former Guomindang general who converted to communism. Moreover, usually both young and old belonging to the upper social stratum had some knowledge of Bin Shen. Reasons for this should be sought along several lines. Since the family history of the majority of these people was somehow entangled with Bin Shen, family history and area history combined, or local history was made significant through lines of family descent. For the old elite now comfortably reestablishing itself in education, administration, and culture, history contains a wide spectrum of possibilities — from selected historical material supporting certain ideas or well-defined aims, such as the historical importance of a cultured elite, to history itself being intentionally created, as is the continuous practice of state power. Amid such interests is an inclination to think that history should be glorious. In its functional dimension, only glorious history is recorded by families and the state alike, tied up with definite social aims in the present, implicitly relating to the pursuit of, or justification for, power.

But why do not the present inhabitants of Bin Shen to any extent link their own history to area characteristics? A factor that could explain this is the correlation between cultural ideals and social accomplishment, which will be discussed in chapter four. Chinese ideals should perhaps be perceived as a totality, implying that historical consciousness is also tied to the awareness of social accomplishment: families unable to live up to Chinese cultural ideals find no reason to investigate or memorize history — neither their own nor that of other people.

The people interviewed used different criteria when locating events in time. Apart from a number of old women who did not know their exact birth years, most people marked their own and their closest relatives' lives by important events in particular years — births, marriages, and deaths. Otherwise they tended to share a traditional type of periodization, placing things and events not at particular points in a continuously flowing history, but within sharp demarcations in the history of society: "Qing dynasty" meaning sometime prior to 1911; "before Liberation," meaning anything from late Qing dynasty to 1949; "before," "during," or "after" the Cultural Revolution, itself covering a decade, meaning sometime between two significant points in history. The old houses in Chang Shun Street and Dong Chenggen Street were referred to as belonging to the period before Liberation, and in some cases to the Qing dynasty. When requested to specify, people would state "more than a hundred years" or "several hundred years" and simultaneously gesticulate as to indicate that it did not matter. When, for instance, the owner of a house in Chang Shun Street rebuilt the interior in order to open a restaurant, several old vertical signboards of the type put up in front of houses and shops in "the old days" appeared. Years back they had been scrapped and, together with other boards, used for the interior partitions. Though nicely carved with characters of fortune-bringing poems and once painted in brown, red, and gold, which suggested that they were quite old, no one showed any interest in them. Neither could anyone read them properly, and they were used as firewood along with the rest of the old timber.

Local community history must be useful if it is to be recorded or memorized. This view of history is not substantially different from the customary view of knowledge that is expressed in interpersonal relations. Seldom is information passed for its own sake. Knowing or not knowing something may be a means of drawing some people closer or maintaining distance to others, giving some people up or protecting friends, creating a certain picture of things or showing no interest at all. Along similar lines, a highly selective historical knowledge may be utilized to avoid official scrutiny and danger. Modern Chinese history may even have strengthened traditional ways as a defense mechanism. The elder generation is, for instance, extremely cautious in relating anything that determines their class background, unless this is known to everyone. An old woman who owned a large house in a side alley claimed that she did not know the former occupation of her husband's deceased father, who had built the house and in whose household she had lived for four decades. If taken at face value, this answer is absurd; it is, of course, to be seen as avoiding answering an unpleasant question. But when the culturally inherent instrumentalization of knowledge is enforced by the post-Liberation politicization of all information, including social background and family history, even the broad narrative of local history becomes distorted. For the anthropologist, it is both a methodological problem and a major frustration, since knowledge of a wide range of matters is lost in collective amnesia.

CHAPTER THREE

Enterprising Households

In Bin Shen the presence of public authorities is not instantly visible. As any urban Chinese locality, however, Bin Shen has all the institutions of a complex society — as well as specific ones. All households are integrated into a network of organizations representing local as well as central government bodies: Public Security, Industrial and Commercial Administration Bureau, Tax Administration, and Public Health clinics are all present in the area. Street and Neighborhood Committees are in charge of well-defined numbers of households in cooperation with the Party organization, which has representatives in all public institutions.

China's individual sector is formally organized under the nationwide Industrial and Commercial Administration Bureau (ICB),[1] a body directly controlled by central government. The ICB in principle is in charge of all affairs of private business as regards the issue of permits, registration, supervision of businesses, and advice on management. As the agency that implements the policy of the central government in this field, the ICB is also responsible for preparing statistical material and otherwise reporting back to the central government on all matters concerning the individual sector. The ICB has a series of departments operating at the provincial and municipal levels. Within the municipality, it has a network of district and local offices; the latter are responsible for a neighborhood comprising a number of streets, according to the density of businesses.

The local offices of the ICB organize managers of individual businesses into the Self-employed Laborers Association,[2] which in turn is divided into branches of businesses within the local area. The association holds regular (usually monthly) meetings, in which ICB representatives and association voluntary assistants inform about state policies and general law and set up guidelines to help the individual shopkeepers avoid possible violations of the law.

Besides the specific organization of businesses, the individual business households are also placed under the standard administrative organization of local areas. A Street Committee[3] office in charge of a quarter somewhat larger than Bin Shen is the lowest level of organization with permanent, state-employed staff members. This agency organizes Neighborhood Committees, each in charge of one street or just a section of a street, according to population. In Bin Shen the Neighborhood Committees consist of between three and eight members and are in charge of somewhere between twenty and a hundred households; the physical layout of dwellings tends to be determinant since every compound or block that shares a common entrance has one or more responsible committee members.

Bin Shen,[4] in ICB administrative terms, is a subdivision of the West Chengdu district. The nine staff members of the Dong Chenggen Street local office are in charge of five Street Committee areas with a total of 1,335 businesses.[5] Out of these, approximately 270 are situated within Bin Shen area itself; the rest are in the remaining four areas comparable in size to Bin Shen. Bin Shen area covers seven streets in which private businesses are found, of which Chang Shun Street is the central. Sixty percent of businesses in the area are here, as is the free market.

All private businesses are organized into the Self-employed Laborers Association, although this organization includes only the managers. Within the association, managers are divided into six branches according to the type of their businesses.[6] The larger branches, such as "catering," are further divided into subgroups; thus all groups are fairly equal in size with approximately ten to fifteen members. Each group has an appointed group head and two deputy group heads responsible to the association. Their duties are primarily to collect taxes, to assist in estimating the turnover of businesses (turnover meaning the total value of business done), to represent the ICB and other authorities in relation to shopkeepers, and to mediate between these levels. They also assist in arranging regular assemblies on the group and street levels.

The administrative organization of Chang Shun Street's approximately 750 households (average four to five persons per household[7]) is divided into six blocks, each with a Neighborhood Committee responsible to the Street Committee above. The administration of the entire Bin Shen area is more complex as it also contains apartment blocks. Neighborhood Committee work is in principle unpaid but serves as an extension of the city administration in a downward direction. The Neighborhood Committees have three main areas of official duties: the environment, health, and security. No special duties exist in relation to private business households apart from assessing the validity of their applications for business licenses. Hereafter they are treated as ordinary households in the handling of daily affairs.

Interviewing

One of the first shops a person going down Chang Shun Street encounters is Mr. Wang's restaurant on the right. Mr. Wang is a retired bank employee and now de facto owner of a prospering business; he exemplifies the model of a successful businessman. In 1987 he was the first entrepreneur to be presented to us by the Industrial and Commercial Administration Bureau official Ms. Yang, a stern-looking woman in her forties. We were duly greeted by Mr. Wang and seated around a small table outside the restaurant; this is the table where Mr. Wang spends his time when the weather permits, chatting with neighbors and customers, operating the abacus, and vigilantly protecting the cash box. During the interview, he willingly answers our questions about his business, occasionally sending a quick glance to Ms. Yang to test her reactions. A turnover of 10,000 yuan[8] per month with a 30 percent profit was controversial until recently. In 1987 it had become the model for development in the official jargon; figures like Mr. Wang are the new development heroes of the media. He openly expresses his pride in his business and his ability through it to gather a large family around him. His two sons have remained in the household with their wives and children, turning the place into a genuine family business. Mr. Wang is the patriarch, head of the household as well as of the business organization and the sole decision maker. The conversation, however, touches points of controversy several times. When questioned about ownership matters, he readily admits, "Well, there is some contradiction in our business. Actually, my son is the license holder; I am only taking care of it until he is old enough to control it himself" (his son is thirty-five). Ms. Yang nods in acceptance. The regulations do not permit a retiree on full pension to run a private business. Later on, when asked about the prospects of developing the business, Mr. Wang reveals the family plans to open another branch of the restaurant, managed by his son: "Of course our purpose is to serve people; this we are devoted to. But we would also like to expand our business. At the moment, we cannot meet the demand of the huge number of customers; we simply cannot provide enough food. The restaurant is too small. So we are looking for a nearby location to open a new branch." Ms. Yang breaks in here: "Thanks to the Open Door Policy and the Party's leading role, Mr. Wang can develop his business to the benefit and development of the whole country." We are witnesses to a double-sided play meticulously staged through formal language.

The play ends when we question the prospects of a changing attitude toward individual businesses, suggesting their attractive profits to be of paramount influence. Ms. Yang interrupts, faithfully reciting another phrase of formal language: "No, it is due to our Party policy and the support of the government to the individual households. The government organizes the managers of individual businesses into the Self-employed Laborers Association. This organization helps to solve the problem of social class. So now the social position of individual households is higher than it was before. We also elect, from individual managers, representatives to the People's Congress." The question of social position is obviously controversial. Ms. Yang soon excuses herself and leaves to see to other duties. During the first week, she participated in our interviews, though with decreasing intensity, and finally stated her confidence in our ability to perform them ourselves.

Mr. Wang's restaurant, the success of which is greatly envied by numerous other restaurant keepers in the street, consists of a fifty-square-meter room equipped with eight round tables. One corner is arranged as an open kitchen; it is separated from the tables only by the counter where meats and vegetables are prepared by the six young employees from the country. They attend to all manual labor in the business. Because it specializes in banquets for family gatherings and cadre meetings, the restaurant has attained a unique position in the street. This is where people go for a treat within the means of a common budget: a one-table banquet seating eight to ten people is 60 yuan. During our presence, a party sits down to a banquet in honor of a deceased grandfather, the head of a large household. They occupy three tables. Because of its unique position Mr. Wang's business not only provides him with a wide range of

contacts in the neighborhood but also secures what he terms "harmonious" relations with local authorities. Mr. Wang is himself a healthy looking man in his late sixties, with a self-confident appearance and a row of shiny white teeth — virtually too white to be his own. He embodies an accomplished Chinese male, brought up in pre-Liberation society. The premises, which consist of the restaurant and a dwelling behind, are actually his birthplace. They belonged to his parents, who ran a teahouse there until the 1950s, when they were taken over by Mr. Wang. He continued the business until the Cultural Revolution eventually closed the place in 1970. With the exception of the fourteen years that have passed until the present restaurant opened, the Wang family has been doing business here for almost a century. The present building was erected about 1900.

Numerous restaurants have opened in Chang Shun Street; apparently the example and profit of Mr. Wang carries great weight. Approximately 30 percent of all businesses are now restaurants. Here, close to where the street leads off the huge Temple Street, they are located side by side to attract the stream of potential customers. The demand for restaurants seems insatiable. In spite of the general assumption in the neighborhood that this type of business depends on a large group of steady customers, most newly opened restaurants are in a matter of weeks able to yield profits that are no less than formidable in the eyes of ordinary wage earners. Even those restaurants opened by people with little or no experience in the business are doing well. At the beginning of the 1980s and up to 1985–86, private groceries were equally profitable. The daring early entrepreneurs who did not hesitate to go private as soon as the new policy was declared made fortunes. The shops became too numerous, however, and scores of them closed. Although the reforms permitting individual business are only a decade old, the phenomenon of "waves" of particular businesses is already well known in the area; groceries, kiosks, a photo printing shop, and now the restaurants are all linked to waves of businesses in Chengdu. As monetary affairs are a major topic of ordinary conversation, news about success and new wealth from private business spreads rapidly by word of mouth in the city. Business strategies are predominantly based on such information. The older people in business, however, find it only normal.[9]

Individual businesses are launched for various reasons, reflecting the life courses of individuals as well as households. Among the individual households, some have very peculiar grounds, indicating that private business may serve as a social refuge as much as an economic safety net in relation to formal society. This was the case for another family who runs a restaurant somewhat farther down Chang Shun Street. In 1983 the Zhang family had an eight-year-old daughter and expected a second child. The unit (a food company) in which the couple worked put pressure on them to abort the pregnancy, and the tension between the two sides increased gradually. The couple refused to give in as they very much desired a son. When the baby, a son, was born, the unit rejected the parents. Street Committee authorities continued the pressure, however, and when the child was old enough to be taken away, the family eventually gave up their struggle. The baby was adopted by relatives (the husband's brother) in the United States in order for him to become an American citizen.

The Zhangs compensated for the lost child economically when they started a private business after leaving the unit. Four employees from the country do the routine jobs of preparing the food, and the business turns over 5,000–10,000 yuan per month; the Zhangs' profit is now more than five times their earnings in their former unit.[10] Although the restaurant covers only twenty-five square meters, it has prospered through their effort to target customers from some wealthy units nearby. The regular customers, including TV stars from the Sichuan Television Broadcasting a few blocks away, are the pride of as well as excellent publicity for the business; Mr. Zhang emphasizes the importance of his customers' social class. Like Mr. Wang's business, the Zhangs' also lacks space to satisfy all the customers. Mentioning their rival Mr. Wang, the Zhangs claim to have secured a share of his customers who were dissatisfied with the quality of his banquets. (Mr. Zhang becomes excited and rather annoyed when talking about his rival.)

Competition relates to *guanxi* as well as to customers. Our reference to Mr. Wang's stated turnover sparks off a bitter remark, probably aimed at Ms. Yang: "It's impossible; it is far more than that, maybe several times more than he says." (The stated turnover is agreed on by the ICB and is the basis for taxation.) Ms. Yang, who at this point has taken a more relaxed position during the interviews, chooses to remain silent. Her face even loosens into a slight smile when another discrepancy between proclaimed policy and local reality is revealed. When asked about the source of the meat and other foodstuffs used in the restaurant, Mr. Zhang claims that the local market is too expensive: "They are not peasants selling their own produce [this should be the case according to regulations], they are retail dealers. They buy it at the same place as we do, and sell it here at a profit." My assistant Liu interrupts, looking sideways at Yang with a grin on his face: "They are stimulating the economy, to say it in newspaper language." When more points of contradiction arise, Ms. Yang is finally disarmed and refrains from citing more phrases of Party politics. During the interview, Zhang states that all his countryside employees are about twenty years of age. (Regulations demand ordinary employees to be above eighteen.) But when asked about a young boy squatting outside to clean the lumps of pork contained in a huge basket, he modifies his words: "Well, he is only sixteen, but those inside are twenty." Mr. Wang is apparently not the only one who has obtained the tax authorities' recognition of rather unrealistic turnover figures. Zhang claims his own turnover to be 5,000-6,000 yuan per month; yet the discussion on buying raw materials on the market reveals that his daily purchase of meat is incredible: a quick calculation estimates his turnover to be 8,000-10,000 yuan on the meat alone.

Private restaurants have won a popularity among both the inhabitants and the businesspeople in the street. This testifies to their invaluable contribution to local social life, although regular eating out is still the privilege of the few. Serving beer and *baijiu* — strong alcohol — has also become an important aspect of the food services sector. One place which has this as a primary source of income is the House of Zhe Xian, named after a famous ancient poet and wine lover. The place is run by Qixuan, a thirty-one-year-old woman. After five years of embarrassing waiting for a job while living with her parents, she finally decided to try private business. After a single month of operation, the small restaurant containing three tables yields her a profit of more than 600 yuan. The two rural employees earn 50 yuan each. A raised eyebrow from Ms. Yang, however, makes Qixuan correct herself: "No, 80 yuan."

The local restaurants tend to become specialized to suit the needs and economic capacity of the differing strata of local life. The very cheapest meals consisting of noodle soup with a few vegetables are served in the restaurants near the market, where the peasants and market vendors depend on light and inexpensive meals served during the day. A meal here can be purchased for 22 fen (0.22 yuan). One such place is the restaurant of another Zhang family, consisting of a thirty-nine-year-old man, his wife, and his mother. The husband had been among the first group of educated youth to settle in the countryside in 1966. He returned to Chengdu in the beginning of the 1970s but could only find temporary employment in different factories.[11] A month before our first visit, he had finally decided to become a restaurant keeper like his father. The excellent location of their house, which faces the market, was the decisive factor; it is now the key to a considerable income. He bought it when he married in 1974 for only 700 yuan — a fraction of its present value. In spite of their recent start, limited experience, and simple meals, the business runs well and secures the household a handsome profit. Always packed with market vendors, soldiers, students, and others wanting a simple meal, the restaurant keeps the family busy, not to speak of the four employees from the country. The crowd of customers bursts into laughter when a solidly built peasant rises from his baskets of eggs in order to have a closer look at my rather formal question sheet during our first visit: "I only know these," he says, running his big index finger down a row of numbers; "that's all I need to count my money."

The restaurant craze is no isolated phenomenon. The great love for food is apparently universal in Chinese society, and it is no less praised today, when it has finally become abundant after decades of, at times, inconceivable distress. The new wealth that at least some have gained is, to a degree that occasionally worries central government, realized extensively through all possible forms of consumption. Expensive food and beverages are only small expenditures compared to the color televisions, tape recorders, and even motorcycles that businesspeople now purchase. Another luxury article that has made inroads into the habits of entrepreneurs is expensive cigarettes, either foreign, if obtainable, or top-quality Chinese, mainly from Yunnan province. When sold in the street, the best Chinese cigarettes are about 3 yuan a packet — the equivalent of a day's wages for a state employee. Consumption carries symbolic value for the nouveax riches. Consumption also indicates a certain distrust for government and its proclaimed political stability. This attitude is summarized in a local expression, probably meant metaphorically as well as literally: "What your stomach contains, no one can take away from you."[12]

Riding on a high tide of consumption is also the baker, whose shop is next to Mr. Wang's restaurant. He produces cakes and biscuits for countless family gatherings such as birthdays, weddings, and funerals and for what he states to be even more important — the numerous spoiled, only children in the neighborhood. Fu, the baker, does business from the very same shop that his father ran before Liberation, though at that time his father sold electrical equipment. Fu is in his late thirties and has an open, ever-smiling face. His round spectacles with one broken lens make him look like something between an overgrown schoolboy and a traditional scholar. He turns out nevertheless to be knowledgeable on the latest government policies — a sort of knowledge that apparently has strained his relations with local authorities. Ms. Yang eyes him like a hawk when, in a rather worried tone, he replies "*keyi*," meaning "not bad," to our questions about his cooperation with local administration. We learned later about the nature of their clashing interests over licenses since Mr. Fu was an exemplary informant, always worth a visit. Fu and his wife launched their bakery not only to make more money, but also out of concern for their child, a seven-year-old son. Because they owned a house, both parents lived separate from their unit of work, and childcare was a permanent problem. In 1987, after carefully analyzing the signals from the central government, Fu decided that the time was ripe for opening a private business. This switch would enable the couple to take care of the child during the day while running the shop. Assisted by two employees from the country, the family lives a comparatively easy life; Mr. Fu purchases raw materials and attends to management affairs, and his wife does the practical business by organizing the employees' labor. In spite of the long opening hours, stretching as long as customers desire, private business affords the Fus plenty of time to rest, spend time with friends and neighbors, or take trips downtown. Mr. Fu is frequently seen at the small table outside the shop, entertaining friends, customers, and passersby. When he refers to his customers as consisting of many from the "upper classes," he uses this concept freely, referring to the cadres and well-educated in the neighborhood. Business goes on all through the week, amounting to a seven-day working week for the employees; Mr. Fu seems to forget, but a gesture from Ms. Yang makes him recall: "Ah — yes, as compensation the employees work only six hours per day."

The growing differentiation of ordinary citizens is gradually becoming more conspicuous. Pushed forward by private business, the inequality in terms of wages or profit among the households in Bin Shen has risen to a level few locals had even dreamed of a decade ago. Furthermore, private business has initiated a clear social stratification or, if seen in a historical perspective, has triggered the reappearance of social categories that for a time had only survived in latency. While some categories of society in the area were easily distinguishable and, like the young employees from the countryside, encumbered with a common disregard, other categories were more ambiguous. The successful managers of individual businesses constitute one such category. A specific situation at an interview illustrates this point. We are seated around a small table outside Shang's tailor shop. It is a tiny place where three apprentices with treadle sewing machines are crammed together and Shang's wife has a small table where she cuts material. Shang receives customers, does some designing, and manages the shop. When he launched it a year and a half ago, he had no experience in tailoring; neither had his wife, who, being disabled, never had an official job. Shang returned from the countryside in 1981. He had only temporary employment for a few years, until he made the decision to launch into business. When we talk about the common disregard for private businesspeople, he says: "Maybe some people look down upon us, but we have more money than they do and we can spend it freely. I am proud of my business and happy to see people wear the clothes I design. I enjoy my art of making clothes." Shang and his wife make at least 500–600 yuan per month through their business and in good periods probably as much as a thousand. From a previous discreet inquiry we had learned that Ms. Yang, who has a high school education and is an experienced official, receives a salary of 100 yuan per month. Liu, my assistant, a competent university graduate in sociology with two foreign languages, makes 120. Although these state employees may receive extra benefits from their units, they are still completely outdistanced by the new entrepreneurs like Shang. He seems to enjoy the situation when he, with special address to them, proclaims his freedom in work: "If I want to go on vacation, I can just close my door. I'm the boss."

The difference in income between private entrepreneurs and the officials in charge of controlling the private economy is, of course, one of the preconditions for various corrupt practices. Far more significant, however, is its challenge to some essential Chinese classifications. That people of little education and no formal position become wealthy has precedent, but the present proportions are controversial. Big private business managers now constitute a group that does not fit into common classifications; they have become a separate stratum in local society.

Entrepreneurs

Among the shopkeepers of Bin Shen approximately 25 percent are from outside Chengdu; another 10 percent claim the earlier mentioned double affiliation by referring to the fact that their families came from other areas, but they themselves were born in Chengdu. About 30 percent are natives of Bin Shen area itself. The elderly inhabitants especially have a strong affiliation with the area; of the present age-group above sixty, practically all are natives of Bin Shen or settled there as children or when quite young. Several inhabitants in Chang Shun Street are over eighty and still reside in their original homes or in houses nearby. A woman of ninety-seven still lives in the former bakery where she arrived as a bride eighty years ago. Her husband, the baker, died from illness in 1942 (fifty-five years old), during their escape to the countryside.

After Ms. Yang had definitively left us on our own, our interviews soon revealed that a substantial number of individuals had never held any official job in a state or collective unit; they were either carrying on a trade that had been their basic livelihood for the major part of their lives or taken up after moving constantly after temporary work in changing units, interrupted by long periods of unemployment. These individuals had escaped the tight social control of the work units and slipped through periods of mass campaigns and cultural revolution by living in the interstices. Others managed only through bitter and often mentally devastating struggle. A sixty-three-year-old woman selling spices from a small stall in Chang Shun Street is an example of someone who never held official positions. With her five children in tow, she used to sell spices from a small trolley in the neighborhood. They actually lived in the streets as they never owned anything that qualified as a home. In 1982 she and her husband purchased their present dwelling with the stipulation that the former occupant, a seventy-three-year-old woman, could live with them until she died. The house, which is nothing more than a ramshackle shed of six square meters, accommodates three adults who sleep in the same bed, as there is space for little more than this and a few personal belongings. The case illustrates that, in addition to the fact that private enterprise itself is rapidly growing, its legalization has become the means of bringing semiclandestine economic activity under the control and registration of the responsible authorities. Individuals within this group clearly belong to the category of doing individual business as the only means of subsistence. Another group of shopkeepers of whom it may be said that circumstances determined the course of their lives is made up of former employees in collective units. Concurrently with economic reforms imposing competition and market orientation on a widening range of enterprises, collective factories (generally smaller than state factories and frequently street based) in particular seem to have suffered. Countless small collective units unable to renew their technology or alter their production processes are failing, and even larger ones are in trouble. Others have exploited the reforms to dispose of surplus manpower that has strained their economy for decades. When these units dismiss their employees, there is no safety net of social security to cushion their fall.[13] The problem has been recognized for a number of years, and its significance in terms of scale and gravity seems to be steadily growing. The problem is particularly grave as those who get fired are typically older people with little education and few skills. If their households are able to care for them, they are secure. For an elderly couple working in the same unit the situation can be critical if they are laid off, however, especially if their children are all married and live elsewhere.

One of the poorest households consists of a sixty-six-year-old woman who lives with her youngest son. After working in a collective factory for seventeen years (she and her husband were assigned work there during the Cultural Revolution after having run a small family business for years), they and thirty other elderly employees were dismissed from the factory with a small pension — a sum equivalent to just five months' wages. Two years ago her husband died, leaving a household of just two members. The woman has no education and is illiterate, as are most women her age. She now makes a living from sewing the upper parts of leather shoes for a collective shop that pays her for piece work. A turnover of merely 60 yuan per month and a profit of 30 yuan added to her son's meager wages amounts to far less than it takes to support a household. She leads a truly miserable life, able to afford only the barest of necessities. In case of illness, she must rely on the mercy of neighbors, since she cannot afford to buy medicine. Her appearance is pitiful; the infection in her face and eyes is badly in need of medical treatment. "I think the factory had ways to take care of us," she says. "We don't deserve to be treated like this. When it developed and got prosperous it just dismissed us. I won't die of starvation, but I'm very much afraid of falling ill, because it's impossible for me to pay for hospitalization."

Individual business reflects the rapidly growing disparity in living standards in Chinese society as it comprises the extremes. Private enterprise typically provides an opportunity to the marginal groups, such as individuals with a distinct entrepreneurial spirit. Driven by the firm belief that their skills can be more efficiently utilized than they are in state units — and that their incentive will yield profit — they set out to prove it. They are energetic and dedicated, which is evidenced in their working hours: twelve or more hours a day, seven days a week, totally eradicating any distinction between work and spare time, between business and family life. They are not quite young, rather between thirty and forty. This is generally the age when people feel their long-standing plans take a "now or never" character and thus need to materialize. Another factor that may exclude the very young is the clear and direct proportionality between investment and profit; success in business generally demands capital beyond their reach.[14] Higher education is no criterion for success, but it certainly helps. It enables one to handle authorities, it generates respectability and trust, and not the least important, it helps in running a business. In fact, among the wealthiest entrepreneurs some have comparatively high educations. By contrast, the illiterate are greatly handicapped in situations of conflicting interests as well as in complying with regulations of growing complexity. As is evident from the profitability of various types of businesses, the true entrepreneur very often sees a restaurant as the fulfillment of his or her ambitions.

Not all shopkeepers can be classified as either victims of circumstance or hard-driving, self-made individuals; a distinct third category of shopkeepers consist of elderly people. In fact, the single largest age group among the interviewed is from sixty-five to seventy years of age. Persons over sixty years old make up 30 percent of the shopkeepers. These people can hardly be expected to be the most active and enterprising of shopkeepers. And apart from a few cases, they actually form a separate group characterized by the desire to live with a suitable level of activity, having in numerous cases returned to their original occupations. The shoemaker has resumed his production of all handmade cloth shoes — a trade he learned more than fifty years ago. The smith is once again producing cake forms from scrap metal. The saddler makes handbags of plastic or, if the customer can afford it, of leather. Elderly people engaged in private business are typically either craftsmen returning to their old trade or cadres who, after an early retirement, still have the energy to start up in a new field.

Depending on the size and composition of the household, businesses vary in their internal organization. Like other households, those in business raise a strong demarcation between inner and outer spheres, which of course greatly affects the sort of answers strangers will receive. This is especially the case in the economic field, the main area of interaction between the household and the outer world and the primary source of conflict with public authorities. The loyalty among family members and openness toward the closest of associates is contrasted by what is usually seen as an almost impenetrable wall of suspicion toward all strangers and authority figures. Relations toward the outside world, however, tend to be perceived as belonging to separate categories, corresponding to the level of "strangeness" and social distance from the family; each category has its own concepts and type of communication. Three successive interviews with one household would result in three different accounts of their success, income, organization, relation with authorities, and ensuing business problems. During the initial interview the household would state: "Thanks to the Open Door Policy and the Communist party we have been able to start a private business, which makes our life much easier than before and contributes to the socialist construction of our country." At a following visit, the statement would be modified: "Because of the Open Door Policy, it is now possible to run private business and become more independent, but it is still very difficult." And when closer ties to the household were established and suspicion diminished, the statement could be changed dramatically or even reversed: "It's impossible to do business under these conditions; maybe some can, but we cannot." Accordingly, statements on essential business matters such as turnover or profit would fit into certain established categories of communication: one set of figures for representatives of authority, one for customers, and presumably another for intimate relations. In the nature of things, intimate relationships could only be established with a small selection of families or key people during fieldwork. The differing levels of communication according to social distance lead to certain language use in certain situations. Especially when anyone associated with bureaucracy and formal authority is involved, the greater the distance, the more the language will approximate the language of the state or what may be termed the "language of power." In this sense such language shows acknowledgment of, and subordination to, authority.

Investigating the internal organization of households we were met with similar problems, although the extremely limited scope for privacy in this type of community left few family affairs concealed from the persistent scrutiny of fellows. Matters of common knowledge to the neighborhood — even rather intimate and unflattering characteristics of individuals — could also be related to strangers. When we visited a couple who, although in their early seventies, still ran a small shop producing clay stoves, the husband said about his wife standing next to him: "We are greatly hampered in business because my wife is crazy (*fengle*). [And the circle of listeners around us all agreed: "Yes, she's crazy, she's crazy."] She went crazy during the Cultural Revolution, when we were molested."[15]

In spite of endless hardship, social unrest, and deliberate harassment, the household (*hu*) is still the life core of common people; it is the primary and dominant factor in all social organization. In relation to public authorities the individual is primarily seen as belonging to a household, as it is expressed in the term *geti hu*, individual household, which is used even if only a single person is registered as a business holder. The households share this perception. When, for instance, the authorities arrange meetings for business-people, another household member than the one registered as shopkeeper is likely to show up — a fact that emphasizes that the household regards itself as a distinct unit in relation to the outside world. The household not only constitutes the basic unit in local society, but also provides personal identity; the work unit or a professional affiliation — that is, the identity assigned the citizen from above — ranks second in people's minds. Social status, name (with family name placed before the personal name), and origin (native place of family regardless of present residence) are the fundamental elements of an organic cooperation wherein individuals share the pleasures and hardship of life according to an established code. The traditional household assigns well-defined roles to individuals within this structure, which emphasizes function and harmony and in which the common denominator is hierarchical relations. As elsewhere in society, however, formal principles are coupled with an informal social reality with numerous channels for deviation. Even the composition of the family and principles of descent can be manipulated by the application of kinship terms: A distant relative can be incorporated into the household by being addressed as uncle or aunt; children of relatives or even strangers can be taken in as sons and daughters; and, in rare cases, friends can be incorporated as brothers and sisters. An estimated 15–20 percent of the interviewed households had incorporated distant relatives or strangers, mainly young but in a few cases elderly people, as full family members. Once incorporated, individuals participate loyally in work and social life according to the prescribed roles. Money as well as other belongings are common property, spent and used as such.

It must be reiterated that this traditional family (*jia*) is a purely abstract concept; it denotes an ideal form of family organization, with only the ideal itself being a static component of tradition. The strong continuity of social ideals in Chinese culture, even when social reality runs astray, is indeed the basis of coherence and cultural integrity. The real-life family is a polymorphous group whose only common characteristics are those of male succession and notions of harmony. Various ways of breaking up, reorganizing, and manipulating family organization exist and may always have existed. The stem family (and if possible the extended family with several nuclear units in the second generation), comprising three or more generations under one roof, still serves as the model, at least for the older generation, and the axis around which variation revolves (only the household of Mr. Wang constituted an extended family). But even so, less than 50 percent of households are stem families. The marginal position of individual enterprising households also becomes clear in this sense; their internal organization tends to display more examples of fragmented and incomplete families than other groups, although no conclusive figures can be given. Elderly discharged workers with no children who stay behind to care for them are forced into the individual economy. Former street vendors who have never had official employment and have never had a standard of living that permitted them to keep their children within the household now also have the smallest families. Another group consists of the handicapped and chronically ill. They are generally excluded from ordinary employment, and some are unable to parent a new generation. At the other end of the scale are some entrepreneurial and freedom-loving young people, for whom one advantage of individual business is the opportunity to escape from the control of family elders. These types of families often stretch over only one or two generations. The main division in relation to stem families is between the eldest and the remaining generations: elderly couples living alone or younger people living with their children but separate from their own parents. Numerous variations are found, for instance, elderly people who raise grandchildren while the middle generation has chosen to live separately. Families may also be split vertically by divorces or external circumstances like distant job assignments or deaths. Yet it is altogether characteristic of most families that ideals are upheld without regard to the present ability to fulfill them.

Organization

Business organization runs parallel to lines of power and authority within the households. As a formally hierarchical organization with authority determined by age and gender, the household is headed by the eldest male. Business is managed accordingly. The authority of male shopkeepers is seldom questioned, even when the actual financial control is not in their hands. Few businesses, however, are as exemplary as Mr. Wang's restaurant. Businesses managed by middle-aged or elderly males with several generations involved are of course closer to the ideal form than others; but even though most people share these ideals for the composition of the household and the business, few may be able to realize them. Cooperation between household members is mostly harmonious, since all family relations tend to be determined by custom. Almost all households state that cooperation is excellent and that family members are preferred in business as it involves fewer contradictions than working with "members of other families."

Individual businesses invariably operate throughout the week. In the words of their owners: "Of course we do; the more we work, the more money we make." Only in the local private kindergarten is there a fixed weekly day of rest. Working hours, however, vary from business to business.[16] Physical labor is regarded as tiring and requiring more rest; it is therefore performed fewer hours per day. The tailor and knitting shops have long working hours, especially at the height of the season, whereas other types of manufacturing demand much less. The chopboard makers in Dong Chenggen Street probably have the shortest actual working hours of all. Their work rarely requires more than a couple of hours of cutting and planing. The remainder of the day is spent waiting for customers to purchase the day's output. Similarly, the bakers, the makers of signboards, and different repair shops generally have far fewer hours of physical work than the number of hours spent in the shop, thus combining light manufacturing with attending to customers.

Service businesses and restaurants have by far the longest average working hours. Restaurants usually offer periods of rest between peak hours, whereas service businesses stay open all day long. In several cases, where shop and dwelling are combined in a single room, opening up for business in the morning and closing up for the night literally signal the waking and retiring of the household. The working hours of owners and employees often varied immensely. The owners of well-established and successful businesses allow themselves long hours of leisure during the day. Some businesses, even some very small ones, were entirely attended to by the employees from the countryside, leaving the owner free to engage in other activities or simply relax. In contrast, the employees generally worked during the whole time the business was open.

All household-based enterprises appear to be well-functioning economic units with relatively little tension over division of labor, periods of work and leisure, and profit sharing. As pointed out by several families, however, if smooth cooperation among the family members could not be predicted, it would hardly have been profitable to launch an individual enterprise. The household heads are of course most sympathetic to family business. In individual businesses they wield an unchallenged authority, which would have been somewhat reduced if all family members had separate jobs. In this respect individual business households are likely to return to true patriarchal leadership by becoming economically independent. A few of the elderly shopkeepers even state that one reason for running a business is to control the young people, who otherwise would be "playing around too much." This was the case with an elderly couple who still had their youngest son with them. Unemployed for a couple of years, he showed little concern for anything other than making the best of his freedom, so his mother opened a bicycle repair shop for him to run. This was the pre-Liberation occupation of the household, and many old tools still remained in their possession. The household head, who came from a long line of smiths, no longer took part in business; instead he retreated to watching television and playing chess in the park.

Contrary to household heads, who are content to have their families gathered under their command, the young generation regularly expresses the desire to emancipate themselves from the authority of their parents and start businesses of their own; such desires are a potential source of conflict. Material circumstances, as well as the wish to avoid discord within the family, eventually make such "not possible" in most cases. In this respect, the young unmarried daughters enjoy more freedom to break away from their households, since this will be the consequence of their marriage anyway. Several individual businesses in the area are run solely by young unmarried women without interference from their parents, whereas this is rarely the case with the young men — but little interference is naturally accompanied by less financial support from the family.

Yet there is little deviation from the common pattern of family relations in harmony (*hesheng*), especially when the family is under pressure from the outside. Elaborations on the concept of harmony as a traditional value included comments on the incorporation of all members into the pattern of authority given by custom and all members carefully attending to the common good. The result is considered to be the joy of working together in an enterprise in which no one feels that his or her labor is exploited by others. "Harmony" thus refers to the conformity of all household members, especially in regard to the unity of the household organization with regard to the outside world. Harmonious relations, however, hardly signify the absence of contradiction and tension; rather, harmony is the ability to overcome, or at least curb, them and in so doing avoid substantial threats to the integrity of the household. Contradiction naturally exists, and not only between the younger and older generations. The role of women is an acknowledged area of conflict. Conspicuous discrepancy exists between the prescribed distribution of roles within the household organization and actual everyday practice. Women's widespread control of finances has already been mentioned with regard to family funds, and the handling of business affairs often corresponds to this informal practice. While household heads prefer to occupy themselves with high-level economic planning and long-term perspectives, the everyday accounting, stock taking, and review of the state of affairs are often in women's hands. Numerous interviews revealed this to be the case. During an interview with a household who run a grocery shop, the household head came forward to answer our questions as a matter of course. When asked specifics about buying and selling, taxation, charges, and the like, he often glanced at his wife, who had been circling around us, partly attending to other matters, partly listening, but had been too shy to interfere. Because her husband faltered in his account she finally took over, delivering more concise and specific information. As soon as anything concerning the future was brought up, however, the husband resumed his account with recaptured authority.

A real threat to maintaining a household in harmony is the divergence of business management from household authority. In the numerous cases in which shopkeepers are women, they commonly manage business themselves but are still subject to male authority within the family. Serious tension is provoked when, as is usually the case, their profits surpass their husbands' wages. The men commonly regard this situation as a serious threat to their hegemony. Household leadership is generally perceived in terms of responsibilities; it derives its legitimacy from the ability to support the family. Therefore, a higher male contribution to the total household income is necessary to maintain the traditional order.[17] Conversely, to be economically dominated by his wife is a source of lasting humiliation for a man. A man who is economically dependent on his wife and thereby incapable of controlling his family is in local metaphors a "soft ear" (*ruan er*), derived from an old belief in the connection between a man's ears and his character. This subject, increasingly relevant with the rise of private business, is always a matter of much entertainment and joviality among women; most husbands prefer to avoid the subject or simply to paraphrase the constitution of the family's business. To solve the problem, husbands frequently assume key functions in their wives' businesses, such as in purchasing goods, establishing useful connections, and developing business plans. In this way they take their share of credit for a successful business. Others oppose their wives' enterprises continuously, and one case of a husband's leaving his wife on the ground of his shattered authority was reported in the neighborhood.

The Experience of Luo and Yang

In many cases, businesses initially launched by women to supplement household income gradually became the main occupation of the entire family. These families' dispositions show the cautiousness derived from historical experience: they adopt a diversified strategy in the beginning and only later finalize their divorce from former units. The grocery shop mentioned above accurately illustrates these considerations, as well as the whole complex of household business. When Luo and Yang were sent to the countryside as "educated youths" in 1970, they were already schoolmates. They had finished primary school and just started middle school. Although they were very young, they soon married, primarily, as they say, "to protect themselves from the wild beasts in the area."[18] It was a remote and roadless rural area in south Sichuan, in which the miserable impoverished peasants were hardly able to feed and clothe themselves: "They only wore shoes at weddings, so their feet looked like wild animal claws." Upon returning to Chengdu in 1978, Luo took over her father's job as a porter in a state unit that loads freight trains. She had to give up her position in 1981 because she lacked the strength to continue. After that time, only temporary employment in different factories was available. In 1986 she decided to start a shop on the ground floor of her husband's family house. The tiny shop had, in pre-Liberation times, been a bean curd shop run by the husband's mother, while the family of nine lived in the fifteen-square-meter dwelling upstairs. In 1951 the shop was collectivized and became the work place for eight employees until it was closed down during the Cultural Revolution. In spite of their extreme poverty, the old woman was punished for belonging to the "tail of capitalism": she had had two employees before Liberation. Since Luo started the small grocery shop in 1986, the family's income has increased significantly, enabling the young couple to move to a new apartment and reach a comparatively high standard of living. Yang, who after their return to Chengdu had been working in a state vegetable unit, saw his salary decline as bonuses dropped at the time the shop opened. Private vendors had taken over the market for vegetables. When his salary reached the bottom standard level of 40 yuan per month, and the unit hardly needed his presence any more, he gradually engaged himself in his wife's business, making purchases, transporting goods, doing the accounting, and so on. He finally quit his job to become the manager of their family business. Although the shop has potential for development, the family hesitates: "After what happened to my mother, I will never take in employees," Yang proclaims. His wife continues: "You will probably see our daughter [thirteen years old] behind the counter before long; she is not doing very well in school, although we had great aspirations for her to educate herself."

Labor Recruitment

Households have various reasons for recruiting employees from outside the family. The low cost of labor is a strong incentive. The distinction between the categories of household members and strangers or between relatives and nonrelatives, however, is often vague and frequently nonexistent. Kinship terms are often applied to close friends of the household — uncle, little sister, big brother, and so on. In the case of close cooperation, such terms are so commonly used that an outsider finds it impossible to distinguish between relations of true kinship and those of friendship. Moreover, relations of distant kinship can be intensified by applying these terms to the individuals actually incorporated into the household. For the sake of simplicity just three categories are here distinguished: "Family members" refers to individuals born into the same household and to spouses and their former household members. "Relatives" refers to others of near or distant kinship. The last category, "others," is a composite group whose main elements are close friends, friends of relatives, and employees from the countryside. When extra labor is required in an individual business, the typical solution is to call on nonresident family members. One can also call on young rural laborers with no potential to become full household members. Because of these laborers' inferior social position, normal (in this sense, intact) households would not even consider taking them in, and the seclusion is in this respect categorical. The distinction is of great importance to common classifications and thus to the whole power structure and question of authority. It shall later be demonstrated that any sort of labor or assistance in household businesses needs reference to positions within a predetermined structure. Whether the service is paid or unpaid — which latter is often the case with relatives — it is supposed to yield a return; only the two alternatives mentioned above appear to be functional.

Rural laborers in private businesses are seldom, if ever, hired directly from the street. When the preferential recruitment of kin is impossible, labor may be hired among distant kinship relations or, alternatively, introduced through kinship relations: friends and neighbors to relatives, in-laws' relatives and their friends, and so on. Consequently, masters and rural apprentices or business owners and laborers frequently share a common affiliation to a certain area. A blacksmith, for instance, employs three young apprentices from his native village, which he left forty years ago. A restaurant owner employs only cooks from his birth town. A female tailor in Chang Shun Street uses even narrower criteria: she employs only girls from her own street, a few blocks away.

The number of households that have incorporated relatives, and in some cases even people of the third category, as full household members is astonishing. The Chinese family is in general considered a strong biologically determined organization, with women being incorporated only through their ability to bear children. The common household organization in Bin Shen, in contrast, points toward principles determined as much by a set of socioeconomic circumstances: in practice, household organization frequently operates across boundaries of consanguinity.[19] Households in private business may in this respect distinguish themselves from others, but many odd combinations seem to exist among all types of households. Two young men who were working for a sofa manufacturer in the area referred to their boss in kinship terms during an interview. The first called him "big brother" (*gege*), and only after repeated questioning did he admit, "Well, he's not my real brother, but I live together with him in his house as if we were brothers." The boss turned out to be a distant relative. The second of the two also called his boss *gege*, as is often the practice when people are on close terms. He also admitted that "he is in fact only a relative." The boss actually turned out to be a friend of a distant relative. An old woman who runs a plastic goods shop needed assistance during the long hours the shop was open. Consequently, she incorporated a young girl into her household consisting of only herself and her husband: "All my children have left home, so she is like a daughter to me." They addressed each other accordingly. The girl was a former neighbor to a distant relative. Another elderly woman who sells textiles had incorporated two children of a distant relative into her household, where they ran the shop. They received no wages but were clothed and fed with the family. The woman's two genuine children were at university and unable to attend to the business. Yet another household had taken in an old barber, also a distant relative, to work and live with them in their barbershop, where he became their "uncle" (*shushu*).

Cases were numerous not only of relatives called on to assist in business, but also of families split up and assembled in new combinations. Some correlation nevertheless exists between the continuity of the family and its wealth or, as another aspect of this, between its integrity and its social position. Socially successful families tend to conform to a higher degree to the ideal Chinese family organization; they presumably possess better means of protecting themselves against hard times, distant job assignments, or other factors commonly threatening the integrity of a family. In the common Chinese perception, there is still a clear correspondence between the number of children, and thereby the size of a household, and its material success. From the parents' standpoint, more children give better chances for one of them to obtain a privileged position that will benefit everyone.

Another connection between household integrity and material wealth is significant among elderly couples whose children were all married off. This group includes some of the poorest households in the area. The aforementioned workers who were dismissed from their collective units with little or no pension, for example, are surviving on a very limited budget, even though many of them have a number of children who are supposedly responsible for their well-being. It was found that old age without social or economic success is frequently accompanied by failing interest and sense of responsibility on the part of the children, hard as it may be for the elderly generation. Some of the poorest old couples have no contact with their children at all. They hardly even know where their children presently work and live. Such is the case with the old couple who make clay kitchen stoves. Because they sell only one or two of the simple stoves every month, they barely survive on their income, and they sleep between the heaps of clay and coal in the single small room they possess. Although the husband is too weak to do other jobs and the wife is disabled, none of their four children keeps in touch with them. This is the only household supported financially by the Street Committee, which grants them 20 yuan a month for basic subsistence.

The composition of "family" (*jia*) became increasingly questionable in the process of penetrating the barriers between public appearance and internal household organization. Was family an organic unit formed by birth and marriage or just a convenient organization determined by a given aim or circumstances in the surrounding environment? In this, as in a number of other aspects of daily life among ordinary people, the elevated Chinese ideals and actual social practice at the local level were often far apart. Subjugation to convention and recognition of traditional authorities play crucial roles in the formation of identity. They often serve as parameters for determining social status in a highly segmented environment: the closer to common ideals, the more cultured and respectable the household in question is. As also appeared relevant to a number of other observations, such social ideals or models for behavior were of far greater importance to those households for whom they were within reach: conventionalism tended to demand a certain economic capacity.

The one-child policy implemented in 1979–80 will inevitably modify the entire conception of *jia* in the coming generation. As it is strictly enforced in all urban areas, no common households will escape its results: a declining number of household members and the eventual termination of families lacking sons. After a single decade of enforcement, ideals have changed only slightly; practically all young families in Bin Shen would like a second child if possible. The desire is particularly strong if the first child is a girl. The one-child policy affects the women deeply. The first question many asked me when they had the opportunity was about family planning: can you have as many children as you wish in your country?

Participants in Businesses

The number of family members, relatives, and employees participating in individual enterprises is not easily assessed. Although usually only one person or a few family members are registered as running the business full time,[20] several others may join in at peak hours, do the purchasing, supply raw materials, look after the shop while the owner is away, and so forth. Children often give a hand after school, spouses do the accounts, and grandmothers cook for family and employees. Although relations of kinship, consanguinal as well as affinal, are typical, they are not exclusive. Other relations of potential *guanxi* can be equally important or at least play an important role in running the business. These include former colleagues or classmates, neighbors, and various dubious connections, any of whom may benefit from the contact. Private businesses frequently support a far larger number of people than local registration suggests, either through direct, full-time involvement or by part-time assistance. The supplying of goods and raw materials that are monopolized by the state or are in short demand constitutes a vast market for semiclandestine economic activities. In recent years, this market has increasingly been taken over by professional middlemen and brokers,[21] of whom there now seem to be hordes, exploiting any shortcoming in the economy and using every possible trick to make extra income. Most of these are well-known figures from pre-Liberation society. Very often, businesses involve a network of considerable size. A restaurant run by a young couple is a good example. Besides themselves, two rural youngsters are employed. The husband's former colleague from the state unit supplies canned foodstuffs. The wife's father supplies lumps of pork, which he buys cheaply from peasants. A neighbor assists with transporting foodstuffs to the restaurant on his own tricycle. A relative supplies sweets, which are sold from the counter in front of the restaurant. The relatives of both the husband and the wife often try to lure new customers to the restaurant. Moreover, the husband frequently meets with former classmates in the restaurant, where they plan additional business.

All participants in private business are supposed to obtain permits and register with local authorities. The number of household members registered in a business is obviously limited to those who do not have employment elsewhere or are studying. Permission to run a business is restricted to the unemployed and those who have been granted leave from their original units. While the registered number of participating family members per business in the area was only 1.3, our survey found that almost every business had extra full-time assistance.[22] This discrepancy suggests that many who work full time in the household business every day are employed elsewhere or are pensioners. The household's demand for security and social status to a large extent accounted for such overlapping employment; the meager wages from the state sector is seldom important in private business. Because businesses are predominantly household operated, the actual number of family members involved in some capacity naturally approximates the total number of family members. We soon discovered, however, that great attention was paid to the education of children in these households. When studying, these children are released from all major duties in regard to business operation (see chapter six for more detail).

Those individuals who simultaneously have permanent connection to a unit and are full-time participants in business typically belong to two categories: retirees from state units or employees in poorly performing, overstaffed state units. Mr. Wang, our initial interviewee, belonged to the first category; as we made our way through the businesses we found it to be exceedingly common. As already indicated, a substantial number of businesses are headed by retirees, although only those from state units have life-long pensions.[23] In numerous cases the businesses are launched by elderly people who want to provide an income opportunity for unemployed children; other businesses are actually established by young people themselves, but as a matter of course managed by elderly people in their capacity as household heads. In the following example, an unemployed youth was the reason for a new business. When a seventy-one-year-old tinsmith retired from a state factory some years ago he soon discovered that he had too much energy to stay idle. Since the household still included his twenty-two-year-old unemployed youngest son, he decided to open a smithy in their house. The two sit together on small stools in front of the template and hammer out baking forms and other kitchen utensils from sheet metal. Working together father and son is a joy for the old man. It enables him to remain active and at the same time train his son to continue the shop: "Learning a craft secures you a stable income all through life," he says; "craftsmen may not get rich, but they will always manage. As we say: 'during droughts the craftsmen won't die.'"[24] His son's attitude reveals an ambivalence toward family business that he shares with most others from his own generation: "Until something better turns up, this will do," he says, while his father is out. "The money we make is not bad, but my interest in the craft is not great."

The second category of people having double employment comprises state workers in poorly managed or unfortunate units. Although such units only pay minimal wages, which are as low as 30–50 yuan, most households are reluctant to abandon their connection to them, primarily because of the relatively high level of security in state units or the converse, the unpredictability of developments in the private sector. Attempts at combining activities at the two places of work, such as making use of one's position in a state unit to benefit the household business, are widespread. Such attempts to boost the family business often touch the bounds of legality or involve actual crime. Easing raw materials and other goods out the back door is common practice, although using them in one's own shop is too risky. Some simply cooperate with others in the unit in organized economic crime, involving the responsible cadres for optimal security. An example of this cooperation was a street cigarette seller who had a household member in a state cigarette wholesale unit; the latter could supply large quantities of famous Yunnan brands, which were otherwise in short supply. Others just exploit skills, tools, or connections obtained from their unit — anything that will give them an advantage over competitors.

Distribution of Labor

The cooperation between the sexes most often implies an unequal distribution of labor strongly in favor of the male. Our initial entry to this matter was the countless vain calls to interview male shopkeepers, who always had a host of reasons for not being in the shop. Males often left the shop entirely to purchase goods, do errands in town, see important people, make business trips to other cities, or sleep long hours upon returning from some of these activities. On these occasions, others would mind the shop. In the cases of truly household-based businesses, this was invariably the wives' task; the superior knowledge they often had on the day-to-day business operation was hereby given perspective. Taking care of a business, a child, and a home can be a tiresome task for the women in private business, and many complain about the heavy burden they bear. "We do all the work," was the common remark; "just look at them, such easy work they do."

This general trend toward making routine jobs the responsibility of women made private business comparable to other sectors of the Chinese economy. After surveying businesses in commerce, we investigated the only state shop left in Chang Shun Street after the reestablishment of the private sector.[25] It is a comparatively large shop selling liquor, wine, and high-quality foodstuffs monopolized by the state. Out of the no fewer than fourteen employees running the shop, eleven are female shop assistants. They serve customers or sit on stools behind the counter and chat the time away during the quiet periods. The three young male employees have the positions of manager, assistant manager, and accountant. One was away when we called one afternoon; the other two were in a small room behind the shop. Seated in a highly relaxed posture they were chatting away, with open newspapers and thermos on the table as the only indications of activity. Asking for basic figures on the turnover of the shop, we soon learned that the accounting was not really done by the staff members themselves, but done centrally in the state wholesale unit delivering the goods. Moreover, it was commonly the case in local state units that managers and cadres refused to pass information on to anyone unless explicitly ordered from above.

Similarly, women in private business are generally expected to do the simple jobs such as serving customers, operating simple machinery, and attending to the employees. These activities tie them to the shop during the day. The local film-processing shop is a fairly typical example of how labor is distributed in a small business. Some years ago, when Fang heard about profits in the order of hundreds of thousands of yuan on film developing, he did not hesitate to give up the grocery shop he was running with his wife and invest all family funds in this novel enterprise. The small grocers had become too numerous, and profits had declined. At the same time the popularity of photography verged on becoming a public mania, and film processing was in great demand. Fired by the idea and the prospect of the family business reaching new heights, he invested no less than 20,000 yuan — a virtual fortune — in photographic printing equipment. None of the family members had any previous knowledge or skills in this craft. When they realized the importance of having such skills, his wife was sent off to Shanghai for a four-week training course at the factory that produces the equipment. The daily routines after opening the shop were as follows: His wife operated the new equipment. Four young rural laborers made advertisements for the local area, served customers, and delivered the pictures. As the manager, Fang had time on his hands to enjoy the prospect of becoming wealthy. Things did not work out the way he had expected, however; insufficient knowledge about the equipment and bad luck in that the market soon flooded with similar equipment resulted in total failure.[26] The dearly bought machine was then practically worthless as superior foreign equipment in the meantime took over the entire market.

The conventional authority of male shopkeepers is seldom questioned, even when actual financial control is not in their hands. Being the household head and representative to the outside world, these patriarchal figures frequently adopt an attitude toward participating in the actual work that seems highly detrimental to the success and further expansion of business. The strong forces of idealized male behavior and self-fulfillment typically motivate the household head to divorce himself from physical labor as soon as circumstances permit and ultimately to dissociate himself from any attention to practical affairs at all. However, the degree to which household heads participate in labor and management varies significantly according to the type and size of business. The larger enterprises in our survey naturally left greater scope for the realization of male ideals. Those with fewer employees and less economic surplus showed a more equal distribution of labor. Another important distinguishing factor was the type of economic activity, typically connected to the differing intentions when launching a business — quick profit hunting or affection for an old trade were the two extremes, with which the evidence of social simulation such as becoming boss rather than just being shopkeeper also varied. Individuals "doing business" revealed values and identities dissimilar from those of self-employed craftsmen. Crafts and workshop production were usually accompanied by full-scale male participation in labor, since the enterprises were based on the professional skills and knowledge of the household head. Even among the more affluent households running small workshop manufacturing, it was rare for the male not to be involved in manual labor.

Most businesses employ extra labor for hard, filthy, or routine jobs; the average is 1.5 such laborers per business. Together with the rather low estimation from our survey indicating 2.1 household members employed full time in businesses, three to four people on average are directly involved in the day-to-day operation of business as managers, assistants, laborers, and apprentices. In estimating the total number of people involved, several other aspects of the businesses must be taken into consideration. All household members are natural dependents of the business, even though some may not participate. If one adds up the family members, employees and, as is frequently the case, one or two relatives, friends, or neighbors having some association with the business without necessarily being paid in cash for their services, a figure of five to seven individuals per business may well be reached. If one considers the total network of participants and dependents, employees, occasional middlemen, and persons otherwise affiliated to one particular business, the figure may prove to be even higher. Because of the highly diversified levels on which private business is practiced, however, few businesses may actually correspond to such a hypothetically standard size.

The majority of employees are rural youngsters, invariably from peasant families which, after the reforms, no longer need their labor.[27] Being surplus labor from contracting farms, they chose to leave, as "there was nothing to do at home." It rarely seemed that they were sent away because their families lacked the means to support them, although they generally came from relatively poor and remote areas with little or no industry. Typically between fourteen and eighteen years of age when arriving in Chengdu, they have hardly any experience outside farming and only very basic schooling. Many are close to illiterate or are semiliterate. In the city, they are employed as hands and apprentices in restaurants, workshops, and other businesses, where they carry out the jobs that city dwellers disdain. Since they cannot legally reside in the city without employment, they work on contract for the individual businesses. Contracts, which usually cover a couple of years of fixed salary and set out work conditions, are worked out by business managers, who also apply for the youths' licenses with the local authorities. Earning from 15 to 60 yuan per month (average 30) plus accommodation, these youths are beyond doubt the most poorly paid in private business — and maybe in society at large. They have the longest working hours of all in private business, frequently working twelve to fourteen hours a day, seven days a week. They normally live and sleep in the shops. They are the first to get up in the morning and the last to retire when all work is done. They are truly the underdogs in local society. Their origin and the nature of their labor relegate them to an inferior social position.

Control over nonrelated employees is straightforward, as all relations between household members and others tend to be characterized by a simple extension of the family power structure downward. The distribution of power and privilege is facilitated by an apparently strong consciousness of position shared by employers and employees alike. Very little tension can be detected in businesses with regard to working conditions, hours of work, and accommodation. A standard type of family enterprise run by several household members and a few rural boys is commonly referred to as a "harmonious" constellation just like the family itself. In this organization of work, all interaction can be governed by "tradition" — in this sense a scheme of prescribed behavior — open to manipulation from both sides but still unchallenged in its general principles. The consensus on this point also applies to the sexes. Even among employees, some division of labor can be found. Male work functions tend to demand less routine work and to offer more frequent breaks and more opportunities for socializing. Again using the restaurants as an example, the cleaning, cutting, and preparing of foodstuffs are generally done by the rural young girls, while the actual cooking is done by the young men — cooking being recognized as an apprenticeship and thus qualifying for better wages and further improvement of social position.

In absolute terms, the youngsters are exploited. The value of their work is often far greater than their wages. In many cases, they do all the work in the shops, leaving the shopkeepers with untold hours of free time and sometimes even with huge profits. Some shopkeepers in the neighborhood only show up to collect the cash box and still make 600-800 yuan per month on the work of two or three "apprentices." This is the case with the two small bakeries making the fried *guokui*[28] cakes near the market. Although unassuming, they are very lucrative businesses. All work involved in preparing and kneading the dough, shaping, frying, and selling the finished cakes is taken care of by two and three apprentices respectively. The owners only supply the simple ingredients needed once a day and return at night to collect the day's proceeds. The apprentices rise at five o'clock in the morning to start the preparations; this allows them just enough time to open the shop at six, when activity starts in the market. They work continuously until noon, when the common rest period slows down all business activities. They rest until about two o'clock, when they resume work, continuing until the shop closes at seven. They are free to spend the remaining hours of the day as they like; most nights they will occupy themselves with watching television in the nearby teahouse. At ten o'clock they fold out their bedding on the floor of the shop, which is just big enough to contain them side by side. During the day, their bedding is folded up and put away in a corner of the tiny shop, together with the two small bundles of personal belongings. The market continues all through the week, and so does their work.

The two households owning the *guokui* shops are secured a comfortable profit despite having to do practically no work during the day. One consists of a divorced man in his forties. He is a mathematician by education but because of the Cultural Revolution never finished his degree. Now he contemplates how to spend his time. In the other household the husband is fully occupied with social work, primarily as group head in the Self-employed Laborers Association, where he arranges meetings and assists in tax collection. Like the woman running the nearby textile shop, we were to meet him again when investigating the local bureaucracy.

The influx of country dwellers into the city creates competition for work, and the wages paid are affected accordingly. The laborers nevertheless seldom complain. To our question concerning the quality of their present life, they tend to agree that "living in the city is more attractive than at home with nothing to do." Being accustomed to hard labor and a simple life, they generally state that their families were in a position to care for them if they wanted to remain, but they chose to leave in search of new opportunities in life: "Life is definitely more interesting here. At home there is absolutely nothing to do. We want to have a function, a job, and so on." The rural laborers are not very talkative when among city people. In fact, they are often so shy that their voices disappear in the noise from the street; their answers are short, hardly reaching a full sentence. They seldom look up when approached by city people, and they rarely ask questions. They are stigmatized by the language they speak; being unable to hide their rural extraction, they are inevitably assigned the lowest social position. When working in the businesses they stick to themselves. Some who are employed alone in a business hardly ever talk: A young lad is employed in a television repair shop to watch the shop when the owner is out and to sleep there at night. He receives no wages but is "studying the skills," which implies watching the owner work and receiving a few meals in return for his duties. The only words he ordinarily uttered were "master is out" when he was alone in the shop. Otherwise he would just move about as a shadow in the shop, gazing over the master's shoulder to watch him work the screwdrivers and simple gauges.

A few businesses employ skilled personnel when they need extra labor. Skilled laborers, who are city as well as country people, are mainly occupied in restaurants as cooks, in barber and hairdressing shops, and in kindergartens as childcare workers. Just three manufacturing enterprises employ skilled laborers: one carpenter works in a kitchen chopboard shop, the sofa maker employs a carpenter and a tailor, and an old hookah producer employs no fewer than fourteen retired metal workers. The skilled workers are generally older and employed at regular wages; only in restaurants do skilled cooks occasionally reside in situ. Skilled and unskilled labor also differ markedly in terms of wages, with skilled workers receiving a salary from 70 to as high as 300 yuan a month in a few cases. The working conditions of skilled workers likewise seem more favorable. Those of city background are often treated with greater respect and frequently approach the status of household members. "We are like one big family" was a remark often made by shopkeepers about their relation with skilled employees of good standing. Being in a position to demand respect or even being equal to shopkeepers in social position is, however, a relation of potential conflict. Skilled workers rarely regard their employment in small private business as permanent. Some may just want a temporary job; others may want to gather experience for starting their own business in the future. In contrast to the rural laborers, who are debarred from starting their own business in the city, the skilled workers already living there have the political means. Widespread accusations are raised against them for "stealing the skills" or building up their own *guanxi* and circle of customers within the shop, then leaving with it all to start on their own. The situation touches upon an attitude toward the outside world that, according to officials as well as elderly people, stems from the old society. Popular sayings hold that "craftsmen don't like to teach their skills."[29] It is also seen to be a feature of modern society. Several cases were told about employees running away with the whole network they had built up, throwing the owner back to where he started. The photographic printing shop run by Fang and his wife experienced this. When they realized that their own skills were insufficient, they employed a talented young man, whom they taught what they already knew and then let develop his own feel for the machine. He actually managed to reach a higher quality of prints than before. During his stay, however, he also managed to bind all the customers to himself. So when he suddenly disappeared, the better part of the shop's customers went with him, greatly contributing to the misery in which Fang and his wife were caught.

That employees may be a threat to future business development probably accounts for the preference of the majority of shopkeepers for rural youngsters. The rural youngsters are cheap, stable because of their dependency on the shopkeeper for licenses, and, what may be of primary importance, can easily be incorporated into the household business without threatening the established order. For most shopkeepers, their employment is a matter of course when labor is needed.

CHAPTER FOUR

The Cultural Economics of Labor

The incorporation of economic activities into kinship organization is indeed the Chinese tradition, shaping the countless numbers of small businesses and handicrafts that dominated production up until the Revolution in 1949.[1] Since then, in the process of industrialization, which involved deliberate attempts to restructure society as well as the minds of individuals, state and family became units of clashing interests. If the aims of the Chinese state were to modernize and synchronize, family strategy could be seen as countering by preserving established values and retreating from public life. Rooted in a firm organization, the Chinese family survived decades of political campaigns and social unrest by withdrawing and confining itself to being merely a unit of social organization. The Chinese family, however, needed merely the signal of legalization contained in the political reforms to revive as an economic unit and eventually gain new vitality and substance from private business.

If animosity toward public authorities prevails, then the conflict is centered on basic ideologies. While for decades central power has propagated the termination of obsolete values and has denounced previous ideologies as the legacy of feudalism, the population of commoners, effectively segregated from political power, naturally incorporate more pragmatic calculations in their struggle for social and material survival. Moreover, in the actual practice of distributing roles in society, futuristic state propaganda has little impact. A focal point of antagonism is over the distribution of labor.

The Position of Labor

In the common perception, work of the mind (*naoli laodong*) is considered superior to work of the hand (*tili laodong*), and few disagree with this perception. Most people, in some way or another, share the fundamental ideal of reaching a position that allows emancipation from manual labor. Related to mind work are the strong concepts of cleanliness (*ganjing*) and nobility (*gaoshang*), essential qualities of high social position. Within this scheme, performing hard physical labor invariably designates the lowest position, less strenuous work a somewhat higher position, and so forth in proportional relations. The tangible qualities implied in this gradation are accompanied by a strong symbolic order. Progress in life thus implies social ascent as gradually leaving strenuous jobs to others with the ultimate goal of doing no manual labor. Such an idealized accomplishment, however, can be achieved only by the male household head who, during his personal development, may hand over hard or routine jobs to other household members as well as to outsiders. The position of women is ambiguous; they are as a matter of course given responsibility for household tasks, and performing them may have symbolic content; but if the household is moving upward, these tasks are frequently passed on to employees. Labor per se is not surrounded by any grandeur or ritualization to the common eye.[2] Quite contrary to being an end in itself, it is rather seen as the path to leisure, provided that no easier roads are negotiable. It follows that upward mobility, the divorce from manual labor, and reaching high position are closely linked to an ultimate quest for freedom.

Labor is therefore regarded as a scarce resource, applied only in careful calculation of its effect. Strenuous, tedious, and superfluous jobs are avoided so that only the bare minimum of labor is performed. Every aspect of business reflects in its own way the rationalization of labor toward pursuing social objectives. The resulting "crass materialism," in the sense that anything in excess of the immediately profitable is left out, is evident from the appearance of shops, level of service, quality of repair jobs, and finish of products.

In Bin Shen area are a number of small workshops where trunks of the Chinese paotong (*caiban*) tree are sawn into disks, which are then planed to be used for kitchen chopboards. The trade is as old as the tools — a large felling saw operated by two men and simple planes for smoothing the surfaces. The location of the shops in this particular street (Dong Chenggen Street) is familiar to any housewife in Chengdu; this is where chopboards have been made for generations. A comparatively high income compensates for the seemingly hard labor involved in this occupation. However, as timber has become increasingly scarce, the number of chopboards sold outside the state monopoly is decreasing,[3] and the occupation is now regarded as merely temporary. Thus there is little incentive for further investment in mechanization or business expansion. An investigation of the actual amount of work performed during the day revealed that a couple of hours was sufficient in any of the shops. What was estimated to be the day's sale would be hurriedly manufactured in the morning. The rest of the day would be spent waiting for customers to buy the finished products. Only when customers such as restaurants or collectives wanted a chopboard of a particular size or thickness that was not immediately available would labor be resumed.

When a potential customer strolls up and down the street to buy her kitchen chopboard (most customers are women), she will discover that prices are fixed and standard. What matters is the weight of the product, and the 70 fen per *jin* is determined by the shopkeepers in relation to the price on raw trunks. Even though no informal organization exists among the five shopkeepers in the trade, a silent agreement on prices prevails.[4] The shops are generally open as long as there is any chance of a sale, following the extensive opening hours of other private businesses. In the afternoon and evening, when business is slow, minor jobs, such as tidying up the shop and repairing tools, are carried out. During the rest of the day, shopkeepers act as dealers, hailing customers, praising the quality of their ware, chatting to friends and visitors, and performing whatever activities they judge required. Totally absent from their business strategy, however, is any attempt to work up the boards to attain a product with a better finish. The coarse surfaces are left as they are. No one tries to increase his share of the market through lowering prices, employing new technology, or finding new materials to replace the rare species of wood. Since little labor is required, few of these shops employ rural laborers. One employs a skilled carpenter; others are assisted by relatives. Only a smith who makes the chopboards as a sideline production employs outside help — three youngsters from his own native village.

One of the shopkeepers is a twenty-seven-year-old man. After leaving school he remained unemployed for seven years until finally opening a chopboard shop on the ground floor of the family house in 1985. Coming from a family with both parents in state employment, he only reluctantly jumped into private business. But he had recently married and had a small child, and his wife's wages were insufficient to support the family. The shop has proved very lucrative. Now, in 1988, after paying the skilled carpenter whom he employs 120 yuan per month, he still makes a profit of at least 300–400 yuan for himself. Nobody passing the shop doubts who is who. The shopkeeper is dressed in a white shirt, a crumpled suit, and high-heeled shoes. The expensive cigarettes he continually smokes and his long nails on his little fingers indicate, if not his present position, then his ambitions. He rarely touches the tools, and the large felling saw he necessarily has to grab one end of in the mornings consistently threatens to knock him off his shoes. He regularly complains about the hard work involved in his business. The employee, a skilled and efficient carpenter, is dressed in a blue worksuit. After a chopboard has been cut from the trunk he can finish it in a few minutes, quickly planing the boards by putting all his weight into every stroke. During the early morning hours, when the shopkeeper participates in manual labor, he obviously works as a craftsman. In contrast, during the long hours of the day when the products are finished and ready to sell, he can return to his identity as a businessman, conspicuously closer to his own ideals and expectations. "When we can't buy the wood anymore, or profits get too low, I'll do some other business," he announces.

That changing one's kind of business seems no hurdle to shopkeepers only stresses the subordination of any type of skills to the more important *guanxi*-relations, to capital and access to premises. Few are willing to acquire an identity as an artisan: the widespread attitude toward such skills is that they can be bought if needed. The vast countryside, after all, can supply ample fairly cheap labor. Only a small group of elderly artisans, all trained by master craftsmen in the old society, rest in and are content with their identity as artisans, even expressing much affection for their old trade. Significantly, the majority of old artisans interviewed were themselves of rural origin and had been sent to the city for apprenticeship when very young. Virtually all other participants in private business cultivate commercial skills or skills in the game of *guanxi* making, considered far more important in the pursuit of profit and far more prestigious in a social context.

Dress as Identity

Everyday life, however relaxed it may be, revolves around a marked consciousness of social position and an occupation with status that seems to spring from inexhaustible sources. Positions allow for mobility and manipulation, but they still retain their original denomination and interrelation. There is a strong symbolic significance of dress and consequently a close correlation between a person's dress and his or her social identity, an unwavering connection that particularly strikes the Western eye. The two apparently merge into a structure that reflects fixed hierarchical positions. It even signifies a certain duality. Although the divorce from manual labor may be manifest in cadre and successful businessman alike, their clothes differ radically. The younger businessman who has no relation to formal organizations and no position in petty officialdom will wear a suit, the "Western dress" (*xifu*). This indicates his adherence to social reform and modernization, which in the colloquial is synonymous with Westernization. A skilled craftsman will wear a blue worksuit, as traditional as the craft usually is. Skilled cooks wear white uniforms, although the color white is in general symbolic, to be associated with cleanliness, rather than an indication of virtue. Unskilled personnel, the rural youngsters, usually wear what they wore when they arrived. These are often their only clothes, which they wear day and night. Deprived of any symbolic quality, such clothes merely belong to the material necessities of a modest life. Some who have good relations to their masters, by being distant relatives for instance, are sometimes donated discarded or outmoded clothes by the households for whom they work, enabling the girls especially to do a bit of washing for themselves.

Petty officials and elderly shopkeepers from a cadre background belong to another hierarchy of positions. The traditional dress (*zhongshi*) consisting of jacket and trousers in blue or gray allows men and women to dress alike. It denotes orthodox thought, conformism, and very often Party membership. The social positions it encompasses range from the highest cadres to the lowest unpaid assistants of local bureaucracy. The identity involved is that of being the Party's medium in guiding the people on the one hand and having good *guanxi* to authorities and access to privileges on the other. Anyone wearing this type of dress is unlikely to participate in any type of manual labor. Thus, the social positions expressed in dress styles mark off two separate career paths. Alike in both, however, is the drive away from manual labor.

Since people normally wear the same clothing all day, rarely changing clothes before or after work, their social identity is maintained. The importance of transferring their social identity into the work sphere lies presumably in the question of authority and the distribution of labor implied.

The people of Bin Shen refer to the inferior position of manual labor as "the way of things." "China has always been like this; it has historical reasons" is the general perception. In addition, the older generation refer to the proverb "Those who work with their brains rule people, and those who work with their brawn are ruled by people."[5] Although this expression has repeatedly been condemned by the regime for being a "reactionary Confucianist view,"[6] it has not lost its relevance for commoners. It belongs to the large stock of standard proverbs, indispensable in the everyday language. Moreover, it is transferred to the next generation through the firm belief that "manual labor takes more effort, and nobody wants their children to 'eat bitterness' (*chi ku*)."

The Social Position Complex

"What are you doing here? It's raining, and tourists don't go out in the rain."

"So maybe I am not a tourist!"

"Well, but you are a foreigner, so what are you doing if you are not a tourist?"

I was standing on a corner in Chang Shun Street waiting for my assistant Liu. It was one of those gray, overcast days in April, when Chengdu is swathed in thick, heavy air, and moisture gathers into ceaseless rain. This woman stopped her bicycle just to watch the phenomenon of a foreigner standing in the rain. Popular categories of thought naturally place tourists among the wealthy, and what she apparently meant was that wealthy Chinese have no need to go out when it is raining, so why did I? Social categories refer not only to status, but also to a large extent to habits; social position is automatically transformed into corresponding privileges. My own interest as a fieldworker was questioned constantly. The wonder expressed by the Social Science Academy over my interest in small private business households was repeated almost daily. When we came to be on friendly terms around many refills of the teacups inside the dark shops, people would overcome their reservation and ask me directly, "Why don't you study international commerce or large business or joint ventures? There should be much more opportunity for you there!" My extensive explanations of the social importance of private business to Chinese society at times sounded odd even to me. Why *was* I doing this? My answers to their inquiries about my relatively good wages from the university made the project intelligible to most; but this necessitated still more complicated explanations: the rate of taxation and the high cost of housing and commodities in my country. But couldn't I get better wages from another job? It was in fact very challenging to explain the logic of an intensely specialized Western society, full of opportunity and yet narrowing down people's concrete choices to the limits of bondage once they have taken their first few steps into a career. It compelled me to reflect on my own work, and I was forced to admit a strong cultural dimension also in my own choice of profession.

Doing our rounds, talking and interviewing even in the heavy Sichuanese rain became important. I believed that persistent inquiries and returning over several years at predictable intervals built up regard and, among a few, even a thorough understanding of the aim: to depict a society in a transitional period, in which private business could play a crucial role. Some felt that I was digging too deep into Chinese affairs. They believed that I was not only viewing Chinese culture from a distance, but was also prying into its weak points. A young woman asked me indignantly, "What are you really, a spy?"

In Bin Shen, as in most Chinese communities, monetary affairs are discussed with an intensity bordering on obsession. Still, money making and the pursuit of profit can hardly be seen as a self-sustained system of incentive, aim, and strategy. Even though a thoroughly materialistic attitude to life seems to prevail, it is mixed with an unwavering consciousness of hierarchical social categories. A materialist approach to life must necessarily take both immediate and long-term strategies into consideration; the quest for social security is indeed the overriding preoccupation of particularly middle-aged and elderly Chinese, who commonly regard the slow and cautious social ascendance as the safest. The social security of a household nevertheless depends as much on an abstract level indicated by position within established social categories as it depends on concrete material welfare.

A remarkable distinction between authority and wealth has developed — although this may not be unique in Chinese history.[7] While formal position still represents authority, it has been completely outstripped by individual business in terms of wealth. The focus of ambition is gradually shifting from prestige and privilege to monetary wealth, a shift that has been facilitated by easier access to consumer goods. Or, to put it differently, money is increasingly becoming the primary road to privileges. Here, private business plays a crucial double role: while providing new attractions to consumers, it also constitutes the means of acquiring more material wealth. This shift evidently gives rise to much friction, not only in terms of clashing group interests within local society, but also in the minds of individuals. The achievement of both authority and a substantial amount of wealth is a common aim. But in practice this is restricted to the highest-ranking cadres: among these alone do wealth and authority coincide easily.

Since the reforms and the return of private business, the previously unidirectional striving for state employment has been challenged. In the reformed society, the average person deciding upon a strategy in life is sooner or later faced with the irreversible choice of social security or material wealth, long-term planning or immediate satisfaction. Once a road is taken, there is no turning back. It is possible to give up a state job, but social marginalization inevitably follows; and the step is by and large irreversible. Thus the average household is now faced with alternative models for ambition, and these models imply radically different strategies. The generation of young school graduates, who are still subject to the authority of the their elders, especially has a dilemma: will they maintain respect and consideration toward family elders, who typically stress social security, or will they, backed by the official policy of encouraging private business, indulge in a more selfish and liberal attitude?

Social classification as expressed by local people does not offer much scope for deviance in its rather schematic correlations between occupation and social prestige. It is almost impossible to detect any effect of post-Liberation political campaigns on the still highly regarded bureaucratic positions or on the debasement of any work involving manual labor. Divorce from real physical labor is an aim with far-reaching implications for Chinese social attitudes; numerous characteristics of private business are explicable in this light, for instance the preference of trade to production, the demonstrated division of labor between employers and employees as well as between the sexes, and the business development strategies employed.

The attitude and aspirations of the members of the younger generation interviewed conspicuously downgraded all activities associated with manual labor. Though many were descendants of households that had been artisans for generations, the young felt no obligation to continue this line. The much longer schooling they received in comparison with their parents, the life in the city, and the general increase in the standard of living had greatly influenced their aspirations. Thus the position of artisans, in spite of political campaigns propagating the nobility of hard work, may even have been lowered, in a relative sense, among city dwellers. The household, already mentioned, that produces the traditional-style hookahs is illustrative of the generation gap. It comprises the extremes. The old craftsman had two reasons for launching the smithy. One was his love for the craft in which he was trained from the age of twelve in pre-Liberation times. Another was his desire to create an opportunity for his youngest son, who had been unemployed for several years. Hence, launching a smithy in premises taken over from a closed collective shop was a logical step for the old man. The business enjoyed quick and unexpected success, and their household prospered. After just twelve months of operation, they had twelve full-time plus a few part-time employees and a handsome turnover from exporting a large share of their produce. The enterprise obviously remains the old smith's trade and he also organizes production, in which he himself participates. His son, in contrast, attends to administrative affairs, and his whole appearance makes it perfectly clear that he does not want to be identified with the craft. While the old man dresses in a blue worksuit and holds some tool or piece of a hookah in his hand as he speaks, his son wears a white shirt and cardigan, has long fingernails, and otherwise signifies his distance from manual labor. He keeps away from the machines when he is in the workshop. The profitable enterprise allows the son to lead an easy life. A new room has been fitted up with modern furniture, refrigerator, color TV, and stereo for him and his wife. His administrative duties in the workshop hardly occupy more than a couple of hours of his time every day, leaving ample time for going to town and seeing friends. Still, his attitude is careless: "So far nothing else has turned up, so I am content."

Parents frequently accuse their offspring of "playing around too much," lacking interest in learning necessary skills, being extravagant, and spending too little time in the shops. The young people complained that their parents were too strict with them and, in regard to manual labor, that "dirty work is less noble than jobs where you are clean when you return at night." "Dirt" apparently has a strong symbolic content, indicating social inferiority and lack of power. Similarly, "clean" is indeed symbolic, since a filthy white shirt is often ranked higher than a clean worksuit.

A picture of occupational classifications emerges from statements and observations. Practically everyone interviewed ranked state employment highest, although comments on the low level of wages usually followed. A marked divergence between parents and children appeared to be growing, however. Parents were invariably content to have their children placed in the secure, life-long employment of state units, even in spite of the low pay, whereas the young generally demanded more. State employment as a ballast in the household is evidently something everybody desires, although not always for him- or herself. If they can manage on a smaller income, many still find state jobs prestigious and welcome them because they secure the social dignity of the household. Still, the routine and strict control in state units were widely described as enervating and senseless. In many of the poorly performing units there was no work at all.

Earlier, collective enterprises supplied the only alternative to state employment and ranked lower in prestige.[8] Collectives still offered the privileges of belonging to a secure *danwei*, however, and in a social sense of belonging to the formal society. Collectives have nevertheless always involved some degree of insecurity. Ever since they were introduced in the 1950s,[9] recurrent economic recessions have thrown smaller ones in particular into bankruptcy and their workers into unemployment. The numerous workers from this sector now doing business for themselves testifies to the crisis faced by the collectives in the late 1980s.

In spite of recent campaigns initiated by central government, private business is still regarded as the very bottom of society. There is no security in it, it has been an ideological scapegoat all through modern history, and it occupies the very lowest social position defined in terms of belonging to a nongroup (the strata of individual households). Attitudes may be changing, but the process is slow at best. How much profit must be made in private business to compete with the attractions of state employment is hard to determine, but it must exceed state wages several times over.

Individuals in private business tend to distribute the bottom social positions among themselves; some envision themselves as upwardly mobile, others are noncommittal. However, disregarding someone's present position in the private sector, it does make a difference whether he or she deliberately made this choice, was squeezed out of state or collective units, or is an outright social outcast. Choosing individual business is likely to be accompanied by a change in values. In the world of individual business, wealth is the guiding principle, indicating a departure from the formal status/value system. Success in business can be measured by one single parameter: the cash return on your investment and labor. Yet the occupation itself is implicitly linked to notions of hierarchical position. Again, the manual labor involved may not be the determining factor, though it is indeed a distinguishing characteristic. Serving others, in the strictest sense of the word, is ubiquitously identified with inferior position, and China is no exception; this country may define social concepts in even more stratified terms than others.[10] The master-servant relationship has been a basic organizational feature of Asian society — not necessarily feudal, but indeed one of position derived from occupation, strong affiliation to an established organization, and hierarchy.

But Chinese society always had, and still has, a pattern of organization that allows the entrepreneur to operate within seemingly contradictory value systems: while occupying a formally inferior social position, he is still master in his own house with control over employees, apprentices, and maybe considerable wealth. And although his business is to serve others, he himself may be able to succeed in his pursuit of the ultimate privilege — the emancipation from labor. Restaurants in modern China may well serve to pinpoint this apparent paradox most accurately. Their owners agree that, even in modern society, they are still identified with an occupation that is perhaps the most ignoble of all; cooking for others holds little dignity with regard to social position. But this very activity is nevertheless chosen by some of the most ambitious of entrepreneurs,[11] and the quick return on investment is of course incentive enough in itself.

Restaurants were by far the most profitable of local businesses with the most secure investments and quickest return.[12] In terms of social prestige, however, their owners rank far lower than state employees — particularly if they drop out of the latter sector to become individual entrepreneurs. They compensate for this by moving up in private business, where success is easily measured and social competition accordingly performed. Starting up a restaurant lowers status in one dimension while it increases personal success and fulfillment in another dimension. As argued later, these represent activities in separate hierarchical systems.

Instant economic success fulfills the aspirations embedded especially in the masculine role. In private economy, it is often accompanied by the reemergence of a traditional division of labor between the sexes. In the more prosperous of restaurants, cooking is done by skilled cooks, cutting and preparing foodstuffs are done by rural "apprentices," serving and organizing are the tasks of women and youngsters. The male household head concerns himself with the cash register or sits comfortably outside his flourishing business and chats with neighbors and passersby; his task is accomplished. Thus, also in this respect, private business comprises the extremes of social accomplishment and in itself offers considerable room for division of labor and, of course, social stratification. Restaurants, in particular, turn out to be Chinese household business in a nutshell; their entire organization confirms the distribution of roles determined by custom, both among family members and between the privileged urban and their subjugated rural employees.

Apart from restaurants, other service enterprises in the area bring admirable positions to their owners. A dry-cleaning service started by a former employee of a collective dry-cleaning factory certainly demands the least effort for good profits. Working on contract with his former unit, which does the actual cleaning, this former employee has secured himself a virtual monopoly in the area. His profit of approximately 400 yuan per month is reached by receiving an average of nine articles of clothing per day. Every second day he makes the short return trip to the dry-cleaning unit and hands the cleaned clothing back over the counter. A rural apprentice is employed to serve customers and to look after the shop whenever the shopkeeper is away; he can in fact stay away all day if he desires. The young unemployed lad across the street, temporarily working in the bicycle repair shop started by his mother to provide for him, often glances toward the dry-cleaning shop while sitting outside their own shop awaiting new customers with flat tires or loose pedals: "He has really done it; that's the sort of business I would like to run."

Among service enterprises, repair shops are probably the least prestigious; they offer low profit, little chance of employing laborers, and endless small jobs. Running a repair shop involves serving others, dirty hands, simple work routines, and little prospect of expansion. A former convict, now released on parole, ran another of the small bicycle repair shops in Chang Shun Street. As he would never be able to return to his former state unit, he was granted permission to run a simple business, both for resocializing and as his only means of income. Being a mechanic by profession, however, he had his visions: repairing motor vehicles was a business promising a great future. With nothing to lose, this very skillful fellow is among the very few individuals who obviously harbor no aversion either to manual labor or dirty hands. Moreover, his genuine interest in mechanics and his indifference to the social position or income involved are indeed unusual among the younger generation.

The present social position of artisans has great similarity to pre-Liberation times,[13] at least within the time span of what the present old craftsmen know. Interviews with them all pointed to a fairly unaltered relative position of their crafts. Although they earn both respect and admiration for skillfully made objects, social classification has always nailed them to the bottom rung of urban society. Nevertheless, in terms of self-respect, the older artisans tend to be proud people, content with life and loving the trade they have practiced for a lifetime. In addition, these skills confer a highly esteemed benefit. Being skilled in a craft ensures a certain stability in life. Although artisans never attain high position and wealth, their craft provides a stable income proportionate to the effort put into the work. The demand for artisans, whether in production or for jobs in private homes, is perpetual. The artisan has derived dignity from usefulness and from having survived a series of social upheavals. Although artisans agree that life in general is much easier now than when they were young, their trade is still only a means of livelihood — comfortable perhaps, but never chosen because of ambitions of prestige or power.

The sharp difference in attitude between the young and older generations toward the dignity of crafts has various origins. The older generation is perhaps more inclined to accept its fate, while the city youth generally entertain greater expectations for life. The urban young associate crafts work with inferior social status and few prospects of improvement. Although wages may be reasonable, they can never compare with wages in real business. So crafts work, which first requires years of apprenticeship at meager wages, brings neither wealth nor elevated status. When it comes to finding a spouse, it is not very advantageous either. Young women usually want men with a higher education and position than themselves or, alternatively, as the young men express it, "someone with a great deal of money who can offer them an easy life."

Traditional Chinese society, if we may use such a term, contained a scheme of incorporating occupations into levels of social prestige. But the clear definition of rank referred only to the main types of occupation. The upper echelons were reserved for the Mandarins, educated through the state examination system. Peasants had the rather symbolic privilege of being second in prestige after the educated few. Craftsmen occupied third place, and at the bottom were the tradesmen. Various interpretations of this scheme can be given,[14] since it, at least in the late imperial society, did not fully reflect the actual material welfare of the groups involved. One aspect of this discrepancy may be a deliberate downgrading of economic activities potentially threatening to the established order. In this interpretation, modern Chinese society appears to perpetuate a system of values that the authorities condemn as obsolete — and in this respect the views of the general population comply conspicuously with tradition, that is, experience — while state policies are more ambiguous.

The Reestablishment of Tradition as a Social Model

In their internal organization, the households in individual business make full use of the social independence they enjoy. Individual business has greatly stimulated the return of a dynamic social organization. For historical reasons, actual families show a great variety; yet they tend to conform to ideals as far as their composition allows. If husband and wife are both present, they immediately take up the roles of such. If grandparents or great-grandparents live in the household, they also adopt their proper roles. And children are invariably brought up to comply with the aim of the family. Into the abstract design of the ideal family, a real-life household plots in its members to fill as many positions as possible, whereafter the hierarchical order, independent of its size, enables it to function. As an organic entity, the family does not demand all its members to reach favorable positions. The common identity can draw on the performance of a single or a few members, as expressed in the proverb "When one man accomplishes, chickens and dogs reach heaven,"[15] meaning that all family members will benefit. This benefit refers to the prestige collected as much as to the material gains through professional nepotism. Likewise, the individual family members are expected to be worthy representatives of the family and if possible to do better than the previous generation.

The last decade of reforms has challenged the outlook and values of the ordinary families by economically awarding activities in the informal, socially debased, private sector. Founded in the experience passed on through generations, few household heads believe that the social position of individual business will ever follow their present economic advantages, and the lowest social position, in this thought, is accompanied by the lowest degree of security: the lower one's position, the higher one's vulnerability to encroachment from above. A diversified strategy is a logical solution to the problem. In this respect the common identity of the family allows it to have some members firmly placed in prestigious positions and others engaged in activities directed toward purely material gain. This has become a common strategy. It is of course convenient if such diverse activities can be combined; private business can greatly benefit from links to bureaucracy, state factories, or wholesale departments. Although a diversified strategy may be the ideal from the view of a traditional outlook, it may not be easily attained. It is much easier for a household of high position to start a business as a sideline than it is for a low-position household in business to improve its overall social rank.

The numerous retired cadres in private business exemplify this situation; retaining their social position and identity, they typically exploit the *guanxi* developed in their professional careers to build their businesses. One such example is the household of Long, a retired cadre from the provincial government administration. When he retired on full pension from his unit, he still felt healthy and energetic. Furthermore, the household still contained his youngest son, who had fine artistic skills but no job. There was economic incentive too. Since the household members had only state employment, the household was unable to maintain its standard of living. The old two-story house they owned in Dong Chenggen Street was ideal for business, for which it had originally been built. A trade even older than the houses was present in this street, which is its center in Chengdu — making wooden signboards with black, hand-painted characters on a white background. Colored acrylic signboards with characters cut out of the same material are now mostly used. So Long naturally chose this type of business: his son had the talent needed, and he himself had the connections to state units, which were to become the major customers for his signboards. Needless to say, the business prospered, securing the household the coveted combination of status and wealth.

Another example of the importance and high esteem in which state employment has been held is the porcelain shop of Madame Dong in Chang Shun Street. The shop was launched because of the desperate situation the family was in. Her husband and two sons all had state employment, but the combination of high inflation and decreasing bonuses in recent years had completely undermined the family's already humble budget. The husband's wages as a low-ranking cadre were limited; the 70 yuan did not go much further than his own daily lunch and cigarettes. The youngest son supported himself from the money he made; as he was quite young and wanted to be independent, the family did not interfere with his affairs. The eldest son, also in state employment, was less fortunate. His unit was in such a scrape that a serious deficit had brought it to the edge of bankruptcy. The employees could only maintain the unit, and their jobs, by contributing economically to help it through the crisis. Madam Dong revealed that this was one reason why she started her shop: her eldest son actually had to pay his unit temporarily to maintain his position as a state employee. Her shop had not been a great success either. The porcelain she could buy from the factory was only second or third grade, since the better grades went for export or to state department stores. The lower price she offered compared to state shops hardly compensated for the poorer quality, and customers were few in spite of the good location near Chang Shun Market. And because of her large stock of porcelain, which had swallowed up all the family savings, she was unable to change her business. The coincidence of adverse circumstances had ruined the household, and the approximately 100 yuan left in the common budget after all expenses were met placed it among the poorest in the street. Hopeless as the situation was, they could not even afford the eldest son's wedding, which had to be postponed indefinitely. Historical experience had made the family cautious: "So far we have no plans to give up our eldest son's position. Of course it depends on the government's policy, and about that you can never be sure."

This attitude reiterates that social status has some foundation in the actual material circumstances. Although it is in no way proportional to material wealth, it is positively linked to security: high social position is commonly regarded as the most effective safeguard against infringement, no matter what the level of wealth or standard of living.

Far more difficult than using previously established social respectability in business is attaining respectability from business itself. The attempts at transforming wealth created in private business into higher social status take various forms, very often linked to work in the local petty officialdom (discussed in the following chapter). Whatever the form, a general characteristic of these attempts remains: the striving for upward mobility frequently uses bureaucracy, either as a tool or as an end in itself. Social categories are firmly attached to the formal hierarchy of state employment, still the only real source of authority in the local community. Prestige, security, or some measure of power can be extracted herefrom by individual businesspeople, but only as an exchange; in this respect, their dependency on bureaucracy never ceases. By purchasing services from officials, the entrepreneur can get a scent of power associated with high social position. Although this is little more than a surrogate, it may give the feeling that the upward struggle is successful.

Moving in the circle of the powerful is an important element of business strategies. The competition among restaurants not only for customers, but also for their social positions, should be viewed in this perspective. Restaurant owners stressed the status and fame of their guests, for instance, that they were TV stars, high cadres, or intellectuals. Other branches of business repeated this. Selling books to cadres is more attractive than selling at the same price to inferiors; baking cakes for the wealthy is preferred to baking for the underprivileged. The relation to local bureaucracy, however, is often a matter of fine balancing for shopkeepers. In relation to other businesses, restaurants are alleged to have a clear advantage. With the commonly shared love for food, consumed in good company and large quantities, it is held that "they have natural means of lowering their taxes and make good *guanxi*." And this is certainly true for businesses like Mr. Wang's and Mr. Zhang's, but when the visiting officials generally expect or even demand favors to be given, the shopkeepers can only hope for a reward in return. The old custom of giving presents to officials from whom one wants favors is continued in the fact that many shopkeepers offer them free meals, goods, and the like as a matter of course.

Some shopkeepers were subject to ruthless exploitation. When Ma returned as a twenty-two-year-old from prison in 1988, he had spent the better part of his time there after graduating from middle school. As is the case for all former convicts, only private business remains a possible livelihood. Fortunately his family owned one of the old houses in Chang Shun Street, close to Temple Street, the site of Mr. Wang's and several other restaurants. And following a new spontaneously arisen wave among private businesses, Ma pulled off a coup. In the autumn of 1988 a craze for "hot pot" (*huoguo*), consisting of a table with a built-in stove and a large boiling pot of soup in which the customers themselves cooked the meats and vegetables, spread in Chengdu.[16] Ma introduced it into Chang Shun Street in a pleasant place called The Labyrinth (*Long men zhen*), a Sichuanese expression for small talk. He was also the first to reintroduce the old colorful banner, proclaiming the name of the business, suspended from a tree in the street. The 5,000 yuan he invested returned quickly; his monthly turnover was at this level. Yet his social position remained unchanged in the eyes of commoners. In spite of his stylish suit and expensive cigarettes people in the street, especially the elderly, frowned. As Ma interpreted their attitude, "They don't like the idea of a prisoner making so much money." Neither did the local authorities. From the beginning he was controlled strictly by the Street Committee, which often sent anonymous representatives to eat in his place "to check his service and attitude"; so did the Public Security Bureau. Their view of him turned from suspicion to open hostility when he was later fined, along with a vast number of other hot pot restaurant owners in Chengdu, for entertaining customers with a good shot of opium in the hot pots.[17] Since then, Ma has been outlawed by local authorities in the sense that any of the local bureaus in practice is free to extract what they want from his business. He claims to spend 4,000–5,000 yuan every year to get his licenses renewed, although these services are supposed to be free or covered by moderate fees. All bureaus threaten to close his business if he does not pay, and several of them continually find shortcomings in his business for which he is charged, for instance unsanitary hygiene, tables too close to the pavement, or the fire extinguisher not in place. He was visited one day by a group of officials from the Public Security Bureau, who ate their fill of expensive hot pot. When Ma asked for payment, they replied: "Do you want to continue your business?" Subsequently, conditions for doing business even worsened.

Representing the extreme end of wealth without status, Ma is more of a deterrent than an ideal, particularly to the older generation; few would want their own children to follow his path. But having lost all chances of being accepted by formal society, he generally expresses that he could not care less. He is one of the few who dare to speak out against the malpractice of local bureaucracy, which he accuses of draining his business, and he is otherwise frequently playing with fire. "Young bullocks don't fear the tiger"[18] is a proverb that the old saddler a few shops away applies to Ma. But his tempered face and glowering looks reveal that he already knows the tiger well from personal experience: "I am not afraid of them; I am ready to tell anyone what they are like."

Conventional Business

The contemporary Chinese private sector is no less in contrast to the bureaucratic state than has been the case earlier. Their clashing interests are evident even in the remotest corners of the economy. In regard to wealth, the struggle over taxes and charges extracted from private businesses is decisive. In regard to power, the strict social control exercised by ruling authorities versus a strong quest for freedom among businesspeople is an area of permanent conflict. The rapidly changing Chinese society nevertheless calls for new types of businesses. In ideological principle, the basis for a change in business strategies has also been provided. The central government's pretension of implementing an open, market-oriented society has clearly had the aim of breaking down informal structures and loyalties, but the lasting ambivalence toward bureaucracy has greatly reduced its effects. Indications of changing patterns became evident when we had made our way through the majority of businesses in Bin Shen.

Diverging practices were seen to originate in either adapting traditional strategies to a new situation or, as in the case of few enterprises, applying new strategies in the prospect of a radically changing society. These differing strategies can be perceived to imply an orientation toward either past or future events, a distinction that is even brought to bear in family organization.

The common strategy of family enterprise, shaped through generations of tight family organization as a safeguard against infringement and exploitation, is to confine the field of operation to discrete, well-defined units, in which all structural relations are replaced by personal ones. In this strategy, expansion of business presupposes an extension of the personal network, the *guanxi*, which in turn is the guarantee for safe operation. Considering the inferior social position of households in crafts and minor businesses, this network has a built-in limitation; it rarely comprises other than local, petty officials of the formal hierarchy. Following such interpretation, business is dependent on having all functions performed within this circle of local confidence or, at most, inside a narrow selection of circles for special functions: purchases, legalization, customers. Although the strategy is strictly functional, with the sole aim of securing steady conditions for business, it is also one of great modesty and with emphasis on stability. It also leaves wide scope for middlemen, bringing services or commodities into the small, confined network of local operation and subsequently making heavy inroads into profits. In terms of licenses and relations to authorities, the stress on intimacy likewise implies stable ties but also predetermined subordination to local officials and consequently exclusion from establishing relations to higher levels of bureaucracy. Only in regard to customers do family enterprises seem to exceed the limits of their own locality, but the lack of boundaries is merely superficial. The total dependency on the local network restricts competition between businesses or transfers competition from selling prices to the level of purchasing — seeking better deals with middlemen and suppliers — and to sales relations — striving to enlarge the circle of steady customers. Advantages accrue from local relationships; the stranger will find no variation in prices among businesses in comparatively large areas.

The question of good *guanxi* as a fundamental precondition for success has far-reaching implications. Linguistically, the word is composed of the characters for *guan* (closed) and *xi* (system, series, department, or faction). The expression "closed faction"[19] is in fact a standard reference to all personal, nonkinship relations. Describing relations within the sphere of public life as determined by seclusion, confinement, or discreteness, and furthermore stressing their functional or even hierarchical nature by association to "system" or "series," suggests a public sphere composed of innumerable discrete units — discrete from the individual's viewpoint, but of course overlapping in absolute terms, as such units rarely coincide with existing organizations. The "closed" character of both the Chinese family and the "public authorities," allowing very restricted access beyond personal acquaintance, thus generates a business environment that, while facilitating the growth of enterprises operating strictly on the local level, strongly impedes their further expansion once the limits of the local market are reached. Additionally, the household organization accompanying these conditions stresses unity and ties that, in principle, are unbreakable. The individual's social dependency on the household, which also defines his or her identity, is reinforced here by economic dependency, as business profits are usually common property controlled by the household head or his wife. In earlier times, occupational identity followed the household's, which often assured the continuity of businesses down through the generations. The seclusion of the public sphere favored large and tightly organized families — a fact that still leaves its stamp on common beliefs. A large family has the capacity to expand with more family members drawn into business, whereas smaller families need to rely on hired labor; and involving nonrelated individuals is always a potential threat to the integrity of the household. Since the household in itself is a self-reliant unit with authority determined by custom, it is only natural that when extra labor is needed, young "apprentices" from the countryside are chosen. The fact that they are cheaper than city dwellers counts, but so does their inferior social position: they may easily be incorporated as an extension of the authoritarian household, on which they are utterly dependent because of a birth-ascribed "geo-social" stratification.[20]

The segregation of the family in relation to the "public" or "outside" world and the passing on of power and identity from generation to generation tend to direct attention backward in time. Power is legitimized through events of the past; the mandate to rule over the family was handed down from the previous generation, which must be duly honored. Family piety thus favors the reproduction of established patterns of behavior, not only within the family organization, but as much in relation to business strategy. A functional attitude and an orientation toward generational continuity in family affairs are likely to be accompanied by similar characteristics in business strategy, stressing ways that have already proved functional and secure and sticking to forms of organization that do not change the internal power structure of the household. This pattern of identical business and household organization leaves little scope for innovation. And internal contradiction can be expected if this type of organization is confronted with external demands for wider commercial ties following expansion of markets, technological development favoring younger generations, employment of skilled labor with specialized knowledge, or radical changes in the division of labor.

The characteristics mentioned above apply particularly to small and medium-sized enterprises in Bin Shen. These may or may not be run by the household as a whole, but generally family cooperation is the ideal. The elderly smith working with his youngest son in their small shop while his wife does the accounting and cooking, the traditional doctor and his wife running a clinic with their daughter assisting after school, or a bakery run by a young couple assisted by her sister and his cousin — these are all examples of family enterprises that operate according to the established pattern, although they contain numerous variations that do not necessarily follow a straight line of male succession.

The largest household among those interviewed, that of Mr. Wang, the restaurant owner, was the very model for family enterprise and, in fact, the wealthiest of all apart from a few enterprises that had developed beyond the level of small workshop manufacturing. The case is illustrative, as it contains the essence of family business in relation to the wider society and suggests the role of family business in the country's economic development. Mr. Wang, a former bank employee and manager of a state shop, runs his restaurant himself, assisted by his two sons and their wives. The five family members are assisted by four cooks and two apprentices. Their own net is considerable, probably monthly approaching what in a total savings sense is required for the status of *wan yuan hu*.[21] Mr. Wang is naturally proud of his business and his success at living up to the traditional ideal of an extended family by incorporating his two sons and their families into it, and he exudes self-confidence. The organization of business follows that of the household: patriarchal leadership under the absolute authority of the eldest male. As regards employees, the organization follows the predictable pattern: all are from the countryside, and all have been introduced by friends — as a guarantee of their safe incorporability into the family business. Cooperation between Mr. Wang and local authorities likewise seems exemplary; the turnover of his business is commonly believed to be several times the figure the Tax Bureau accepts. In sum, the business appears to have an entirely traditional organization, in all areas operating within a closed circle of dependable and efficient relations, with the minimum involvement of outsiders to achieve a given aim.

The identity of Mr. Wang's household is noteworthy. In answer to the routine question as to his native place, Mr. Wang claims Mongol origin; his ancestors came to Chengdu sometime during the Qing dynasty. "But of course we are also Chinese," he adds. This pattern is generally found among the elderly: "We belong to this or that province, but I was born here."[22] This orientation in identity pointing backward is clearly linked to family organization: authority today is legitimized by reference to the past. The whole organizational setting is indeed one of extrapolating events of the past into the present society. In personal affairs, too, this traditional outlook looks to the past. The fact that Mr. Wang's wife died more than twenty years ago and that out of reverence to her he did not remarry earns him great respect in the neighborhood. His face still clouds when he mentions her.

The type of business the Wangs run is in itself a logical consequence of this strategy of economic seclusion. A restaurant satisfies the desire to shun the unknown. Raw foodstuffs are easily purchased at the local free market, customers are mainly local and many are personal aquaintances, and all licenses required for safe operation are issued by local officials.

Although their turnover is still increasing slightly, the limit of expansion has probably been reached. Their great desire for further development is hampered by the physical surroundings. The size of the premises sets a clear limit to an increase in turnover, as does the fixed meal-time hours of the Bin Sheners, which means that the place becomes packed with people at peak hours and deserted in between. The Wangs have considered investing a substantial amount of ready capital in opening a new branch to be managed by one son, but the "right place" has not yet been found. Furthermore, Mr. Wang maintains that his adult son still lacks enough experience. For a family enterprise this is probably the crucial stage of development. Business proliferation involves partial surrender of power to the younger generation, something inconsistent with the established pattern of authority within traditional family organization. Employing nonfamily members to manage a branch of a family enterprise is out of the question. Also, opening a new branch entails either running two places within the same locality, for which getting a license may be a problem, or starting up in a new area where neither officials nor customers are known, a step that is only hesitantly taken.

Future Orientation

Like family organization, family business organization as a model is rarely questioned. It demands neither far-reaching schemes nor idealistic visions of a changing set of business conditions. The few businesses that break with this pattern nevertheless have great impact. Comparing Mr. Wang's family business to the two largest private enterprises in the area reveals major differences. In fact, these two larger enterprises, both in manufacturing, are not family businesses in the strict sense of the term, and their internal organization is of another kind. One of the enterprises is run solely by an engineer according to a proclaimed policy of avoiding all relations of kinship. The other is the one started up by the old hookah smith to provide an opportunity in life for his youngest unemployed son, whereupon the father would retire. All employees in this enterprise are nonkinship relations, chosen especially for their skills. Both enterprises have a far wider network of relations to the outside world than the other local enterprises have; this extended network is, of course, fundamental for their operation. One manufactures mainly for export, the other for a large selection of enterprises in the modern sector. Such markets imply external ties of nonpersonal acquaintance and cooperation with public authorities far beyond the local level.

The engineer producing plastic containers especially displays a future orientation that dissociates his business from any similarity to family enterprise. His products are of a new type, and among his customers are several contractors with foreign companies. His business is altogether a venture into the unknown; when launched, it was registered as a collective enterprise in order to avoid the restrictions on the individual economy — and in the hope that the political winds would further favor the private sector. His market and the technology and competition involved are factors that offer very little security in business. In frequently referring to central government policy and pointing out the discrepancy between this and local implementation, he refuses to accept the local rule of custom. For him, as for others in the neighborhood, future orientation goes in concordance with relating one's business to the aims of central government, which through the media employs highly futuristic terms in its propaganda.

The second of the larger enterprises shows that the strategy of operating beyond the bounds of the local area is not exclusive to the younger shopkeepers, although it tends to be more prevalent among them. The sixty-six-year-old hookah producer has combined his purely traditional design with new techniques and a new business organization. His staff of retired smiths and metalworkers is indeed a deviation from the organization of family enterprise as it relies on a far wider network of nonpersonal acquaintances. Labor organization emphasizes efficiency and optimal utilization of everybody's skills, and wages are paid accordingly. In relation to authorities, their enterprise operates on a level where family businesses rarely venture out, as their main customer is a nationwide state trading and exporting company. Toward the local bureaus they stick to pragmatic and impersonal arrangements.

Thus strategies of business, interpreted here as expressions of the general outlook of the families or shopkeepers in question, appear to fall into two clearly distinguishable categories. One is characterized by a strong orientation toward tradition — internally headed by a patriarchal leader and outwardly expressing the cautiousness against an unstable and insecure environment derived from a repressive regime. The second strategy is modernistic. However, considering the strong futuristic orientation adopted by the central government, "future orientation" may be a more appropriate term. The strategy is founded on a firm belief in continued and succesful reforms, as it has the open society as a prerequisite. Both strategies have pronounced effects on the organization of the business and its relations to authorities, customers, and the like. An important question arises as to the social origin of these differing attitudes, whether they can be related to class, age, locality, or even subcultures within the Chinese society.

The predominant family-type organization in the individual economy may reflect the low educational level of its participants. As class in a strict sense usually corresponds to position in the formal hierarchy, it also tends to indicate educational level, although events in recent Chinese history temporarily altered this trend. But as things return to normal, higher education is again becoming a prerequisite for achieving a high social position.[23] In regard to business, the argument is that one's personal *guanxi* power is determined by class and education. A well-educated person, who is often somehow connected to the ruling stratum, has not only a comparatively high-level entrance into bureaucracy if employed there, but also a natural initial advantage for doing business that permits operation beyond the local level. Higher-ranking officials are accessible to such an individual because they are equals or near-equals; the self-confidence, literary skills, and knowledge of central government policies that accompany education often facilitate the quick handling of affairs, issue of permits, and so forth. And the backing of an influential family can itself be crucial when services from local bureaucracy are needed. Education carries prestige in a seemingly unidimensional perception, the level on which exams are passed being the all-important feature without regard to content or discipline. Several among the small group of better-educated individuals in private business expressed the quality of their schooling in terms like "I think the officials respect me because of my education," in the sense that having a high school diploma would implicitly secure a better deal with the Tax Bureau than having only primary schooling or being illiterate. In contrast many noted that "they [officials] don't respect us individual businesspeople" when one's identity could not be attached to any formal education.[24]

Age indirectly plays an important role in the formation of business strategies. With the rising educational level the younger generation's outlook has changed. The bounds of the neighborhood are often too narrow to satisfy their desire for personal development and a richer social life than their parents enjoy. Evidently inspired by the development fantasy of the media, they want their businesses to develop fast, to obtain locations for business in the city center, and quickly to pass over the decisive demarcation from work of the body to work of the mind. Circumstances rarely permit these rapid achievements, however, and the young in individual business are often left with no escape from their households, on which they are utterly dependent. But when succeeding, the young tend to experiment with forms of organization other than that of the family, for instance, working by themselves to avoid the control of elders; working with friends, relatives, and spouses in various combinations; or working with a staff of employees as common wage earners. Examples are a glazier working with his cousin, a hairdresser working with a friend from Beijing, or a chopboard maker working with his wife and a former classmate. These young people who in some ways have departed from the family organization typically express views strongly in favor of individual business: "There is no future in state jobs" or "I will never even think about going back to a state job; the wages are ridiculous." The strategy of the young is often to a far greater degree in line with stated government policies than are the strategies of the older generations, but the degree of success in business puts a limit to their fulfillment of these novel ideals. The less successful frequently end up with a small family business of their own, maybe assisted by a few employees or apprentices.

Gender and locality play little role in this respect. At least within the city of Chengdu, no significant differences can be registered in regard to fundamental strategies toward authorities, market, or customers. What is of importance, however, is the reemerging conspicuousness of social stratification. The young in particular carry such correspondence between social background and general outlook, and the growing competition for education and employment has created the circumstances for a marked consciousness of stratification (this discussion will be resumed in chapter six).

As suggested in the preceding interpretation, the outlook and strategy of shopkeepers typically fall within two separate categories, closely coinciding with an orientation toward the ideals of tradition or the model of future, both rather abstract concepts as they tend to represent only prescribed patterns of organization, behavior, language, and thinking. But why did these two categories emerge? Apart from the contrast between tradition and modernity that manifests itself in any society undergoing rapid transition, some characteristics of Chinese society strike through. Apparently the thought polarities contained in these strategies represent a long-standing contradiction in Chinese society, namely, one of family versus state as forms of organization and focuses of loyalty. Tradition is indeed perpetuated by the organization of the family, the power structure of which rests heavily in what was earlier the powerful ancestor worship. The modern form does only hesitatingly extend beyond the bounds of the living, but it still retains the principle of male authority succession through the generations. If the outlook of the family is turned toward the past and toward repetition in life, the outlook enforced by the modern state glorifies the future, with development reached through controlled action being the objective. Although the state no longer directly infringes on family affairs, the heavy controls on the media and countless campaigns concerning all aspects of life still leave their mark. The atomizing of the traditional family is apparently of great concern to the state in its push for modernization, even if this may have an immense and unforeseeable impact on society. This "modern" attitude propagated by central authorities also promotes release from the morals and responsibilities of the family, without such responsibilities to any significant degree being replaced by similar systems of social regulation.[25] Thus the effect of breaking with established values is often expressed in an extremely selfish attitude of the young and in their all-absorbing concern for material wealth. In business, the modern outlook is commonly accompanied by uninhibited profit hunting and the pursuit of unrestricted expansion.

Deviating from Tradition

The common Chinese ideals concerning family organization, social dignity, and cultured behavior tend to demand acceptance as a totality; essential classifications mold them into a body of thought that honors completeness more than depth in any of its individual aspects or institutions. Any inability to conform to idealized behavior and respect for institutions can entail a total rejection of prescribed etiquette. Extreme poverty, broken up family organization, or social marginalization is often the immediate cause for a departure from common virtues.

The teahouse in Chang Shun Street represents the reverse side of society — but not in the sense that its customers in any way are outcast or marginal to local society. Yet the atmosphere inside the dark saloon with its roofed extension outside on the pavement is indeed one of relaxed manners and profane language. It is the sanctuary of the elderly population, especially the male part, who do their best to maintain the traditional noon and late afternoon visits to the saloon. But other groups use the teahouse during their resting periods or whenever possible. There are elderly housewives, young construction workers, farmers from the market, and some private shopkeepers from the street. The teahouse operated throughout the Cultural Revolution thanks to the hosts, who only by an extraordinarily radical interpretation could be branded as capitalists. If the saloon has a simple, down-to-earth atmosphere, it emanates from their appearance. The old folks are definitely in a class by themselves: he is seventy-six, physically frail, his face burned out from excessive alcohol consumption, but that he still has a lucid mind is evident from the coarse jokes he unceasingly throws at customers. When asked about his background, he is startled: "When I came to Chengdu in 1924 I worked as an apprentice picking up dog shit," he says. "I have also worked at digging mud, sawing timber and selling ice cream. But I never had an official job." His wife is a bit younger, without knowing it in any detail. Her wry face is ravaged from a rough life, and her squinting eyes flicker about in their sockets. But she understands the questions we ask her, turning them over in her mind before answering them carefully. The old couple have the rags that apparently no longer will detach from their bodies in common. The place merges into an organic unit with the hosts. They have taken root in each other in both mind and matter; the same filth is spreading on the earthen floor, growing up along the walls, hanging from the ceiling, and absorbing everything in its timelessness. This is a place where people spit fiercely on the floor while jawing and scolding as their hearts desire. After an endless row of formal interviews, this is also a bit of a relief for us. No illusions about hygiene and no feigned proclamations about serving others are expressed. The teahouse assistant is peacefully snoring under the staircase during his early afternoon resting period. With his head dropped backward over the chair and his long legs stretched out, he is blocking the way for the hostess, who allots him a fierce kick every time she passes. His bare legs have only few spots revealing the color of his skin. The rest is one with Mother Earth. However, employers and employees rank equal here on the darkest spot of the private sector: the 50 yuan the assistant earns is among the highest wages in the street and equals what each of the hosts can make. The 15 fen that customers pay for tea leaves with as many refills as they want can hardly support the old couple. "My husband likes to drink wine," she says, "and if he doesn't drink he has no energy and cannot work."

Besides the television, around which people gather at night, the teahouse provides a forum for discussions — or at least an outlet for anger and frustration. Businesspeople especially feel free to vent their views here. A woman who runs a small restaurant boisterously curses the state department selling sugar because it generally refuses to supply the quantities needed in private businesses. "Life as a private businesswomen is damned hard. No leisure, just work, and our profits are decreasing at the moment. I think you ought to know!" Others complain about the cost of living. The elderly housewives seem to agree that life was easier in the 1950s right after the Liberation. "At that time wages were lower, but lasted longer. My wage was 30 yuan. But the price of meat was only 28 fen per *jin;* now it is 2 yuan." The fake peasants trading at the market are also targets for their anger. But they are calmed down by others maintaining that this practice has always existed. Much of the discussion in the saloon is about money, a favorite topic in all public places. The combination of guests in the teahouse varies significantly during the day, and from day to day; it has become a forum for exchanging local gossip, information, and business experience.

Rationality and Belief

It has been the aim to describe basic ideologies in terms of how they are entrenched in the social structure. However, the picture would be incomplete or even distorted if it did not embrace ideas about the rationality of life in a wider sense. No matter how strong the odds are in favor of a household, it will never escape the workings of the unknown, commonly perceived as fate or destiny (*mingyun*). Decades of criminalizing all heterodox thought have had profound effects on modern Chinese society. Such criminalization has clearly hammered a wedge between "otherworldly" practices and their linguistic expressions. After even the word became an offense against ruling authorities, practices directed toward the invisible forces survived only in the confines of the home and were usually surrounded by silence. Elder and younger generations thus share only the surface of these beliefs, while only the elder generation possesses systematic knowledge of the correlation of these beliefs. Basic attitudes involving nonmaterialist conceptions often prevail across generations, however.

Notions of the old cosmology were frequently touched upon during interviews, although no one felt qualified to connect them to a consistent set of ideas. Ideas about the power of fate seemed particularly widespread and common.

The scholarly baker was the one to put the pieces together. Having been born just before the Liberation and brought up in one of the wealthiest households in the street at that time, he was one of the few to retain knowledge of these ideas in full. So one afternoon while we were sitting outside the bakery in the bustling atmosphere of Chang Shun Street, a local underworld of legendary beings suddenly disclosed itself (as everywhere in China it appears as a mixture of standardized components and local variation). The superior spirits are the Godly Spirit (*shenling*), which decides fate, and Governor Yan (*Yan wang*), which controls birth and death. Governor Yan, though ruled by the Godly Spirit, is closer to people's lives. A common expression for dying is still "to see Governor Yan." The Godly Spirit is remote; he represents a universal force more than a concrete being, and the power he has over people's lives is also beyond the influence of the living. This supramundane deity thus controls the larger structures of life. Predetermined events are already marked on people at birth and can be read by, for instance, lines in the hand. Governor Yan is the authority to which people are responsible after birth. He is the ruler of both heaven and hell, where people will be led according to their individual deserts. Governor Yan has four assisting spirits, who all come to earth to lead people, either to heaven or to hell. These are the Four Entrusted Spirits (*si da jingang*, known in Buddhism as the Four Guardian Warriors). They all have the capacity to lead people, but by different means derived from their appearance. Secondary God Wu (*Wu er ye*) has a human image and is the consultant of Governor Yan. Chicken Claw Spirit (*jijiao shen*) has a human body, but chicken head and claws, by which he carries people. Cow's Head (*niu tou*) carries people on his head. Horse Face (*ma mian*) takes people with his nose. The four spirits all have regular contact with human beings, as they are the assistants of Governor Yan. Because they are close, they are often used to scare and control children when they are misbehaving. Invisible beings in general (*gui*) occur in many aspects of life. They are believed to hang around graves, they appear in the darkness, and they occur in dreams.

When people die, they must see Governor Yan to have their destiny determined. But first they need to cross Nai River bridge

(Naiheqiao), the bridge between life and death. Those who practiced good cross the river easily and meet Governor Yan. Those who lived evil lives, however, fall off the bridge to be punished in various fashions: burned, fried, boiled, or carried away to walk over mountains with sharp peaks. Still, in principle, all have to see the governor to be examined and have their destiny decided. Life in heaven is like the life of fairies. Some may have the chance to come back to earth. The purpose of these beliefs is to encourage people to do good, not evil, according to the local people, who hold that the beliefs are unconsciously transferred from one generation to another. Behind the life in heaven lies the Mystery (*shenmi*), making it impossible to tell the exact details of life beyond.

This pattern combines with universal ancestor worship, which has also been practiced in the area as everywhere else. Some still possess ancestor tablets going back dozens of generations. Ancestor worship has reappeared in public all over China in recent years. In cities like Chengdu it is still limited to the Buddhist and Taoist temples; few would openly burn paper money or put out meals for their deceased in front of their homes. Funerals, though, have in the matter of a few years become surrounded by pre-Liberation rituals. Several families in Chang Shun Street have recently erected mourning rooms of cloth and plastic from the facade of their house and into the street at the death of family members, sometimes blocking the traffic in the street. Big, colorful wreaths with the name of the deceased, large strips of paper painted with characters, and long rows of folded pieces of cloth from friends and relatives, each with a strip of paper attached to it, were set out facing the street on three sides. Inside, a table turned into an altar was crowned with a large photograph of the deceased; underneath were candles, fine dishes, and fruit for the deceased family member to enjoy. Many of these ideas about the nonmaterial world seem contradictory, such as, for instance, the position of deceased family members. Are they in heaven or are they still taking part in family life as spirits as some believe? But apparant paradoxes in the spiritual world have never caused anxiety among ordinary Chinese; ideas about multiple souls have been widespread. Bin Sheners also admit that there are many variations to the ideas about gods and spirits, although they elaborate on the same basic notions.

The notion of fate as a set of conditions that does not allow manipulation penetrates the variety of views of the spiritual world. The work of *shenling* is beyond human control. Just as the individual stands alone when confronted with death, so also is his fate singular; it does not involve the institution of marriage, the family, or social groups. On the contrary, the individual frequently regards his or her family as an aspect of fate; it is to be accepted and made the best of throughout life. Thus the merits of the individual are also strictly personal.

Whether established social thought or pragmatic adaptation, the notion that all may have their turn is predominant in present society. The rise to fortune of certain classes of individuals sharing a number of characteristics is unlikely to be followed by these manifesting themselves as a group in society. Fortune, in the common perception, occurs to an individual, and consequently to his or her household. It can be pursued in multiple ways, although some are more negotiable than others at a given time. But even this is subject to rapid change. Much can be attained through practical skills, ingenuity, cunning, and so on. But to hit the right spot at the right time is equally important, and in this respect good luck is considered a significant aspect of business.

The practitioners of magic and the fortunetellers who were abundant in the old society are of course gone, although fortunetellers now and again appear in Chang Shun Street. Among the elderly population, however, old beliefs are becoming more conspicuous. The majority of the old men once again go to the Taoist and Buddhist temples regularly. In private homes the old beliefs manifest themselves more often, but even here most people only reluctantly revive practices of the past. Another area where a certain measure of magic has survived is traditional medicine, the only continuously practiced system of the old society; in the early stage of Communist rule it received the blue stamp as an integrated set of ideas. Although the local doctor hardly would agree to be called a magician, clear elements of magic are certainly among his crafts and remedies. His success in the local community also emphasizes that people have gained more freedom in turning to practitioners closer to their own beliefs. The presence and strong position as the primary medical system of traditional Chinese medicine — which does not employ the division between body and mind, physically effective drugs and psycho-social stimulation, or science and magic found in modern medicine — point to a cosmology in sharp contrast to the crude rationalism of Chinese authorities.

Summary

Since this chapter has dealt with various expressions of household ideology, but also was intended to prepare for the more abstract discussion of ideology in chapter eight, a short summary is in order here. The distribution of labor in society, both locally and at large, is a prominent factor in the formation of household ideology. The superior position of work of the mind over work of the hand is a notion shared by the vast majority and is typically incorporated into strategies of work. An almost categorical graduation of the attractiveness of work as related to degrees of manual labor has shaped a conviction that labor, surrounded by social symbolism such as dress styles, is a scarce resource to be very consciously administered. The social value attached to manual labor has apparently been lowered in the socialist urban society, partly because of the vast expansion of the state sector, which until recently absorbed all attractive career possibilities. Today, this balance is being challenged, since a new informal hierarchy of private entrepreneurs, shopkeepers, and subordinates is rapidly developing.

Somewhat contradictory value systems operate. While common classifications place state jobs over collective and private employment and office work over manual labor and serving others, positions downgraded according to convention may have another potential. Private businesses such as restaurants are on the one hand inferior undertakings, but on the other hand they allow their proprietors to build their own prosperous little domains, with themselves on top, freed from hard work. Private businesses in the area are mainly household businesses, typically extending only as far as the household network and the local market allow. The few local businesses that radically deviate from this picture by employing only nonrelatives and skilled labor orient themselves toward far larger markets and goals. These businesses are closer to the future visions contained in Chinese state propaganda. Thus we may discern a conflict between a traditional form of organization, based on family ties, and a modern or futuristic form of organization operating in the faith that society is gradually opening up to form a large free market as presented in state propaganda. Orientations toward either family sphere or state sphere are significant aspects of business strategies, depicting inevitable contrasts in a society undergoing state-governed reform.

Household ideology is more complex and embraces more variation than these major dispositions. In spite of intensive state propaganda, an undercurrent of an old cosmology is still felt — among the older generation in the form of religious beliefs and among the younger generation as a derived belief in fate. Rational strivings in the material world are necessary conditions but not sufficient conditions for winning in private enterprise.

CHAPTER FIVE

The Continuity of Bureaucratic Power

Our first encounter with representatives of local bureaucracy was with employees from the ICB office. Apart from Ms. Yang, who had introduced us to the first shopkeepers, we had little contact with the office for several months. Mr. Long, however, the head of the local office, was anxious to meet me, the foreigner. So I was invited for a banquet in Mr. Wang's restaurant. Turning it into an excursion, the entire ICB staff arrived in their fine blue uniforms, which they wear only at very special occasions. Also present was Mr. Wang himself and his neighbor Fu, the baker, whose previous conflict with the ICB had apparently been settled. Mr. Long was the jolly senior officer, who with great relish utilized any opportunity to turn meetings and other events into banquets, preferably in Mr. Wang's place. Equipped with liberal ICB funds, the whole office indulged in these special occasions. Compared to the rather basic meals customary to most state employees, such a banquet is a real treat. So many and lavish are the dishes that the big round table is not big enough; dishes are placed on top of each other in several layers. Meat, fish, and poultry are the all-important dishes, with lesser plates of vegetables and bowls of soup. With several Sichuan specialties among the ordinary dishes, these events are almost orgiastic excesses. Dishes are passed around or portions placed in bowls faster than anyone can possibly keep pace with. Rice is brought in only toward the end of the banquet in case anybody still has an empty corner in his stomach. Plenty of beer and *baijiu* (strong alcohol) come with the food. Through endless *ganbei* (empty cup) rituals we were initiated into the local drinking habits — and presumably, the custom of *guanxi*-making. At least such events had repercussions for the rest of the day and into the next. Particularly demanding were the endless notions and sayings about foreigners' drinking habits and Long's experiments with their truthfulness. Eating out is closely associated with friendship, which it both establishes and maintains. The scholarly baker searched his immense stock of old proverbs for the most pertinent: "After three days with nothing to eat, a man pretends to sell rice."[1]

Mr. Long's office became a place we often visited; with the neatly arranged teacups in the meeting room and an open atmosphere, it was always a good place to spend an hour or two with endless refills, Chinese sweets, and a chat. Mentioning professional matters, however, often sparked a touch of uneasiness among the senior officials. Their favorite topics were definitely food, family affairs, and foreigners. Apparently the whole situation of private business was outgrowing their office: they complained of strained relations between central and local authority, new regulations being impossible to implement, and contradictions among local bureaus. And like everybody else in official employment, they felt the decreasing value of their wages heavily: the salary of a senior official was outdistanced by even the humblest cigarette seller in Chang Shun Street — a fact they failed to see in any glorious light.[2] Representing a central government body (Ministry of Industry and Commerce), the ICB normally stands alone on the domain of local Party-dominated organs. Since local administration is embedded in an intricate web of *guanxi* relations and contrasting interests, it may appear equally impenetrable to both the internal and the external observer.

From the viewpoint of people in private business, local bureaucracy (*guanfu*) is a unified structure in the sense that it operates according to established rules, unwritten though they may be, and has fairly predictable responses. In local society, it is the main counterpart to private enterprise; as an obstacle to expansion of business and profit making it constitutes a gathered force, held together by "bureaucrats shielding one another" (*guan guan xiang hu*). The cadres (*ganbu*) of bureaucracy derive their position from their rank in a hierarchy defined by the state, regardless of their actual bureau of work. Yet the local administration with which the entrepreneurs are confronted consists of a long series of individual bureaus[3] that all need to be gratified independently.

Cooperation among various departments of local administration is of increasing political interest because the present structure responds only vaguely to reforms.[4] The enormous size of the local administration is in itself a reason for rationalizing, especially where local bureaus work in related fields, carrying out, for instance, similar programs of central government concerning job creation, education, or control of individual business. During interviews, practically all bureaus mentioned that they were undergoing reforms. Little consistency, however, could be found in their accounts of cooperation, areas of responsibility, and internal structure. For example, the Street Committee (dominated by Party interests) maintained that a total reorganization of the local bureaucracy was close at hand; in a few months the local ICB (which in principle reported directly to central government) as well as the Tax Bureau would be incorporated into the Street Committee as a unified structure and the employees of the other bureaus transferred there, thus increasing the power of the Street Committee and providing for more independence in the use of funds from tax collection to carry out the programs suggested by central government.

Confronted with this picture, the ICB flatly repudiated imminent subordination to the Street Committee. On the contrary, it was maintained that the ICB had just been reorganized to operate more efficiently on street level and that each newly employed staff member had a single street or neighborhood as his or her responsibility. A young girl was presented as responsible for Chang Shun Street. She eventually turned out to play a double role, as she also appeared in the Street Committee, where it was maintained that she was on staff. Further investigation into the structure of local bureaucracy only increased the confusion. The Street Committee claimed as its responsibility educational programs and other affairs of the Self-employed Laborers Association, whereas the formal structure places all responsibility for the individual sector with the ICB.

The apparent mystery of local bureaucracy may cover several different phenomena. Local authorities tend to confine their work to well-defined spheres, and distinction among these is often based on local, even personal, interpretations rather than compliance with legal duties. Interdepartmental cooperation is minimal. Bureaus reproduce a pattern of organization as required by central government, but contradictory to their formal purpose. Bureaucratic seclusion within discrete units and the almost absolute power of leading cadres of each bureau offer ample opportunity for malpractice. Examples of such are the deliberate abuse of power, overlapping personal and professional interests, or, as it is still frequently the case, insufficient knowledge of state policies and current regulations. Contradiction between the "supreme order" and integrational efforts on one side and convenient local interpretations on the other is inherent to the system — and is not to be confused with contradiction between central and local powers.

In addition to the high-handed manner of leading cadres and the local competition for power, the prevalent local-central contradiction is liable to be crucial. The administrative system is obviously undergoing reform that, in line with central government policies, has dual aims. Rationalizing the huge local administration and disposing of, in particular, its middle levels are stated policies,[5] but for a number of years in the 1980s they were coupled with attempts to alter the balance between civil administration and Party organization. For this reason the central-local power struggle frequently turns out on the local level to be one between state policy and Party dominance. In this game the ICB clearly represents the state level, whereas the Tax Bureau is responsible to local government. The Street Committee has always been a Party domain, and the social control it exerts, a main area of Party interest. During the fieldwork, areas of Party dominance were commonly detected by an extremely closed attitude of the personnel and inaccessibility of the institutions in question. Party-dominated institutions fully conform to the locals' perception of traditional power: they represent absolute authority which may address subjects but which may be dangerous for subjects to address.[6] By contrast, the ICB generally showed openness and offered ready assistance from its office.

The relation between bureaucracy and private businesses is also affected by these differing attitudes, and among businesspeople the ICB was unquestionably the most popular of authorities as it represented the most positive attitude toward individual households, at least until 1989. Complex relations exist with all authorities, however, and simply to depict the sides as structurally opposed is merely a partial truth. As local bureaucracy extends downward in a huge network of unpaid positions and duties, it simultaneously offers a taste of the prestige connected to office in the formal hierarchy. That numerous businesspeople volunteer to do social work for local authorities suggests that such work is accompanied by personal benefits, either in the form of improved status or in access to certain privileges in the neighborhood: A small income may be had from a possible surplus of the sum placed at the disposal of Neighborhood Committees for social work. Taxes may be lowered for these semiofficials. Finally, they may be entitled to start up small businesses on behalf of the Street Committee.

The Self-employed Laborers Association

The bureaucratic control of individual businesses is chiefly effectuated through the Self-employed Laborers Association, organized by the Industrial and Commercial Administration Bureau. That the association primarily is an instrument of control is evident from the fact that it comprises only household heads/business managers; other household members and employees are excluded from participating; control of these is entrusted to household heads along the lines laid down by the ICB. Thus the association is a pseudo-organization in terms of safeguarding the interests of businesspeople or their employees. In this field, as in others, the ruling authorities accept no spontaneous organization. The formal structure of private business emphasizes bureaucratic order and standardized organizational units that form natural parts of the universal structure of the Chinese state. All "businesses" — whether that means large, prosperous enterprises with numerous employees or just denotes an old woman trading in a few spices outside her humble dwelling — come under this single category of economic activity and are contained in the one and only association, divided into comparable groups, and in principle treated equally by the responsible bureaus. In a social perspective, however, this seeming hodgepodge makes sense. The concept of *geti hu* stresses their status as a category of households, separate from the formal organization of society. Although defined as an economic category, *geti hu* thus has strong social connotations. Their social marginality forms the basis of this classification, which refers neither to the actual type of economic activity nor to the level on which it is practiced.

Constituting a social rather than a professional category, the individual households are subordinated to institutions whose social organizational content is more important than their economic content. The association may even be depicted as a preventive measure to assure that no unions, societies, or guilds develop outside the reach of bureaucracy. Belonging to a *danwei* is so fundamental in modern China that even though individual households occupy what is formally an external position, they are still incorporated into a structure resembling work units within the formal society. The Self-employed Laborers Association embraces only the actual shopkeepers, as they share the social position of *geti hu*. Thus shopkeepers are also generally expected to be household heads, implying that business and family organization run parallel. The peculiar way that the association coincides with social organization emphasizes that *geti hu* is treated by the authorities as a social rather than an economic category; the association is an extension of household organization and the integration of this into the universal bodies of social control.

The association is responsible for educational programs, social security schemes for businesspeople, and in cooperation with the Street Committee, job creation for unemployed youth. The meager funds it collects from individual businesses do not enable it to carry out these programs itself. However, these objectives are of major importance to its legitimacy as part of the local apparatus. They are essential to the authority that the association extracts from its position as a mass organization, supposed to realize the policies of central government. The problem of businesspeople being without access to common social services, for instance, is recognized by government, and the association takes certain measures, described below, to fill that lack.

The individual households are initially organized according to their location. Chang Shun Street with its approximately 160 businesses constitutes one such administrative unit.[7] The businesses are divided into branches of businesses, of which six out of the seven tabulated by central government are present: handicrafts and manufacturing, transportation, commerce, catering, service and barbershops, and repair shops. The size of these branches is regulated; the largest are divided to assure that the groups consist of approximately ten to fifteen businesses. The few groups that have more will be divided if they grow further. Chang Shun Street thus has nine groups, the two largest branches of business, catering and commerce, being divided into three and two respectively. Membership in the association is mandatory for all managers of private businesses. The group head (*zhuren*) and two deputy group heads (*fu zhuren*) are appointed by the ICB. The duties of the association are described as social work (*shehui gongzuo*) or social service (*shehui fuwu*) by the ICB and its members alike. The ICB appoints people who respect the four principles of the constitution[8] and who are prepared to "serve the people by doing social work." In one of the old compounds off Chang Shun Street, the association has an office where the application forms and files of each individual business are kept. The eight volunteer employees work part-time, handling new applications, requisitioning files from the applicants' former units, issuing and renewing licenses, preparing statistics, and so forth. This office only executes orders from the bureaucracy, however, as it has no formal authority itself. The obligations of group heads and deputy group heads are to assist in the organization of meetings, assist local authorities in carrying out government policies, mediate between shopkeepers and authorities, and assist in tax collection. In practice they are the tools of the bureaucracy, as little communication is directed from below upward. Shopkeepers volunteering for the association are generally managers of fairly lucrative and stable businesses that barely need their presence.

The motivation for engaging in association work may vaguely be described as "compliance with tradition," accompanied, for instance, by the opportunity to wear the cadre dress and surround oneself with a bit of a cadre's authority and perhaps get the feeling of totality in life for reaching a position identified with working for the country. For a number of local people, especially among the older generation, this is a genuine enough reason. However, as will be shown later, an active compliance with the ruling dogma is usually accompanied by substantial material gains.

One of the most active group heads in Chang Shun Street is Ms. Wu, who runs the textile shop in Chang Shun Street. Being one of the mediators for the local Street Committee as well as working for the association, she is occupied with social work practically all through the day. She is a tidy little woman in her sixties, always impeccably dressed in a gray cadre suit. The neat little lounge behind her shop has a new plastic sofa set and a color TV. Endless framed awards are on display on the walls: model individual worker, model representative of the association, awards for mediation, and the like; she eagerly shows them all to visitors. Being a Party member, she faithfully speaks in the official jargon as far as her simple education takes her.[9] She continually pronounces the masses' benefits from government and Party politics. To the individual shopkeepers she propagates the bright prospect for their future:

> Generally we have nothing to worry about in individual business. We should not let ourselves be influenced by conservative ideology concerning social position. From central government to local administration they pay attention to us.

> And thanks to the policies formulated by the Communist party and carried out by central government, the problems of social guarantees are being solved. Now we can pay 1 yuan every month and receive free medical treatment [nothing but an individual savings account]. Also, through individual business the problem of unemployed youths has been solved.

Confronted with the facts that many young in the area are unemployed, that unemployment is again rising, and that unemployed young make up only a small minority of shopkeepers, she states her denial: "Unemployed young make up 30 percent of shopkeepers, just as the Party has recommended it to be on the national level."[10] She answers mechanically all questions concerning key areas of Party interests. Because of her allegiance to Party politics, local bureaus use her services when disagreements with shopkeepers arise and peaceful resolution is preferred. The Tax Bureau also uses her as a trusted collector.

For elderly people like Ms. Wu the veracity of ideological statements is nothing but the effect of their utterance; such is the personal experience of the representatives of her generation. When Ms. Wu's collective unit was shut down in 1962, circumstances forced her to start a small business. Because her husband was assigned work in the countryside and she had four children to care for, the local authorities allowed her to continue her business all through the Cultural Revolution. They could assign her no other means of survival.[11] It was just a humble little shop, barely ensuring the family's survival. Nevertheless, she suffered physical as well as psychological mistreatment when she and her business became the target of leftist accusations of taking the capitalist road. The events of this period are still traumatic for her to recall. Her business nevertheless was one of the very few that remained operating all through the 1960s and 1970s. The liberalization since 1980 has been a great personal relief, and the full legalization of her business has evidently been of great economic benefit. Although she approximated her profits to be but 120 yuan per month, one of her relatives operating the shop later revealed them to be closer to 1,000. The two distant relatives in the shop, both rural youngsters, work for no pay but have been more or less incorporated into the family. The house, which combines the shop with a large dwelling inside and upstairs, was bought with the 250-yuan allowance from her former unit when she was dismissed; the house is now assessed at 50,000 yuan. Ms. Wu is among the people whom the reforms made wealthy overnight.

But the experiences of her past still linger. The two youngest of her own children are studying at university; they are always very well dressed and are relieved from duties in her business. "My children are influenced by conservative ideas," she says, "and I don't want them to do individual business. I think in the future, if people are not educated they will not occupy any stable place in society."

Another of the active association workers in Bin Shen is Mr. Wang, who runs one of the small *guokui* bakeries near the market. He worked in a restaurant as a skilled cook until he retired in 1982. Then he started his own restaurant but had to close it down a few years later because the building was torn down by the City Reconstruction Bureau. In 1985 he started his present place, which is operated by a single employee supervised by his wife. Mr. Wang is also in his early sixties, has only primary school education, and runs a business not requiring his presence. In his blue cadre clothes he spends his day doing social work for the association. He describes his election to this position as an expression of the "will of the masses": "They need my help. I know this street very well and I like to offer my service to it. Society needs communication, and I know both the masses and the government departments. So the neighborhood has chosen me as a social worker, and the government departments have approved it." Wang is, apparently because of his unique qualities, doing three kinds of social work. He is first assistant of the Tax Bureau — "because I always give the correct figures, so the masses and the government approve me as an assistant. I think I only do what I should." He is also in charge of fire inspection for the local police station and group head of the health and environment inspection organized by the Street Committee. Wang's own business secures his household a stable income with little effort, presumably much higher than the 200 yuan stated. But he is aiming for bigger business still. Presently he is waiting for a new building to be finished in his earlier location so he can start up anew.

Volunteer workers for the association are exclusively the shopkeepers, as they are its only members. The nature of the jobs they perform is tightly connected to the neighborhood and to private knowledge about virtually all shopkeepers in their own group. Employees and apprentices have no organization, and their conditions of work are left entirely in the hands of the household heads; the association informs employers about relevant regulations at their regular meetings but never engages in any control of or work for employees. Only in cases of serious disagreement between employer and employee are any authorities involved, first the local mediators[12] and subsequently Public Security. Local authorities are not otherwise concerned with labor relations in individual businesses.

Apart from those actively participating in the association as social workers, few others regard it as anything else than an extension of the bureaucratic control executed here in correspondence with all other ramifications of state and Party authorities. The younger shopkeepers in particular openly express the discrepancy between the association's presumed goals and its actual functioning or simply show indifference toward its work. No one in the neighborhood, except the volunteers, expresses any confidence in the association as a safeguard for business interests. It is mostly treated with indifference; when mentioned, it is in terms such as "It has no real value," "It can do nothing for us," "When it comes to real trouble, there is nothing it can do," "It has no practical role; it just encourages us to pay taxes and charges. It is moralizing from above," or "It is set up to control us." The association is tolerated as a measure of control, however, especially so by former employees of state units, who are used to much stricter discipline. To them, being a private business manager is relative freedom.

An Association Assembly

The government's assertion that the association is a businesspeople's organization is given the lie in the attendance at assemblies. Monthly meetings are held in all groups, and in addition regular assemblies are held for the whole Bin Shen area. Participation is compulsory for shopkeepers, who are here informed about government policies, new regulations concerning private business, and new taxes and charges by the ICB. These meetings are also considered the basis of the political education given to shopkeepers. When central government demands the masses to study certain topics, as was the case in 1988 when all were to "study the law," the association is the organization through which the individual households are reached; it thus serves as a direct parallel to ordinary work units. A common general assembly in the association can proceed as follows:

All shopkeepers are called in for a meeting to be held at nine o'clock in the morning. A large tea saloon on the first floor of a state restaurant on one of the main streets is used for the purpose; it is five hundred meters away from the Bin Shen area, which has no accommodation of this size. It is a gray and dreary hall with a dirty concrete floor, hard wooden benches, and no decoration on the old walls, which badly need paint. The association treats everyone to tea, served by an old employee from the restaurant below. His hands and clothes are in accordance with the overall impression of the hygienic standard of the place. The businesspeople start coming in about nine, one by one or in small groups, engaged in animated conversation about business affairs. Many are late for the meeting, and even after its start several groups of young people linger near the entrance, refusing to sit closer to the front where the speakers can be heard. Out of the well over 200 people (probably 250) obliged to attend, about 170 actually appear. And it quickly becomes evident that many shopkeepers have sent substitutes: Old grandparents, spouses, sons and daughters, distant relatives, and even employees are numerous; the actual shopkeepers apparently make up just a small minority of the participants. Those in the bigger businesses especially, such as Wang, Zhang, Fu the baker, and others, are nowhere to be seen. The main topic of the meeting is the introduction of an education charge to the central Education Bureau; the charge consists of a compulsory one-time sum to be paid by all citizens in Chengdu. The organizers of the meeting talk at length about the necessity of this charge. The main speaker at the meeting is a Mr. Wei, an individual shopkeeper who has been promoted to volunteer for the West City level of the ICB. For half an hour he speaks wholeheartedly about the need to educate the young, and with equal enthusiasm he urges the shopkeepers not only to pay the compulsory charge, but even to exceed it.[13] While he talks people are yawning, chatting, walking to and from the lavatory; their attitude collectively expresses the triviality of these matters, as new charges are constantly introduced. Many have placed themselves behind pillars or in distant corners of the room where they cannot possibly follow the speeches. After Mr. Wei has finished his monologue, he rushes off to the next meeting in another local area to repeat his performance. A local representative takes over, while some shopkeepers start leaving before the show has ended; "time is money in private business," as one of the young near the entrance states, an entirely new phrase taken from newspaper accounts of the capitalist West.

The meetings consist exclusively of one-way communication. Comments from the floor or open criticism is unheard of. Yet the inattentive participants clearly reveal their view. Some of the organizers admit that "individual households are more difficult to control than ordinary *danwei,* where the organization is more strict." The representatives receive a 3-yuan allowance from the ICB for every day's work for the association. But they readily admit that it also gives prestige in the neighborhood to work for the authorities. They are all dressed as cadres, clearly distinguishable from the individual shopkeepers. The prestige gained from performing these semiofficial duties is of a kind that may allow conversion. As one of the shopkeepers expressed: "Yes, it gives them a certain prestige, but they also do it to protect their own businesses. You cannot criticize officials. If we criticized an official, we would not be able to face him afterwards, even these small ones."

From the standpoint of individual businesspeople, the bureaucracy is a multilineal system of parallel hierarchies; functions may be specialized, but in situations of actual confrontation it is indiscriminately perceived as representing potential danger to and infringement on family affairs. The notion that "the bigger your business, the more officials you are visited by" is common among individual households. Whether founded in out-dated beliefs or personal experience, bureaucratic power is taken for granted; rarely if ever does anyone venture to check with higher authorities when met with commands from local officials. Either requests are silently complied with or attempts are made to manipulate them within a *guanxi*-type of relationship. No one in the area has attempted to stand up for his or her rights using the association as a representative. Rather, the association functions as a buffer between shopkeepers and the authorities holding the actual power, as we shall see in discussing the local Tax Bureau. Some recorded attempts at defying the local authority by addressing higher levels of bureaucracy will be discussed later.

Tax Bureau

In its relation to bureaucracy the Self-employed Laborers Association plays a crucial role in the private business environment. Taxation is naturally a matter of potential conflict, and the relationship between the local Tax Bureau and the association is illustrative. After a long series of interviews had brought anything but clarification about tax-paying procedures,[14] we decided to turn directly to the source of the mystery. In a narrow lane slanting off Chang Shun Street right where it connects to Temple Street is the compound of the Bin Shen Tax Affairs Office (Bin Shen Shuiwu Suo), securely confined behind the old gray wall. Our dropping in on the local Tax Bureau aroused a storm. Several of the approximately fifteen employees in the old buildings around the courtyard jumped out of their chairs and marched against us, evidently terrified by the intruders. In an agitated voice and with a face running out of control, one secretary informed us about our offense. Nobody, least of all a foreigner, could visit the Tax Bureau without invitation. Letters of introduction were to no avail: the secretary assured us that no such letters were powerful enough to open their doors. The employees' reaction aroused our interest in the bureau. (My assistant Liu was virtually dying of laughter when we exited the gate). Through contacts on the level of provincial government, the Provincial Tax Administration was requested to receive us, and the order was passed down through all levels to end with our local bureau. The bureau, however, reacted by demanding an additional permit from the Street Committee, which we also obtained. When we met their last demand — that all questions be delivered in written Chinese the day before our visit (usually the token of bureaus under virtual Party control) — the way was finally cleared for a short visit to their little kingdom.

Dressed considerably better than a mere state wage should permit, a man claiming to be the responsible officer for tax collection among private businesses received us. He answered our prepared questions about the taxation rates and procedures for collection politely, but not informatively. The interview gave an impression of the taxation system as logical and standardized, allowing for no manipulation or discrimination. The only shortcoming was, according to this official, the inability to assess the turnover of businesses by "scientific means." Tax collection in the area was performed by a couple of chosen employees of the Tax Bureau and these alone. The turnover of every business was assessed collectively at regular meetings in which all shopkeepers from one group participated.[15]

Checking this account with local businesspeople revealed quite a different procedure than that stated by the Tax Bureau. Tax was in principle assessed at meetings but was invariably collected not by the tax officials themselves, but by association members according to the tax officials' directives. That the businesspeople were compelled to collect tax among themselves points to an important function of the association. The tight organization of every branch group with no less than one group head, two deputy heads, and other duties distributed within the group had as one of its aims to facilitate efficient tax collection. Shopkeepers within the group were commonly confronted; some tax relief was promised in return for estimating the turnover of others, for instance, among restaurants. The association clearly appeared here as an instrument of bureaucratic control and an impediment to extrabureaucratic alliances. The animosity often detected among shopkeepers — for instance, toward Mr. Wang, who ran the largest restaurant — resulted from the fact that some attained a better deal in taxation matters than others. Also, letting businesspeople themselves collect the taxes shifted the responsibility for eventual overcharging from the officials to the members of the association who acted on their behalf.

The Tax Bureau had earned a reputation for being the most corrupt among local bureaus. Checking the bills issued to individual shops certainly pointed in that direction. Even the closest scrutiny failed to establish the precise principles for calculation. Not even the well-educated among the businesspeople could discern how the amount they paid was actually reached. And by the end of the year, everyone was required to pay an extra charge, frequently amounting to several hundred yuan, assessed by the Tax Bureau for no discernible reason. The utterly impenetrable principles for tax collection, if principled at all, were a constant source of conflict. There were no consistent methods for assessing turnover and computing taxes, and the Tax Bureau's statement that it was without the "scientific means" to determine turnover in many cases appeared to be an excuse for maintaining serious discrimination. Tax evasion proved to be out of the question for some, possible for others, and a matter of course for a few of the wealthiest households and those with direct connection to the bureau via association work.

De facto procedures for tax collection show another side of

bureaucratic authority. While the Tax Bureau itself works as a hermetically sealed apparatus, its extension, the stratum of association members working as its petty officials, frequently must operate in a fashion that is bound to disclose its practice. In the local free market, vegetable vendors are exempt from paying tax, whereas meat vendors pay according to a figure estimated for their turnover. We often met the tax collector on her rounds. A stone-faced woman in her fifties, she carries a small tablet of forms. The carbon paper has colored her hand blue right up to her wrist. She writes out tax bills with no mercy and pays little attention to the skillful argumentation of the merchants — that they come from distant places where they already pay tax, that the turnover is bad because of low prices this month, that they only trade a single basketful every day, and so forth. Merchants who have fixed locations in the market pay only once a month; those who appear occasionally are charged every day they are present. My chatting with the tax collector revealed that assessments were not made solely according to turnover. Cooperativeness was also a factor, which in this context may be a way of recognizing local authority. "And if any of them carry out illegal trade we charge them extra. If, for instance, they pump up chickens with water or sell products of inferior quality — in these cases tax can be as high as 30 percent, depending on their political attitude, their agreement with government policies, and their attitude toward us." Her comments certainly brought earlier Communist legal practice to our minds. Thus, caught in the stew of central government policy, interests of the Tax Bureau, and the officer's personal interpretation, taxation is a central theme in local society. It expresses the way that the "system" — the grand order of society — reaches out to the tiniest corners of the economy, such as the small farmers and secondary dealers trading at the market. But it does so in a fashion largely uncontrollable by central government institutions. Talking to market vendors rendered probable our suspicion that the majority of them are actually operating on the margin of regulations. They tend to be secondary dealers who buy up loads in suburban markets in the morning and sell them in Chengdu during the day. Although not operating on permits and certainly not registered with the ICB, they still pay tax.

Several shopkeepers expressed rather cynical ideas about tax collection. Ms. Luo, who operates one of the grocery shops, listed the most important factors:

> Everybody pays differently. First of all it depends on your

> *guanxi* — the quality of your relations to the officials. And of course, if you are doing jobs for the officials, you pay less. Also, when the tax collector comes, it depends on your power of speech and how persistent you are. But if you are too aggressive, they will get you in another way; they always win in the end, of course. People who have their own houses also pay more, because tax collectors know they are richer. And if you have a motorbike you are also charged more; that's why I never ride my small motorbike right up to my shop but always park it at a distance when I get here in the morning. Also, if you in any other way show off your wealth, like wearing expensive clothes or watches, they charge you more, so you must be careful what you wear, too.

Others stressed the importance of respectability and education as an expression of social standing. For instance, the bakery owner, Ms. Zhang, who had a high school diploma and an always cultured appearance to match, noted: "I think the officials respect me because of my education, so we are always treated reasonably." The majority of entrepreneurs, however, rejected this attitude, simply concluding that "they don't respect any of us individual households; it only depends on how much you give them."

The mutual distrust between officials and shopkeepers indeed reaches its peak when taxation matters are involved. Some shopkeepers had ideals of always keeping clean relations with authorities when they started business. The traditional doctor, who previously had strained relations to certain authorities, started out this way: "The Tax Bureau doesn't seem to use any accurate methods to estimate the tax," he says. "In the beginning I always told them the truth, but they never believed me, and always demanded me to pay more at the end of the year. Of course, I still tell the truth, but I can understand why some people don't." Some of the younger people were frequently caught in this game between two sides. Starting off by stating fairly true figures, believing in the righteousness of local authority, they ended up paying far higher rates than required. Some learned, however, that taxation depended on their attitude as much as their turnover. A young lad had turned this situation into part of his profession: by eloquently speaking about Party policies whenever visited, he was eventually able to make the collectors accept a figure far lower than his real turnover. Living and sleeping in the tiny little clothes shop the family was running, he was one of the few to win the sympathy of local authority without engaging in volunteer work. And stressing his own positive attitude to overnment and Party, he even referred openly to his pious fraud.

Bureaucracy and the Law: Clashing Ideologies

Discrepancy between the expressed national order and actual local practice is inherent in the Chinese political culture. Tension is evident everywhere in the Chinese administration, primarily between the attempt from above to integrate through the rule of law and the strategy from below to build up secluded totalities. Arbitrariness in bureaucratic practice and personal interpretation of regulations fill up the space between them. Local examples are plentiful from situations concerning the officials' issue of permits, implementation of regulations, and participation in illegal economic activities. The strongest manifestations of legal relativism are found in tax collection. Because it concerns the distribution and redistribution of wealth, it is a focal point of conflict, giving rise to tension on several levels of local society. Apart from the obvious contradiction between the tax-collecting authorities and the taxed businesspeople, it also conveys the discrepancy between regulations demanding legal absolutism and local practice frequently employing legal relativism. Based on the figure for turnover, taxation is idealized as calculated from "true figures." From the stance of bureaucracy, however, "truth" (*zhenshi*) in taxation is a concept involving not only business matters, but in addition the personal qualities, moral character, and political conviction of the entrepreneur; it may even be open to negotiation.

From the stance of businesspeople, "truth" depends in addition on the setting: be they stated among close friends, in relation to customers, toward competitors, in the presence of strangers, or before local authority, "true" figures vary significantly. A businessman among equals will state a relatively high figure for his business: his success in business will influence his prestige in the crowd. Confronted with representatives of local authority, the businessman will definitely state lower figures. If a state worker among his customers inquires about his earnings, however, he will be prone to further underestimate them in order to diminish the social distance between himself and the customer. Figures are indiscriminately attached to social values. Yet the different statements hold true in a relative sense, for every setting constitutes a separate framework. A customer inquiring about the turnover of different shops will receive a fairly accurate picture about the relative size of the businesses; a tax official or a total stranger likewise, although they may all receive differing sets of figures. Thus "truth" tends to apply to certain established categories of social relations, which define separate frames of reference and depend on social distance.

When new tax regulations were issued by central government in the spring of 1988, the local tax authority demanded everyone to start keeping accounts of their turnover. And so everyone did, laboriously stating all figures for their buying and selling. But when subsequently collecting tax, the officials rejected the figures, even as a basis for negotiation. Tax is still collected according to the responsible official's intuitive assessment of the "true figure." In a more concrete sense taxation is still a powerful instrument in social control, necessary to maintain the existing power structure. "The only one they cannot control is the son of Deng Xiaoping," as one said when rumors were circulating about his grand business transactions.

Regulations on individual business are publicized by central government in a small book that everyone is compelled to buy when setting up business.[16] It gives all the basic regulations on registration, employees, taxation, and the like in a comprehensive form. It even states the rights of individual households. In everyday life nobody ever refers to this book, neither businessmen nor officials. And for long periods it has been sold out from the ICB, with the result that it is a rare thing in the shops. In a certain respect it makes sense that local authority is unwilling to distribute the book; their practices deviate more than a little from those prescribed. But individual businesspeople do not find the book, which is supposed to represent the law, useful either. Very few shopkeepers were acquainted with its content or paid any attention to its existence. If the book was mentioned, a common remark would be that "it does not matter; the officials just make their own regulations if they don't agree with the book," which was frequently accompanied by "we businesspeople have no one to protect us anyway."

The tension between the absolutism of the written word expressing universal ideals and the relativism of actual adopted practice pinpoints the characteristics of bureaucratic power.

Nationwide policies and regulations are perceived as belonging to a different dimension than the handling of local affairs. Politics form the power basis by providing the abstract authoritarian rhetoric needed to establish powerful positions, which are duplicated down through bureaucratic institutions. The actual power exercise, however, is of another category, largely unaffected by current ideologies. Bureaucratic office is perceived as an individual privilege by officials and subjects alike; the charismatic personage ascending in bureaucracy especially somehow earns the respect of all, disregarding the means, since "might is right." The persistent survival of established practices in this field has hitherto been silently accepted, presumably as a prerequisite for maintaining national integration. Grave cases of power abuse have been attacked by central government and also given much publicity, but the national face thus preserved by central government and everyday practice are without similarity in this regard. In the local community such as Bin Shen, the numerous rectification campaigns are merely faint signals. Local power is personalized to such a degree that the law is identical to the officials in power, and legality is their specific way of employing such power. Thus the scope for private entrepreneurship is laid down by the practice of local bureaus, and the public reactions toward them concern their "fairness," rather than their legality. The concept of "fair treatment" (*zhengdang*) is in fact far more commonly used than references to law. Some local officials even admitted that these were common principles. When asked about the legality of some of the charges extracted from individual businesses, the head of the ICB local office answered after some contemplation: "I don't think it is a question of whether they are legal, but if they are reasonable."

Illegal practices exist among businesspeople as well, logically following similar lines: illegal in relation to the law defined by central government, yet enjoying some measure of acceptance from local authority. The reputation for cheating, selling fakes, and so forth that the individual sector has gained among many ordinary citizens is steadily nourished by some of its unscrupulous representatives. Such activity is most commonly restrained, not by local authority, but by the immense cautiousness exhibited by customers. One mobile stall in Bin Shen, for instance, openly sells illegal copies of casette tape recordings of famous stars, but the low price corresponds to their quality. Few of the permanent shops can survive on inferior goods or service, however. The travelling salesmen are the ones people watch out for, since their tricks are numerous and often sophisticated. Some sell fake medical herbs. Another travelling salesman, a gifted speaker, sold a bicycle polishing-liquid in fancy-looking bottles. Consisting of vinegar and red coloring, the liquid had a limited effect, and after a few days everyone knew it. Still, the vendor was able to talk strangers passing down the street into buying the stuff, often to the amusement of the nearby shopkeepers, and he made a good profit in spite of being taxed heavily by the collector in Chang Shun Street.

Several shops sold or processed goods and materials that cannot possibly be bought legally by individual households. The hookah workshop molds the hookah bodies in a chromium alloy that is in very short supply and distributed only to key state industries. It is procured from an electrical appliances factory in large amounts by a relative and claimed to be scrap metal; the finished hookah sells at a price presumably lower than the world market value of the material used. The plastic container producer buys his raw materials, also monopolized by the state, through channels that "take a lot more than just good *guanxi*." Another shop sells clothes made for export by a state factory. They are sold on commission for a neighbor who has relatives working at the factory in question. A smithy cannot buy the sheet metal at the price determined by the state wholesale department; since it is in high demand, the state shop sells it at a negotiated price, approximately double, making a huge profit. Many restaurants use cooking oil of inferior quality; it is mixed with oil extracted from pig skin, highly unsuitable for consumption, and everybody knows it. Cigarette sellers in the street openly trade foreign cigarettes purchased on the black market, often in connection with illegal money changing with foreigners.

When confronted with such irregularities, the local bureaucracy remains passive. If it interferes, it is usually by securing a share of the profit gained through illegal means. Likewise complaints from people who have been cheated are generally futile. Disputes between residents in the area are mostly sorted out by the volunteer mediators and only in grave cases transferred to the Public Security Bureau. Cases involving strangers are rarely investigated, as the bureau claims to lack the power and personnel to operate across administrative boundaries. This was the case when a young girl, who had just started her shop after being unemployed for a number of years, was cheated by two peasants. One day someone posing as a small peasant came to her shop to sell her a small quantity of "lotus-root flour," telling her that it was becoming increasingly popular for cooking. He persuaded her to buy a single packet, just to see if she was able to sell it. The next day another man walked by. As he passed her shop he cried out in joy pointing to her lotus-root flour. "I have been looking for this for ages," he said; "can you get me some more? I want to buy a large quantity." The third day the small peasant returned and after receiving her order supplied her with the quantity required. The young girl got stuck with the whole load of useless flour and lost all her savings. All the security office did was suggest she be more careful. Ordinary thefts reported by shopkeepers were rarely investigated.

In contrast to the attitude of indifference toward illegal economic activity, local bureaucracy reacts with firmness when its authority is challenged. Cases of struggle between entrepreneurs and bureaucracy concerning criminal acts were few, and apparently easily solved. Far more serious and long lasting were the conflicts over their decision-making authority. Very few entrepreneurs ever dared to speak out against the local administration or dispute the legality of its authority. The few who did were mostly better educated and possessed the confidence and intellectual capacity to fight for their views. Several cases involved shopkeepers refusing to accept the high-handed manners of certain officials. One such shopkeeper was the traditional doctor, practicing near the market in Chang Shun Street. Toughened from his Cultural Revolution experiences, he knew bureaucratic practices very well, and in addition he knew some of the highest cadres in the local bureaus; several of them still hold their positions.[17] The doctor can tell countless stories about their abuse of power, which had dire consequences for his own life.

Zhong was educated as a traditional doctor in the late 1950s by a combination of studies at university and subsequent years of practice as assistant to a famous doctor of traditional medicine. In 1961 he opened his own clinic at the present spot, a shop already too small from the beginning. But in spite of the tiny clinic in 1964 he was accused of taking the capitalist road; even more serious accusations were based on his background as the son of a former Guomindang officer. In 1966 he was attacked again; this time he was physically molested, brutally dragged through the streets, and literally came close to losing his head when the fanatic gangs made him kneel in front of a dagger. His clinic was closed and all the expensive medicine and equipment seized by the local police (when he tried to claim it back later he found that it had disappeared, just like everything else seized in the neighborhood at that time). He was put to work as a porter, pulling a cart with heavy loads of coal between Chengdu and a factory eight kilometers away. More harassment from the police followed. Because of his unruly behavior, his wife was publicly forced to take a stand, either for or against him. This resulted in their divorce, in which everything was taken away from him because of his unfavorable class background. When he later opened a little secondhand book shop, the police came after him again. Officials and other people freely stole his books, and when he complained to the police, they sided with the thieves. One day the head of the police station confiscated several of his books, including a copy of *Lady Chatterley's Lover*, which also disappeared. After this incident he complained continually to higher level authorities, always in vain. Once an official in the Sichuan provincial government administration responded sympathetically, but backed out when he learned the target for Zhong's complaints: "Isn't it because the books have a morally polluting content?" he asked. "No," said the doctor, "they are all approved books." "But where did you get them?" "I got them from the state book shop." "But can they still be bought there?" "No, they are sold out, because they were all best sellers." "Well, but if the state book shop no longer sells them, there isn't any reason why you should sell them." And that was how it ended.

Zhong's conflicts with local authority continue today. In 1984, when he reckoned private business was becoming safe, he reopened his little clinic. But his license is only for selling medicine. Although he was reexamined for his medical skills, the authorities refused to give him a license to practice medicine. Instead, they demanded that he choose one of the two, which they claimed to be different professions. In his view this makes traditional medicine impossible to practice, and he has defied their verdict. "Of course there are ways you can get around it." He laughs heartily; he is always in high spirits when he talks about the corrupt practices of the officials:

> And that's what it is all about. Actually they have already prepared a permit for me, I have seen it. It is printed on a very large piece of paper — which means that it is very expensive too. First of all I don't have that much money, and secondly I don't want to pay for something I have the right to get for nothing. I will continue fighting for my case. But my conflicts with these authorities have accumulated ever since 1966. Some

> of them are the same people, but I will never yield.

During his discussion with the Health Bureau he said that he would write to a certain journal of traditional medicine. They replied that he was welcome to do so. When he contacted the journal he was told that they only had the right to determine how people should be informed, and he had the right to manage his own shop. This way to redress was obviously closed.

In spite of his defiance, the authorities are reluctant to close down Zhong's clinic. It is a lively place, where a constant stream of customers is a testimony to its popularity in the local community. The little bench is mostly occupied with his patients waiting for their turn. The doctor feels pulses, examines eyes, gives injections and acupuncture, and prescribes medicine. His present wife prepares the medicine, which the apprentice fetches for her from the countless drawers or from bags hanging from the ceiling. Zhong's new strategy is to tell all his customers about the trouble he has had with local authorities, hoping that the pressure he creates will at least prevent his business from being closed. He talks so loudly that even people outside the shop can follow his accounts:

> China has never paid any attention to its intellectuals. It was more conspicuous during the Cultural Revolution, but before and after it was the same. Doctors have always been looked down upon — it is the same now as in the old China. That's probably one of the very big mistakes. But at least now you can talk about it.

Other cases exist of local struggles over authority rather than the law. Another shopkeeper who challenged bureaucracy was the plastic container and labels manufacturer, an enterprising and farsighted thirty-five-year-old engineer educated at a university in Beijing. His case also reveals the numerous invisible barriers impeding such private production.

After spending a number of years in a government forestry department, the engineer felt discouraged about his career and the prospect of spending the rest of his working life in this unit. Strained relations with the unit's management strengthened his desire to leave and start up individual production, a step that requires the approval of these authorities. But permission to leave is in principle not granted to professionally trained engineers and technicians because state units are constantly short of them. So permission was denied. But he continued resolutely, and after several years of struggle that threatened to ruin his whole career, leave was finally granted. He pays a permanent compensation of 50 percent of his original wages to the unit. This, however, is no heavy burden. After leaving, he decided to produce plastic containers, as state units are very sluggish in this field and cannot meet the rising demand. "But it could have been anything," he claims. With no other expertise than his general technical knowledge, he invested less than 10,000 yuan in some abandoned pieces of machinery from a state unit. He gave the equipment an overhaul and subsequently started a small production. Success came rapidly. Because he was a flexible and fast producer of new items, orders rushed in from state, collective, and individual customers alike. A small factory with thirty employees was quickly established, and the turnover proved his efforts worthwhile. In a matter of four months his business reached a total turnover of no less than 260,000 yuan, giving the engineer a personal income of approximately 5,000 yuan per month and in addition a large capital is placed in the bank.

Further expansion has only been limited by continuous controversy with various authorities. As a formal limit of seven employees to one individual enterprise has always existed, he managed to register his enterprise as a collective unit, hoping that the Thirteenth Party Congress in November 1987 would widen the scope for private production.[18] Registration as collective enterprise is practiced by scores of private businesses in Chengdu, made possible through agreements with the local Street Committees, which usually charge something like 1 percent of the turnover for this "service." But still practically all local bureaus put pressure on him for various reasons. Only the Industrial and Commercial Bureau has offered a lasting agreement. The Public Security Bureau especially creates difficulties for him over the question of the organization of the work force, which it demands comply with that of the ordinary *danwei*. Another source of continual contention is the control of all financial affairs by the state bank, which maintains a monopoly on decision making regarding financial transactions of all larger collective enterprises. "If I need a large sum for investment, and the bank doesn't agree, I simply don't get it." The bank demands that all his business transactions as well as payments pass through its channels.

Likewise, the local Tax Bureau gives him sleepless nights.

Although his personal tax allegedly amounts to 40 percent of his personal income, he is still unable to reach a lasting agreement with this authority, which has a policy of constantly changing conditions for renewal. "There is a clear contradiction between central policy and local implementation here. The tax officials seem to rely on their own interpretation of the current policy — or rather, they chiefly look after their own interests. It's a historical phenomenon!" says the engineer. Yet another obstacle is the purchase of raw plastic, also monopolized by state departments. The essence of his conflict with local bureaus is that he refuses to accept their individual interpretations of current regulations and individual solutions, usually involving monetary compensation. He consequently addresses his applications to higher authorities when possible. "I think it will be easier to run private business in the future; hopefully the Party Congress will allow us more freedom. But anything can happen. Maybe I am not here in a couple of years. I think most of us who run business are afraid and uncertain about what the future may bring."

As mentioned, Chinese authorities in charge of the individual economy are presently reorganizing so they will be able to handle more efficiently the affairs and correspondence between central policy making and local implementation. The outcome of these efforts has so far been difficult to detect by shopkeepers, and of course the Chinese special bureaucratic tradition poses a problem in itself. Apart from arbitrary use of power and some officials' high-handed tactics, local bureaus are characterized by operating autonomously rather than cooperating with other departmental bureaus. This tendency toward departmentalism, each bureau becoming a secluded entity within the bureaucratic structure, has significant effects on the business environment in general. "Small or large, but complete"[19] may not only be the slogan of the bureaucracy, but is likely to necessitate a similar type of organization in the businesses dependent on them for legalization and services. Becoming integrated into a closed network of personal ties secures the smooth running of the business but tends to bind it tightly to local operation and can even become a straitjacket when expansion is desired. Still, the issue of licenses is an area in which favoritism, nepotism, and corruption flourishes. Totally dependent on licenses for the legality of their businesses, the shopkeepers are in the pocket of the ICB. Once the license has been granted, this bureau rarely causes trouble; having the shopkeepers on the hook only once may, of course, incite the ICB to exploit this opportunity in full. To some shopkeepers, obtaining the licenses is easy, and the fees are insignificant. Some obtain them easily in spite of being formally debarred from private business — for instance, the old cadres who register their children or relatives as shopkeepers. Others pay what they consider reasonable fees. A few of the more forthright admitted, however, that they were compelled to pay large sums of money for a license that they were supposedly rightfully entitled to. Fu, the baker, was one of these:

> There is always conflict between central government policy and local administration. Central government promotes private business, but in reality it is extremely difficult to get the license. The local offices seem to have their personal interpretations of everything. When I applied for the license, the ICB sent me back and forth between a number of different offices: Health Bureau, Tax Bureau, etc., which all proved to be blind alleys. But when you hit a wall you have to find a way round it. It took me four months, but when I reached an agreement with the ICB, I could set up my business even before I got the license.

A central theme in the struggles taking place in local society, and one that penetrates the practices of the local bureaus, is the display of conformity — in this respect, centered on submission to authority. Whether genuine or just assumed in the pursuit of privileges, conformity in the outer appearance of things tends to be the rule of the game. It assures those in office that their authority can be transformed into privileges, and it provides the people below with a recognizable procedure and builds a feeling of security that only those possessing the proper status or charisma move to the top by gradually building up their authority. Conformity belongs to the shared values of social thought. Bureaucratic power is still viewed as the "nature of things," and to some degree it rests on consensus. It belongs to "tradition" — which can be manipulated, but nevertheless makes up the common starting point. Old proverbs and expressions for officials are countless. They stress the officials' lack of morals and their ruthlessness and covetousness. They are the "uncrowned Kings" who "divide and rule." And "when the gods fight, the people suffer" — for instance, when "the officials burn houses while commoners are not permitted to burn oil lamps." The officials are even compared to traditional landlords when taking away excessive taxes: "to work for

Master Liu" means to work without getting the fruits of your own labor.[20]

Most shopkeepers still accept and submit to these unwritten codes of local society. The disciplinary effects of bureaucratic power are obvious. The social control enforced on individual households is not directly one of securing the interests of Party and government. Collective registration of businesses, for instance, is still the preference of the ruling authorities, but it is often carried out for other reasons than intended — for instance, extracting money for hiding their actual private entrepreneurship. Ideological control of businesspeople is attempted through the association but is carried out by officials with different incentives. The power structure of society in itself, including the unrestricted authority of local bureaus, is the indirect source of a systematized disciplining. Obviously, the discrepancy between formal order and informal practice is steadily nourished.

However, to depict the interaction between bureaucrats and commoners as that between rulers and the ruled may paint a distorted picture. The bureaucratic display of personalized authority must be seen against the background of practices that ordinary people adopt in their mutual relations; often, these virtually reproduce the bureaucrats' way of making optimal use of any potential power. The general economic situation has worsened for a large section of the population since the reforms. Likewise, the competition for securing one's personal survival is getting harder. The last of the smiths working in Chang Shun Street proper experienced this when his landlord broke their contract and evicted him. The landlord had been given an offer from another shopkeeper who, because of the severe shortage of housing, was willing to pay considerably more. Although having to withdraw to the compound of his home, the smith could still practice his craft for a circle of steady customers. But the weak position he was in brought more misfortune. The owner of the house in which the smith rented a few rooms for himself and his family lost his state job. After that the landlord's only source of income was the rent from the extra rooms occupied by the smith. So he raised the rent. And shortly afterward, he demanded to become the smith's partner in business. This implied receiving 50 percent of his profit. Any such private arrangement is without interest to local administration and open to exploitation. "Big fish eats small fish, small fish eats shrimp" is a pertinent colloquial expression for this order.[21] Hence, it may be equally true among ordinary people that a person exploits any power he or she has, emphasizing the strong demarcation between the inner and outer circles of social relations and loyalties.

The strategies that individual households adopt toward local bureaucracy are ambiguous. As shown, there are certain patterns in these strategies: either conformity and the pursuit of privileges by following the rules set by those in office or, on the other extreme, resistance to bureaucracy in order to avoid all personalized relations. The heavy pressure that bureaucracy puts on anyone with ample economic resources makes balancing between the involvement and noninvolvement strategies difficult. Thus, the highly esteemed conformity in local society means indeed following the rule of custom, rather than the rule of law, as opposed they may be. Just as conformity within the family is tied to respect for traditional authorities, so does behavior in the external setting revolve around the recognition and manipulation of bureaucratic authority. As is shown below, bureaucracy tends to extend downward to encompass all relations of potential power in local society, far beyond the level of its paid officials. By swallowing up all authority, bureaucracy itself becomes the very scene for ambitions and upward mobility for a large section of the population.

Participating in social work and local administration is indeed an established value in society, although it is primarily performed by people well over fifty years of age. In business, such participation tends to be connected to pragmatic strategies, strongly linked to local reputation, personalized connections, and ultimately to security. Some instances were recorded in which doing jobs for bureaucracy had positive consequences such as distracting public attention from one's personal affairs or compensating for shortcomings in other fields. But in the structure of local society, social work plays a more specific role.

Petty Officialdom: Systematized Exchange

As previously noted, a substantial number of people in Bin Shen are somehow involved in the local bureaucracy. They receive no regular payment, but they frequently get small monetary benefits from the work they perform. Equipped with a semiofficial status, they are the extension of the bureaus, themselves hierarchically organized institutions. They are employed in the areas of public administration, taxation, public security, health and hygiene inspection, all sorts of registration, propaganda, mediation, and other aspects of public organization. The Street Committee, the Neighborhood Committee, and the Self-employed Laborers Association are mainly the institutions for which they work. The collective enterprises also have their own organization similar to that of the individual businesses; it too involves a number of volunteer workers.

While the Street Committee has employees on regular wages as well as volunteers, the Neighborhood Committees below it have only volunteer workers. Since both are integral parts of the civil administration, with firm control and intimate knowledge of every household under their jurisdiction, these social workers (*shehui fuwuzhe*) are indispensable. The Neighborhood Committees in Chang Shun Street have volunteers in charge of public security, health inspection, and fire surveillance. In addition to organizing the Neighborhood Committees, the Street Committee has various other functions. It is in charge of all state propaganda and runs propaganda offices and it has actual programs in birth control and job creation, teaches evening classes and compulsory political study courses, and the like. Several of these functions also involve volunteer social workers. The Street Committee is also responsible for local mediation in marriage affairs, quarrels among neighbors, disagreements in business, and other quarrels and fights in the street. All mediators are volunteers, too. Volunteers in miniature offices, often just consisting of a small table in a private home and a sign next to the door, register all guests and visitors staying more than a day in the neighborhood. Others register regular traders and vendors in the street and at the market.

The association with its numerous social workers has already been described. As earlier stated, an estimated one out of every three households in the area has one or more members with semiofficial duties. The simplest tasks of social work involve being aware of certain affairs in one's environment, like the cleanliness of streets or courtyards. Others involve a few hours every day or regular shifts during the night for those on the public security line, on guard for thieves or other irregular activities. Other assistants are fully occupied throughout the day. These are the association organizers and tax collectors and the mediators and volunteer workers in the Street Committee's offices. Some of the active members of the association receive small tokens for the time spent: for instance, the 3 yuan for a day's work organizing the assemblies. The responsible social workers in the Neighborhood Committee receive only indirect payment. The Street Committee gives the Neighborhood Committee a monthly allowance to meet its expenses. If the monthly budget can be kept below this, the balance may be shared by the members. But as the budget is only modest, this rarely amounts to more than 10 yuan per person. It can certainly be said for all social workers that the direct or indirect payment for all jobs performed is far below the return on similar efforts in the private sector.

It is evident that engaging in social work has other motivation than the direct monetary benefits. Motivation for engaging in local community life among the elder generation is the positive compliance with tradition — an expression of surplus in one's own household that allows for donating one's time and energy to the common good or, in the phrases of the present leadership, the benefit of the masses. Doing social work brings the volunteers into contact with a number of other people and because of the high demand for sociability among most locals is an important reward. For some of the elderly, volunteer work gives meaning to everyday life, just as some of the elderly shopkeepers run a business as much to entertain themselves as for profit. The registration office of the association, for instance, is staffed every day by far more people than the simple work requires. But the old, dusty office, sparsely furnished but nicely situated in an old compound, provides a stimulating milieu for some of the elderly people. It combines attending to simple jobs with sociability. Local gossip and hearsay thrive in these places, and many meetings are held.

Working in the compounds of the former elite and performing bureaucratic work may signify an ascending social position for a household. For the average individual who has spent his or her working life in a secure but static position, it may also support personal fulfillment and a sense of totality. Authority is supposed to be achieved steadily through life; old age without authority is often associated with failure. Working for the community, and through this gaining higher status, is how the volunteer social workers themselves express their commitment. As an additional perquisite, social work permits them to wear the dress commonly associated with a cadre.

Apart from social status, more material aims could well be expected to influence people's motives, and such was often hinted at by others, especially among people in private business. Again, historical experience must be considered. Accusations of "taking the capitalist road" were so widespread in the late 1960s that they involved practically everybody in private business. Almost half of the present shopkeepers who were also running business then were publicly exposed to violence.[22] After the reforms, the public debate on private enterprise has time and again touched upon the question of its integration into the socialist system — in which instances it is acceptable and in which instances it turns into capitalism (e.g., Xia 1987). It has frequently been argued that when small businesses are run by an individual who himself participates in the labor, it is not capitalism. Shopkeepers, however, generally harbor no intention of participating in the labor except when absolutely necessary. Several shopkeepers run businesses in which their presence is unimportant, such as Wang's *guokui* bakery or Ms. Wu's textiles shop. For these shopkeepers, participating in association work is presumably the better bargain for safeguarding the continued legality of their businesses. In addition to providing security, this solution may even increase their general respectability.

Still closer to everyday life and material aims is the return on energy invested in the association. Local bureaucracy evidently accepts far lower figures on the turnover of businesses run by the people with positions in the association. Ms. Wu's and Mr. Wang's stated turnover may be less than half of what should be expected or what their employees estimate. Tax therefore is a lighter burden for association members than for others. And the additional charges collected by local bureaus are likely to follow this pattern. While certain officials' helpers or association representatives may collect charges at random in businesses like the The Labyrinth, for instance, they will think twice before doing something similar in the shops of Wu or Wang, for in that case they would be collecting from their colleagues and equals.

In such a perspective, the petty officials in the neighborhood become part of a much larger and far more significant power structure. They become the lowest level of strict nomenclature, in which the small officials in the local bureau were previously the lowest; they are the informal extension of the formal hierarchy. Consequently, they merge into the pattern of systematized exchange relations: conformity and unqualified loyalty toward the superior levels in exchange for privileges and security. By performing the tasks of bureaucracy, they acquire part of the status connected to it. And by speaking the language of authority, they acquire a small fraction of this authority themselves.

Propagating the interests of bureaucracy does not necessarily mean compromising conscience for the sake of wealth. The behaviors described are simply the rules of the game. In regard to local reputation, no one really expects officials or semiofficials to speak from conscience. The emotions of the inner self have evidently no direct relation to public performance. Even though the more cynical among shopkeepers may remark that they only act in such ways "to protect their own businesses," the measures these petty officials take are not qualitatively different from those taken by the shopkeepers. The measures just reflect different strategies that different people employ according to their own experience, faculty, and goal. Against the background of a highly unpredictable regime, the protection of businesses is paramount to all. These strategies commonly have as their core a highly materialist attitude toward life and business that is equally shared by all.

Good morality, conformity, and loyalty toward superiors can be repaid in kind. Although morality, when applied to the public sphere, always explicitly directs itself toward the benefit of the masses, it obviously carries implicit meanings. A semantic change is effected by its combination with a highly symbolic language, in which the principal phrases are current ideology, emitted from the Center. Such phrases imply the recognition of the central authorities that derive their legitimacy from operating in the name of the masses: Tax Authority of the People's Republic, People's Health Bureau, Street and Neighborhood Committees, Public Security, not to mention the Chinese Communist party. By monopolizing interpretations of the "will of the masses," these bodies concentrate all power accordingly. Power and privileges are redistributed through the channels open to propagation; authorities reproduce lesser authorities in their own image.

Succeeding levels of bureaucracy employ similar means to secure their positions, forming a long series of exchanges. The system transmits two currents. Loyalty and expression of conformity travel upward, while the countercurrent is one of power and privilege — easily changed into material benefits. For this reason the power structure of local society is highly contradictory to any legal construction in which individuals are equally positioned. Thus local authority builds its existence on principles that obstruct all attempts by central government to enforce the rule of law.[23]

A central theme is precisely the rule of law — not only the practice of bureaucracy, but how concepts of law are placed in the interaction between bureaucracy and individual businesses. Petty officialdom is a key in this interaction. It has earlier been mentioned that petty officials can function as a tool of the local bureaus in covering up their malpractice. By this means, bureaucracy has a firm grip on everybody; it is virtually impossible for the average person to sort out who is exploiting his or her business — whether it is the state through excessive state taxes, the local bureaus through the more or less casual additional charges, or the local collector, who is of his own kind. For businesspeople, infringement comes not only from above, but from anyone in a position of power that allows it. All know that it is not possible for the association or any other organization to speak out or defend their rights. The bureaucratic practice of deliberately implicating people from within the group and binding them to their superiors through lines of authority and privileges secures stable ties. Being implicated excludes the return to any defense of the rule of law such as propagated by government bodies. Thus alliances in local society tend to run along vertical lines. In these petty officialdom is the all-important ingredient. Petty officials actively discourage all potential alliances along horizontal lines expressing stratum, class, or common business interests. The strong hold in tradition that these alliances take is emphasized by the actual people involved. The elderly people with little education, who not only recognize local authorities but also have interests in raising their own status, make up the majority of volunteers. These are the people who in other areas also are defenders of convention; in family organization and outlook they are easy prey for local bureaus.

Examples of vertical alliances involving particular officials on top are difficult to extract; generally, these alliances follow the hierarchy of the individual bureaus. The heads of bureaus deal with lower officials, who then arrange things with representatives of the association, Neighborhood Committees, and the like. Many of the petty officials presumably have particular officials toward whom they are responsible — that is, there are personal followings inside the bureaucracy. The head of the local police station had a very special reputation for blatantly building his own kingdom. Through binding a large number of officials and petty officials to his own person he ruthlessly extracted large sums of money for the "security" of all businesses in his district.

Local bureaucracy, the petty officials, and a large part of the remaining population have a common attitude toward the law. As all important interactions between the average person and public authorities make use of the personalized connections of the *guanxi* type, law and order also tends to be a question of individual application. The tradition of moralizing authorities[24] combined with unrestricted personalized power has also prevailed in Bin Shen. For the elderly population, varying regimes have altered little in this respect; for the young the Cultural Revolution especially carried this custom to the extreme. Common people thus regard regulations introduced by central government as something belonging to the sphere of ideology; they have no practical implications for everyday life. Although the Self-employed Laborers Association is formally organized by the ICB, it is unlikely to be a reliable instrument in introducing legal principles. Since it is subordinated to various local bureaus, it can only continue their practices. Consequently, those active in the association have no other relation to legal matters than the practices of their superiors. Law in the abstract sense remains part of the language of the Center; it may itself be logical and consistent, but it has little coincidence with local life.

Individuals relating to any abstract social aims are few and tend to be marginal, if not downright isolated. A few local intellectuals such as doctor Zhong, baker Fu, and engineer Chang consistently referred to the law when discussing private businesses, always mentioning the discrepancy between central government policies and local bureaucratic procedures. For them, the defects of the local society were caused by the "rigid thought" that the officials applied to everything. They generally saw historical reasons behind this; the absolute power of these officials and the small kingdoms they erected were the traditional benefits of officialdom. They did not believe that increasing the wages in official employment would bring about any real changes. "It is a historical phenomenon," as one of them said; "power and privilege go hand in hand. Local officials use their own interpretations of government's policy; they always follow their own interests. They use every power in their possession, and they always will."

CHAPTER SIX

The Young in Business

Doctor Zhong complains about his teenage daughter when we pay him a short visit one afternoon. Customers arrive unceasingly in the tiny shop, and some leave again because the wait is too long. The daughter, who Zhong had hoped would study medicine to become his successor in the clinic, is still sleeping upstairs. She is badly needed to measure out medicine and assist, which she often does in her spare time. But she is becoming increasingly unwilling to spend her time in the shop. And according to Zhong, that goes for studying and attending classes too: "They had a party again last night; it's the only thing they really care about now. All her classmates gather to dance somewhere here in the neighborhood. They say that they are only celebrating birthdays, and of course you cannot forbid that. But there are fifty students in her class, so every week it is someone's birthday. They stage it Saturday!"

Zhong's daughter is one of the countless teenagers to whom studying seems more and more a waste of time. In her own words: "There is no reason to study at my age. It is hard work, and even if you pass the exams, you cannot use it for anything. There are no jobs for us from our school when we graduate, and going to university is almost impossible. Many of my classmates want to leave school now to do private business. They want to make money quickly to buy nice clothes and things."[1]

Many more her age in the street are in the same situation. Ms. Luo, who runs the small grocery shop across the street, tells a similar story about her daughter, who is now fifteen: "We would like her to go to university, but she doesn't bother. She just wants to enjoy herself, drink Pepsi, smoke expensive cigarettes, and make herself pretty in front of the mirror. So she just wants to make money." And the daughter has good reasons for leaving school. No one from her class will go to university, and consequently 80 percent of the students just want to leave school to start making money. Divided already from primary school according to marks, the best students go to the best schools, the less good students go to the less good schools, and so forth. Practically none of the students ending up in the lowest grade schools will reach higher education. And the majority of children from individual business households end up in such schools. With little hope of ever obtaining state employment, they are most likely to follow in the footsteps of their parents. But if their offspring ended up in private business they were toward the end of the 1980s accompanied by scores of other young people who, in spite of an ordinary background, had no other future.

Personal Emancipation or Victims of Modernization?

Initial investigation among young secondary school graduates revealed that after a year only about half of them had found a job, and after two years the number was not much higher. For the rest, the inevitable could be postponed as long as their parents would support them, but eventually they would end up in some sort of private business. One example is a small outdoors bookstall run by a sister and a brother. Such a stall requires a permit for the spot it occupies, and they were lucky when they had their place assigned by the Street Committee. The stream of potential customers is endless here at the junction between Chang Shun Street and Temple Street. Their selection of books and magazines is popular. They have all the colorful magazines that young people are keen on — magazines about romances, movies, pop stars, science, and space travel. Books on politics and a few new novels are also on display. From this small stall, the size of a dinner table, they make 600–900 yuan per month between them — an income that is out of reach in official employment. Their respective attitudes toward the present trade are instructive, however, since they tend to be customary. The sister, aged twenty-five and married to an engineer, was unemployed for almost five years before gaining this opportunity. For her, selling books and magazines is a pleasure. She likes to read, and there is plenty of time for reading during the day. The income allows her nuclear family a freedom and lifestyle that would otherwise be impossible, and she declares that she is prepared to sell books for the rest of her life if policies allow. In contrast, her brother, aged nineteen, treats the business with conspicuous indifference. He is interested in books, yes, but not selling them! He was unemployed for a year and felt that he needed to do something for a living. More than half the students from his class managed to obtain state jobs. But he did not get the chance; he was never offered a job, and he has found nothing worth applying for so far. But he surely prefers state employment. To the direct question on the quality of state employment, however, he just shrugs his shoulders: "I don't know; the money is good here, but I would take a state job if I were offered one."

Their parents are both ordinary workers in a state unit. As the offspring of a household that, in terms of social status, belongs to the mainstream of society, these two young people who run a bookstall signify a new trend in the private sector. Through 1988, and particularly in early 1989, a number of new businesses of this type opened in Bin Shen; as a result the young became noticeable in business. A TV-games shop in Chang Shun Street is another example. Numerous are the young customers sitting on the long bench before the three TV sets, and many more follow the games intensely over their shoulders. The glittering new TVs produced by a joint-venture with Japanese investors and the Japanese private power supply stand in odd contrast to their accommodation: the old walls, cracked beams, and earthen floor of the house appear dilapidated, almost untouched since their construction, and the shop is otherwise empty. Fangshui, a young girl dressed in Chengdu's fanciest clothes, runs the shop. She was employed at a bottle factory in Chengdu after spending one or two years without work. It was filthy and hard work in three shifts, and the air in the factory was unbearably hot and polluted. Monthly pay was 48 yuan with no extra benefits because the factory was poorly managed. When on the night shift, she stayed in a dormitory at the factory; at other shifts, with her parents. When she married, she decided to break out from the course of life set for her. With the assistance of both her own and her husband's family she bought the equipment worth 16,000 yuan, a substantial investment that nonetheless seems quite safe. Her monthly income easily reaches 500 yuan according to her own statements. When we mention the social status issue, she comments:

> I actually think my social status is higher now. Compared to working in that filthy factory nearly going broke this is quite

> an improvement. Now I have a business that is easy to run, and I can wear clean clothes. Most of the money I make goes to our new home and to clothes. Many of my former colleagues now admire me for breaking out and want to do the same thing.

Getting permission to leave the factory was uncomplicated; she was just requested to pay a monthly charge of 50 percent of her former income. Obtaining the private business permit alone proved to be "very difficult." The only remaining threat to her business is the dramatically rising charges assessed by the local bureaucracy. "They envy us and take advantage of private businesses," she says.

More young people have chosen the games trade, a novelty in Chang Shun Street. A billiard saloon has been opened in a large room just recently turned into a shop. The twenty-three-year-old son of a local family runs the place. This is his first activity since he graduated four years ago. He waited in vain for a state job; upon realizing that private business was the only alternative, he decided on a billiard saloon. There are usually plenty of customers playing at the two tables, but heavy inroads are made on his turnover of 500 yuan a month: 200 to the landlord, 100 to the special "culture charge" on all games businesses, and 50–100 on tax and additional charges.

There are a variety of solutions to unemployment in the area. For some, the local market provides convenient jobs. Since a highly liberal attitude prevails toward the market among the authorities — provided that everyone receives his or her proper fees — the major obstacle for city dwellers trading at the market is their own social consciousness. Being identified with the peasantry is a sufficiently frightful thought to restrain the vast majority of young and old alike. The few who break with these socio-spatial classifications are invariably young women. Four or five of the locally registered unemployed young women gain their livelihood at the market by selling fruit or homemade bean curd and bean paste. Two of them sell pears and apples side by side at the far end of the market. Several years with nothing to do eased their aversion for the trade. One was unemployed for almost five years before starting at the market; the other had a job in a kindergarten, paying 35 yuan a month. At seven o'clock in the morning they travel to a suburban fruit market to buy a tricycle load full of fruit to take back. They spend the rest of the day serving customers or sitting on the bench behind them, chatting the time away. Although not very challenging, it is an easy job, considering the 300–400 yuan a month they each can earn. "What I made per month in the kindergarten I can almost make in a good day here at the market." The young woman's small child sleeps on the bench next to her. Customers can be far apart when activity slows down toward the afternoon, but the young women will usually stay at the market until five or six at night.

They have plenty of company between customers. The old bench they occupy leans against the wall of the Street Committee's billiard saloon; numerous young men from the neighborhood, usually in high spirits, lean out the window. The billiard parlor is run with the sole purpose of providing entertainment for the unemployed young, but undoubtedly with a mind to what they otherwise might be up to. But whatever the motive, the parlor is crowded with people all through the day; the two billiard tables and the single employee are always busy. The billiard players are, with rare exceptions, young men. Some have regular jobs but spend their lunch breaks there. A few countryside laborers from a nearby restaurant spend their noon resting period by the billiard table. The majority, however, are unemployed young men. Some have been so for a year or two, others up to seven years. In spite of the local authorities' denial of the problem, the billiard saloon is clearly a testimony to unemployment looming large. How extensive it is no one can really tell since no unified registration of the phenomenon exists. Some of the young may be registered with the official job allocation system.[2] Some are registered with the Street Committee. Others are registered as unemployed in their parents' work units. Since these administrative bodies can presumably transfer individuals among them to be registered elsewhere, they may all in accordance with the Street Committee and state authorities conveniently announce that "unemployment is only very small."

The attendant in the billiard saloon is a thirty-five-year-old former worker in a collective unit. He too was unemployed for a couple of years before working for the Street Committee. Now, he is paid a standard wage plus the 5 fen that the players pay per game. His job is just to be there, teaching them the basics of the game and controlling the crowd. Though employed by the committee he feels no obligation to speak for its views: "Yes, there are many unemployed in this area. Every street has a number of them. Of course, if they only have to wait a year or two after graduating, it is no problem. But many of them come here for years with nothing else to do. It also strains the relationship with their parents." The crowd of young in the billiard saloon is largest around noon when the jobless get company from those with regular jobs. Many are former classmates. With or without job, everyone wears a suit, except for the couple of rural laborers who occasionally show up. The quality of the suits indicates the respective positions of the young. Some of the unemployed are unlikely to have anything else but this single set; some other customers are very expensively dressed. There is, for instance, a young taxi driver whose family put all their savings into his future by investing in a car. He is the one to whom the others point as an example to follow: "He is rich!" And so is anyone with a private car in Chengdu. Others are less fortunate. Qingrong, aged twenty-four, holds the record among those present by having never had a job since he graduated seven years ago. He has never been offered one and has never been able to find one himself. Neither have his parents been able to place him in their units, and since they are relatively young state workers, he cannot expect to replace them for the time being: "I don't think much about it any more, because there is nothing I can do. My family can support me. But I depend on them for everything, that's the biggest trouble. Every time I need to buy things I have to ask them for money, and they don't have much either." Without an income there is also little chance of marrying; few girls would want a husband who cannot support even himself. Consequently he is stuck, in both a social and an economic sense. So how about private business? "No, and it's also too difficult to find a place. If I could get my own car I would like to become taxi driver, but that is not possible." Selling fruit in the market? "No way." So time passes with billiards and seeing friends; as the girls comment from outside the window: "They can only play. They play billiards in the daytime, and at night they gather somewhere in a private home to play *mazhang*, you can depend on that."

The Street Committee also has job creation on its agenda — a way of indirectly recognizing the seriousness of the problem. According to decrees from central government, it is supposed to establish new economic activities in the fields possible. A few small stalls near the market were, for instance, rented by the Street Committee and turned into collectives with two or three young unemployed in each. One sold state-produced posters and pictures otherwise not available in the area; the other sold books. But they were only short-lived since the young gained only a small profit and apparently lacked interest in the project. They were required, of course, to operate as collectives and found themselves strictly controlled by the Street Committee.

Hence, local authorities such as the Street Committee find themselves in a dilemma when confronted with serious unemployment. No responsible cadres on a local level want their own statistics to differ radically from the nationwide or provincial figures, which often express elevated ideals rather than reality; there is a strong drive toward conformity in this field. Being in line with central government in as many areas as possible is an expression of successful control and management of local affairs — and, presumably, submission to central authority. Cadres frequently refer to the national level when proving their own statistics to be "normal," in this sense meaning in no way being subject to public attention. The freedom they enjoy in handling local affairs is linked to submission to higher authorities. But when central government ordains Street Committees to combat unemployment and simultaneously issue statistics cloaking the problem,[3] the political culture of the past is obviously maintained. Street Committee, Neighborhood Committee, and petty officials all harmoniously deny the problem. As Ms. Wu in the association stated, "No, there are hardly any unemployed in this street. When a shopkeeper asked us to help him hire an assistant we could not even give him a list of names." But shopkeepers hiring hands through any organization is highly unusual, or rather unheard of.

When individual business was reintroduced after 1979, one of its formal and primary aims was to control the mass unemployment threatening the young school graduates from years of booming birth rates. State units were unable to absorb the influx into the work force of almost ten million individuals per year. The businesses in Bin Shen surprisingly comprise very few of these "job-waiting" (*daiye*) young. In 1987–88, only 8 percent of the households visited stated as their main reason for starting up a business the wish to provide for jobless offspring, and in only 5 percent of the households were these young people the actual shopkeepers. In contrast, the age group often referred to as "the lost generation," because their schooling was interrupted by the Cultural Revolution, is well represented in businesses. After years of only unskilled labor and some only recently returned from the countryside, they typically saw private business as the path to a brighter future. In 1989, the number of young school leavers running private business had increased somewhat (to approximately 12 percent), but the newcomers were mostly on the lowest level: simple mobile arrangements in the street or at the market. But, as the young people concordantly state, the preconditions for successful business are good connections, capital, and access to premises. These conditions favor the elder generations and tend to shut out the young, however talented or skillful they may be.

Rising Contradiction

While an increasing number of young people was driven toward self-employment in search of a livelihood, another development from 1988 to 1989 worsened the conditions for private enterprise dramatically, and in fact threatened to undermine the entire private sector. A discursion is necessary in order to expose the socioeconomic circumstances the young people faced. National economic stagnation, revealed gradually through 1988, was followed by a serious recession in the Sichuanese economy, which again affected the overall level of bonuses in the state-run enterprises. From reaching the highest level ever in 1986–87, bonuses suddenly dropped in the following years according to the common assessment of local people. Reports on state enterprises unable to pay more than standard wages rose markedly in the beginning of 1989. For the masses of workers in state and collective enterprises, wages did not keep pace with inflation (assessed to be as high as 25 percent[4]), and for many the situation turned grotesque: while the cost of living rose steadily, their pay had shrunk from the year before. In Bin Shen, it became obvious to everyone that the average state employee now belonged to the poorest group of people. Established social categories were threatened. A commonplace tendency toward personal solutions to economic difficulties (*daoye*) was rapidly developing, and in the cities like Chengdu an old saying that "everybody has his own ways" regained its truth. This was also the case with officials from the various bureaus in charge of the private sector; the period from 1987 onward brought new taxes, surcharges, and fees to businesses like never before. In Bin Shen, supplementary fees, in addition to the business tax paid to central government, increased 100–200 percent in this period, and the number of bureaus collecting them increased from five to approximately ten. The new charges introduced were security charge, paid to the local police station; culture charge, paid to the Municipal Culture Bureau;

education charge, paid to the Bureau of Education; city reconstruction charge, paid to the Chengdu Bureau of City Reconstruction; and temporary residence charge for employees, paid by shopkeepers to the Street Committee. Casual charges were collected in addition. For the smaller businesses, the additional fees far exceeded the state tax. The individual sector had become the happy hunting ground for the "uncrowned kings" of local authorities who exploited every possible means to extract more money. The officials' inventiveness in regard to new charges seemed unlimited. Such was the situation in the spring of 1989 that even Taoist and Buddhist monks appeared in Chang Shun Street and attempted to collect fees from private businesses, but because they were suspected to be swindlers, their proceeds were low. Local observers noted that the whole picture became more and more similar to the large state units, where a great many live off the work of a few.

Several local shopkeepers felt that their businesses were seriously threatened and were about to give up. This applied particularly to the smaller shops and workshops run by elderly people — for instance, the old saddler, one smith, and some retail shops. But relations with local authority worsened considerably for middle-sized businesses as well. The average total taxes and charges these businesses paid had apparently doubled in a single year, while turnover had increased only moderately. Even some of the elderly shopkeepers who had silently experienced the entire Communist epoch began to vent their views. An old couple running a tailor shop at the level of basic subsistence began to speak out:

> Before the Liberation we hardly paid any tax. Now all charges are so high, even if you sell a few vegetables at the market you are charged. And the association does nothing for us. Once a year they give us an assembly where they serve tea, peanuts, and melon seeds. We say thank you, and they say oh, you paid yourselves. Inside we agree. They do nothing but collect money and then they give us a paper wreath (*huaquan*) when we die. The association is like the chairman of the country. The government gives him to us, and then they say he was elected by the whole people. It's the same with association members; they are appointed by the Street Committee — no democracy."[5]

The rising conflict between bureaucracy and individual households brought about a decline in moral standards that could be sensed everywhere. It vented itself in more than just personal profit making. A common phenomenon is what the shopkeepers call the "red eyes disease"[6] — envy, from neighbors and officials alike. It is a straightforward expression of the frustration directed by those with formal position and low income toward the monied businesspeople. Most often, it means accusing the more fortunate people of misdeeds, rather than analyzing the cause of one's own situation. This is especially the case with officials in higher positions who find it impossible to accept a situation in which the distribution of real wealth does not follow social rank. Since private businesses mainly belong to the lowest stratum in society, they are the easiest to exploit. The red eyes disease has of course existed ever since private business yielded good profits; but with living standards declining for a large section of the population, the attitude toward the individual households became ever more reproachful and hostile.

The Media

If widespread social friction was the consequence of stiffer competition for scarce resources, the public media were certainly fanning the fire. Whereas the central government–controlled media encouraged private enterprise in principle, and often tried to lure people with rosy success stories, the local Party-controlled media were at best skeptical, and often downright hostile to the individual households. In 1989 such animosity frequently found overt expression. This was, for instance, the case in an article on the front page of the *Chengdu Evening News* (*Chengdu wanbao*), entitled "We Cannot Allow Them to Become Rich through Tax Evasion."[7] The article employs Cultural Revolution rhetoric and generalizations, stating that "many individual households have come from investments of a few tens or a few hundred yuan to having nowadays assets of several tens of thousands, several hundred thousand, up to one million yuan. But their tax payments have not increased with the same speed." The article maintains that the individual households in Chengdu pay on average only 31 yuan monthly in taxes. After mentioning that a famous mosquito net producer in Chengdu nicknamed "One Million Yang" owed more than 150,000 yuan in back taxes and that another well-known entrepreneur evaded tax of more than 90,000 yuan, the article discusses the problems of the tax authority. An unnamed tax bureau official states that "practically 100 percent of individual households all evade tax (*tou lou shui*); tax evasion is at least 70 percent. The businessmen even have a saying: 'If you want to get rich, just snatch the tax' (*chi shui*)." The article ends by referring to a new Shanghai incentive aimed at exposing tax evasion. "Should not our city employ similar measures?" the article asks.

Although this is only a single case out of many, the style and rhetoric are instructive. To evaluate the message of such an article, some basic facts must be considered. First, tax assessments in individual businesses are still not based on accounts, but on the tax officials' and their helpers' estimates of the turnover in every business. Tax officials have the final word; businesspeople cannot appeal the officials' decisions. Second, in December 1988, taxes were increased by 50 percent all over Chengdu simply by increasing the estimated turnover of all businesses. Third, the situation for small businesses presently is that the charges paid to local bureaus exceed the taxes; if average taxes are only 31 yuan as stated by the paper, the total fees for an average individual business are much higher (50–100 yuan). In Bin Shen, for example, the monthly "security fee" paid to the local police station (*pai chu suo*) averaged 15 yuan. Fourth, field data indicate that tax evasion among small businesses was limited, while the bigger businesses had better means of lowering their taxes by using their *guanxi*.

Certain details in the article mentioned above also deserve comment. The mosquito net producer probably no longer runs a purely private business. People from his neighborhood claim to know that he was forced to convert his business into a joint state-private enterprise because he was becoming "too powerful." On the level of local gossip, which provides a substantial part of all everyday information in Chinese cities, tax officials are in a dubious position when criticizing private businesspeople: despite their very basic official wages, they are generally considered to be wealthy. A young couple living in Bin Shen was often mentioned as an example on this matter. One was a tax official, the other employed in the Customs Bureau; their combined wages should have amounted to about 200 yuan a month. But their large private flat was reportedly something like an exhibition in modern consumer goods: wall-to-wall woolen carpets, color TV and video recorder, stereo, refrigerator, and automatic washing machine — all, of course, foreign made.

Apart from providing some basic figures on private business, such articles obviously present a highly distorted picture. The subcontextual message, however, may be the most important. It presumably represents the attitude that the Party organization in 1988–89 had adopted toward private business. Such writings constituted clear signals to local authorities and to the businesspeople. To the bureaus in question, the article emphasized support for their practices, and even gave the green light to go further. To businesspeople, it delivered a warning that local authority would be strengthened and that the development of local power at the expense of central government, even where it entailed disregard of new regulations, was backed by the Party organization. Local media helped justify the display of force that businesspeople experienced from the officials on whom they depend for operating permits and for maintenance of their legal status.

We inquired with some local businesspeople if they had read the article in question; most of them had. One of the better educated had this comment:

> It expresses the writer's own imagination. Some of it may be true, but most of it is pure fantasy. And the attitude is very bad; it fires people up with hatred toward businesspeople. But we often see this attitude; it's very common in the local media. The envy is tremendous; it's a main problem in China. It's an old thing that you cannot get away with being different.

We also asked Ms. Wu for her comment on the article, which she also had read. She agilely avoided our question; only after our persistent return to it did she say: "I think the journalist has the right to express his attitude." But she admitted that businesspeople's income made common people increasingly envious.

In a wider social context, the writings of the Party-controlled media, put forward at a time when many state employees are seeing a decrease in the purchasing power of their wages, may strike a public response. Accusations of creating inflation are often directed toward private businesses, since in most areas they are free to set their own prices. The local media have thus attempted to inflame public opinion by confirming prejudices, as well as fabricating new ones, against private businesses. In the Party line of thought the causes for the success of private businesses are usually that "they get rich through swindle and tax evasion;"[8] this thinking largely ignores the positive impact of higher efficiency. These accusations thus touch the widespread frustrations among state employees and tend to direct aggression toward individual businesses by insinuating that they contribute to, or are even responsible for, China's economic difficulties. Far more realistic, however, are worries expressed in Party circles that the rise of private business represents a threat to the leading role of the Party. When a growing number of households leave their *danwei* to launch private businesses, Party power declines. Local authorities may be able to infringe on the entrepreneurs' profits, but not to control their lives. The monopoly on information that the Party has established for itself also indicates that the local Party organization is unable to engage in a dialogue with informal groups. Local authorities, in the words of businesspeople, "do not tolerate one sentence of criticism." Conversely, the media direct their criticism downward, toward the marginal groups of people who lack the channels to defend themselves publicly. Private businesspeople are barred from expressing their views. In the spring of 1989 they increasingly complained: "We cannot speak for ourselves."

The consistent use of the media for specific ends leaves little room for anything else, and often the deliberate distortion of reality reaches heights where it has reverse effects. When, for instance, the new "education charge" was introduced at meetings in the association all over Chengdu, the *Chengdu Evening News* simultaneously printed reports on private businesspeople donating large sums of money for the purpose. A certain Wang was reported to have contributed no less than 30,000 yuan.[9] But the missing specifications on the businessman's full name, trade, and address tell any skilled reader that the report is bogus. Rather, it is an example of the deliberate emphasis on the ideal in times when practice is running out of control. The new charge was met with passive resistance everywhere.

Education as Reproduction of Status

Thus, attacks on the private sector escalated and political conflicts in local society sharpened at the time when a growing number of young had to rely on private business for their subsistence. Another factor contributing to the frustration the young felt, and perhaps to their eventual involvement in the private sector, was the elitist drive in education. Once opportunities in the state sector narrowed, recruitment to the state sector tended to concentrate on fewer channels.

Educational elitism is another effect of the reforms.[10] Since 1980 it has been a stated policy to "develop talents" even from the lowest levels. Emphasis was put on the "key schools" (actually *zhongdian* "center of gravity") and on a number of alternative specialized vocational schools (*zhiye zhongxue*) that teach nonliterary skills at the level of upper middle school. Although the schools were designed to give students higher professional abilities, graduates from the vocational lines find it as difficult as ever to find employment. Consequently, adolescents generally feel that their destiny, as far as employment is concerned, is already determined when they reach junior middle school (*chuzhong*).[11] Against the background of entire classes, or practically entire schools, from which not one of the students reaches university, the endeavor seems fruitless. In the average mediocre schools from which a few may reach higher education, the outcome of the struggle may be equally predetermined. The endless exams and tests have already divided the students into hierarchical positions according to marks, which are the sole criteria for moving on in the educational system. However, the availability of state employment is the crucial factor to the vast majority of young who are standard school graduates.[12] Here the reforms have had their most negative side effects. Staff cuts necessitated by the struggle for better economic performance have altered the whole prospect of studying for a large group of young people who have neither high marks nor connections to pave the way to secure employment.

By definition, the sons and daughters of small individual business households lack any such connections to power and privilege. Their achievements rest on their own efforts alone. The marginal position of their households is a hidden impediment to a formal career. Though strongly emphasizing the importance of education, the individual households often lack the means to supply a suitable room for study, intellectual stimulation, and clearly articulated ambitions. As opposed to ambitions for high status, their households inspire the quest for immediate material satisfaction. They stimulate the short-term strategy rather than years of study and sacrifice. So what parents commonly desire for their children, they tend to counteract by their own example.

Although education in itself is commonly upheld as an absolute value in the Chinese ethos, following Confucian ideals being a measure of the individual's level of culture (*wenhua shuiping*), there is reason to believe that a highly pragmatic approach to education prevails. According to informal norms, basic literacy is considered a prerequisite for urban identity, but beyond this level it is thought of as an investment, expected to yield profit in terms of either wealth or privilege. Faced with failing opportunities, ordinary middle school students are already likely to question the purpose of studying. In recent years, a serious dropout problem has presented itself in city and country alike. It has affected all levels of education from primary school to universities with evident consequences for the national literacy level.[13] Dropping out may not only affect careers, but may destabilize family relations. For urban youth, dropping out is frequently a reaction to the double pressure they are under. It is directed toward education as an undertaking of little promise as well as toward the various authorities controlling their lives.

Conflicts over education are ever present in Bin Shen. People living in the area send their small children to some of the mediocre school in neighboring areas. However, right in the middle of the Bin Shen area, with an entrance from Chang Shun Street next to a couple of old Manchu households, is perhaps the finest primary school in Chengdu. It is nicknamed "The Emperor's Primary School' (*huangjia xiaoxue*) because it is run by the provincial government administration, situated only half a mile away (at the site where the old palace stood). It is restricted to the children of the higher cadres within the provincial government. In this school the children receive the best possible start on their later careers: they have the best teachers and teaching material, fewest students per class, and highest funding. The active and devoted teachers are paid several times more than standard wages. Because of the education they receive here and the stimulation they presumably receive in their homes, most of these children will later reach university. As expressive of the general move from privilege to monetary wealth as denominator in society, however, children from outside the government unit can now be enrolled here for a sum of money. They are called "ten thousand–yuan children" (*yi wan yi hai'r*), since the enrollment fee is more than 10,000 yuan. People who can pay this amount of money to place small children in a primary school are the wealthiest in private business, who in this fashion attempt to transform wealth into higher social position. For the school it is a convenient way of meeting the demand for increasing economic self-reliance in educational institutions. Every class thus has a few of these "gilded" students whose parents are prepared to pay anything to ease them out of the private business environment and promote them into prestigious standing.

After six years of primary school, the children are divided according to their marks before continuing into junior middle school. If the children from individual business households do not reach the distinguishing marks, their parents commonly pay for an extra year. The division after primary school determines a student's educational path. All schools are hierarchically positioned according to the success their students have in the compulsory exams; their success rate here indicates their ability to send the students further into the best schools on senior middle school (*gaozhong*) level with possible access to universities. From the best primary schools, 30–50 percent of the children are expected to reach university — against the national average of 1.2 percent. At the level of junior middle school, the percentage will increase. The best senior middle school in Chengdu will send almost 90 percent of its students to university. With the extremely limited per capita university student capacity (which makes China rank 110th in the world out of 137 countries[14]), the result of elitist thinking in the educational reforms has created an immense divide between the few key institutions and the vast majority, in which any competition for marks and exams may seem fruitless. On all levels of education, practice is quite different from the ideal system of equal opportunity for all. Reforms have not been able to rule out the overwhelming importance of *guanxi*, which can help people around the examinations when placing their offspring in the desired institutions. The one-child policy has sharpened the competition for education markedly and pushed the crucial barriers forward to earlier stages. Getting a child enrolled in a preschool and kindergarten of high standing is now the means to assure that this only child will bring glory to the family and promote other household members — that he or she will lead "chicks and dogs to heaven."

The sharp distinction between good and poor schools is easily detected in the attitude of the students. The sons and daughters of ordinary businesspeople have usually realized at an early stage that they lack the capacity to fulfill their parents' ambitions for them. Many of the local adolescents move at the edge of their parents' tolerance with their studies. While people like doctor Zhong have a relaxed attitude toward their children, others use their authority to keep them studying. Moreover, much more is expected of sons than of daughters. So it is mostly true for the boys that increasing competition for skills and proficiency has made their households channel more aspirations through them, irrespective of the older generation's success. This situation emphasizes what has already been suggested: that the ideology concerning social status is fairly intact in spite of occasional reinterpretation.

Contrary to some local middle schools in the lower end of the hierarchy lacking both discipline and ambitions, the old pre-Liberation elite schools quickly regained their prestige after the Cultural Revolution. After having familiarized myself with the difficulties the young Bin Sheners faced, I felt a need to compare their situation with that of a radically different group, the best of formal society's offspring. By investigating the contrasts and at the same time inquiring about their attitudes toward private business, I hoped to get a clearer idea about the formation of the two basic flows in society. Not far south of Bin Shen is the oldest school in Chengdu, the Shi shi zhongxue (Stone Chamber Middle School), an old Confucian school dating back to 141 B.C. While only one of its pre-Liberation buildings, the Confucian temple (which during the Cultural Revolution was turned into a factory) still stands, the school has otherwise resumed its purpose of educating the elite. Its mottos are: "Prepare for the Four Modernizations, face the world, and look toward the future. Help the students develop morally, intellectually, and physically. Help them achieve individual satisfaction as contributing and socialist-minded citizens armed with modern scientific knowledge and in good health."[15] The large buildings with pointed roofs, huge courtyards, and traditional-style gateways symbolize the prestige that surrounds the school. Today the vast majority of the students are offspring of the university-educated, the higher cadres, and the intellectuals, and everybody aims at university. From this school, 70 percent of the senior middle school graduates enter university directly after examination. Many of those who fail in their first attempt, however, study another year for reexamination and a new chance to reach the required marks, which brings the total up to 80–90 percent of the students entering university.

After going through the formalities required for visiting any public institution, we are admitted to the school for interviewing. Only the masters are obliged to receive us; no students have been assigned to join in. Only those who volunteer to be interviewed are sent to the nicely furnished meeting room. Shy to start with, a large group of students finally gathers. The students from Shi shi have in common the enthusiasm they express for the future of the mother country (*guojia*) and for themselves. (Paragraph one in the student regulations states: Love the country, love the people. Support the Leadership of the Chinese Communist party. Study hard to make contributions to the Four Modernizations.) They all know English and are all uniformly oriented toward the key areas of national interest and prestige: science and technology, economic management, and foreign relations. They have confidence in the new China, bound to develop and regain its position among the world powers. At least when speaking publicly, the students vividly anticipate the return of national dignity (*guoge*). As a young man expresses it: "I think my country needs me to study hard, so we can make up the gap between China and America. I want to study physics and nuclear technology, so we can advance in these areas. I would also like to go abroad to study." Another characteristic statement concerns studying abroad, especially in the United States: "America is very good and very beautiful. I want to go there to study chemistry. I want to study hard for my country." We ask him what will happen if he is not able to go. "Oh, I haven't thought about this question; I work so hard that I have no time to think about this. Soon we will have our examination, and I want to be good. I listen to my parents and the teachers."

Maintaining socialist goals while praising the United States, cultivating individual talents while working selflessly for the Four Modernizations, and educating oneself for privileged elite position while attaining the socialist mind set are clear manifestation of the immense divide between ideal and practice on both the state level and personal levels; in addition these dichotomies point to ambiguity in the Chinese normative universe.[16]

Judging from the enthusiasm of the students, nothing can block their way ahead. They appear to be assured of success and enjoy all the support of their privileged families, who in many cases have the capacity to further them in the educational system and secure them favorable positions irrespective of their marks. Contrary to all other schools at this level, Shi shi has no drop-out problem. If the students have no need to be anxious about their future employment, they are certainly affected by the decreasing value of state wages and very conscious about the problem. We ask them about the correspondence between wages and social position. One says: "Yes, I pay much attention to social position; it is very important. The present situation is unfair, and I think it will change in the future. I want to have a high position with high wages. So a university education is the best way to achieve this." Most of the student we talk to agree with this view. Some just refer to given circumstances: "My parents are both university educated, so I just follow the pattern of my family." Confronted with the question of individual business, most students strongly dissociate themselves from the idea of such a career. However, when one of them states that he is actually willing to work for any business, provided it offers him sufficient challenge and can develop its technology, an interesting discussion on concepts arises. One says: "I think the concept of *geti hu* is wrong. Maybe if it were changed it would be more attractive to enter it. Also, if they developed into bigger businesses more people would join them." The students generally agree that the concept of *geti hu* has connotations of smallness, marginality, and even selfishness. Thus larger units categorized as *siying qiye* (private enterprises) are far more agreeable. Raising the question helps several of the young to detach themselves from the formal language they have hitherto employed. The conversation is slowly turned toward the insecurity that many of them feel. In spite of their fine social backgrounds, several are from families that lack the proper connections. The competition for favorable positions is also intensifying in their environment. Some openly state that they fear unemployment after graduation.

Among the students are a few from individual households, which have to pay high tuition. A local furniture manufacturer, for instance, has his two children studying at the school. He is willing and able to pay any sum of money to have them educated, and his plans are that they go abroad to study. His children follow the classes, but at examinations their marks are a bit lower than the others'. But if necessary this lack of success will be compensated for with an extra year.

Notwithstanding difficulties for some of the students, Shi shi provides the best possible platform for attaining the desired prominence. It boasts immense resources compared to standard schools, including huge facilities, national priority, and honorably titled teachers. A small elite is conspicuously developing in the futuristic image created by the Chinese government. It receives the highest education in fields that usually secure access to authority, the opportunity to travel abroad, and whatever else is usually associated with the freedom that high position gives. That essential Chinese values are defended appears from the school's emphasis not only on individual talents, but also on fine arts, which have returned as a supplement to aimed education.[17]

Division by Sex and Status

The consciousness of class (*jieji*) and social position (*shehui diwei* / *shenfen*) is still profound among all groups in Chinese society, although class as an absolute position in society is probably an alien concept in China. Thus class consciousness is not eradicated by the mere disappearance of previous social groups and the emergence of new ones. The important concept of social origin (*chushen*) firmly attaches people to their family background. As individualization emerges among the new generation, such classifications could be expected to fade. This, however, is hardly the case. According to established values not only occupation, but also secondary expressions such as language, clothes, and manners are indicators of an individual's level of culture, and among the young, this perception tends to be unaltered. The spoken language, ranging from short, simple sentences to refined articulation, is a powerful classifier. It locates people geographically as well as educationally, and both locations are easily turned into stratified social positions.

The highly futuristic ideology adopted by the Chinese government after Deng Xiaoping's return to power affected the young more profoundly than the older generations, which are hardened from repeated periods of tumultuous change. But what competition has contributed to the Chinese economy, it has also contributed to making social stratification more conspicuous. Underlying divisions that may have persisted since the Liberation now find expression among the young, who have lived their teenage years during a period of unprecedented freedom. The deviating values that certain groups of young have picked up have been carried too far in the eyes of the regime, which regularly announces new measures to curb crime, Westernization, and ideological polution. In general, however, the young are as much internally opposed to one another as they are toward the regime. Fierce competition and mutual envy exist between those whose education has not paid off and those who have become wealthy without earning respect. Outright contempt is frequently expressed between them, and the educated do not play a modest role in this polarization.

The educated still stigmatize young private businesspeople as the "lowest people" in society because of their "low level of culture" and their "common" manners; formal education and level of culture are used synonymously. Even when a businessperson is seated in the international coffeeshop of the Jinjiang Hotel, a single glance at or a single sentence uttered by that person will reveal his or her social background to someone passing by. The observation that the lower the businesspeople's position, the more they lean on conspicuous consumption is generally true. Wearing stylish clothes while spitting on the floor or smoking expensive American cigarettes while revealing a faulty set of teeth is an obvious social denominator. These businesspeople live in a world in which anything new in regard to commodities is seen as "modern," and anything different in regard to social behavior is taken for "Western." The ideology regarding social position is nevertheless seen to be deeply embedded in the minds of even these new "kings of consumption." This observation becomes evident when one looks at those private businesspeople who possess both wealth and a certain measure of social prestige derived from their previous occupation or level of education. University graduates or other well-educated individuals who have given up their assigned jobs tend to display quite different patterns of consumption: at least in public, they tend not to exhibit any considerable wealth in excess of the ordinary, and in many cases they also adopt longer-range strategies in their business investments.

With the present youth as with previous generations, schooling is the principal element of social distinction in city life. It not only determines one's immediate place in society but also has a profound influence on one's personal relations for life. Relationships formed across social strata are not encouraged by any institution in society and are exceedingly rare even among the young. Because extrafamily relations are typically of the *guanxi* type, they tend to run along the lines of given relations: apart from relatives, one's associates are typically former classmates, colleagues, and others of equal standing. Such alliances are stressed in matrimony as well. Hence the young tend to be divided by social background as well as present social position — classifiers that are on one hand vaguely defined and relative and on the other hand powerful and deterministic. Most of the young socialize primarily among their equals: have parties, help one another, find close friends and partners. Business relations and partnerships are generally sought along similar lines. The young are apparently becoming more stratified than they have ever been during the People's Republic. I have already noted that a rising number of young people were driven into private business by the lack of prestigious state jobs; at least in the outset, their situation made them equals, particularly if they engaged in private business in their local area. But the Open Door Policy has not only created an entirely new sector in the Chinese economy by allowing foreign investments, it has also expanded the range of social positions derived from professional affiliations. Joint ventures and branches of foreign companies have become such popular employers that they threaten the leading position of official employment. With higher wages and trips abroad, they attract young employees from the group of university graduates in the state sector. Following the Sichuanese recession in the late 1980s, many of the new graduates turned their attention toward the representatives of foreign economies. The better educated are not only likely to he hired by such companies, but they are also more aware of opportunities outside their local community. Moreover, they possess the self-confidence necessary to leave home to try their luck elsewhere; many university graduates seeking employment leave for the southern provinces and Special Economic Zones (SEZs). Thus foreign economic presence has challenged the social thought concerning private business and has even created a new hierarchy among these: the bigger and the more closely tied to foreign economies, the more prestigious the place of work is.

As Western and Japanese consumer goods of superior quality steadily make their way into the Chinese market, modernity becomes associated with foreign consumption. Although symbols of "Westernization" for only a minority of the young, foreign consumer goods are a powerful attraction to all groups. And independent of social values, the young have a consciousness about world centers that differs radically from that of their parents. They nevertheless share the notion about distance from and relation to the Center as a conspicuous determinant in social status positions. While only a few reach foreign universities or are able to leave as technicians and engineers, these privileged few draw behind them a long trail of lesser privileged positions: jobs with foreign companies in China, authorities dealing with these, subcontractors, and import and export corporations. This effect continues all the way down to the street level, where the instant trading of new foreign goods such as canned soft drinks and cigarettes provides the shopkeeper who can offer these items with a tiny advantage over those who cannot.

The division of labor between the sexes has changed little with the generation of young. Private businesses run by young people vary little from those run by elders in this respect: they all duplicate the pattern found in society at large. Young men are as embarrassed as older men when their wives produce incomes higher than their own, and many simply forbid their wives to become involved in private business. Again, higher education and status go with stronger adherence to the ideals of formal society, or the "Chinese" ideals as such. Numerous manifestations of everyday life indicate that social prestige and social status positions are of tremendous concern to young men, whereas women commonly have a far more relaxed attitude to their professional life and are far more prone to compromise. Starting private business, trading in the market, selling books, and the like, all appear to be less complicated and surrounded by less need for compensation for the young women. They seem to take unemployment as less of a personal disaster than do their male counterparts. Families still expect more of their sons, who traditionally carry on the family line. Although the young men frequently react negatively to the authority of their parents and do not fulfill their parents' desire for them to stay in the household, they are still highly conscious of their own and the household's social position. When they marry and set up a new household, they identify their household's position with their own, and as a rule they take responsibility for maintaining their present position at least, and preferably improving it. The choice of a marriage partner follows convention, although some deviance is beginning to be felt. When private business was legalized, young men in business found it difficult to marry because their status did not permit them to find a suitable partner. Since the private sector has expanded and has produced unprecedented wealth, businesspeople are no longer isolated in this respect. However, marriages between young from radically different backgrounds are exceedingly rare; marriage between a girl of high status and a young man of low is close to impossible.[18]

Thus the male universe is highly competitive: for education, prestigious positions, and *guanxi* for some, and for money, consumer goods, Westernization, and modernity among others. They meet in an ideology that contains a strong urge to measure and stratify, to interpret social positions and manipulate and reinterpret them in a never-ending game of becoming more powerful in the social world. Although the female side is less competitive, it is in a larger perspective no less concerned with status, which reveals itself at marriage. Young women may spend a number of years doing casual jobs, of which they demand little more than enough to support their life, but at marriage they frequently reconsider their situation. Moreover, their choices of partners correspond well with the vyings for high positions common among the young men. As has always been the marriage custom, young women marry equal or a step higher in the social hierarchy, never below their own level.

Women in Business

Women in private business households frequently complain about their husbands' humble contribution to actual labor. Young women are no less critical of their husbands, but their criticism tends to touch more fundamental areas of married life. In the modernizing society new demands, such as showing their feelings and involving themselves in their wives' psychological and intellectual requirements, are placed on the young men. Private business may strengthen the overall position of the young women, both before and after marriage, since divorce has become a common solution to matrimonial troubles.[19] The local mediators are always involved in divorces, which earlier meant long periods of talks and attempts at reconciliation. Today the process is fairly easy: authorities usually approve of divorces if both parties agree. But like anything else in society, divorces are subject to exploitation, and not only by officials. Among successful businesspeople enormous sums of money are frequently involved when one of the partners wants to buy back his or her freedom. Cases were reported of more than one businessman paying his wife up to 100,000 yuan for her signature when he wanted to marry anew.

It is nevertheless before marriage — which has always been a period when young women enjoyed a certain freedom in work — that young women manifest themselves most forcefully. If they do private business they may even postpone marriage. Inspired by Taiwanese pop singers, Hong Kong film stars, magazines from the overseas

Chinese world, and occasional Western movies like *Love Story* (*Aiqing gushi*), young girls set out to hunt affairs that are "romantic" (*luomantike*). They search for "love" (*aiqing*) and true "feelings" (*ganqing*), concepts that are extremely abstract for their parents' generation. From the background of a highly pragmatic attitude to marriage, in which common requirements concerned social status and appearance and only thirdly asked that the partners like (*xihuan*) each other, the leap into romantic love tends to perplex the young more than emancipate them.

The lessened control on social life is of course making possible more casual relations among the young possible.[20] When a young girl who opened a hairdressing salon put up a sign in the window announcing that "sexual liberation needs prostitutes,"[21] she was arrested the very next day, and the shop closed down. Before the sign was noticed by the local authorities, however, the news spread all over the city to the amusement of everyone. Among the changes that the young have brought to Chinese society, the cry for sexual liberation (*xing jiefang*) may be the most explosive. It is a challenge to a society that, at least on the surface, is highly puritanical.

Since 1985, dance halls have sprung up all over Chengdu, a number of discotheques have opened in the big hotels, and a few coffeeshops and bars have set up at the Jinjiang River bank in the downtown area. Although all places are in principle supervised by the local authorities, whose representatives control the entrance, prohibit alcohol in the dance halls, supervise the dancing, and so forth, the gathering of the youth itself brings about far more activities than desired by the responsible authorities. One such activity is prostitution, which flourishes in the convenient settings that the dance halls provide. The prices asked restrict customers to the young businesspeople, but their high number and relative wealth will support many "small cats" (*xiao mao*) among the frequent guests in the dance halls. Everybody apparently knows who the girls are, and the phenomenon is surrounded by much joking; neither in this field is much privacy expected. When I visited one such place in the suburbs, four to five *xiao mao* were pointed out to me among the approximately hundred young. At another place, two Bin Shen girls observed a young businessman on a brand new motorbike picking up a girl outside the dance hall: "He asked her for the price, but when he heard it he just sat silently thinking it over for a long time [*xiangle ban tian*, 'was thinking half a day']; we could see that he was considering all the other nice things he could buy for the money. Then finally he nodded, and she jumped on the back of his bike." Also annoying to the authorities are the drinking and gambling taking place in private homes, often in connection with visits to discotheques and dance halls. The dance halls are frequently surrounded by disorder, and occasionally there is fighting in the streets at night. Open aggression and fights in the streets increased enormously and inexplicably during the latter part of the 1980s.

It is primarily the young from private business who frequent the dance halls and discotheques; the entrance fee, let alone the drinking and gambling, is too costly for state employees. But the countless private dance parties are a significant victory for the young, if not a revolution, compared to the tightly controlled social life that lasted until the mid-1980s. In this respect, Chengdu and a number of other peripheral cities have enjoyed far more freedom and earlier relaxing of control than has been the case closer to Beijing. But for all places the emergence of the private sector has provided a powerful catalyst for social liberation. Those who have gone to the extremes are the first cracked down upon when new signals are emitted from the Center; ordinary young people can enjoy a large measure of freedom in their shadow.

That the concept of sexual liberation has stronger relevance to women is obvious from the practice of some high-flying male entrepreneurs. Being married while openly having a concubine in the form of a countryside maid employed for this and other household tasks is becoming increasingly common. The immense distance between some businessmen's income and ordinary wages has created a market for any possible service. Installed in separate rooms, some of these young women have reached such a status that the household head will buy one clothes and presents and virtually treat her as a second wife.

On the fringe of Bin Shen is one of the newly established labor markets for private employment (*laodong shangchang*), which acts as an intermediary between workers and employers. Supervised and controlled by the West City Administration, which houses it in the courtyard of a local office, the market is open to out-of-town workers seeking employment in Chengdu. All the twenty to thirty people who usually come to sit on the long benches to wait for employment are women. The majority of them are sixteen to twenty years old; the rest are elderly women. All are from rural families who do not need their labor. The small pay they receive — 35–40 yuan a month plus accommodation — means that every family who can afford it uses the girls' services. The employers thus are wealthy businesspeople and privileged state employees who live in their own apartments separate from family elders. The main problem is in fact not the pay, but the accommodation. Only the larger apartments have a separate room for the maids. Elsewhere they sleep in living rooms or kitchens or on balconies. During the day, they perform all cooking, cleaning, and washing for the family. Most of the young women who arrive at the market find a position within a few days; the older women need longer, or obtain only temporary work. The employers arrive in couples or singly to walk around and examine the women; when they have decided on one, they will sit down beside her to discuss the terms. Many of the young rural women find families with state employment the most attractive to work for. Some deliberately avoid other kinds of families; as they say, "Individual business households are too complicated." Others are influenced only by the size of the payment.

Emancipation through Private Business

Cut off from a formal career and influenced by television, movies, and literature, the young people are eager to try new ways — for instance, to realize another lifestyle while supporting themselves on private business. A common complaint among ordinary private business households is that children are drifting away from the control of their parents, thus contributing to a disintegrating social organization. Countless are the parents who do not want their children to engage in private business and simply forbid them to start. The parents are not always successful, as some instances proved. One young girl from a family of state employees was dissatisfied with the prospect of working in a state clothes factory for the rest of her life. She felt that the senseless control the unit imposed on her prevented her from developing her "skills and energy." In order to secure her personal development, and in addition a better income, she planned to open her own tailor shop. This decision enraged her parents, who felt that the entire family would be discredited if any family member started in individual business. She defied her parents and left the state unit to start her own business. Renting a shop in a small alley off Chang Shun Street, she started with the assistance of one apprentice. Her efforts were rewarded with far better income than she had received in her original unit, but at the sacrifice of relations with her parents, who had never accepted the move. Only when she married a year later and moved to her husband's family was there some reconciliation since she no longer belonged to her parents' household.

A number of households maintain similar restrictions for their offspring. In one household, which ran a successful business securing everybody a comfortable living, the younger brother of the household head forbade his own children to go into private business, stating that he would rather see them unemployed indefinitely. In a few instances families split up over the issue of private business. A young mechanic who had previously been working in a state garage was offered a job in a new private garage in town. This enterprise was able to guarantee a minimum wage four times what he earned in the state unit and far more variety and freedom in work. He complained that in the state unit everyone was endlessly in disagreement with the leaders, who were always criticizing people and were nearly always unreasonable. Because of their position, nobody could criticize them when they made mistakes themselves — and they made mistakes more often than others because of their poor education and insufficient technical skills. His parents rigorously resisted the change of employer but were unable to restrain him. Defying his parents' authority left him with no other choice than to find another place to live. Here again private business proved its potential for radical solutions; with the far higher wages in the new job, the young man had no difficulty starting up his own home.

Thus a break on one front frequently leads young people to a major departure from the established society. In the process of emancipation from one authority, there is only a small step to disregard for them all, since they tend to represent equal challenges to the individual. The respect that all authorities in society demand apparently forces the young into categorical and far-reaching decisions; in the educational system, official employment, and family relations, they are presented with the choice between unconditional subjugation or departure.

Sometimes severe clashes are seen when individuals move between the strictly controlled *danwei* and the private sector. A specific case was that of Xiaomin, a young schoolteacher living in Bin

Shen. After graduation she was assigned to teach in a village school several hundred kilometers from Chengdu. Being without family and friends, she felt miserable in the village, and even more so at the prospect of spending the rest of her life there. Moreover, as a university graduate in music, she felt overqualified to teach singing lessons to primary school children. After one year, she started applying for a transfer back to Chengdu, which of course was denied. Then she began influencing the authorities by traditional means, that is, establishing *guanxi*. She found a middle school in Chengdu in which the leading cadre hinted that he would accept her and sort out the formalities. During the next eight months she travelled back and forth to Chengdu whenever possible, taking gifts to the cadre in question. The famous brands of liquor, cigarettes, and foodstuffs consumed half her wages (only 45 yuan) in this period, which left so little for herself that her health was seriously threatened by her poor diet. She was skin and bones when she was finally granted the transfer to Chengdu. Although her situation improved, it still allowed for only an extremely simple life, since the new unit could not offer her accommodation. This she had to find privately, and the small room she rented took 25 of her monthly salary of 65 yuan. Being alone and without parents to support her (one had died and the other moved away to live with relatives elsewhere), she lived at a subsistence level for the following couple of years. But she was a talented musician and singer, and when a number of new dance halls opened all over Chengdu in 1987–88, she soon found employment with a private band (a new aspect of private enterprise) and performed in a dance hall four nights a week. At the pay of 10 yuan for two hours per night, this was a revolution in her life, allowing her a better diet and new clothes. Because middle school teachers teach only twelve lessons a week, she felt fully capable of maintaining her position. But the Communist party secretary of the school soon found reason to inquire about the cause of her new clothes. When he learned that she was singing in a band at night, he demanded that her income from this source be deposited at the school immediately. He also forbade her to wear the new clothes when teaching as they presented a "bad example to the children." She refused. The secretary responded by withdrawing all her holidays and her sick pay. She still refused. The Party secretary next insisted that she stay at the school all through the day (8 A.M. to 6 P.M., Monday through Saturday) even though she was only teaching two lessons a day on average and like everyone else usually left in the early afternoon when the work was done. This schedule tired her out so much that she could hardly keep singing in the band, which assembled at 7 P.M. when they performed. To solve her problem, the Party secretary strongly recommended that she marry and follow a normal course of life, showing respect to the school and the Party. She finally gave in and told the secretary that she had finished with the band, and she started wearing her old clothes again when teaching. But she kept singing in the band at night, hoping no one would discover. The secretary was eventually told about this and reacted promptly by threatening her with the use of ultimate force: he insinuated that criminal charges would be raised against her if she did not obey.[22] At this point she was standing alone against the authorities of the school. At an earlier stage the young teachers especially had supported her in private; but when the conflict hardened, even her closest friends backed out in fear of the consequences. No one dared talk to her at the school. When she gave up the band, a period of reconciliation followed, but in the beginning of 1989 she left the school to work for a private employer, presumably without any hope of ever returning to official employment. Her own attitude also had hardened indeed: "Long live the Chinese Communist party — I shall die from hatred!"[23]

Emancipation from controlling authorities usually implies physical distance following the demands of "face"; for this reason many young people choose to leave their local area, and the extent of this would be far greater if housing only permitted. A few of the young businesspeople in Bin Shen are runaways from the control of parents in their home town. The two young men running a hairdressing salon in Chang Shun Street are such a pair. In 1989 their salon was by its Western style the only place to depart radically from the common appearance of shops in the street. Coming from Beijing and Guangzhou, they moved to Chengdu to live together in a relationship that presumably would be obscene in their home towns; being out of reach of their families and doing business among strangers gives them freedom to choose their own lifestyle.

For the local young, doing business in the downtown area is the dream, as it is for practically everybody in private business; location in the central area is equally important to earnings. The Young People's Street (Qingnian lu), where there are endless rows of stalls and shops selling fashion clothes, is especially attractive. It is not just that the fashion shops, restaurants, stereo shops, and the like in this area gather young people from all over Chengdu; the street is also the center for everything considered modern, Western, or just different enough to be absorbed in the new youth culture. The enormous profits that anyone lucky enough to obtain a permit can make in this area have created a platform for a new modernist vanguard among the young. Defiant to anything in formal society, they have set out to prove themselves through making money — the more and the quicker, the better — and through whatever money can buy. The successful young businesspeople now constitute a separate stratum in society, low in formal status, but with a huge capacity for consumption: Japanese motorbikes, privately owned flats with expensive Western-style furnishing and fully equipped with Japanese electronics, American cigarettes, and restaurant or hot pot meals that would cost the loyal state employee up to a full month's wages. At night they often gather at the coffeeshop in the Jinjiang International Hotel to sit among foreigners or frequent the discotheques. In addition, this new stratum has created a market for human labor and services — anything from countryside maids doing household work for the wealthy to simple prostitution, which flourishes in this new environment. Any discussion of social status is now met by the entrepreneurs with remarks like "He who has the money is now the king."[24] The young women dress as close as they can to the models in foreign fashion magazines. They are only limited by China's import restrictions. Their thick makeup and big, shiny, imitation jewelry seem to emphasize their identity; the self-sacrifice and socialist modesty propagated by the authorities are met with cynicism. Their male counterparts dress in dark suits and white shirts, with sleeves lifted to reveal their huge watches, while they continuously smoke their American cigarettes.

The young are natural exponents of a larger process in society. In the wake of radically changing conditions of life, new strategies are made and new identities are formed accordingly. Not only is a profound reinterpretation of values taking place, but this even appears to be rapidly accelerating; while the young are eager to try new ways in their showdown with the established society, mainstream society is itself engaged in reshaping. In the spring of 1989, tension had increased markedly in Bin Shen as compared to previous years and was felt to be rapidly accelerating during the fieldwork period. What contributed to the general feeling of uneasiness was the decline of the state sector, a decline that influenced both wages and career opportunities. With the failure of reforms becoming increasingly visible, Chinese society was thrown into dramatic upheaval.

CHAPTER SEVEN

A New Cycle of Business

June 4, 1989, was already long gone when I returned to Bin Shen in 1991 after almost two years' absence.[1] While Chinese student organizations abroad, together with the Western media, had cried out their message never to forget June 4, now termed *liu si* (6/4), to place it firmly within Chinese history, parallel to *wu si* (5/4; May 4, 1919), few Bin Sheners now mentioned the happenings. Even the term *liu si* itself was not immediately understood by most people asked about the events. The revolutionary spirit and fearful events of those few weeks had only added a new layer to the sediment of historical experience. Moreover, my inquiries about the impact of June 4 on Bin Shen were met with a mixture of bewilderment and irritation: of what interest was that to me or to anybody now? The involvement of a large number of Bin Sheners was nevertheless a fact, although Bin Shen itself had not been affected directly by the demonstrations and turmoil that was nothing short of an uprising. I knew from private correspondence that fighting had been fierce in Chengdu: thousands had taken to the streets, and mobs had attacked a number of official buildings. By interviewing the usual groups in Bin Shen, I could establish a picture of which groups had participated.

Party authorities, however, had not forgotten their near overthrow. When June 4 approached, the municipal government organized a street carnival in the downtown area with compulsory processions from large state units; the carnival was clearly a preventive measure, running for several days before and after the anniversary. The stairs in front of the Mao statue overlooking the People's South Boulevard, where students spontaneously met two years earlier to express their protest, had been covered entirely with an abundance of heavy cases of green grass.

Little had changed in the physical appearance of Chang Shun

Street over these two years; it was by and large intact since the army unit had not made use of its permit to expropriate a section of the street. Although its new hotel was running well from renting office space as well as individual rooms, the economic recession and the continued absence of foreign businesses had limited further construction. So the old houses were still there, though largely in bad repair because of their uncertain future. Chang Shun Upper Street, the section from Temple Street to the market, was slowly becoming a restaurant street as many had predicted already three or four years earlier. From Temple Street, restaurants now occupied all shops on either side of the street for some 50 meters, gradually thinning out behind. Mr. Wang's restaurant had had its interior rebuilt once more, and Mr. Fu, Wang's neighbor, had turned his bakery into a restaurant involving both the old courtyard behind his house and the household who occupied the lot beyond. On the other side of the street, several small restaurants had been opened, among which one had already built up a reputation as the best noodle place of its kind in Chengdu. The total number of restaurants in Chang Shun Street was thirty-two in 1987, fifty in 1991 (in the remaining Bin Shen area the number was fifteen in 1987, thirteen in 1991). The total number of businesses in the entire Bin Shen area had increased steadily, from approximately 270 in 1987 to 290 in 1989 and 330 in 1991 — an increase that was by and large confirmed by members of the association. Handicraft and small production had decreased considerably, from 14 percent of businesses in 1987 to only 9 percent in 1991.[2] Conversely, the percentage of businesses in service and commerce had increased, especially hairdressers and clothes and textiles shops; groceries were also increasing in numbers again. The modern hairdresser salons, which previously had been found only in the downtown area, had made their way into Chang Shun Street, where a veritable wave was propagating from a few successful shops close to the restaurant mall. Four very similar salons occupied four neighboring shops on one side of the street, and seven other salons were opened or about to open within a short distance.

Changes had occurred elsewhere in Bin Shen, especially in Dong Chenggen Street. Here a long row of the oldest houses in the area had been torn down and a new concrete apartment block with shop space below had been erected. As was expected, the businesses that had occupied the old premises were gone, to be replaced primarily by collective units. The blacksmith with his three apprentices, the signboard shop run by the old cadre, a kitchen chopboard maker, and a few others were gone. Inquiries about them were fruitless. Some people thought they had received compensation enabling them to run businesses elsewhere, perhaps in a neighboring area; others believed they had moved to the outskirts of Chengdu. However, despite considerable efforts put into the attempt, they could not be traced. The traditional location of woodworking shops in this street was perhaps coming to an end: the lack of suitable premises, pressure from the authorities to modernize facades and shops, and presumably a slow change in consumption patterns all contributed to this demise. In 1991 only two chopboard makers and two signboard makers remained.

The blurred distinction between the public and private sectors that developed from the mid-1980s had become particularly evident in Dong Chenggen Street. A number of shops launched and owned by collective units had in recent years been transferred to individuals on contract with the unit. Through this arrangement the units maintained their rights to the premises, while the contractors could run shops that otherwise were out of reach to them, in terms of both commodities and premises. A few clothes shops and a groceries wholesaler were operating in this fashion. In a number of other cases individuals were simply gaining control over old, or establishing new, businesses under "the red umbrella."

Along this line a number of Chengdu hospitals opened clinics in local areas, especially in 1990, apparently owing to increasing demands of budgetary self-reliance. People working in state and collective units without special agreements with medical units would get expenses from treatment in such local clinics refunded. In Bin Shen no fewer than six different units[3] had established themselves, giving doctor Zhong a hard time keeping his patients. Despite the competition among the new clinics, a number of hospital doctors chose to work in them since the clinics allowed them both freer working conditions and higher pay. Elderly medical professors also traded on their reputations and began seeing private patients in the local clinics. One clinic in Chang Shun Street had seven famous old professors seeing patients in turn through the day. Other doctors used the clinics to sell their self-produced herbal medicine or to practice special therapies.

Changes were also under way in the western part of Bin Shen. A large program for repatriating retired Guomindang people and members of the former elite had followed upon the normalization of relations with Taiwan. Since Bin Shen had been the residential area of many of these people, it was chosen for the program. In the small alleys west of the Chang Shun market a large lot was being prepared for construction of traditional-style housing, to be offered to the repatriates at sky-high prices. The lot and the low houses previously occupying it had been expropriated by the municipal government, and the inhabitants received compensation that, theoretically, could buy them the same floor space in new apartment blocks in the south-eastern suburbs. The projected building ground also contained a rare English villa from the 1910s, the only entirely European-style building in Bin Shen. Build solidly to last for generations, its two floors with high stucco ceilings and its basement — also the only one in Bin Shen — had been the common living quarters of eight households since the Liberation. Because not a single repair had been carried out since then, the basement and one room on the ground floor had become uninhabitable in recent years, primarily owing to the missing glass in the windows. Of a much heavier construction than the surrounding houses, which were torn apart in a single day, the house survived some months longer until motorized equipment could be dispatched. A descendant of the original owner of the house was said to have had his claim on the inheritance recognized recently and thus to have become a rich man owning three new flats.

In a way, the repatriation program affected the entire Bin Shen area. To make the area more appealing and restore some of its quiet and secluded pre-Liberation atmosphere, it was decided that all street-facing walls and facades should be painted. The Street Committee engaged a number of contractors to do the job, and they hired a number of rural hands on the labor market to do the manual work involved. Streets and neighborhoods were assigned particular colors thought to resemble their original ones. Some streets had white-washed walls with red woodwork, some with blue woodwork. One area had all walls painted dark gray, and in Hongqiang (Red Wall) Alley, everything was painted red as it had been once. The brush-up certainly gave a refreshing impression and restored the Chinese characteristics of the walled streets — without, however, attending much to delicateness and refinement in the work performed. Chang Shun Street, being an open street with little partition between street and household, had not had prescribed any particular pattern for its decoration. So far the City Reconstruction Bureau had only demanded that all facades be renewed or painted at the owners' own initiative and expense, that all signboards be renewed, and that the shops in general have a thorough clean-up. Several of the best restaurants already reported a steadily increasing number of Taiwanese guests, who were becoming a new group of target customers.

Business Almost as Usual

My yearly rounds in the Bin Shen area already seemed institutionalized to many locals. "You did not come last year, did you?" was the most common remark I met when revisiting the old businesses. Mr. Fu's transformation from baker into operator of a large restaurant next to Mr. Wang's had cooled the relationship between them somewhat since it had turned them into competitors. Fu's explanation was that the bakery had clear limits to its development because it catered only to the local community, whereas the scope for a restaurant was far larger. So he sold the baking equipment to his sister-in-law and changed profession. But another motive revealed itself from the layout of his new restaurant. The former bakery had occupied only the ground floor of the front building, which had an unbroken facade toward the street. With the restaurant, however, an old passage, about eight feet wide, through the house to a courtyard in the interior was reestablished. Thus the new restaurant occupied the old bakery, the passage, the quiet courtyard — which was its main attraction — and in addition two of the three rooms in a large, detached house facing the courtyard. This house, which was constructed in a heavy stone and concrete version of the traditional style with two bulky columns supporting the gateway, had been shut off from the street for decades. It had been built by Mr. Fu's parents a few years before the Liberation, and it expressed in all its prominence the wealth of the family then. Its three high rooms with wooden floors and windows framed in square patterns had been preserved. After 1949 the house had been allotted to another family, and the Fus were transferred to the front building, where they also did business. The new restaurant was registered as run by two families (altogether four adults) since Fu had persuaded the family across the courtyard to join him in his business and to move their living quarters to rented space in a neighboring house. This arrangement allowed Fu to gain control of almost the entire compound that had belonged to his parents. "You may speak of sentimental value, but of course it means a lot to me to be able to sit in the rooms where I lived with my parents when I was a child." His parents' old living room is now used for entertaining special guests and for offering exclusive banquets to customers.

The new business was a great success from the start, easily supporting the now altogether sixteen people involved as owners, cooks, and laborers. With four tables indoors and three outdoors, the restaurant could hold more than thirty people. Among its attractions, the restaurant boasted a small fish pond from which customers could choose their own fresh fish. As the only one of its kind in Bin Shen, this was another benefit of having the comparatively large courtyard at their disposal. And anything new could provide a business with a temporary advantage; for instance, it could attract some of the artists and celebrities working at the nearby Sichuan television station. Also contributing to Fu's success was the falling popularity of hot-pot restaurants in Chengdu; these were no longer a trend, and their former customers were searching for novelties.

The Chengdu downtown area was approaching Bin Shen, and there were signs that it would slowly absorb the entire area as the city developed. This meant an increasing flow of people through the streets, from which of course all businesses could benefit, albeit it brought in another clientele. Hitherto Bin Shen had not known informal organizations such as secret societies to any significant degree. But such groups were making themselves visible recently, and restaurants were the prime targets for their activities. A number of restaurants had been called on by small groups of men who threatened the owners and demanded free meals. They would repeat their visits a few times, testing the owner's power of resistance, and then demand sums of money for protection against "harassment and attack on the business."

A few restaurant keepers had submitted to their threats and paid them small sums for being left alone; most owners refused to pay, hoping that a few free meals would satisfy them. But trouble was under way in several restaurants, where the owners preferred to hire people to retaliate if the gangs made good on their threats. Nevertheless, the gangs indicated a new development in the local community by either representing secret organizations themselves or giving rise to others in the search for protection against them. Yet the formal Self-employed Laborers Association and the tight grip the authorities had on the private sector through it dampened such formations considerably. The criminal gangs threatening the restaurants were presumably organized by a blend of experienced criminals and "job-waiting youth," many of whom were not so very young any more since they had waited for a decade. Some individuals among them had been identified as belonging to an area north of Bin Shen. The gangs obviously chose another locality than their own for their crime. Local authorities did nothing to prevent the gangs from establishing themselves in Bin Shen, and their indifference started speculations on their own involvement. Some suggested that the police cooperated with the gangs, obtaining assistance from them in tracing hard criminals in exchange for granting them a certain freedom to extort from the private sector. Speculation apart, a new exploitative agent was added to the numerous others.

Business and Bureaucracy after 1989

Certain adjustments in the bureaucracy's practice toward private enterprise had taken place since June 4. The renewed adherence to ideological leadership also brought a whole series of new rectification campaigns against pornography, tax evasion, false registration, and, at least on the surface, against abuse of bureaucratic power.[4] A number of cases on the national level concerning the exposure and punishment of bureaucrats had sent shock waves down through the hierarchy. Though none of these campaigns had direct influence on daily life in Bin Shen, they all contributed to greater caution on both sides. A bold youth running a books and magazine stall with colorful foreign magazines under the counter had chosen to close. Moreover, the illegal recording tapes, pseudo bicycle polish, and fake medicinal herbs had disappeared with their light-footed salesmen, and cases of cheating and deceiving among commoners had positively declined. Bureaucrats had become more careful when spending public funds, and complaints were heard among restaurant owners, since the officials' diminishing use of banquets had reduced the restaurants' turnovers slightly.

As expected, the new policy had only confirmed the fears of a number of businesspeople. A widespread view was that their future was already planned from above: "It is all determined for us. We can develop, but not over a certain level, where we would pose a threat to the order of society — just like in traditional times." Some interpreted it as the government's fear of a new middle class (*zhongchan jieji*) articulating itself as a powerful group demanding a change of the social order.[5] Some businesspeople found that the events had stabilized their relations to bureaucracy, but much disagreement over the issue prevailed. What could be measured was of course the size of the taxes and charges paid. One of the greatest nuisances, the police station, had lowered its "security fee" significantly. In 1989 many households paid 15 yuan per month, but in 1991 the same households were paying only 25 yuan every three months, presumably for the same services.

Despite new moderation in some bureaus, the number of them who joined the assaults on private business continued to increase. If the new regime had inspired a certain discipline among its officials, it had simultaneously signalled the repression of private enterprise, thus leaving private businesses open to exploitation by any authority. Thus more departments and bureaus turned to the private sector in search of new sources of income. While businesspeople in 1989 were troubled with ten different taxes, they now had to cope with about twenty. Among the new ones were grain price-levelling taxes (approximately 5 yuan per month per head paid to both municipal and provincial funds), a pork price-levelling tax, an energy tax, and a new sanitation charge.[6] Consequently, the total taxation, legal and illegal, was still increasing ruthlessly, and the small businessowners, in particular, were bitter.

Tax was calculated and collected with the same lack of consistency as before. Nowhere was tax calculated according to accounts as had repeatedly been stipulated by central government since 1987.[7] Moreover, in October 1990 the tax authorities' creative thinking had produced a new "self-evaluation — make up for evasion" (*zicha bubao*) tax, paid in October every year. The maneuver was that everyone through contemplation — and under guidance from tax officials interviewing everyone — would estimate his or her own tax evasion and then pay the balance. Then at a general meeting in October everyone was supposed to expose this evasion in front of the others. The tax officials would activate people's memories and make use of comparisons and confrontations among the businesspeople of the same trade. As a result, at the end of the year business owners paid between fifty and several hundred yuan as "voluntary" settlement. The real change from before was that everyone was now forced into a kind of public self-criticism — with which all were familiar and at which they could only laugh because they knew the background of everyone participating on either side. But as always, it was difficult for the authorities to make businesspeople show up at meetings. Excuses were many and often clumsy. Consider, for instance, the one later produced with a grin by the old saddlemaker who was still in business: "I thought I would stay here in my business, so I asked my wife to go — you know, it is actually her license. But eventually she got sick and did not go either. But it is always the same, anyway. First they want to educate you, and then they ask you to pay more taxes."

Some personnel changes had occurred in the association after an interval of reproach and upbraiding. Ms. Wu had left the association as, she claimed, her eyes were getting bad and she could not read properly.[8] And since she already had two three-year terms behind her, she felt that others should take over: "Everyone has the right to elect, and the right to be elected." This is her perception of local democracy: everyone must take a turn in the association and be elected by the others. Ms. Wu's living room right behind her textiles shop had gone through a metamorphosis. The brown plastic sofa set had large patches torn off, and filling was coming out everywhere. Gone were the huge framed awards that used to adorn the walls. The cabinet in which silver cups had been on display was missing. Tea was no longer served in the shining Russian-style tea glasses but in humble, cracked, enamel cups. The authority she surrounded herself with was suddenly replaced by servility. But Ms. Wu explained that she has a good life now: her children have all left and are in secure positions, and because she has only her husband and herself to care for, there is affluence in her household.

Idle Money Abounds

It is a common saying in Bin Shen that "those who are really rich you cannot distinguish." They are said to be silently and inconspicuously accumulating their wealth over the years, perhaps operating a small, insignificant shop as a cover for their leading endeavor. After having heard this repeatedly since 1987, but never being able to put names on paper, we decided to try to determine whether this was more than gossip. After certain hints, we eventually found one such person in

1991. To my surprise at least, he openly admitted the rumors to be correct when we adressed him. Mr. Zhang, of Manchu descent, runs a small kiosk in his house in Chang Shun Lower Street, where businesses are thinning out since customers are few. The shop looks dilapidated. The few articles on display are dusty and in disarray. During the day, his wife looks after the shop and serves the occasional customers. Mr. Zhang, however, is usually away, tending to his main business, a groceries wholesale store in a large shopping area nearer the center. It is not that this business is illegal. Mr. Zhang just does not want the authorities in Bin Shen to know about it. Neither does he want to change his status in the area.

The wholesale store belongs to a large collective unit, which runs several of its kind in Chengdu. Since the unit was in crisis, it offered contracts for running several of its least profitable stores. Mr. Zhang's operation, he said,

> used to have more than ten employees and was awfully disorganized until I contracted it two years ago. The unit considered it unprofitable and offered it to me since I already knew someone there. Now I run the business together with a single helper. The unit still supplies the store with all the goods, which we sell to groceries, both private ones and other collectives. So it is fairly easy business, and my own profit is very good.

Mr. Zhang estimates his earnings to be 4,000–5,000 yuan per month, and the profit tax is only 10 percent, owing to the collective status of the store. He can spend very little of the money himself: "We do not want anyone to know we are rich, so we lead very ordinary lives and spend little." Mr. Zhang cannot put his money in the bank. He has a savings account containing "a few ten thousands," but anything in excess of such an amount will raise questions. During his two years running the wholesale store, he has accumulated considerably more:

> I lent a friend a hundred thousand to start up a business; otherwise I just save up for my old age. I still have several hundred thousands, which I have to take care of myself. I bought a house a bit further down this street, where we will move to when we get old. I would also like to buy a car if it became possible once. I would try to arrange someone to place my money in a Hong Kong bank, but it is very risky; he could just run away with it all.

Mr. Zhang belongs to the descendants of the old Manchu community in Bin Shen and still registers as Manchu. He also belongs to the Manchu Association, which arranges social gatherings several times a month for its few hundred members. But Zhang thinks his generation will be the last to register as Manchu. His children do not care, and in general the young Manchus tend to intermarry with Han people. There are, however, certain benefits in being Manchu. He can freely send his daughter to a fine secondary school in the area, since this school belonged previously to the Manchu community and still has a certain quota reserved for Manchu students.

For a period the political instability after 1989 made people more careful when spending money and making further investments in businesses. The slow activity in the state sector, and in particular the only meager improvement in the standard of living of state employees despite improvement in the national economy, widened the gap between most state employees and the most properous members of the business community. A certain regained freedom could be registered in that a number of people talked frivolously about their wealth. Luo and Yang, who run one of the small groceries, had saved up a large amount during those two years, enabling them to buy a new flat and take out life insurance. Moreover, they do not bother to hide their motorcycle anymore; mounted with a sidecar, it is used for transporting goods, and it is often parked right outside the shop in Chang Shun Street.

Many business households now watch over considerable amounts of cash. The plastic producer managed, through his foreign connections, to place his money in Hong Kong. This act gives him an immense freedom compared to others, at least until 1997. But he is a rare case. Common to everyone else is the lack of placement and investment possibilities. The bakers have money, a couple of the former signboard makers are wealthy, the textile shops are quite profitable, a hairdresser can make a fortune if she owns and runs the place herself, and even the tiny groceries and kiosks can yield substantial profits. If a single group stands out, however, it is the restaurant owners, of whom the majority have substantial capital. The aggregate wealth in the neighborhood easily runs into millions of yuan, mostly kept in cash in order to provide for old age and for the unexpected: sickness, bad fortune, and periods of erratic political struggle.

The Young

For the young in Bin Shen, the economic slowdown after 1989 further aggravated circumstances. Rising taxes and stricter policies had squeezed out a number of young people doing small business in the street — for instance, the brother and sister running a bookstall, the girl with the TV games, the young man with the billiard saloon, and several others. The total participation of youth in private businesses had dropped to its 1987 level, or even below, in spite of the fact that in 1991 the economy had recovered somewhat and people had more money to spend than in 1990 and 1989 after June 4. Another new policy, which prohibited state employees from easing their children into their units, had been enforced in most places; the young had to wait until their parents retired, and then take over the vacated jobs.

Moreover, those jobs available to the young still held little attraction. Ms. Luo's now seventeen-year-old daughter had, together with a number of other young people from her school, found temporary work as a gardener in the Du Fu garden outside Chengdu. But at 75 yuan per month, the work was neither well paid nor particularly demanding. She would either leave home at 9 A.M. and be back at 11 or go to work a little before 3 P.M. and be back soon after 4. She was free the rest of the time, so she did not find enough motivation to regard the job as a real career. Doctor Zhong's twenty-year-old daughter, his oldest, had done nothing for three years now. Her pretty looks had earned her a contract as a future receptionist in a private hotel under construction. She had undergone a three-month training course, for which her father had paid 300 yuan, to prepare her for starting work when the hotel opened. Presumably because of the crisis in the tourist industry, however, completion of the hotel had been postponed. In the contract the hotel had agreed to pay her 40 yuan a month while she waited for a full-time job. Meanwhile, word had reached her father that the hotel wanted another 200 yuan for a training course, since it asserted that her previous training was becoming obsolete. So this far the deal had been in the hotel's favor, and the doctor felt he was being cheated: "You don't know what to believe; at a certain point I thought that they were con men exploiting people's concern for their unemployed children, but a friend of mine tells that they are really building something where they say — so I don't know!"

The number of young unemployed had grown steadily. Meanwhile the category of "job-waiting young" had been narrowed by stipulation that it applied only to people under thirty years of age. Thus those without a job, but over thirty, were no longer counted unemployed by the local authorities; they belonged to a new, nameless category. In their despair, the long-term unemployed regarded themselves as a new class of "social waste" (*shehui feiwu*); they found it ironic that in spite of their unenviable class affiliation their numbers were steadily increasing. Apparently, all those who had been long-term unemployed in 1989 were still without jobs in 1991. The Street Committee's unwillingness or inability to produce reliable data on the unemployed was explained by a number of the young: "They would not know how many we are, because they do not bother even to note our names when we register with them." The unemployed's own estimates of their numbers in Bin Shen ranged from 30 to 50 percent of the young. It was a common feeling among them that the local authorities did not care about them whatsoever.

The youngest school-leavers had less difficulty in finding at least temporary jobs, primarily in factories. If there was a vacancy, the employer would prefer either the rural young or the least educated urban young having reached only junior middle school since these groups were presumed to be the easiest to control and to be willing to work harder for less pay. At the other end, the graduates from the new specialized technical schools (*zhuanye xuexiao*) were in high demand and were almost certain to get good jobs, frequently implying cadre status. Between these extremes, those ordinary young people who graduated from the statutory minimum of senior secondary school were even harder hit than before.

It had definitely become more difficult for the young to start private business. Discouraging rumors of others' difficulties were spreading; a common attitude was that one could start a business now only if he or she had old connections or extraordinary financial means to establish new connections. The main obstacle was the even more entrenched practice of demanding large sums of money for all pertinent licenses, involving long periods of "pending" when the parties would try out each other — the applicant offering increasing amounts of cigarettes, liquor, and cash payments without knowing the effect, and the official playing with the upper limits of the applicant's capacity. People felt that they were subject to the conscious calculations comparable to how much a cow can be milked or how much the cart can be loaded before the horse perishes. Some individuals, apparently those whom certain officials regarded as troublesome, found that a license was out of reach even though they possessed the money: "You want to pay homage to the Buddha, but you cannot find the entrance to the temple."

A young man wanted to establish himself as a tailor in a small alley in Bin Shen. With 2,000 yuan borrowed from his family for investment, he reckoned it could be done. The ICB and the Street Committee let him start the shop, a tiny room rented from a family possessing a humble little house, without giving him the license at once. In the following months, the various bureaus of administration sent him round in circles. Asking for documents he had never heard of, they all demanded money for their services. Now, four months later, he still spends well over 200 yuan per month for "services" connected to the completion of his license, not counting the large sum he paid when starting the shop. Not much is left after another 200 yuan for taxes and 100 for the landlord. He sleeps in the shop. At this point he has started doubting whether he can finish the formalities before his investment is lost altogether. The landlord herself ran a little restaurant in the same room but gave up recently because of exorbitant taxes: "Look at that tree outside. I planted it myself many years ago and I have taken care of it since. I put up a paper sign when I ran my little place and was fined 50 yuan by someone passing by."

The raging unemployment among the young has become another subject of exploitation. Someone can make money on other people's concern for their children and their subsequent vulnerable position. Next door to the young tailor, a retiree opened a tiny barbershop to help his unemployed son obtain a taxi driver's license. At once, the state real estate bureau owning the house increased the rent from 1 to 30 yuan. Nonlegal taxes soon followed and amount presently to at least 100 yuan per month. And new bureaus still join in. When he took out his tiny stove for boiling tea water and placed it outdoors against the wall, he was charged an extra 15 yuan per month even though it is placed under his own roof. After a long series of further complaints he says, aimed at me: "If you find out why the officials act as they do, you have the key to China's problem."

A small group of young men usually gather next to the teahouse in Chang Shun Street, where the parents of one of the men own a house. If the weather is nice they will put out a small bamboo table and stools on the pavement so they can sit there during the day and watch street life, drink tea, and chat. They have evidently not washed for some time; their clothes are in rags, they wear plastic sandals or are barefooted, and in summer their upper bodies are naked. They are between twenty and thirty years of age, and they have been unemployed for periods ranging from a few years up to fourteen years; among the six of them present this day, no one has ever had a decent job. They also have in common the fact that they rely on their parents. "I can only hope that my parents will live forever," says the eldest with bitter sarcasm. In exchange for being supported, they usually cook for their families at night. Otherwise they pass time by sleeping long hours, drinking tea, or playing *mazhang*, which, however, is an indoor activity because of the illegal betting involved. Some claim to make a little pocket money on *mazhang*. However, since "playing *mazhang*" is frequently used to explain incomes not gained from ordinary work, it has become synonymous with crime in some segments of society.

For these youth daily life is boredom. Their families do not have the means to help them establish business or get an education. There are no unemployment programs, and local authorities tend to ignore their existence. They are neither supported nor controlled, just left to themselves. Many know how to make money on odd jobs such as painting or doing carpentry for friends and acquaintances, helping in restaurants, or working as porters or pedicab drivers when someone needs them a day or two. Such small and relatively easy jobs were always available in Bin Shen, and a few marginal individuals have lived on them for decades. But petty theft by individuals and casual small groups is also widespread among the young — frequently connected to the attraction that gambling has for them. Large amounts of money change hands during the nightly gambling sessions in private homes and in the back of some restaurants, where businessmen, criminals, fortune hunters, and the young social outcasts meet. On the big nights, the pool in each game may run into hundreds of yuan, and sometimes more than a thousand. In this environment, criminal gangs recruit their members, but make them operate outside Bin Shen of course. This environment also contains the strongest articulation of opposition to "the system," since people here have no access to the privileges distributed in formal society and have little to lose in terms of social position. They sense no distinction between central and local power or between Party and government interests.

They find the system intolerable and in need of fundamental change. But they have little confidence that another political system would bring about such change. What a number of other people would only insinuate, they would speak out clearly: "The real problem is Chinese culture — the lack of freedom, the power abuse, the extortion that makes it impossible to build something for yourself." Inside, around the gambling table, the conversation is radically different from outside. A young shopkeeper who runs a perfectly legal business will by day express his opposition to the local bureaucracy commenting that "their illegal taxes make it impossible to do proper business." But at night, in the liberated atmosphere of the gambling dens, he will voice the reproachful opinion that "it is Chinese culture to want something from other people."

During the demonstrations leading up to June 4, 1989, practically everyone among the young unemployed went down to watch. The students from all colleges in Chengdu took the lead when the protest started, but they were soon joined by other groups of young. As the demonstrators gained ground and the revolt developed, those young people who were less integrated into the established society became more conspicuous. They apparently went further than the students and the organized wage earners — who all had their careers to think of — in terms of direct attacks on personnel and property when fighting broke out in the last days. They were in the front line when two government buildings were attacked, the People's Exhibition Hall and several apartment blocks set on fire, the gift shops on the ground floor of the Jinjiang International Hotel looted and the coffee shop set on fire, and buses and military vehicles seized and burned in the first days of June.

And the young unemployed indeed took the heaviest blows when the armed forces recaptured the streets of Chengdu. Hundreds were beaten unconscious with iron clubs by the People's Armed Police, and there were heavy casualties. Of Bin Sheners one is still lying unconscious in a hospital, one was sentenced to life imprisonment for throwing a piece of wood into the burning department store, several are still imprisoned, and some have been released after serving minor sentences. In the public media's denunciation of demonstrators as criminals and counterrevolutionaries, private businesspeople repeatedly were accused of being both instigators and arms dealers, against whom public action should be taked through campaigns.[9] The role of the job-waiting young was simultaneously downplayed, since this group is grossly underestimated in the official record. Official statements notwithstanding, none of the established businesspeople in Bin Shen was known to have participated in the demonstrations.

The young people who sit in the sunshine in Chang Shun Street are much concerned with the death penalty and its zealous application in their country.[10] Small groups of convicts are regularly paraded in open trucks through the main streets of Chengdu on the way to the execution ground. One afternoon, five young people who belong to the class of social waste were taken there. Yet when confronted in public, these young maintain that "no one here participated" even though at least one has served a prison sentence — as opposed to the flocks of young Chinese who have applied for residence permits in the West since June 4, 1989, all claiming to have been involved as demonstrators or student leaders.[11]

It is not only the young who perceive history as being something flexible, somehow tied to the human mind in mutual dependence. The general view of history in Bin Shen, which was addressed in chapter two, directs little attention to historical processes in their own right. Abstract issues such as the formation of social groups or the development of private business are subjugated to personal experiences and motives. Another example of a flexible interpretation of history concerns the private enterprises (*siying qiye*) in Bin Shen. In 1987–89 investigation of their possible occurrence in the area had shown that none existed in all of Chengdu, few knew about the concept, and among the few who knew, the common explanation was that no businessman "wanted to go first." In the meantime, the central government had put increasing weight and authority into the both the registration and control of private businesses, emphasizing their correct classification.[12] Yet the total system reacted sluggishly in conveying the message. Still, in 1991, few businesspeople in Bin Shen even knew about the possibility of registering as private enterprise, and when it was mentioned to them, most commented that "you would be stupid to register in such a way." Shang, the bicycle repairman with his own shop in Chang Shun Street, still had no license at all. The plastics producer was still operating on a collective license, now in fine understanding with responsible authorities who received their appropriate charges. With his thrity employees and obvious personal control of the company, he should have been among the first to be informed about the new policy — at least in the outsider's view. Yet he claimed never to have heard about "private enterprises." The authorities' attitude to Mr. Wang's expanding restaurant is another case attesting to the discrepancy between government policy and local practice. With sixteen employees in 1991, Wang was far past the limit for household business. However, instead of suggesting that he transfer to an individual enterprise license, which unquestionably the law prescribes, two different organs have put increasing pressure on him to register as a collective. But their internal disagreement has so far been his rescue; both the Street Committee and the Industrial and Commercial Administration Bureau wanted him to surrender to their organization as a responsible unit, thus for a time making it possible for him to play one against the other. He states that he will remain private as long as possible: "In China, you cannot do business on worries."

Great was our surprise when a private enterprise suddenly sprang up in Bin Shen, even claiming years of registration as such. An association worker mentioned it to us during a short encounter in the midst of Chang Shun Street's throng. We decided to investigate the case immediately. The mysterious enterprise was a sewing school, which occupied a private ground-floor flat in the residential quarter behind the army hotel. To enlarge the facilities, an odd-looking wooden extension without windows was built out into the courtyard between the concrete apartment blocks. A middle-aged woman named Gou runs the school. Inside it is dark as night. Half-finished clothes hang everywhere, and treadle sewing machines, dummies, and piles of material mix with Ms. Gou's private belongings. The school offers basic training in the tailoring of women's garments in particular. The school had been the training center of a collective unit. According to Ms. Gou, the coincidence of several events made her decide to segregate it as an individual household business: it had become possible after 1979, and when she in the beginning of the 1980s lost her voice when she developed a goiter, her only option was to become private. She has run since the school by herself, only recently assisted by two young people, who work as part-time accountant and cashier to comply with the regulations for private enterprises.

The sewing school is also a factory, in addition to Ms. Gou's home consisting of two independent shops outside Bin Shen that produce large quantities of women's clothes by the labor of approximately twenty students. The students stay for periods of three months to about a year, learning basic skills by alternately receiving instructions from Ms. Gou and working in one of the shops. The students pay no tuition fee. Neither are they paid for their work in the factory. Among the students are a number of local girls from the job-waiting category. Ms. Gou says that she cooperates with the local authorities by running their courses, and she even holds a title in the association herself. Ms. Gou thus answered the question of how both the association and the Street Committee could claim to run their own tailoring courses for the job-waiting young; the association would simply refer them to private initiatives under its jurisdiction such as Ms. Gou's, and the Street Committee would also have the option to refer them to evening classes organized by municipal authorities.

Today, Ms. Gou claims private enterprise status in Bin Shen dating back to 1987 — at which time even responsible authorities, including the Tax Bureau, hardly knew of the concept and strongly denied that any such existed. The success of Ms. Gou's training program, which provides her students with an improvised diploma in return for their unpaid labor, depends entirely on the support of local authorities. The expansion of the school-factory's production in recent years must have been accompanied by local authorities' tightening in on her. By writing back her business as a private enterprise, Ms. Gou presumably helps the local authorities fulfill their new quotas and thus satisfy higher levels of the bureaucracy. In exchange, the arrangement permits Ms. Gou to run several shops and, even more important, to sell her products to state shops, which would never be possible on an ordinary individual business license.

Ms. Gou is frank in relating her story; like everyone else, she complains openly about the state of affairs: taxes and charges are impossible to calculate, and the relentless introduction of new fees is becoming unbearable. The new grain tax of approximately 40 yuan per employee per year[13] hits hard because all her students are counted as employees.

Though seemingly open-minded and willing to talk, Ms. Gou has no qualms about adjusting her business' history to the social needs of the present moment. Some facts in her story hardly fit. In 1987–89 her business was not listed in the association archives of *geti hu;* although these were found not to be fully updated, our inquiries among the officials presumably brought forth all businesses within the branch of small production, whether listed or not. Therefore, it is highly unlikely that Ms. Gou's school was then registered as being run privately, whether as *geti hu* or *siying qiye.* At one point during the conversation Ms. Gou confused the time at which her school allegedly became private. The suspicion arose that her business, presumably quite recently, transferred directly from collective to private status after pressure from local authorities. They may have been urged by higher levels to expose a certain number of *siying qiye.* The alleged former *geti hu* status would then have been her own means of justifying her private enterprise status as a logical step from smaller to larger business. The ICB and the association's writing back her business history was presumably extended by Ms. Gou for the purpose of an ordered exposition, thoroughly contextual as it is.

A Cycle of Business

As we followed the rise and fall of businesses in Bin Shen since 1987, a picture of the life cycle of a typical private household business emerged. This is not to maintain that all businesses develop along a single line and are abandoned after a predictable period — quite the contrary; significant variation was recorded, among certain types of businesses more than others. An underlying pattern was always present, without, however, covering every concrete aspect of business.

A fundamental characteristic of the businesses in the community appeared to be the absence of any firm correspondence between the identity of the household and the type of business. While only handicraft businesses to any degree were tied to the skills of their managers, frequently trained by other master craftsmen before the Liberation, few others regarded it as a prerequisite to have training or experience in that particular branch of business they considered entering. Thus, branch of business was decided upon after contemplation of what size or scope of business was suitable to one's capital, energy, ambitions, connections, and accessible premises. To single out one of these, one's amount of ready capital is more important than previous experience when finding the most auspicious business to open. Consequently, handicraft businesses seemed to maintain a high stability compared to others, in terms of both life span and size. But other factors counteracted such tendency. The old generation of artisans is slowly pulling out of business, and the authorities' attempts to move workshop production out from the center works in the same direction. In terms of stability, people are prone to give a good business a longer life than a bad one, but on the other hand, ready capital from a profitable business offers new opportunities. Apart from handicraft workshops, which were mainly discontinued because of inevitable circumstances, restaurants also exhibited a considerable, somehow unexpected stability. Yet most businesses share a number of characteristics.

Conformity and competition go hand in hand in private enterprise. The power of the example looms large in the minds of most households starting up a business. Rather than abstract considerations as to what is possible, what does not exist already, or what activity may be the most satisfactory to engage in in the long run, it is the range of concrete examples that counts; moreover, these model examples are local, with few exceptions seen in the closest vicinity or in a neighboring area. There are few innovators in household business; the closest to such is the entrepreneur who introduces an activity from another area into his own. Since private businesspeople are already marginalized by their label, there is little encouragement to establish a truly original business or otherwise venture out into the unknown. Yet everyone wishes to link up with the endless waves of fashion and public expressions of modernity in Chinese society, suddenly bringing a certain type of consumption into focus. Be it cooking, film processing, or hairdressing, the chance that someone in the household can learn it is usually taken for granted; in this aspect of business, a high degree of self-confidence is shown by business households. Rather than being the first with a new business, an entrepreneur may want to become the first to introduce, to his or her own area, a business that has already proved to be a hit elsewhere. Strong competition awaits; the entrepreneur will be watched and studied, his customers counted, his tax receipts checked; if he succeeds, the word will spread like ripples in a pond. If he has proved a path negotiable, he will eventually be copied — not by a single or a few businesses of the same type, but by a whole chain of them, after which he can only hope for respite in the further proliferation of his trade. The entrepreneur can only defend his or her advantage by playing on "reputation," "experience," and the mutual value of "steady customers." When starting up business, there is no concern for keeping up good neighborly relations; most people would rather sacrifice them than restrain themselves if they spot a lucrative business. It was a common experience in restaurants, hairdressing salons, and kiosks that relations deteriorated when neighbors became competitors. Thus, at times, the entire climate is one of frantic competition on a very limited space of operation, where a genuinely innovative entrepreneur is compelled to scoop up his profit as quickly as possible before the crowd of successful opportunists takes the wind out of his sails.

Judging from experience in Bin Shen, the Chinese universal praise of "steady customers" is a highly relative concept, or even bogus. The concept relates to the perception of history, tradition, and continuity — entities that may be shaped according to immediate needs. Local restaurants claim to have steady customers after one month; the new hairdressing salons in Chang Shun Street all claimed to have their own steady customers, even though some of the shops had opened just a few months before. A young girl opening a textiles shop in Chang Shun Street, competing with Ms. Wu, managed to reach a monthly turnover in the proximity of 10,000 yuan in a few months. To the question of how long it takes to build up steady customers, she answers after some contemplation: "Maybe one month, if you treat people well and do not cheat."

After a business is established follow stages of changing work patterns and distribution of labor. Whether the business is of the traditional outlook or adheres to modernistic aims as described in chapter four, patterns of leadership, employment, and business strategies vary accordingly. In the traditional type of business, adjustments inside the household are commonplace, particularly so if the business is launched by a woman while the male head of the household has other employment. To preserve harmony, control over the business should comply with authority over the household, so that the male household head is in the long run forced to leave his job and take full responsibility over the business. Among elderly couples at the end of their careers, deviation is more acceptable. That work organization follows household organization with the addition of a bottom layer of rural laborers has also been shown. The male detachment from manual labor is conspicuous even at an early stage, granting credibility to the Chinese expression of a *cao jiao lao ban,* a word play consisting of "a busy leader" and "lifting up one's feet."

As a business grows and its success becomes more visible, the household that runs it is put under increasing pressure. Local bureaucracy extorts the businesses for money — the more conspicuous the wealth of the household, the more so, as has been amply shown. What is equally difficult for a number of households but far less admitted and discussed, however, is the pressure they are put under by friends and relatives. It is a theme as old as Chinese literature that wealth attracts relatives so that families tend to grow in correspondence with economic success. Although less outspoken in the modern Chinese society, such basic rules are still applied, not the least to successful businesspeople. Among the business households in Bin Shen, the wealthiest households can afford to let sons stay in the household with their wives and children as is the case with Mr. Wang's, the hookah producer's, and several others. Similarly, a household like Ms. Wu's can grant its young the freedom to study, while distant relatives are incorporated to attend to the business. But these dependents who are not actively participating in business are only the surface of social obligation and represent only the responsibilities desired by the household itself.

Far more complex are connections to various persons on the household's periphery; some state that this is in fact the most complicated aspect of private business. It was only toward the end of my fieldwork that I realized the extent of many successful businesspeople's obligations toward friends and relatives. In the city, where ordinary people's relations reach far beyond the local area, obtaining an overview of social structures and obligations is of course impossible. But repeated questioning as to what the surplus from business was used for finally opened up accounts of the obligations entailed in being comparatively rich. One example illustrates the problem best: Mr. Yuan and his household, including his son and daughter-in-law, run a restaurant in Bin Shen. It is among the largest in the area and has six employees to assist the Yuans. Thus, in the inner circle, the business supports the six Yuans and the six employees. In the next circle, several people do minor jobs and services for the business, either on Mr. Yuan's request or by their own initiative and subsequently acknowledged by him. One neighbor supplies oil from a state unit, a relative has a connection that can procure fresh fish, another acquaintance buys the vegetables needed on the market in the mornings and transports them to the restaurant, and so on. Altogether seven or eight people have a certain income from such services, and Mr. Yuan is constantly met with offers concerning foodstuffs and services for the restaurant, frequently accompanied by outspoken expectations playing on neighborship or old acquaintance.

Let us move from business relations to the household's kinship bonds and personal acquaintances. Here exchanges tend to shift from a purely material basis to involve abstract values as well. To assist relatives and to engage relatives in one's business when needed is considered only natural. No successful businessman will frown at having to support his children and their families, his own brothers and sisters, or his parents. But since the Chinese kinship system assigns precise terms to a large range of relatives in several generations above and below oneself, a great number of people can usually claim kinship to a businessman. Mr. Yuan has a brother, a cousin, and two uncles who regularly receive some support from him. Apart from relatives, Mr. Yuan has a number of old classmates and friends who, since they are in trouble now because of crises in the state sector, have approached him for support. He estimates that he supports five or six of his old friends, either by giving them some tens of or a hundred yuan every month or by occasionally giving them a few hundred yuan, for instance, at the spring festival. Mr. Yuan is of course proud of his healthy business and his ability to support a large number of other people. Yet he sometimes feels exploited. He knows that one of his old classmates, whom he had not seen for years, approached him after having heard about his business from another classmate. "First he dropped in for a meal, pretending not to know about my running the restaurant. Then he came back after some time and asked for money."

Mr. Wang, who still runs the largest private restaurant in Bin Shen, estimates that, apart from his household and employees, as many as fifteen to twenty people receive support from him, either monthly or occasionally: "When you ask me how I spend the money from my business, you should know how many people expect something from me. It is not only in relation to the officials that you have to *yanjiu yanjiu* [word play saying study-study, or study cigarettes and liquor, meaning "everybody must study, but business-people must pay attention to special means"]; it goes for a far wider range of people." Together with his large household of seven, his sixteen employees, his beneficiaries, and his many suppliers, the number of people receiving an income from his business is simply incredible — according to his own estimate it easily reaches fifty, not counting various officials and units of bureaucracy.

A hairdressing salon in Chang Shun Street provides another example of the ratio of income earners to workers. The household owning the eight-square-meter premises receives 300 yuan per month, which is pure profit. The contractor who rents the shop does not run the business himself. He receives 700 yuan per month from the two young Guangdong hairdressers running the salon, from which he pays the rent. The two hairdressers are on leave from their former units, but may go back. To maintain their positions, each pays his unit 50 percent of his former wages, which amounts to 100 yuan per person per month. The business runs well, giving them a comfortable income since they are both single. However, when there are busy days before public holidays or when one of them has other things to do, they pay some of their friends to assist them in the shop. Three young men regularly work in the salon. A fellow in the neighborhood has pressed himself on them and attained rights to deliver shampoo and conditioner. Moreover, since they are new in the area, they do not know the customary limits of casual taxes and tend to pay more than others.

It is evidently difficult to establish the ratio of work-free to work-dependent profit from a business like this and furthermore to estimate how many people benefit from the work of those seen in the shop. However, a total figure in the range of a fifty-fifty share between work-free and work-dependent incomes after registered taxes and charges seems realistic. When a business is running well, outsiders' extraction of funds is no heavy burden, and less so to those businesspeople who own their premises. Yet it may put a limit on the businessperson's ability, and even on the desire, to invest further. And in times of crises, this proliferation of dependents can become a real nuisance. Added to the constant squeeze from bureaucracy and maybe even threats from the criminal gangs, the search for a way out may encourage the businessperson to consider starting up a new business. If this step is actually taken, it may for a time provide the arguments that ward off the dependents and allow some breathing space. Much rests on the businessperson's ability to handle both a successful business and the social network that rises spontaneously around it. Some locals suggest that handling "social relations," including those with the bureaucracy, is even more important than skills in doing business.

Another factor in the downfall of a business is the lack of interest, or conversely, the desire for innovation, which is particularly outspoken among the male business managers. The engineer running the plastic container factory readily admits it:

> I have been running this business for four years now, and I cannot complain. But it is too boring — eight hours at work,

> eight hours being with the family and eight hours asleep. It does not hold my interest any more. I want to try something new and prove myself through something bigger. I have heard from friends that East Europe is a good place to do business right now. At the moment, I am trying everything I can to establish myself there. A friend is investing some money for me to start a business in Bulgaria, where it is possible for Chinese to obtain a residence permit. Then when you have stayed there for some years maybe you can go to Russia. I think prospects are better there than in China. Maybe I will try to sell clothes, but it does not matter what type of business. It just has to be trade, not production any more.

Ma, the hot-pot entrepreneur, is not seen in his restaurant anymore. A young girl takes care of it in his stead. The story is that he found a girl friend some time ago. At that time, she ran a clothes shop in the northern part of Chengdu. After a while, they started helping each other in their businesses. When Ma's mother, who had helped him, died in a traffic accident, he started losing interest in his restaurant. So the two young people simply swapped for a time: he sells clothes, and she runs the hot-pot restaurant. They both think it is good to try something new and to gain diverse experiences in business: "We want to pool our resources and maybe go to Shenzhen and run a business there. Maybe next year we will go."

In an attempt to overcome the dejection in a life of routine without visible improvements, much money and energy are spent on quick restylings. Those who can afford it will constantly rebuild, remodel, and change their environment, without necessarily improving the quality of their businesses, since the quality of the renovations is often dubious. Rather, these moves may seem as the sublimation of a dull life. Mr. Wang, for instance, has renovated his restaurant every year since 1987, Fu redid his bakery several times before opening a restaurant, several of the small grocery shops have been changed, and even the traditional doctor is seen from year to year to move his counters and paraphernalia from one side of the room to the other, making his shop a mirror image of what it was before.

Again, the old craftsmen stand out in maintaining a stable environment in their workshops. However, if a certain affiliation with a specific trade and a well-defined environment is detected among the artisans in Bin Shen, it should be seen in the light of their own rural background. They commonly belong to the first generation of city dwellers in their families. The second generation, their children, born in the city, definitely expressed higher expectations for their careers; and with few exceptions born out of necessity, the second generation commonly prefers staying unemployed to becoming overemployed in manual labor — such is by definition reserved for rural people.

The End of Business

In retrospect, the businesses in Bin Shen underwent changes, but not radical ones during the fieldwork years. There was a continuous flow of businesses being launched and abandoned, apparently without political events having a dramatic influence on their numbers and structural changes. Of the sixty businesses with indoors facilities that were thoroughly investigated in 1987, approximately thirty-three were still in existence in 1991, with businesses in handicrafts and services showing equal frequency of survival. Apart from only one of the five tailors interviewed remaining in business, there was no clear pattern of specific businesses being more temporary than others. Restaurants appeared to be relatively stable, however, with approximately 70 percent still operating in 1991. The disappearance of a number of highly specialized businesses — for instance, the photo printing shop, the sofa maker, the cloth shoemaker, and the noddles producer — narrowed the range of specialization somewhat in the private sector, since a great number of newcomers were in the trendy branches such as restaurants, hairdressing, and textiles.

Several factors make it nearly impossible to accurately estimate the average life span of businesses in Bin Shen. Private business has a short history, having begun only after 1979. A few of these businesses started in the early years are still in existence; at the other extreme, a number of businesses survived only a few months or just a few weeks, thereby escaping our surveys and also quickly passing out of people's memories. Thus, in this as in other matters involving hard data on private businesses, one can only speak of ranges. Of the thirty-three businesses still in existence in 1991, five or six can be expected to be discontinued soon because of old age, lack of interest, greater ambitions, and so forth. Hence a fall-out in the range of 15 percent per year is realistic. If these assumptions are correct, the average life span of a business would be four to five years, with 25 percent surviving less than two years and 20 percent surviving more than ten years — provided, of course, that a fairly stable environment prevails as was the case through the 1980s.

Concluding from the experience from Bin Shen, a business cycle can be signified by the entrepreneur's initial enthusiasm, full devotion for a few years, transformation of surplus into prestige and showing off in the form of conspicuous consumption, followed by a stage of frequent renovations and succeeded by loss of interest altogether before the entrepreneur wants to start something new. Age, family affairs, and external circumstances greatly influence the progress from one stage to the next and may even halt the process completely. Yet the model remains applicable to a vast number of businesses in Bin Shen as well as in similar environments. In this scheme of things one can speak of household business, but certainly not family business in the sense of a well-defined family group being tied to a certain economic activity over generations. Neither was the following of genealogical goals a principal driving force in the type of businesses that unfolded in Bin Shen during the 1980s.

If the private businesses were less enduring than was believed to be the case in pre-Liberation society — and certainly less stable than one would expect from the reputation of Chinese overseas business — this could be a matter of rational adaptation to the set of external circumstances prevalent in contemporary Chinese society. However, building on experience from Bin Shen, such argument may in fact be reversed. Following this conception, the claim is that the overall conditions offered by the Chinese state power, its socialist label aside, is as much an expression of an underlying cultural exposition: a shared system of ideology, strategy, and action applied by individuals in all sections of society. This system incorporates and reproduces the cycle: the inherent notion of surviving the low tides in order to prosper in the high tides, and the quick moves that are effected by such patterns of thought. Particularly in the final stage of socialism, when unprecedented opportunities emerge, the antagonism embedded in the relation between Chinese business and bureaucracy can only be expected to sharpen.

CHAPTER EIGHT

The Dialectics of Household Strategies

> You know, it is the social system that causes the problems, not the people. Leaders are people who press themselves forward, placing themselves on top of structures built by the people — like Li Peng and Zhou Enlai, they were not the leaders that were promoted. But too few take responsibility. No one dares to stand out, that's why it is so easy for them. Everybody just follows their families or groups or the lines that are laid out for them [businessman, off the record].

This chapter analyzes household strategies in regard to business and bureaucracy in the local community. The point of departure will be the identification and classification of some basic contradictions crucial to the formation of household strategies. Relations of both potential and actual conflict obviously exist in local society; but while some clearly manifest themselves in the clashing interests of various strata, households, and individuals at a given time, others may become apparent only after we clarify their wider structural setting — that is, place local society within the context of the Chinese state. Thus, from the basic conflicts in Bin Shen some structural oppositions will be derived, and some reflections on them will be molded into a hypothesis concerning the essential conditions shaping household ideology and action.

In the following analysis the criteria are maintained that the structural oppositions established are not merely constructions of the Western intellectual milieu or just of the anthropologist, but at least in colloquial terms, permit recognition in local society. They must expose, or be part of, the current discussions on the state of economic and political affairs and on modernization in Bin Shen as in other similar Chinese communities and thereby contribute to the ongoing discourse of culture. Still, it is a reflective account in that it is made by a Westerner, writing for a Western audience, and touching upon aspects of Chinese culture that are usually emotional property rather than subjects of writing.

This is of course an expression of a dissatisfaction with a great number of existing accounts of contemporary Chinese society[1] that address issues relating to socialism, class formation, or political ideologies involving democratization. In the post-Liberation era, the Chinese state adopted Marxist terms as its formal language. This language takes the form of a monologue rather than a dialogue, and it is without parallel in local society; the authority that derives from paraphrasing it, though, is extensively used and will be examined. Comparisons will be made with other Chinese community studies and relevant additional sources. Studies of Chinese business and bureaucracy per se are only treated as subordinate to the principal concern: a sketch of local society in terms of abstract household orientations and positions and how these are played out in the pursuit of social and material aims.

As a prerequisite for drawing in parallel sources related in type rather than in origin, a specific issue should be considered. It has been widely debated whether Chinese culture can be profitably analyzed as a whole or whether regional, provincial, or even local variations defy all such attempts.[2] Some writers insist that a profound cultural diversity rules out all generalizations. The stand taken here is nevertheless "generalist": as the Chinese themselves generally consider their culture to be a coherent whole and refer to it as such, the particularists' task seems difficult. With Francis Hsu one can infer that the significance of such diversity still needs to be convincingly demonstrated: "It has not been shown how different groups of Chinese differ in their approach to men, gods and things" (1971:24). An assumption concerning the long presence of centralized power will be made: aspects of family organization, bureaucracy, social status connected to the Center, and household strategies formed against the background of a powerful state are all areas in which common principles may appropriately be asserted to prevail and where unifying values may be traced.

Theoretical inspiration is drawn from works focused on such consistent aspects of Chinese culture — for instance, Max Weber (1920), Marcel Granet (1922), C. K. Yang (1961), Maurice Freedman (1979), and Stephan Feutchwang (1992), all emanating from the systemic interpretation of Chinese religion[3] but with far-reaching implications for the study of the synthesizing aspects of Chinese culture. Inflating this to comprise a common frame of distinct "Chineseness" as done by Freedman (ibid.) is not the point, however, although the concept has a certain value in demonstrating Chinese cultural classifications.

A "liberal" dialectical conception based on empirical inductions from the fieldwork material will be pursued. Viewed explicitly in a domestic group perspective, which will be maintained, the first "class" of phenomena refers to the relation between family group and state power in Chinese culture, since these two are units of analogous abstractions and also tend to be universal organizational models. Next, in regard to local community interaction, business and bureaucracy are seen as alternative paths in both Chinese social thought and corresponding life or career strategies, consequently making up two parallel systems. Finally, approaching ideology formation within the household, I discuss the recurring issue of ideal culture contra actually registered practices. Emerging are three fundamental issues, which will remain our objects of analysis: state versus family, formal versus informal hierarchies, and ideal versus social practice.

State versus Family

Seen in the domestic group perspective, the Chinese state embodies a specific set of circumstances that in the common account is derived from its nature and historical continuity. Conversely, the requirements of the omnipresent Chinese state tend to polarize all social organization into the realms of state and family, into what belongs to the state's own sphere of interest and what lies outside. The distinction between state and family as two major polarized forms of association does not imply essentially different types of relations, loyalties, and identities; rather, it is a moral distinction.

I shall first turn to literary sources, since countless writers, both Chinese and Western, have pondered the subject. State and family in Chinese society are commonly characterized as analogous organizations and power structures (e.g., Chai 1962:94), for instance, depicted as "society as a magnified family" (Bodde 1981:265), with a single sense of solidarity (Levy 1949:164–5). The Chinese concepts applied to both, or more precisely, the domestic character of the terms applied to the state level (state as Mother, leader as Father, nation as Country-home [*guojia*]), point to definite patterns of identification, which have been maintained through modern history. In 1915 Hobshouse wrote in the introduction to a work on Chinese social institutions by two of his Chinese students:

> The family as a great undying corporate unity, embracing the ancestors, the whole body of the living kindred, the unborn members who are to maintain its honour and perpetuate the memory of the forefathers, reveals itself as the heart of the Chinese social structure. Neither writer can get far from the family for long, whatever topic he is discussing, for all Chinese custom, all literature, ethics, art, religion, and government itself, start from the family life and end in it again. (Leong and Tao 1915:viii)

The parallel is described as equally important in imperial society. The emperor as the pater familias, the patriarchal order on a grand scale, apparently had its foundation in the Confucian integrational ideals of "China as one person" and was indirectly expressed in the Confucian basic Five Relations of the social hierarchy (*wu lun*) (e.g., Baker 1979:10). Independent of Confucianism, the category of "oneness" is of central importance to Chinese culture, and no less so in its political dimension. "Millions as one man" is a theme repeated in modern propaganda and in the national anthem. Powerful ambitions for *Universismus*, bringing the world to one, connect past and present in the tradition of Chinese state authority.[4] The Communist regime has put renewed efforts in particular into the strengthening of loyalty toward a strong, unified state of dynastic dimensions, inevitably and expressly at the expense of the powerful family organizations — which in turn only stresses the significance of the family as the model of all interdependence: "There are not two suns in Heaven, there are not two kings on Earth, there are not two masters in a family, there are not two superiors in the same position" (J. Croll 1989:8).

Viewed in a historical perspective, the state-family continuity may reveal changing characteristics. At the turn of the century, the Chinese regime was depicted as "despotic," but essentially anarchistic, a laissez-faire regime that interfered little with the life of the great majority (Leong and Tao 1915:71). With the steady growth of state involvement in local affairs, a development initiated in the late nineteenth century, the Chinese state has undergone an immense expansion as an institution in society, apparently greater than in other countries in the modernization process and historically independent from Communist rule.[5] In a macrohistorical context, central power may always have alternated with powerful, local-based clan organization. As Weber wrote in 1920,

> [T]he sib developed to an extent unknown elsewhere — even in India. The patrimonial rule from above clashed with the sib's strong counterbalance from below. To the present day, a considerable proportion of all politically dangerous "secret societies" has consisted of sibs. (86)

In postrevolutionary Chinese society, state and family do not form a continuum within a comprehensive structure, and it is questionable if they ever did; it is noteworthy that after the Communist takeover, the forced modernization of social institutions implied raising the status of the individual as compared to family and clan organizations, of which the latter explicitly were to be overthrown. Mao's dialectical thought, as developed before the Great Leap Forward in 1958, evolved through the recognition and resolution of contradictions; one such was the contradiction between state and collective interest and individual interest, one among the Ten Great Relationships (Schurmann 1968:77). Thus, incorporated into the theory of social classes consisting of peasants, workers, intellectuals, and bourgeoisie was the assumption of the emancipated individual.[6] Since ideology first and foremost was a basis for action, principles for social reorganization dictated individual responsibilities. Conversely, Mao's consistent refusal to deal with or even mention the Chinese family in his works after 1949 may be indicative of the true character of this organization as an immense and ineffable obstacle to his grand scheme.

The postrevolutionary state soon came to build on the tight *baojia* organization of households into small, numerically standardized units, reintroduced to China by the Japanese and taken over by the Guomindang (Schurmann 1968:368). Carrying the process of change to its extreme, the Chinese state after 1949 eradicated and substituted all previous local independent institutions in both rural and urban social life: clan and village elder councils, independent town administrations, urban commercial guilds, clubs, native-place or neighborhood associations, and the like were replaced by, in principle, state-controlled institutions. (In regard to the urban work force, 69 percent of workers were under state control in 1957, and 79 percent in 1977 [Whyte and Parish 1984:29]).

As parallel organizations both demanding subordination to exclusive authority, originally in close analogy, state and family may be seen in a dichotomous relationship as competing centers for authority, loyalty, and identity in regard to the individual. When state and family are viewed historically, the assumption is warranted that they have developed from having a set of comparable characteristics into, in analytical terms, constituting one of the basic polarities in modern Chinese society. This has become manifest in three specific aspects of social life, experienced for instance in Bin Shen.

First, in terms of authority, while authority within the family has to a large extent been preserved as corresponding to the patriarchal pattern, authorities in society at large have been seriously challenged. In this respect, deliberate action from the Mao Zedong regime aimed at breaking down all intermediate-level authorities between the individual and the leader has merged with the general modernization process. Second, in terms of morality, there is general agreement that morality in the Chinese world is primarily cultivated within the family. However, whereas traditional morality has survived in domestic affairs (where moral code can be sanctioned), the utter lack of morality when people act on the public level has become a major obstacle to the development of the open society. Third, in terms of strategies, while all state institutions ideally presuppose an open public sphere in which individuals are thought to act,[7] the strategy of the family runs conspicuously counter. Family- and kinship-based relations are now again the prime instruments in satisfying the needs of the individual in regard to providing economic security, defending basic rights, furnishing mutual assistance, and competing for scarce commodities and services.

The affiliation of the individual is exactly the point of clashing ideologies between state and family. The *danwei,* and the Self-employed Laborers Association as its substitute in private business, is the socio-spatial identity placed on the individual from above, enforced through the use of *danwei* identity cards and registration whenever the individual is confronted with authorities. In modern society few apparently regard the *danwei* as anything else than a unit of work and habitation, within which, however, useful and intimate relations may be developed.[8] For the individual, family relations commonly remain the principal sources of identity.[9] In contrast to official rhetoric, the individual's position in society is given by birth, a fact that some term "birth-ascribed stratification" and others bluntly refer to as the creation of "a caste society by giving everybody labels that derived their status from fathers and grandfathers."[10] Attempts by central government to change the balance between Party organization and civil administration in favor of the latter, the centrally curbed media, and the accelerated drive for central control in legislation are all contributing to the state level's becoming the main representative of the "outside" in the family's outlook.

The omnipresent Chinese bureaucracy (although its authority is being depersonalized through imposing "the rule of law") is an important factor in the molding of the family business ideology. Max Weber, in his examination of the divergent origins of the Chinese business mentality and the Western Puritan Ethic, highlighted the ambivalence in the commoners' relation to authority:

> The hatred and the distrust of the subjects, which is common to all patrimonialism, in China as elsewhere turned above all against the lower levels of the hierarchy, who came into the closest practical contact with the population. The subjects' apolitical avoidance of all contact with "the state" which was not absolutely necessary was typical for China as for all other patrimonial systems. But this apolitical attitude did not detract from the significance of the official education for the character formation of the Chinese people. (1948:438)

State interference in the fieldwork area has been expanding; modern history has to an unprecedented degree brought central government authorities into intimate contact with local life (in a historical sense, Sichuan has experienced a gradual integration into the Chinese empire, an integration not completed until after the Liberation). In this process, traditional authoritarian leaders of mostly local origin have been replaced by ambiguous central authorities; although their representatives may defend private interests, they are firmly attached to a nationwide, centrally controlled structure. Although Street Committees, for instance, generally are strongholds of Party dominance, securing the privileges of their leading cadres, they are both the central pattern of authority and local personalized power in one. Thus, in the view of the individual business households, exploiters are of an increasingly diffuse kind: before Liberation rich landlords and powerful generals extracted monstrous rents; since the Communist takeover, policies of the central government have determined the scope of private business, while the centralized Party organization provides the power structure enabling local bureaucracy to continue the practice of ages. When mentioning their opposition to the "above" (*shangbian*), local people stress the presence both of particular bureaucratic "uncrowned kings" and of the central authorities. But today the latter are by far the most dreaded: local authorities defending private interests are predictable exploiters, whereas the ideological struggles of the Center determine the entire foundation for private business. Particularly feared, and by many somehow anticipated to return, is the collectivization drive of 1952–53, as well as specifically aimed ideological campaigns, which surfaced again in 1989.

In terms of business matters, contradiction between state and family obviously exists; yet in another dimension, state power and family group may be placed on a continuum. In regard to essential values, private business households in Bin Shen are rarely seen to deviate from the conventional: prestige drawn from attachment to the Center, emphasis on formal education of their offspring, and patriarchal authority. The internal power structure of households appears as an extension of the hierarchical organization of society, seen, for instance, in the fact that the association incorporates household heads only. Thus the top/Center notion is somehow always represented in local community life and even internalized into the domestic group as an important basis for authority.

If we are to judge from the Bin Shen material, the relationship between family organization and state power is tense, ambivalent, and evidently changing. Radical state interference has not yet effected the social transformation usually associated with modernization: disintegration of the big family ideal and the partial replacement of family bonds by institutions based on legal codes. In their execution, state and family authority are evidently incompatible features of Chinese culture. The development of the Chinese state from a laissez-faire institution modelling the family to a powerful, omnipresent authority clashes with family coherence. Their close analogy is the source: patriarchal exclusive authority, the requirements for absolute loyalty in the search for wealth and power, action and devotion through the powerful concepts of past glory and future prospects, a dynamic approach to social and economic life, and, as will be shown, a verbally unbridgeable discrepancy between ideal and practice. A conclusion may be that the traditional Chinese state, founded on the ideal of constructing a universal order through moral armaments, is incompatible with its own striving to realize the notion of omnipresence. The vast expansion of the state domain, bringing it into direct contact with the family organization while maintaining its essential characteristics, is inconsistent with civicism. While the state during the 1960s and 1970s offered social security, it is no longer able to take responsibility for the individual. It still competes with the family, however, by demanding an even stronger allegiance: postponing marriages for the sake of the nation, leaving the family for distant job assignments, "eating bitterness" (*chi ku*) for the state, informing against family members, and so forth.

We may further perspectivize the state-family relation by turning to the overseas Chinese world. Comparison to overseas Chinese business communities suggests that basic household ideologies do not differ radically in an economically developed environment or will at least maintain comparable characteristics. A linkage between the rise of private business and the emergence of "civil society" in the PRC has often been asserted, particularly by sociologists.[11] Whether or not civil society implies images of a Western society, the development models constructed hereupon prove unsatisfactory to the Chinese case; on the basis of an investigation of Xiamen entrepreneurs, Wank (1993) identifies symbiotic power relations between state and society with a complex resource exchange. Wong (1985) shows a strong cyclical process of enterprise formation, centralization, segmentation, and disintegration across the Chinese world; Chinese enterprises are found to be impermanent, rarely extending over more than three generations. Moreover, Wong argues that "the family firm as a major form of Chinese business organization is not restricted to a particular locale or a special line of economic endeavour" (60). It may be suggested that either the economic ideology of the Chinese household is not a reaction to a certain type of state power or that ideology is seen to be preserved for generations (an aspect of changing ideology will later be shown). Along this line, household strategies are rarely seen to embrace abstract "state," "public," or other extragenealogical goals in Taiwan, Hong Kong, or other overseas Chinese communities. Although social prestige now as before is highly communicative within the Chinese world, with explicit reference to the cultural center and to socio-spatial hierarchy, economic life is astonishingly noncommunicative, referring to people's own household experience and to information through *guanxi* channels. Even in the rapidly urbanizing Taiwan, anthropological fieldwork points to strictly local models even for industrial entrepreneurship aimed at the export market, operating through an extensive brokers network, with person-to-person communication within narrow confines (Niehoff 1987). Apparently, this is not far from the case in industrializing Chinese villages, equally marked by "waves" of identical economic activities through exclusive local economic reference (Zhou and Du 1984:69) and certainly confirmed by experience from Bin Shen.

Studies of Chinese restaurants in the West also emphasize the strong economic self-containment to which such enterprises seem to give priority. The kinship organization is generally used to maximize loyalty and profit, as well as to avoid official scrutiny. One such study is that of Wilson and Pusey (1982); but, as much as this study depicts Chinese restaurants as the epitome of Chinese organizational patterns, it is itself sociological analysis in a nutshell. By defining a universally Chinese "achievement motivation" based on distinct social and psychological patterns stressing group obligations and "face" consciousness, the writers set out to prove such motivation and patterns by means of a sample of Chinese college students and one Chinese restaurant. Throughout the analysis, empirical findings are intertwined with reference to "traditional" attitudes, obligations, loyalties, suspicions, and so forth. The writers naturally conclude as they began: that traditional Chinese business is essentially traditional and that the family is the group that motivates achievement. However, rebutting their own hypothesis of stable patterns in social loyalties from imperial times, they foresee that the "modern Chinese may well be able to work long, hard hours for benefits that largely accrue to a particular social unit, or even to society as a whole" (207), quite unlike "individualist Westerners" (synonymous with Americans).

Formal versus Informal Hierarchies

From the wider ties and references between family group and state power, I will move closer to the articulations of local community hierarchies. Whereas the state-family dichotomy relates to a vertical distinction, the formal-informal hierarchy dichotomy incorporates a horizontal distinction: it explicitly refers to concrete coordinate organizations, which constitute the frame of reference for the strategies that households adopt in their outward activities.

Before assessing the roles of formal and informal hierarchies, we should again briefly consider the general process of change in Chinese society. A dual set of hierarchies may seem of chiefly historical interest as it relates to late imperial China, where the mandarinate was opposed to a large, diversified gentry-merchant stratum, and may only in a structural sense be applied to contemporary society. However, in several respects these hierarchies become useful concepts by suggesting fundamental social orientations among separate groups, or strata, in local society: strategies tend to form separate lines according to the actors' point of departure. From the perspective of political culture, the concepts relate to the issue of the development of civil public associations in late imperial society without the development of civic power turned against the state (e.g., Huang 1991:320ff.), and in terms of present society, they may elucidate the priority of vertical over horizontal loyalties at the local community level.

Judged from literary sources, traditional society appears to have contained a power structure in which formal authority radiated from the Center, but in no way reigned supreme. As one historian writing about Sichuan noted:

> The government of Szechwan (Sichuan) in 1898 was dual. On the one hand, there was the formal hierarchy: governor-general, top provincial officials, taotais, prefects, local magistrates, military commanders; all non-Szechwanese, all designated by Peking or by people themselves appointed by Peking; a hierarchy which held a monopoly of legal authority. On the other hand, there was the informal hierarchy: a group of local notables, a provincial establishment; mainly but not wholly Szechwanese, mainly but not wholly resident in the province; a hierarchy with few legally defined rights but considerable extra-legal powers. (Adshead 1984:9)

Confronting the bureaucracy as both its colleague and rival, the informal hierarchy represented landowners, businessmen, bankers, and the like — a group of people holding considerably more wealth and controlling more people than the formal hierarchy. (Sichuan always had a distinct division between Chengdu as the center of government and Chongqing as the great commercial hub). With the Communist takeover in 1949, the "informal hierarchy" was hastily eradicated; the gentry lost its property, and only diminutive private enterprises escaped the collectivizations. Since then, the Communist regime has built a society with a power concentration unprecedented in Chinese history. Chinese society has also been thoroughly militarized as the consequence of these efforts, which, however, only continued pre-Liberation developments (see also n.5).

The reforms after 1979 had profound impact on the whole structure of society and on both rural and urban economies. The reforms not only brought about slackened social control and beginning demilitarization but in addition evoked alternative lines of career. Private business rapidly developed into a separate strategy for pursuing material ends. But despite extensive state propaganda all private business relapsed into an inferior position in a social sense, while it simultaneously turned out to be highly lucrative. While private business in its initial stage only embraced minor, primarily household-based businesses, it soon gave rise to larger units with considerable numbers of employees (e.g., S. Young 1989). Several characteristics justify conceiving private business as the structural continuation of a prerevolutionary informal hierarchy: as its sole aim is to create wealth, it is in opposition to the formal society, headed by bureaucracy, to which authority and privilege are decisive. It has developed an internal stratification, where social position carries increasing weight; employers and employees often belong to definitely distinguishable strata.[12] Furthermore, on both local and national levels it appears that private business and formal society enter into mutual exchange relations: intensified by the fact that a substantial number of the successful businessmen were formerly state employees, wealth, favors, privileges, and access to position flow between the two sectors of society through *guanxi* networks.

Thus representing "two streams" (*liangge chuan*), clearly distinguishable but mutually dependent and constructed around a common normative setup, formal and informal hierarchies may be appropriate terms. The stereotypical striving toward emancipation from manual labor is their common source, and they form separate paths to apparently identical goals: social ascendance and material satisfaction. One presupposes education, the other, skills and ingenuity. One is the ideal approach, the other, pragmatic. One is the conventional, the other, unorthodox and generally debased. The consequence is two opposed, or competing, entries to corresponding ends. They coincide in the fact that these ends are reached only through powerful positions: either the privileged, formal authority or the informal power operating through material wealth. Both are characterized by their principals' absolute authority and stretch downward in meticulously defined positions. They generate equally coveted values in compliance with Chinese ideals of the "good life" (*hao huo*) (figure 3).

FIGURE 3

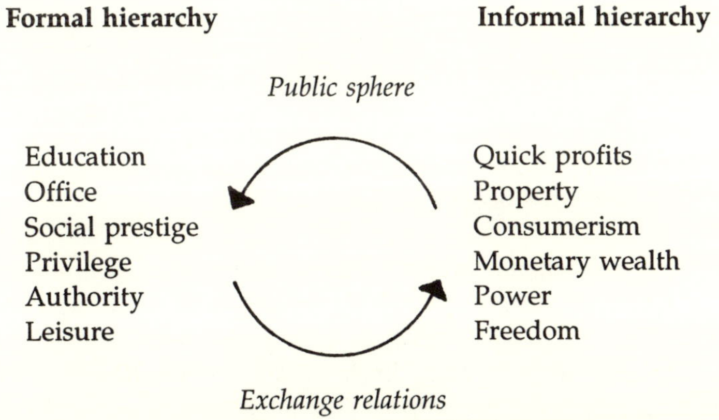

The formal hierarchy relies on the state *nomenklatura* system,[13] which reaches downward to embrace ordinary citizens. Varying bureaus and departments are allotted a number of given rank positions to comply with this universal structure. The informal hierarchy operates along lines of custom. Partly geographically determined, it places city dwellers over country people, it links up with social status in general, and it applies the power structure of the family. But it also involves highly dynamic relations. Ultimately determined by the ability to amass power, wealth, and connections, it has a wide range of people as potential principals and participants.

Chinese society is, and has apparently since ancient times always been, highly stratified. Even prolonged Communist rule has hardly achieved radical change in the basic components in Chinese social thought. Though Chinese society is stratified, it is becoming increasingly evident that the concept of class as expressed in Marxist theory (and repeated in sociological works on China) is alien to Chinese thought. Peasants were formerly stratified according to the size of their property, but among the urban population no concepts referred to class. Rather, the concept of *jieji*, before it was taken over by the Communists, was an ideographic compound referring to hierarchical positions. As Kuhn noted (1984):

> Originally, the ideograph "*jie*" seems to mean steps, like rungs on a ladder; and "*ji*" is the order or threads in a fabric. The term thus connotes hierarchical degrees on a continuum, rather than groups of people. (17)
>
> The idea of "*jieji*" as "rungs on a ladder" was still current when Liang Qichao first used the term in 1899. (18)
>
> So by the third decade of this century, Chinese thinkers were still having trouble relating the Western concept of class to their own sense of social organization. (19)

(This view has gained support among others, e.g., Schram 1984.) Behind Chinese concepts involving hierarchical relations lies the notion of change / transformation. In imperial times, social boundaries were not drawn along lines of relative wealth or poverty. Differences between rich and poor and between landlord and laborer were not understood as belonging to the eternal order of society. "The oscillation of family fortunes was accepted as a principle of heaven and earth" (Kuhn 1984:25). A number of sources support the assertion that traditional society was highly dynamic when viewed through the history of individual families (e.g., Ho 1962; Hu [1933] 1963).

If we return to the concept of dual hierarchies, the perpetual question of alliances along the lines of class arises, as countless writers, Chinese and foreign alike, still envisage the transformation of Chinese society in such terms.[14] Is the repression from state and Party authorities sufficiently effective to prevent the formation of genuine classes with articulate ideologies and aims? Why, for instance, do not small businesspeople form alliances to speak up against injustice and protect themselves against infringement? And why do not the employees in the larger businesses unionize to gain better wages and working conditions? On empirical grounds such notions must be rejected; nothing in the area of fieldwork indicated such attempts. Nor have anthropological fieldworkers registered significant "class consciousness" among workers in Hong Kong or Taiwan; quite the contrary: in the case of Taiwanese factory women, their "perceptions of work, . . . involve factors that go beyond the nature of the tasks they perform; and the satisfactions that they find in work derive in large part from the social context they themselves create" (Kung 1981:209). Usually, such work is regarded as merely an intermediate stage. In our local area, businesspeople who engaged in association work were well aware that their work was highly detrimental to common group interests, and rural laborers will remain loyal to their masters if just a crude material minimum is satisfied. Theories of unconscious subjugation to political domination through formalization of power (e.g., Bloch 1975) appear absurd considering both the conscious political actions involved in local petty bureaucracy and the calculating ideologies in the economic field. The explanation must be sought in terms of vertical loyalties rather than horizontal. The spontaneous hierarchization of social institutions results from the type of loyalties that are embedded in paternalism, consciously reproduced or further developed through the practice of *guanxi* cultivation — and a strong element of conscious competition is ever present. "Class" affiliation is only the immediate result of one's striving; internalized consciousness of affiliation to this particular step in a hierarchy of positions would be not only highly detrimental but also exceedingly provocative toward the collective life strategy of one's household (in line with the original meaning of *jieji*).

Chinese social hierarchies have a conspicuous spatial dimension. It is an important fact that social status in general terms make sense only when seen in relation to the space into which it is entrenched. Completeness is attained only when the spatial dimension of one's social position is satisfied. To quote Juri Croll on "traditional" (archaic) society:

> The laxity of social ties on the state level was reflected in the notion of a discrete space; it was thought of as compartmentalized, divided into heterogeneous sections of different value that were deemed the more valuable, the nearer to the most valuable part of space, the center, they were situated. Space was considered to be monocentric, its compartments forming a hierarchy. Its only center was identified with that of the world. (1989:2)

Spatial hierarchies are still manifest: the upward social mobility connected to migration to the city, running a business in the center of city, provincial government authorities situated in the exact center of Chengdu at the site of the former palace, and the social decline in any job assignments in the periphery all testify to its importance. Similarly, affiliation to a certain area may be a source of social affiliation; as we have seen, many elderly craftsmen and businessmen themselves originating in the countryside may seek apprentices from their native area, a source of dependable loyalty.

In Bin Shen a strong symbolic demarcation is seen between business and bureaucracy in terms of public appearance. Dress, manner of consumption, and modes of speech express clearly defined positions. But although structurally opposed, business and bureaucracy between themselves reveal a certain continuity. As one's identification lies with one's household rather than with profession and employment, the performance of individuals is more fruitfully seen in terms of the entire household. Few households seek simply to maintain their social standing. Against the background of an unpredictably changing society, a higher position is sought to increase the status of the household, much is allotted to security, and great emphasis is put on the education of children by all groups. The high number of business households engaging in the petty bureaucracy support the impression that basic ideological components are shared between business and bureaucracy.

Households in official employment and those in private business share consensus on essential values and life goals, although some households may be in better positions to realize such ideals. Thus, the separate hierarchical structures represent different paths to a common goal, along already proven and laid-out flows. They are socially sanctioned tracks for investing energy in order to compete for socially sanctioned ends. Thus they permit people to pursue superior positions without standing out too much.

Regarding overseas Chinese business communities, it was mentioned earlier that sociological analyses sometimes classify Chinese business as a universal organization across geographical space. Although its internal organization may correspond to such a pattern, however, there is a certain deviation in its outlook. It has been shown that values of business households, influenced by the "traditional" Chinese state, invariably incorporate formal position. By contrast, the dual hierarchical structure may dissolve under the influence of another type of state power, significantly weakening the orientation toward formal position and bureaucracy. The large Hong Kong, Taiwanese, and Singaporean commercial corporations are apparently independent, kingdomlike structures expressive of a rejection of the state as a source of prestige, although Taiwanese society, for instance, has developed a strong separation along ethnic lines between political power and commercial activity. Unsurprisingly, overseas Chinese business communities under non-Chinese state power have also either abandoned the state as a source of prestige or reproduce the images of formal society in a range of invented societies.

Dual Hierarchies and Modes of Speech

The structural validity of the dichotomy between formal and informal hierarchies may be qualified by another approach. While native Bin Sheners do not distinguish between separate hierarchies, they fully recognize the hierarchical structure of society at large, frequently in terms of "higher" (*shangmian*) or "lower" (*xiamian*) people. Yet when it comes to a career, the two main paths are fully recognized. The same is true in relation to modes of speech. The anthropological study of political language (the term is ethnocentric; it would be "speaking bureaucratic" in the vernacular) has come up with some points of specific interest regarding the creation and distribution of power. Maurice Bloch (1975) tended to see political culture as determining who is in authority and how he/she speaks; it formalizes vocabulary and style and supports the preservation of traditional authority, which of course is the source of social control. Behind Bloch's hypothesis of "unconsciously accepted authority" (3) apparently hides a dichotomy of "false" and "true" consciousness. By contrast, and in critique of Bloch, most recent writers are inclined to a softer view: they stress negotiation and interaction among differing modes of speech drawing on different powers, virtually developing into an idea of "society as discourse." Much fieldwork suggests that political oratory combines elements of formalization and creativity and also that political culture is tied to dichotomous modes of speech. Such modes may be exemplified by Tshidi politicians, who use both rigid formal speech and a different style, emphasizing their own personal qualities

(Comaroff 1975); by the switching between formal ideological speech and rational discussion that occurs in Kenyan bureaucratic communication (Parkin 1975); by the differences in Ilongot traditional "crooked" speech, which emphasizes individual creativity, and modern "straight" speech, the oratory of authoritarian hierarchy (Rosaldo 1973); and by a number of other native distinctions. Parkin (1984) summarizes such cases in critique of Bloch:

> As is clear from the above examples, it is the idea of fixity rather than its practice that most typifies oratory among most peoples. Or if there does exist a fixed style, then there is inevitably an alternative oratorical style which allows for more flexible and creative interpretive exchange between speaker and audience. To remain with the hypothesis that traditional political language stifles creativity and reinforces control comes dangerously close to a tautology: any speech style that deviates from this, or any audience response which is of questioning nature, can so easily cause us to assume that the form of oratory is nontraditional, perhaps no more than an innovation. (351)

In the preceding chapters I have recurrently referred to formal language usage in situations involving bureaucratic authority: ICB representatives' performance allegedly defending state and party interests, all local bureaus exercising authority over private businesses in similar terms, and association petty officials drawing on bureaucratic language in the encounter with fellow businesspeople. Formal language strictly refers to current policies of the Center: paraphrasing these denotes that the speaker draws, or intends to draw, on its authority. Thus the contents of "speaking bureaucratic" (*da guanqiang*) are inconstant and subordinate to form, which is preserved (there is no demand of internalized consistency with moral dictates, truth, remorse, and so forth, although this of course is a noncharacteristic). The conceptual use of *da guanqiang* marks its opposition to ordinary language (*kouyu*). However, by drawing on extralocal authority, bureaucratic language is not only in opposition to ordinary language, but also to speaking in proverbs (*chengyu*; in sets of four characters), which draws on other external sources: high Chinese literary tradition (endless ancient and new dictionaries of proverbs exist), coupled with the dynamically creative capacity of local community speakers. Proverbs are constantly invented or reshaped. Speaking in metaphorically rich proverbs is performatory art, but more than that. It correlates with alternative sources of authority by drawing on ancient wisdom, local historical experience, and common sense. Moreover, by relating to classical learning, it challenges the nonreflective bureaucratic language, which may use proverbs, but generally uncomplicated and ideologically purified ones emanating from the Center with simplified moral content rather than metaphor.

Proverbs constitute an institution in oratory as strong as the bureaucratic institution in social organization. Metaphorical/proverbial language runs conspicuously counter to current bureaucratic/political rhetoric. Whatever the subject of concern to ordinary people, it is bound to find expression through the immense stock of proverbs available in the vernacular. Proverbs directed toward public authorities certainly abound. Some mentioned earlier include "Big fish eats small fish, small fish eats shrimp," "When the gods fight, the people suffer," and "The officials burn houses, while the commoners are not allowed to burn oil lamps." One that has been particularly condemned by the regime is the Confucian "Those who work with the mind rule, those who work with their brawn are ruled" (chap. 4, n. 6). But although proverbs were earlier aimed at local officials' ruthless behavior, they have since the Liberation increasingly been directed toward authorities of a more abstract type. One proverb created after the Liberation was "The Nationalist party (Guomindang) imposed many taxes, the Communist party (Gongchandang) imposes many meetings" — in recent years amended to run "The Communist party imposes many taxes and many meetings."

Equal to formal language, proverbs have a strong moral tone, but they oppose formal oratory by viewing hierarchies from below. It is significant that both forms of oratory refer to the lowest levels, whence they derive their legitimacy: formal language refers to the "will of the masses" and the "dictatorship of the proletariat," simultaneously expressed through a neocanonic literature; proverbs, drawing on a Confucian conception, refer to moral behavior toward the masses. We find that the construction of "reason" incorporates canonic tradition, which may appeal to emotions as much as to intellect, to heart as much as to head, or even to chains of associations. It may further be suggested that any exercise of power or authority takes as a prerequisite an explicit reference to the common good of the household, the community, or the masses — and such references belong to a common stock of symbolic language. Evidently, the dichotomous phenomena of which modes of speech are expressive are complementary aspects of a single reality.

While informal talk invariably involves metaphors, formal speech tends to operate through symbols and metonymes (another concept used by Robert Paine [1981] is "enthymeme," signifying a condensed statement, leaving something unstated [13]). To quote Paine (1981) on the political aspects of metonymes:

> Metaphor . . . is the trope of development and extension of thought; metaphor breaks old boundaries. At the same time metaphor is widely recognized as evoking similarity. . . . it is often an unexpected similarity that is evoked . . . it is partial similarity, . . . but not similarity itself. Such incompleteness, again, is a source of some of the power of metaphor; . . . If metaphor affords perspective, metonyme is a process of reduction. . . . Whereas metaphor is an instrument in the development of a language of ideas, metonymy transposes the intangible back into the tangible so that, for example, "emotions" become "heart", and "shame" becomes "a movement of the eye" . . . I suggest therefore that the first "mission" of metonyme is, contrary to that of metaphor, to withhold the slip into change. (188–89)

Although metonymy should not exclusively be identified with the language of power and vice versa (and switches between metonyme and metaphor are of course attempted frequently), the strong content of metonyme in formal language points to a structural opposition: it seems warranted to infer that Chinese bureaucratic language in its pure form is counteracted by another mode of speech. Thus, "speaking in proverbs" can play the role of the oppositional component in political oratory, related to the space of informal power.

Modes of speech denote specific types of relationships and the pursuit of specific ends and have a certain connection to dual sources of power. It is not, however, beneficial to pin persons to specific positions within such structure; rather than confining individuals to strata, they depict differentiated situations of predominantly hierarchical relations: a midranking official may use different combinations of speech modes when wanting to express his loyalty and subordination to his superior, when emphasizing his authority over his inferior, or when confronting businesspeople. Thus the tropes contained in speech modes belong to a repertoire; rather than implying strict classification, particular tropes belong to particular points of departure toward a common field of exchange relations.

When defining an informal hierarchy in which political oratory is a factor in the distribution of power, I assume spontaneous, or at least extrabureaucratic, local organization. Forced into the straitjacket of state- and Party-controlled organizations, people have little space left to realize alternatives. "Politics" as competing ideologies is absent; there are many potential speakers, and there is an audience when the association assembles, but the two are effectively cut off from each other. As Paine noted (1981), propaganda is rejected rhetoric; while propaganda may be propositional, the audience doubts the sincerity of the speaker. In the unrestricted teahouse conversation, in the uncontrollable small gatherings of businesspeople, and in all *guanxi* relations, the use of antiformal metaphorical language may be associated with moral trustworthiness and reliability in transactions. Since all reference to literary learning is a source of social prestige, drawing on such in ordinary speech is an aspect of Center-periphery and rural-urban distinctions and has considerable bearing on occupational classifications. In building up local family reputation, drawing on literary learning as contained in proverbs is also significant. Returning to Bloch, it is of course true for the Chinese case that formal status arrangements tend to predetermine everything, but formalized political language itself has little capacity for domination; linguistic domination depends entirely on a strong apparatus of social domination, not as Bloch sees it as drawing its power from culture itself. Moreover, concerning the current views of rhetoric as devoted to persuasion or to negotiation between speaker and audience (Paine 1981:1) through the construction of "meaning," Chinese bureaucratic language in its current form is difficult to place within these concepts. For many locals, its simple efficacy in a total sense has priority over persuasion and conviction. To develop this issue, we now examine the final dichotomy.

Ideal versus Social Practice

When discussing the tension between convention and actual behavior, one is of course moving closer to the individual and also reaching the limits of the domestic group perspective, since such discrepancies belong to a sphere of Chinese culture that tends to abide in inarticulate convolution — not that this inconsistency is greater than what is experienced elsewhere, but it is indeed profound in Chinese society when viewed from the outside. Yet an internal analysis is maintained; this dichotomy may be said to go beyond the domestic group perspective, and it certainly fulfills the criterion of local recognition: a vast number of people in the fieldwork area pointed to such a discrepancy from various angles and with different phrases and terminologies.

The phenomenon of the elevated Chinese ideal, as expressed in both spoken and written language (and covering both bureaucratic and ordinary speech), and its varying degrees of application to social practice have been underlying themes throughout the present study. Various phenomena are expressive of this discrepancy, which penetrates practically all levels of social life.

To recapitulate: At the political level a number of dissimilarities between proclaimed government policy and local reality in Bin Shen have been noted: business households must struggle for social acceptance in spite of the fact that central media praise them, licenses are issued to others than those intended, the young are not very prominent among established businesspeople, legalization of business tends to follow local rule of custom, extensive exchange relations between business and bureaucracy counteract the rule of law propagated by central government, and so forth. The role of local bureaucracy in particular departs from the picture created by official rhetoric in that a profound legal relativism prevails, frequently expressive of the cadres' personal interests. Moreover, in contrast to formal policy, the *guanxi* relations are all-important for economic activities and the entire structure of the local community. On the level of local community interaction, private businesses frequently present themselves similarly. A formal conformity appears to be crucial. Businesses pretend to observe standards of hygiene and to be almost ritually concerned about cleanliness, operate according to the slogan of "serving others," and in general give the appearance of obedience to regulations and bureaucracy. A large number of households engage in association "social work" in the name of the common good. Formal language with reference to such ideals is used in a number of defined situations involving public appearance and the competition for authority and privileges. On the household level, a focal question arises: What is the Chinese family? and accordingly, Is there anything called family business? Contrasts are conspicuous: The opposition between male formal authority and female informal power is often seen in business activities and frequently in actual financial control. Demanding work is often left to women despite the fact that convention ascribes it to men. Real-life families are of great variety and frequently incorporate relatives or even strangers to restore form. Unsuccessful elderly people especially are frequently neglected by their children. Through formal conformity is expressed a strong adherence to an ideal state of things that may never be within reach. However, adherence to common ideals tends to be a matter of absoluteness, allowing for no deviating interpretations. In a certain sense, family integrity correlates to high social position and wealth. The ideal form is either continuously striven for or entirely abandoned; some households on the fringe of society reject the common ideals altogether.

A clear historical dimension to such contrasts may be found in literary sources, their universal dimension apart. In an interesting volume, two Chinese historians offer a novel interpretation of the process of historical change in China (Pong and Fung 1985). They have chosen "Ideal and Reality" as the title that binds the individual essays together:

> This volume, . . . aims at providing a fresh perspective on modern Chinese history. In general terms, it focuses on the ideals and aspirations of people in and out of government and on how these people tried to further their objectives. By studying the interplay between ideal and reality in each case, the chapters collectively shed new light on the period 1860–1949 and contribute to a better understanding of the forces that subsequently helped shape China. (1)
>
> In a larger sense, efforts at national reconstruction after 1949 can be subsumed under the quest for wealth and power and for reducing the gap between ideal and reality to a tolerable level — goals pursued by successive governments since 1860. . . . It is our belief that the gap between the two holds one of the keys to understanding the broad sweep of modern Chinese history. (4)

Speculating that the ideal and reality will act upon each other like yin and yang, the authors turn their attention to central concepts applied to political and social change. They argue that the Chinese response to foreign influence, aggression, superiority, and the like in the midnineteenth century was idealistically conveyed. Through the revival of ancient concepts and the creation of new ones with traditional connotations, the officials in power aimed at moral rearmament: self-strengthening (*ziqiang*), reform (*gaige*), search for wealth and power (*fuqiang*), restoration of a sense of national grace (*guochi*), regeneration (*zizhen*), and cultivation of useful talents (*shiyong zhi cai*) (25ff.). Their concepts are not necessarily Confucian, although Confucianism may have been a main carrier of the gap between ideas and practice (Bodde 1981:291), but they all reveal essentially Chinese notions: reform without change of structure, restoring the lost dignity of the Middle Kingdom (to which the writers Pong and Fung also adhere by stating that after the Four Modernizations China is "finally and firmly set on a path to wealth and power"), and the grace found in tradition — all idealistic conceptual tools operating at the level of commonly recognized values. The depiction of a glorious past, which is projected into the future, leaves the present social reality merely a vaguely defined intermediate stage. What is of specific interest here, however, is that most of these concepts are also directly applicable to family organization.

The early anthropology of China noted the collective reference to "ideal culture." Francis Hsu writing on his West Town (1948) points out that "actual life . . . may differ considerably from these socially upheld norms. The differences are, naturally, more apparent in the more well-defined relationships than in others" (64). Consequently, the most clearly defined types of relations deviated most significantly from their ideal state: the relationship between father and son was one of identification and mutual dependency rather than one of absolute authority, and the unconditional obedience that wives should show their husbands was contrasted with their various informal powers; a large number of uxorilocally married husbands actually held a position in the household no higher than that usually ascribed to a daughter-in-law. It is significant that such local deviations did not affect the general adherence to high Chinese norms.

Turning to modern society, we see that the various levels of social interaction — family, neighborhood, local community, and so forth up to the state level — all involve defined relationships that tend to imply strongly idealized models for conduct, making the distinction between the convergent and divergent, and ultimately between good and evil, a matter of accurate definition.

Principal Relationships

As a unified force, the elevation of ideals concerning the principal relationships is a perpetual trend in the life of ordinary Chinese. In a pure, personalized form, ideals are transmitted from childhood; they occur as dutiful children, devoted students, self-sacrificing parents, rightful masters, and visionary sages. Later they appear as model workers and model cadres, selfless revolutionary heroes, cultural heroes, modernization heroes, kings, and emperors.[15] The deification of humans is a perennial aspect of Chinese religion. Ideals are ever-present in Chinese proverbs. The public media exploit them endlessly — in social and moral affairs, in production and politics, in sports and cultural life. Whenever a point is emphasized, it is in strongly moral terms attached to one such figure. These personalized carriers of virtue are the advocates of convention.

That the personalized ideals are not necessarily truthful representatives of this world, and may not even be depicted as such, emerges from the disciplinary function they administer. They set forth the example to follow, but simultaneously they insinuate a secondary message: their immaculately pure form that precludes interpretation and their unswerving adherence to virtue suggest that the attitude toward offenders is implacable. Within the family, in school, in work units, and in public life, the respective authorities in principle demand conformity as expressed through such ideal behavior. Thus these authorities enjoy the privilege of making use of their powers to any extent they deem justified.

The concordance or discordance between ideal and practice for these reasons does not form a continuum of possibilities. The all-embracing ideal of family organization, as, for instance, expressed in Confucianism, is the patriarchally headed and strictly patrilineal group, encompassing five generations. The Confucian Five Relations (*wu lun*) for all basic relations in society also contain the sacred five in number. Five generations under one roof is of course exceedingly rare. But the model of the family as encompassing all generations in the male line persists, although practiced by a mere minority. The traditional Chinese family has also seemingly been a highly dynamic unit in its size and composition, depending not least on economic circumstances.[16] In terms of control, the position of women has often been overlooked (Parish and Whyte 1978:200ff.; Ebrey and Watson 1986:274ff.); the financial control that women commonly exert may be only the most conspicuous of their powers. Some argue that traditional society was virtually ruled by women, especially elderly women, as family despots (Hu [1933] 1963:4). Moreover, it has been noted that the Communist organization of society may have reduced the informal influence of women (e.g., Parish and Whyte 1978:242). If this was the case, then the tendency has probably been reversed in recent years; there are indications that women now have significant powers through private business, high-paying jobs, and the like. As for the composition of households, present fieldwork shows that those in private business are based on a high degree of social and economic pragmatism compared with common descent: "family" relations contain dynamic elements that under special circumstances allow for radical deviation. In regard to distribution of labor, "convention" and reality seem far apart (in agriculture, too, the distribution of manual labor tends to be in favor of males[17]). The filial piety emphasized in the Chinese ethos is frequently violated. The reverence toward family elders tends apparently to diminish with physical distance, when "face" is not threatened.

Similar patterns can be found to varying degrees at other levels of social interaction. The secretive Party organization operating in the name of the masses is presumably the successor to imperial bureaucracy operating in the name of Confucian morality. At the state level, the proclaimed civil rights including freedom of speech are invalidated by the ruling four principles (chap. 5, n. 8). Many more phenomena with immediate relevance to daily life could be listed.

As social practice is frequently contrasted with idealized conduct or, to put it differently, as social practice deviates from the prescribed, it progressively enters a space of nondefinition, naturally open to manipulation (for instance, by referring to other items of idealized conduct, counteracting the first). Defined relationships belonging to separate levels may be contradictory. To return to a local example of the family versus state polarity, in which a number of such contradictions are obvious: while an association petty official naturally takes an interest in his family, of which he is the head and for which he is economically responsible, the commonly upheld ideal of affectionately doing social work for state and local community authorities draws him away from home for long hours, frequently spent in socializing. As labor is needed in business, rural employees are used, or even exploited, to substitute for the petty official's own work along with that of other family members. In case of conflict, he can use the association to excuse himself in his household and his household responsibilities to excuse himself when confronted with the demands of the association. The dictates of "convention" may be mutually neutralizing, leaving ample space for individual action. Similarly, the ideal for a woman to be a "good wife and loving mother" (*xian qi liang mu*) emphasizing domestic duties may stand in a similar relationship to general expectations regarding her economic activities. A practice of leaving large areas to be his or her "own business" (e.g., Hsu, 1948, chap.3; also confirmed by present fieldwork) neutralizes tight marital control, especially when economic matters are involved.

In many instances, ordinary language tends not to cover deviating practices. On the contrary, in direct communication a frequent reaction to deviating behavior will be to use phrases that progressively emphasize social ideals, thus acting in a symmetric relation to observed reality. One can also refer to the incident as *not* something: not good, not right, nonconformist, antisocial, counterrevolutionary, and so forth, depending on people and circumstances. The parallel between family and state organization is pronounced also in this respect. As they both rest on a morally founded authoritarian leadership, which normally judges inside the moral dichotomy of good or bad, open contradiction will never be tolerated. Response to the exercise of authority will either be to praise the ideal by expressing conformity verbally or to let it pass in silence. We may suggest that not only formal language but also any other verbal communication to a large degree refers to defined relationships, which constitute established categories of thought and action. Consequently, conformity and submission are verbalized, whereas deviation and defiance tend to be nonverbal.

Other conditions must be considered when looking at language as an exponent for idealized behavior. Language tends to follow the formal/informal distinction already discussed; it points to the well-defined boundaries between use inside the family and in the outer world, between use toward individuals of higher rank and toward those at one's own level. To a certain degree, it corresponds to social categories in society at large, although not to be comprehended as classes. Application of formal language tropes thus expresses recognition of hierarchical organizations and sharp demarcations in social interaction. Some local thinkers in the fieldwork area pointed to three different types of language: what one uses toward very high ranking officials, what one uses toward smaller officials, and what people use among their equals. This variation implies that confronting officials necessitates skills in the proper vocabulary and style, skills that commonly presuppose education and/or charisma (charisma is itself generally drawn from accomplished education). Linguistic relativism is the consequence both of these demarcations and of the use of certain language as expressing submission to authority. For any discussion of social ideals, the role of the Chinese language is significant.[18]

Turning to the concept of "tradition," we see the common social ideals manifesting themselves again. In Chinese civilization, "tradition" (*chuantong*) is closely linked to "culture/cultured" (*wenhua*), in the sense that they are both seen to be upheld primarily through education. Thus tradition is to be seen as the purified ideal, the model for perfectly cultured behavior, unattainable in itself, but still the cardinal point around which the dynamics of social practices move. Also in regard to space, tradition presumably represents an abstraction alone. Rather than being high culture radiating from the Center, tradition is constructed from the unifying ideals, neither central nor local, but present anywhere as an indispensable element of the Chinese language. In an extreme interpretation, language as the mediator between ideal and practice may itself be an important ingredient in the continuous reproduction of a cultural center.

Tradition and convention unambiguously define what is Chinese and what is not. They classify certain phenomena into a strongly coherent conceptualization of "Chineseness" (here used as what is Chinese in an abstract sense) and reject other phenomena as belonging to other unspecified nationalities and areas. In this interpretation, Chineseness is a coherent scheme of defined relationships, not unlike the old five *wu lun*. Social and physical phenomena that do not fulfill the ideals for Chineseness are ascribed to the outside world in a scheme of geocharacteristics (which is the root of widespread xenophobia). This scheme tends to further enlarge the discrepancy between ideal and practice; it purifies the ideal rather than confronts practice. It places Chineseness as the axis for moral behavior, contrasted with the morally impoverished world without. Thus evil doing and demoralizing behavior are easily ascribed to non-Chinese influence; the victims of such influence can be distinguished as a group and by simple transcription turned into scapegoats for the entire community — for instance, when the distinction between modernization and Westernization is derived.

Further reference to local Bin Shen life may give substance to this axiom. When businesspeople express idealized intentions toward the outside world to protect themselves, it should in no way be perceived as a deliberate strategy specially adopted for the occasion. Endless incidents analogous to such public expression are contained in ordinary Chinese family life (presumably one of its roots). When children grow up and seek greater independence, this pattern of expression is extremely common. What needs to be protected from the controlling interest of parents is skillfully transcripted into idealized behavior. "I just tell them what they want to believe; it makes them satisfied," as one girl said about her explanation to her parents when they inquired about her performance in school. She seldom actually attended school, but instead did business with a friend. Often such transcription of reality serves as a respite, until the unpleasant message has gradually been delivered and the actual state of affairs revealed. Another example from family life is more controversial. A girl married a Hong Kong engineer and went to live with his family in Hong Kong. After the first excitement of living in Hong Kong had cooled off, her marriage ran into trouble. Her husband exploited her weak position, far removed from her home, and in addition took advantage of his own position toward other women. After just six months, she left her husband and went to live alone. In the following period, she often went back to live with her own family for a number of weeks at a time. Whenever her marriage was mentioned she pretended to live an ideal married life in Hong Kong. The individual family members were gradually informed about the breakup of the marriage, first one sister, then the next, and then her mother. Her father, the old patriarch, was the last to be informed indirectly about the state of affairs. But even after this, several months passed in which everyone gathered around the dining table and talked as if her marriage were still in effect, asking after her husband and so on, well aware that everyone present knew the real situation.

Personal Relations

The concept of *guanxi* and the use of *guanxi* for exchange purposes clearly belong to the practical strategies of everyday life, distinct from the defined relationships of ideal culture. It is important that *guanxi* relations encompass all relationships outside the defined categories of family and kinship and are therefore matters of everyday life. *Guanxi* commonly runs along nonfamily lines of given relations: schoolmates (*tongxue*), colleagues (*tongshi*), same locality (*tongxiang*), or same country if abroad (*tongbao*) are all relations of natural *guanxi*. It is implied, however, that people share something either in the past or at a lower level of geographical space than where they meet. Former classmates have natural *guanxi* when they meet in a new setting, for instance, in a work unit, and people from a certain village have natural *guanxi* when they meet in the city. *Guanxi* emphasizes the logic of the situational context. As noted, all acquaintances people may have outside the family are *guanxi*, without distinction between friendly relations and those of potential utilitarian value. Chinese personal relations are commonly characterized by instrumentalism.[19] Similarly, a common neutral phrase for inquiring about the link between two persons will be "What is their *guanxi*?" meaning anything from dubious connections to ordinary friendly relations. Thus the argument that all casual outward relations are potentially useful *guanxi* would not be far from the point; they are governed by objective rather than subjective considerations. *La guanxi* — to pull *guanxi* — is the term for exploiting these particularistic relations for special personal ends. Virtually everyone has networks (*guanxiwang*) involving other individuals or households (*guanxihu*) in mutual help (*huli*) relations. Reciprocity is explicitly contained in the concept of *baoda* — reciprocal assistance.

Guanxi is not only the notion that some connection may become useful; it is a distinct strategy of employing informal instead of prescribed channels. It is used by everyone in all walks of society; what distinguishes elite from mass society is merely elite society's access to "good *guanxi*" (*hao guanxi*), not the actual exercise. As *guanxi* is perceived as reciprocal, it follows that access to *guanxi* commonly implies personal assets to exchange: powerful position, privilege, and wealth. But unreturned favors are often seen; apparently the ability to grant favors is associated with power, and prestige can be drawn from it. The whole complex of informal channels behind the facade of egalitarian mass organizations is probably the most essential feature of Chinese society, without which "things could not be done."

Ordinary citizens do not address public authorities unless they have *guanxi* within their offices, or, the other way round, people will make sure that they establish *guanxi* if they need public service. But even though high social status has fallen out of step with material wealth, status is still an important factor in determining at what level *guanxi* relations may be established. In the fieldwork area few businesspeople would contact the local bureaus unless circumstances forced them to do so — when renewing licenses, for instance. Notions that such contact involves danger persist. Still, a few of the well-educated in the area actually made such contact, not only confronting local bureaucracy, but even venturing to address higher bureaus. The self-confidence that, for instance, the local doctor and the plastic container–producing engineer express is rooted in their assets as university graduates. To know someone of high education is in itself good *guanxi* regardless of the person's ability to make use of his or her position; it rests in the simple assumption that social position equates with power. Therefore the better educated will under normal circumstances enjoy more freedom than others in the local community (which may count for the animosity toward them shown by central authorities, who regard them as a potential danger).

Summary: The Dialectics of Local Life

A synthesis of household strategies may now be established by extracting common features in Bin Shen. Household strategies have been depicted as a conglomerate of various considerations, contradictions, and compromises, merging into what represents itself as a unified strategy in the household's outer appearance — all held together by paternalist norms and the ideal of family relations being in harmony. When apparently dichotomous phenomena are placed against their wider background, they become aspects of social processes, passing through stages of divergence and convergence and alternating between contradiction and unification over basic cultural features — complementary aspects, as it were, of a single reality.

A dialectical analysis of the empirically derived major contradictions in local community has been attempted. But it is questionable whether they are in fact contradictions. Are they merely a frame of reference, marking the outer edges of defined "Chineseness"? Or do they, in both verbal and nonverbal forms, determine the "rules of the game" regarding how to acquire the largest share of given resources within the Chinese normative universe? Tension between the distinctly normative morals and social practice is evident. Within this it appears that "tradition," "convention," and "things Chinese" are interpreted or manipulated to create the widest space for individual action: the more closely such concepts are defined from the outside, the more they dissolve into pragmatic pursuits, revolving around the competition for wealth and authority, materialized into visible social superiority. "Tradition" is definitely an abstraction, covering dynamic rationalization in a given set of circumstances.

Values are essentially dual, referring either to high cultured ideals or informal practices, relating either to the unspoken, quick material gains or to cultured conformity to prestigious social pursuits. Between them a rational adaptation to the modernizing society, or virtually any society, is possible: predominance of one is redressed by emphasis on the other in a search for a social/material equilibrium. Within this framework, totality is a key concept in any labor or household strategy. Household strategies of families in structurally different positions tend to converge: business and bureaucracy alike merely represent means of attaining the good life. Both successful business and bureaucratic office are key power positions for exchange relations. High culture and the world of "traditional" ideals consist of defined relationships in a dynamic perception. Both family authority and external positions are streamlike structures, in which, as prescribed by convention, the individual may be carried through all hierarchical positions. A series conception of social structures is predominant, contributing to the activist, positive approach to life.

The ultimate goal of any labor or household strategy is freedom from toil and the achievement of a superior position. The means are unfaltering social alertness and activism. Long-term strategies are applied to all fields relating to "Chineseness": genealogical goals, formal education and position, attaining high social esteem, and so forth. In contrast, nondefined relations are characteristic of the informal society, and short-term strategies are typically applied here: business quickly set up, frequently abandoned, and reestablished for maximization. Seen in a domestic group perspective, socializing is business, and business is socializing. Pure and simple economic interaction is nonexistent. Simultaneous multilevel communication is invariably present and intensifies competition. Similarly, any interaction is evaluated socially, resulting in the personalization of economic life.

Compared to other types of approaches to Chinese studies, the anthropological approach is of course ambitious; but rather than pretending to reveal any absolute facts or positivistic truths about China as may be the intentions in, for instance, sinological or sociological approaches, only a single facet has been presented here: a piece of the complex mosaic of contemporary Chinese society.

CHAPTER NINE

Conclusion

As I mentioned in chapter one, over the course of my fieldwork the local people gradually became good friends and eventually felt free to request that I grant them the favor of speaking for them in return for their openness and hospitality. Although this scholarly study does not permit such taking sides politically with the individual households, it is still hoped that the account of their situation — under the sway of a monolithic state, exploited by a corrupt bureaucracy, and amid a society in ceaseless turbulence — will in itself serve their cause.

It has been the aim of the present study to contribute to empirical accounts of contemporary Chinese society, accounts sorely needed in the social sciences. An anthropological approach to local society was followed — that is, local society was viewed through its basic institutions. Although the study is based on direct contact with the people of the fieldwork area during long periods and often intimate relationships and making use of observation, interviews, dinners, banquets, ordinary visits, and just being in the area, it was never possible to reside in the neighborhood. The anthropologist's calling upon the residents, rather than both parties being in equal position to call spontaneously, naturally hampered leisurely communion. Still, the freedom enjoyed during the research was extensive and somehow unexpected. The study is one of citydwellers, carried out by a citydweller.

To avoid the anthropological "village syndrome," it was found imperative to involve institutions representing wider society. Thus the present work differs markedly from field accounts depicting Chinese villages as totalities or accounts based on interviews with groups of emigrants from a specific rural area. Although an empirical study of individual households, it involved a wide perspective in order to contemplate the constitution of social esteem, values, and ambitions, all with reference to the unifying aspects of Chinese culture. Consequently, to reach a fuller understanding of the complexities influencing the lives of ordinary households, both local bureaucracy and the Chinese state were drawn in. Following this approach, the inquiry had to embrace several dimensions. If the reemergence of dual hierarchies and the related socio-spatial categories represented one dimension of local society, another dimension clearly revealed social transformation, sustained by some entrepreneurial segments as well as the young in general.

These two dimensions accurately pinpoint the seeming paradox in which the Western view of contemporary China is easily caught. We observe a society that is returning to conventional structures — in, for instance, its patriarchal economic organization, the power abuse of its bureaucracy, and the state temporarily retreating to a laissez-faire role — and is simultaneously being thrown into a formidable process of transition — in fact, a genuine revolution, though still unnamed. In the meantime, a reinterpretation of values is taking place. Whether this marks a return to traditional values or a shift to new ones is a matter of definition: as has been demonstrated, the concept of "tradition" tends to be abstract in the context of social life, as it generally refers to "ideal" culture or "ideal" behavior, representing the unifying model rather than social realities. Thus a wide range of value interpretations is possible; they can be articulated or manipulated in multiple ways, all of which allow "tradition" to be upheld and remain Chinese in character.

Therefore, although Chinese society in this transitional period has revealed trends strikingly similar to what keen observers like J. J. M. de Groot, Arthur Smith, and Max Weber depicted at the end of the dynastic period, one must not commit the fallacy of ascribing these phenomena to an abstract and inconclusive "tradition," whether ascribed to Confucianism, Chineseness, the dynastic legacy, or Chinese historical socialist predispositions. Tradition per se must be rejected by the social sciences as an explanatory determinant: contemporary Chinese society consists of contemporary social institutions, rooted in the socialization process of their present individual actors. Bearing this in mind, the observer may be able to free him- or herself from the blinding ideological disputes that have restrained Chinese studies for decades. Still, both history and tradition provide us with patterns that are suggestive for the study of contemporary social institutions — and vice versa: our knowledge of contemporary society may even inspire reinterpretation of Chinese history.

Summarizing my empirical findings, first I noted the spontaneous reemergence of pre-Liberation socioeconomic forms of organization in Bin Shen: the Chinese household as the unit of business, presenting the main alternative to formal employment. A number of the present entrepreneurial households are merely resuming activities that were interrupted at the Great Leap Forward; artisan households especially were strongly represented among these. However, as household businesses predominated in the pre-Liberation economic structure of the area, as well as of Chengdu at large, the majority of the present business households had in their recent history some connection to business. Just as the concepts of household (*hu*) and family (*jia*) are frequently used synonymously, household structure builds on family structure, which is extended to embrace the rural apprentices and employees in hierarchical relations. It was also noted that the existing Chinese "family" tends to be a highly adaptive unit, moving between ideal and functional patterns, even able to replace missing members with nonrelatives to restore form.

Individual business households in the area of study can hardly be said to offer any separate lifestyle, ideology, or organized alternative in relation to formal society. Comprising a wide range of people and enterprises, the individual sector exists primarily as a negatively defined, nonpublic category. It exists within a society with a monolithic stamp and with very limited tolerance of deviation. If particular patterns can be identified in regard to the way private entrepreneurs think of themselves, it is a question of reacting to a common influence rather than sharing a common identity. In a wider perspective, the economic ideologies enacted in the individual sector do not distinguish themselves significantly from what is typical of mainstream Chinese society. The powerful aspirations of the Chinese household toward social ascendance make the formal and informal sectors signify sources of values and types of strategies. The respective sectors rarely determine the individual's identity and certainly do not signify a permanent economic affiliation. In the macroperspective, the growth of individual business is thus more truly depicted as an effect of economic circumstances, calling for new solutions, rather than an expression of radically changing values. Both sectors of society share the basic notions of totality and order, expressed through strategies that relate to a golden mean. Conformity requires the conscious balancing of seemingly contradictory endeavors and taking care never to reach out further than one's backing permits.

On the level of fundamental institutions, a dichotomy with reference to the unifying aspects of Chinese culture was derived: family and state as the all-embracing idealized abstractions. In a historical perspective these ethically and conceptually interrelated organizations have evidently alternated in the decline of one and simultaneous ascendance of the other. The four decades since the founding of the People's Republic have been marked by the unprecedented rise to power and authority of the Chinese state, a centralized and monopolized authority that in principle only continued the ideals of previous dynasties but in practice went far beyond by enlarging its domain to embrace every institution in society. Although the latest reforms have lessened control in some spheres of life, they have also brought new central authorities into close contact with local life. On a grand scale, the efforts of the Chinese state toward moral rearmament, idealistically perceived reform, and strengthened authority are continued: economic liberalization is prompted while political structure is preserved. As Chinese patriarchal authorities tend to demand absolute submission, possible reactions to them fall within a limited repertoire: formal obedience, turning away in silent defiance, or open revolt.

Local authorities such as the Street Committee, Public Security Office, Tax Bureau, and the Self-employed Laborers Association still impose considerable social control on individual business households and in that respect work in extension of Party and government interests; presumably there is a strong coincidence of interests here between higher and lower levels. This is not the case in matters relating to the local departments' own key interests, in which their combination of relative autonomy and undisputed authority have a very different outcome. Giving free play for lawless entrepreneurship among both bureaucrats and businesspeople and thereby providing formidable obstacles to the implementation of the open market society as propounded by the state, bureaucracy is in itself a major force in the reproduction of "tradition." However, because a large number of people actually involve themselves in the local bureaucracy, a clear division between ordinary citizens and bureaucrats does not exist. Rather, the character of Chinese state power concurs with the apparent steadfastness of traditional bureaucracy, which again may be said to coincide with vital aspects of household ideology.

As has been demonstrated, household business ideology inevitably relates to the total situation of the household and the aggregate social and economic capital of all its members. Thus the household and its collective endeavor is the relevant unit of analysis. From this viewpoint, it is clear that the state sector, or formal hierarchy, is equally important to a private business household and any other household in its focal role of championing social values and providing ideals for collective ambitions.

While the private sector, for a number of years, has primarily contained groups that, in a social sense, could be branded as marginal, recent developments suggest that this is no longer the case. Equally important for the interflow and interdependence between state and private sectors is that the vast majority of businesspeople of the older generation were earlier in life employees of state and collective units, just as the majority of young now joining the individual sector have entertained clear ambitions of state employment. But of principal importance is that private business, or as it has been termed here, the "informal hierarchy," is analyzed as a socioeconomic "strategic space" rather than as clearly stipulated categories and groups of people; this conceptualization corresponds to the outlook of the Chinese household. In the modernization process, all forms of private business play crucial roles in providing "space" for the formation of new ideologies and facilitating the spontaneous development of new forms of social organization. In this respect private business has indeed the potential for accomplishing what mass campaigns earlier aimed at in modernizing social institutions but were never able to carry through.

During the period of study, individual business was in relative terms becoming increasingly attractive to people in the fieldwork area and presumably to urban residents in general, although corruption rose accordingly. The individual sector was joined by an increasing number of ordinary state and collective workers who definitively severed their ties to their former units. Their breaking off from the tightly organized *danwei* constitutes a significant trend in the structure of Chinese urban society. And as seen among the young, it has sown seeds of rebellion against the monolithic state. Along with other movements in urban society, the continuous growth of private business all over China has contributed to the end of an era in Chinese history.

Although the events in the spring of 1989 temporarily halted the expansion of the private sector, neither government nor businesspeople dwelled on them for long. After a pause, new growth in private business was evident, and the slow process of its destigmatization also recommenced. With Deng Xiaoping's tour to the south in early 1992 came the final breakthrough after much accumulated uncertainty. His comments on the benefits of using capitalist methods in the economy, though only sporadically reported in the Chinese media, were regarded as a landmark in the further liberalization of the economy and for millions of people the signal to go ahead. Leaving government departments and research institutes almost entirely deserted, scores of state employees went out to attend to private projects. Deng's remarks were apparently given more weight than the Fourteenth Party Congress in October 1992, which confirmed the full-scale transfer to a market economy and finally gave the blue stamp of approval to "capitalist methods" in the economy. In the state sector these events sparked new sayings such as "You either change your ideas or you change your position." Afterward the political climate in China was intensely focused on growth through a complete transfer to a market economy. In the gross liberalization of the economy, even the Communist party is getting a new role in society: local branches are now instructed to go out and teach market economy to peasants and workers. In spite of the momentum that private enterprise presently has gained, there is no reason to believe that the established pattern of alternating laissez-faire policy and intervention has dissolved. Moreover, private enterprise will hardly replace the state, even though it takes a new guise and adopts a new language of power, as the ultimate focus for social orientations, which remain as being toward Center, social competition, and formal authority.

Notes

Authorities present in Bin Shen area:

Industrial and Commercial Administration Bureau (Gong Shang Ju)
Self-employed Laborers Association (Geti Laodongzhe Xiehui)
Street Committee (Jiedao Banshi Cu)
Neighborhood Committee (Jumin Weiyuan Hui)
Tax Bureau (Shuiwu Suo)
Police Station (Gongan Ju)
Public Security Local Office (Paichu Suo)

Notes to Chapter One

1. This is not to exclude any other type of fieldwork aiming at a thorough investigation of the household's affairs — for instance, the "guerrilla interviewing" among small businesspeople outlined by Thomas Gold (1989a). Even systematic interviewing of households may be conducted within a homogeneous selection of neighborhoods or villages, with one or two picked in each place. However, in the delicate balance between bureaucratic authority and private enterprise the local society often adopt creative solutions or develop original substructures that neither is prone to reveal.
2. When this was later revealed to me, it brought to my mind an old book by a British consul to China, who in the 1880s found that a sedan chair was a sine qua non when visiting public authorities: Hosie 1890.
3. See Bruun 1988. This report also includes statistical material on the interviewed household businesses in Bin Shen and discusses development issues related to private business.
4. According to *Chengdu wanbao*, 22 March 1989.

Notes to Chapter Two

1. The free markets were opened all over China as a result of the Open Door Policy and economic reforms after 1979. Chengdu city has

approximately twenty such markets, many at pre-Liberation market sites. In Sichuan at large, there is one market per fifteen thousand people (*Sichuan jingji nianjian* 1988). In practice anyone can trade at the markets since local authorities tend to regard them as a source of income: taxes are collected indiscriminately from all vendors.

2. Chang Shun Street already existed in the Qing dynasty, where it constituted the main street in the Manchu quarter, itself a walled-off area inside the city walls of Chengdu. As the street led up to the military commander's palace, it had no name; it was inhabited by the Manchu guard, divided into "the eight banners" (*baqi*), who occupied separate sections of the street. The street is clearly depicted on a city map from 1880 (Sichuan sheng wenshiguan 1986). Previous maps made by the imperial administration are very sketchy. Chang Shun Street got its name after the founding of the Republic in 1911.

3. Situated at the site of the former Guomindang headquarters, which again was the palace of the Qing dynasty military commander-general (*jiangjun shuai fu*).

4. In 1987 a section of Chang Shun Upper Street was expected soon to be torn down to make room for the army unit's expansion. The army hotel is not only to accommodate army personnel, but also contribute to the unit's economy by renting out office space, for which the demand was thought to be unlimited in the mid-1980s.

5. An immense variety of goods was apparently available to customers in pre-Liberation urban society. In 1906 a missionary counted no fewer than 150 different trades performed by these itinerants in Chengdu (Vale 1906; see also Sewell 1986). Today most of the itinerants sell fruit and handmade goods from rural families, although some work as craftsmen.

6. A few Manchu households still live in the street. Being descendants of the Manchu guard, they still occupy the original Qing dynasty houses. A few old Manchus speak with an accent and still remember the Manchu dialect they were brought up with. Some have also preserved the old Manchu uniforms. Until the Liberation in 1949, the Manchu households were comparatively wealthy, and a clear distinction existed between them and the neighboring Han Chinese households. Many of the present-day adults were brought up with a keen awareness of these different identities. Reference to a conversation with a Manchu businessman is found in chapter 7.

7. The concept of *geti hu* has a strong negative connotation in ordinary language since it is associated with the unwanted qualities of individualism: selfishness, low level of culture, and social deviation. Being marginal implies low social status. The concept of *geti* (individual) is only used in an economic sense (individual producer,

worker, farmer, etc.) relating to professions. Semantically *geti hu* is a paradox. The characters for *geti* stand for "one body," whereas *hu* is "household," synonymous with *jia*, which is "family."

8. *Nüren shan li cai.* Another expression is *guan jia po* (old woman controlling the family) or *qi guan yuan* ("men have goiter," phonetically similar to "controlled by women").

9. The nuclear family tends to be approved and supported by Chinese authorities. As noted by Hugh Baker: "The ideal family of traditional times no longer holds attraction for the Chinese rulers, and every effort has been made through law and exhortation to eradicate Big Family mentality and its supporting institutions" (1979:189). Whether seen as a deliberate attack on traditional social organization or just as a parameter of successful modernization, the nuclear family is the model propagated by Chinese media and the model for the construction of new housing, for registration in villages and in work units, and so on.

10. All urban citizens are in principle organized into *danwei* (work units), which is their place of work, encompassing from a few up to several thousand people. The *danwei* is a socio-spatial unit usually demarcated by a wall and containing all facilities and services for the member families. The concept and organization of *danwei* has been addressed by Björklund (1986), who concludes that by providing its members with a common identity, it has a potential for being "an effective unit of spatial organization in the transformation of society" (28). This view is opposed in chapter 8 (see n. 8).

11. In 1987 the distribution of businesses was handicraft and production, 10 percent; transportation, 1 percent; commerce, 49 percent; catering, 28 percent; service including barbershops, 7 percent; and repair shops, 4 percent. See Bruun 1988 or 1990 for statistics.

12. The concept of *guanxi* stands in conspicuous contrast to the Western concept of "relation," associated with a line or connection between two points. Also the Chinese concept of *guanxihu* (*guanxi* households) points to networks and connections tied to households rather than individuals.

13. These streets also originate from the Qing dynasty and are depicted on old maps. However, the houses vary greatly in age: some may be several hundred years old, presumably built by the ruling Manchu families, while others were constructed by wealthy Han families after the Revolution in 1911. Many Guomindang officers lived in this area. None of the present inhabitants know anything about the history of the houses they occupy, except that they are "from before the Liberation." It is a general trend that the history and age of houses are insignificant to their inhabitants, unless they

are tied to their own family line. For instance, a woman of ninety-seven who moved into a house in Chang Shun Street almost eighty years ago only knows that the house was already old then. The area also contains the Guandi Temple, which has been preserved and turned into a traditional paintings exhibition. Among other famous sites is the building of a former business university, Business Street (Shangye Jie) derives its name from this school.

14. In terms of education, the staff members of the local bureaus usually have senior middle school exams supplemented with administrative and political training, except for those individuals employed when correct class background was the all-important criterion. The average schooling among businesspeople was 5.5 years, but it varied greatly with different age groups, from 0–2 years with the fifty-five to sixty-five age group to 9–10 years with the fifteen to twenty-five age group (see Bruun 1988). However, a few individuals had studied at university. That the officials on average have higher educations than businesspeople also relates to the fact that there is now a majority of younger people employed in the local bureaus, while most established businesses with indoor facilities belong to middle-aged and elderly people.

That the social position of businesspeople generally is low may not hold for all locations in China; for both historical and political reasons the southern coastal regions developed large private enterprises earlier and more easily than the north and the interior, where connection to the Center was more prestigious.

15. On the recent history of private business in China see, for instance, Hershkovitz 1985; Kraus 1991; Liu 1992; Ma 1988; Rosen 1987–88; Solinger 1984, 1992; Taubman and Heberer 1988; S. Young 1989; Yudkin 1986. On its social impact particularly, see Gold 1989b, 1990.

16. Especially in late imperial times, Sichuan was praised by foreigners and Chinese alike for its fertile lands, abundance of rivers and streams, and immense variety of cereals, vegetables, and fruit, not to mention its handicraft production, which showed an equally high level of variety and sophistication. The inhabitants seemed to enjoy a degree of ease and well-being uncommon in other provinces. In Alexander Hosie's words, "Ssu-chu'an is really a picture of what peace, contentment, industry, and consequent trade are able to accomplish" (1890:207), a picture that was confirmed by, for instance, Richthofen 1873; Blackburn 1898; Davidson and Mason 1905; Adshead 1984; and a number of other writers up until the warlord era. See also Hosie 1922 on industry in Sichuan. For a fascinating account of a missionary family's life in Chengdu in the early twentieth century, see Service 1989.

17. Liu Wenhui was the brother of the notorious landlord Liu Wencai (chap. 5, n. 20). In Republican China, Liu Wenhui was a military commander and from 1928–33 Sichuan provincial governor; he was one of the key figures in the civil war through the 1930s. At the retreat of the Nationalists from Sichuan in 1949, he declared allegiance to the Communists, and in the following years he achieved important posts, the last as minister of forestry. For decades his conversion to communism has been used for propaganda, and schoolchildren have been taken to his former home in Bin Shen.

Notes to Chapter Three

1. The ICB is in charge of all industry and commerce within its area of jurisdiction, including the state, collective, and private sectors. See also chap. 5, n. 3.
2. The SELA was established in 1980 as a local initiative among eight hundred businesspeople in Harbin in the northeast. As a spontaneous organization aiming at representing and promoting the interests of individual businesspeople it quickly spread to other cities. In the process the organization metamorphosed: by being incorporated into the formal structure of society it came under the control of the ICB, which manned its posts (Yudkin 1986). The SELA is now a "mass organization" of businesspeople with compulsory membership.
3. Street Committees were set up all over China right after the Liberation in 1949 to organize and mobilize the inhabitants.
4. *Bin Shen xiaqu*.
5. This figure is from August 1987. In 1988 the administrative units were changed, and statistics on private businesses were thus impossible to follow from this year to the next. An approximation of the number of businesses in Bin Shen from 1987 to 1991 is given in chapter 7.
6. These branches are handicraft and production, transportation, commerce, catering, service and barbershops, and repair shops. The nationwide division has an extra category of construction, which is not represented in the area.
7. Statistical average for Chengdu, 3.8.
8. 3.7 yuan to 1 US$ in 1987, 5.4 yuan to 1 US$ in 1992.
9. A common expression for such model following is *gan chaoliu* (catch the flood) This phenomenon is reported elsewhere in the Chinese world — e.g., Niehoff (1987), who refers to the Taiwanese expression of "a swarm of bees" (*yi wo feng*). Niehoff stresses the importance of entrepreneurial households as models for new economic ideologies in a rural area: by evaluating the attractiveness of the entrepreneur-

ship of others, households relate to a particular concrete model rather than an abstract ideology. See also discussion in chapter 8, "State versus Family."

10. Stated turnover and profit often differed considerably from what we could estimate from inquiring about purchases of raw foodstuffs and number of customers. In this case the household reported a turnover and profit of 5,500 yuan and 900 yuan, whereas our own estimates reached 9,000 yuan and 2,000 yuan. Generally, in the businesses where we could make estimates of basic figures, these were usually 50–100 percent higher than the reported figures. See also Bruun 1988.
11. The local educated youth who in the beginning of the Cultural Revolution were sent to the countryside rarely had more than junior middle school education (see chap. 6, n. 11), and the majority of the young had not even finished this. Upon returning in the late 1970s, and some as late as recently, they found themselves without means to find steady employment. Moreover, their interrupted schooling had left them with an inferior education compared to that of later school-leavers. Since the reforms, many young returnees have gone into private business.
12. *Bu keneng qiang zui li de shi.*
13. About 8 percent of present shopkeepers in the area are former collective workers let go with tiny pensions.
14. The survey in 1987–88 showed a clear pattern in the relation between average investments and profits: businesses with little or no investment had average monthly profits in the range of 100–200 yuan, investments of 2,000–3,000 yuan gave monthly profits of 300–400 yuan, investments of 4,000–5,000 yuan gave monthly profits of 600–700 yuan, and so on (calculated from stated figures only).
15. Almost half the elderly people who have returned to private businesses since the reforms said that they were seriously molested during the Cultural Revolution, many to a degree causing permanent physical or mental disablement (see also chap. 5, n. 22).
16. All businesses operate through the week, giving both owners and employees a seven-day work week. The work day in service and commerce is usually ten to twelve hours; in handicraft and production it seemed considerably shorter — rarely more than six to eight hours if the job was physically demanding, and frequently less.
17. Numerous field accounts mention that maintaining "harmony" necessitates a higher male contribution to household income; see, for example Chan, Madsen, and Unger (1984), relating that in Chen village the men insisted that no man should be allowed to slip below any woman in the scale of prestige defined by work points in the

commune (92). Also Mosher (1983) reports that in Sandhead women would never reach the number of work points assigned to men in spite of their often harder work. Attempts at equal pay were met with resistance from the men, afraid of losing face (204–5).

18. Other locals claimed that peasants in the Sichuanese rural areas raped many of the city girls and beat up many of the boys because they had no husbands or families to protect them. Many of the urban young people married to improve their respectability and legal status or assimilated in peasant households as sons and daughters.

19. Baker (1979) also notes the distinction between the ideal (generally extended) family and the actual family of many varieties, which has been the source of confusion (1). Further, in traditional society family size was greatly influenced by economic circumstances; the wealthier the family, the better means it had of realizing ideals. Widespread adoption or selling of children for others to bring up has been practiced in all periods, contributing to the "pragmatic family" construction in times of need. But while the adoption of girls was simple, the adoption of male children was less common, and often subject to restrictions specified by law. Qing dynasty legal code demanded that heirless families wanting to adopt boys search within specified lines of kinship (82). High death rates frequently called for such arrangements. A survey from 1930 revealed an average family size of only 5.0, compared to 4.0 in France (Parish and Whyte 1978:132). On Taiwan, present average family size is 4.2, compared to 5.0 in 1978 (Tseng 1988), and complex families count for only 23.6 percent (Chen 1988).

 Reforms are also reported to have affected family organization in contemporary rural society. E. Croll (1987) defines the "aggregate family," involving several households related primarily by kinship, as a new form of maximizing labor and use of resources.

20. Local average is 1.3 family members registered as operators of a business. But many cannot register since they belong to, or receive a pension from, a *danwei*.

21. The role of present-day brokers is often compared to similar arrangements in traditional society; the percentage they draw, however, is now far higher since their undertaking is usually illegal (e.g., Zafanolli 1985).

22. The survey suggested a figure of 2.1 family members directly involved in the day-to-day running of business. This figure is based on the shopkeepers' own statements and direct observation of individuals present every day.

23. Retired state workers and cadres usually receive life-long pensions. Retired cadres, of which there are plenty in private business,

commonly collect about 100 yuan per month.

24. Old proverb: *Tian gan er bu si shouyi ren.*
25. Also left are the state outlets for rice and flour products and a few outlets for collective meat units. Otherwise the entire economy of the street is in private hands. However, as in society in general, the distinction between collective and private enterprise is blurred. A few family businesses were deliberately registered as collectives, using the "red umbrella," for protection.
26. A large number of collectives engaged in this trade when profits rocketed. By exploiting their advantage over individual businesses in being permitted to import goods, they had access to cheap foreign paper, whereas the individual businesses could only buy the paper from collectives at negotiated prices. Consequently, collectives soon took over almost the entire market.
27. Out of the total ninety-one employees in the 1987–88 sample survey, fifty-nine were such rural young. The remaining thirty-two laborers were skilled in their profession and of both rural and urban origin.
28. *Guokui* are fired on a flat pan. The dough consists of flour, brown sugar, and oil.
29. The head of the Street Committee maintained this to be a major obstacle in integrating private businesses into the national economy and making full use of their skills, for instance through apprenticeship. Some craftsmen admitted that such may have been the case in the old society, where competition was sharp and survival difficult. Yet it is a common attitude among all that "only stupid people tell everything they know." Elvin (1973:29) mentions Han dynasty artisans "jealously guarding their professional secrets." Weber also notes that occasionally the guilds secured craft secrets ([1920] 1951:18, 19, 257) .

Notes to Chapter Four

1. See chap. 2, n. 16 on manufacturing in traditional Sichuan; chap. 3, n. 29 on craft secrets being kept in the family; chap. 4, n. 13 on social classifications relating to the household's economic activity.
2. There is reason to believe that this is no isolated urban phenomenon. Similar attitudes are also reported in rural areas, e.g., Mosher 1983:41: "The Chinese never cherished any illusion about work. They regarded it not as the divinely ordained purpose of life — there was no Confucian, Taoist, or Buddhist work ethic. . . . The goal of Chinese peasants was to escape toil by accumulating a little land, hiring tenants to till it, and living off the sweat of others. This dream of leisure lent their labors a hopeful energy, even a certain dignity."

Niehoff (1987) also finds among rural Taiwanese households in entrepreneurship that they are "demanding maximum efforts of themselves in the present with the belief that it will lead to a more comfortable set of circumstances in the future" (302).

3. Trading this timber is in principle monopolized by the state timber department. Widespread private felling, trade, and transport are nevertheless undisguisedly taking place from the West Sichuan mountain areas into the cities.

4. No traces of secret societies, guilds, or informal organizations influencing prices could be traced in the area. The Self-employed Laborers Association presumably rests too heavily on all businesses and certainly has the eradication and prevention of all other organizations among its purposes. In 1991, however, criminal gangs attempted to establish themselves in the area (see chap. 7).

5. *Laoxinzhe zhi ren, laolizhe zhi yu ren* (classical statement by Mencius).

6. Since the proverb has strong associative value to common people and has been impossible to eradicate, Chinese authorities have been much aware of it; in 1983, for instance, Hu Yaobang termed it "an obsolete and wrong way of thinking" (*Renmin ribao*, 14 March 1983). Even a standard Chinese-English dictionary comments upon this proverb: "This is a reactionary Confucianist view" (*Han ying cidian* 1985).

7. It is noteworthy that in imperial times, although wealth was commonly accumulated through activities in the informal hierarchy, status in society was invariably drawn from position in the universally defined, formal hierarchy. Wealth, power, family connections, and individual charisma were all important in the quest for personal success. But a prerequisite for fulfillment within the Chinese ethos was going the cumbersome way through state examinations to a degree, and preferably to office. Much has been written about the low esteem in which industry and particularly commerce were held in traditional China and the consequences for economic development this may have had (e.g., Needham 1969:40; Elvin 1972, 1973:203ff.). But nothing suggests that the ruling stratum desisted from engaging in these activities. Rather, wealth gained from economic activities and status derived from a professional career can be perceived as belonging to differing categories within the dualism of Chinese thought, being aspects of the sensitive dichotomy between ideal and social practice. Among the aristocracy, it is probably true that wealth in itself was only an intermediate stage, a halfway mark on the road to personal perfection, which, when fully accomplished, in Chinese thought allowed human beings to stand in a divine light. Self-perfection through education in the classics was a deep-rooted Confucian concept, basic to all literary

achievement.

8. Chinese authorities have always incorporated the three sectors of the economy (state, collective, private) into a hierarchical structure that simultaneously denotes their economic priority and the social status involved in being employed in them. However, these are often expressed in reverse terms — for example, the countless newspaper articles encouraging private business, stating that the private entrepreneurs are useful to society or the joint notice the central ministries issued in 1981 stipulating that private businesses should be sold supplies on an equal footing with state and collective units (S. Young 1989:60), while simultaneously ideological discussions take place concerning how to control the private sector or secure its dependency on the public sector.

9. Collectives were always unstable since they were politically enforced establishments, mainly set up during the two urban collectivization campaigns in 1952–53 and 1958–59. In the second period, a large number of vaguely defined "urban communes" were established, but they quickly disintegrated; see, for instance, Schurmann (1968:380).

10. There is close connection between the Confucian Five Relations, indicating relationships of superiority / inferiority, and the distribution of tasks and service. Superiority is commonly perceived as freedom from labor and responsibilities, indicating the strong agrarian roots of Chinese classifications. The striving toward superior position in the state hierarchy associated with freedom and leisure is returned to in chapter 8.

11. The attraction of running a restaurant is probably a combination of high profit and a structure easy to control. The issue of the Chinese restaurant as traditional relationship in a nutshell has been addressed by Wilson and Pusey 1982, which is discussed in chapter 8.

12. Restaurants were the most costly investments in the area (average nearly 4,000 yuan) and had by far the highest profitability, with average monthly profits of almost 700 yuan (as stated by owners).

13. The Confucian social order operated with four large occupational groups: scholars, agriculturalists, artisans, and merchants. Every category forms a complete system that is generally assumed to imply hierarchy (Kuhn 1984:20); "agriculturalists," for instance, embraces both landlords and peasants. That artisans occupy the second lowest category, below scholars and peasants but above merchants, expresses the state distinction between root and subsidiary occupations. Also, state fiscal interests presumably placed farmers second after scholars. Needham has called attention to traditional China's respect and esteem for its craftsmen (e.g., 1974). However, the general perception is that craftsmen occupied low positions and

were ascribed little significance in the needs of society (e.g. Elvin 1973:32 [technical skill as a quality of slaves]; 165 [unregistered artisans buried alive along with merchants]; 270 [advanced crafts and industrialization primarily connected to rural sideline production]; 278 [spinners, weavers, etc., working at home on contract with big businesses]).

14. E.g., Elvin 1973:285, bureaucratic restrictions on commerce.
15. Old proverb: *Yi ren de dao, ji quan shang tian.*
16. Hundreds of such places were established in the matter of a few months, another example of the "tidal waves" in private business. Their popularity diminished after one or two years, and many of them were converted into ordinary restaurants.
17. Opium is widely used in *huoguo*, not only for the immediate effect, but also to make customers return. Unconditioned eaters will experience sleepless nights. Opium is easily purchased from Tibetans trading in Chengdu. A control team from the municipal health authorities roams the city to take samples of the soup (*Chengdu wanbao*, 12 December 1988), according to restaurant owners, frequently eating in the places without revealing their identity until asked for payment.
18. Old proverb: *Chu sheng niu du bu pa hu.*
19. The discussion of the social significance of *guanxi* as a strategy will be continued in chapter 8, "Personal Relations."
20. See Potter 1983. The distinction between urban and rural dwellers is a stratification following their unequal valuation by the state, a long-standing distinction. Potter quotes a Zhou dynasty official: "The duty of the local officials is to adjust matters between town and country, to harmonize clashing interests" (465). Potter argues that after 1949 the contradiction between urban and rural populations may even have increased.
21. In 1989 his registered turnover was actually raised to 20,000 yuan per month.
22. Questioned "Where are you from?" or "Where were you born?" The phenomenon is universal in Chinese culture and has been reported, for instance, by Hosie 1890 and Hinton 1966:287.
23. This is, for instance, seen from the rising educational level of Party cadres and Party members in general. At the beginning of the 1980s only half the forty-two million Party members had more than primary school education, and only 4 percent had gone to university (Pan 1987:159); by 1987 the percentage of university graduates had increased to 7 percent. Hu Yaobang, especially, called for the reconstitution of China's leadership and for involving more intellectual and specialized cadres (e.g., scientists and engineers) (see

Judd 1983–84). Hu's controversial views led to his fall during the student unrest in 1985–86.

24. Business owners on average had five and a half years of schooling, with approximately 20 percent stating illiteracy and another 7 percent being able to read but not write. The level of schooling varied considerably between age groups, however, with those in their early to mid sixties having received next to nothing, and the present twenty-year-olds having the highest level. Those now thirty-five to thirty-nine years old also had a low level of education because of the Cultural Revolution.

25. The traditional family is not only a unit of organization; it also forms the basic unit for morality in Chinese society in the sense that moral obligations are primarily directed toward family or toward family-type relations in the outer society (e.g., Tseng 1988:15).

Notes to Chapter Five

1. Old proverb: *San tian bu chi fan, jia zhuang mai mi han.* A very cryptic proverb to use, since it signifies a person who hides weakness, poverty, or incapability by simulating the opposite.

2. Even senior officials in local bureaus rarely earn more than 120–140 yuan per month. But as the *People's Daily* declared in 1985 on behalf of the Party cadres: "In the situation where some people get rich first and the rest get rich later, in order to let the masses get rich first, we are willing to wait to get rich later. If this may be said to be losing out, then this loss is necessary. If this may be said to be a sacrifice, then this sacrifice is glorious" (*Renmin ribao*, 30 March 1985).

3. Chinese administration is divided into *bu* (ministry), *ju* (bureau), *chu* (section), and *ke* (office). The external departments have varying designations; for instance, the Industrial and Commercial Bureau belongs to the Shangye Bu (Ministry of Commerce); the provincial level is Gong Shang Sheng Ting, the city level is Gong Shang Ju, and local level is Gong Shang Fen Ju. The Public Security Bureau and the Tax Bureau are on the local level divided into *suo*: Pai Chu Suo and Shui Wu Suo.

4. In 1987 and 1988 several central government initiatives were aimed at separating Party and state interests in administration — for instance, the 1 August 1988, proclamation to abolish Party cells in every ministry under the state council (see, e.g., Manoharan 1990).

5. The middle levels in the administrative system are frequently the Party and provincially dominated "block organizations," akin to the state "line organizations." The intermediate Party-dominated levels of administration are generally seen as obstacles to reform (e.g., Pan

1987:40).

6. The "traditional" cautiousness of addressing public authorities still prevails in all fields: Public Security, Tax Bureau, Street Committee, etc. Examples will be given.
7. The administrative division of local areas is presently undergoing reform aimed at more efficient control and better knowledge of local affairs. This reform, however, applies only to state-controlled organizations (such as the ICB); the Party-dominated institutions (such as the Street Bureau) remain unchanged.
8. Four principles of the constitution: Adherence to the socialist road, dictatorship of the proletariat, the leading role of the Communist Party, and upholding Marxism-Leninism and Mao Zedong thought.
9. Few elderly women have more than very basic schooling, and many are illiterate. See also chap. 4, nn. 23, 24.
10. Liew 1989:5 "The emphasis on centralism over democracy lowers the quality of information available to the center . . . [I]nformation flowing to the center is often deliberately biased towards policies favoured by the center, regardless of local objective conditions. . . . This proved disastrous during the Great Leap Forward."
11. Local authorities allowed very few businesses to operate during the Cultural Revolution, just a couple in Chang Shun Street and a few in the neighboring streets. They were all small and insignificant; of those reported, one sold spices, another secondhand books and magazines, and another secondhand clothes and shoes.
12. According to *China Daily* (18 March 1989) China has about six million registered mediators, organized in committees of a few to about ten members. They allegedly have kept more than seven million disputes away from courts and "saved the lives of nearly 120,000 persons."
13. Simultaneously articles were published in the *Chengdu wanbao* about shopkeepers donating large sums of money for this purpose (e.g., *Chengdu wanbao*, 13 April 1989). See also chapter 6, "Rising Contradiction."
14. The standard tax determined by central government is 5 percent for businesses in manufacturing and 3 percent for all other branches, to be taken on total turnover.
15. The central government had already demanded bookkeeping as a basis of taxation in 1987 and repeated the demand in the spring of 1988 and in 1989 (e.g., *Renmin ribao*, 5 August 1987; *Beijing Review*, no. 10, 1989). But along with several other regulations designed by the central government (e.g., the distinction between individual households and private enterprises), it had not been implemented in the autumn of 1988, nor in the spring of 1989.
16. Sichuan sheng cheng xiang gong shang ye guanli banfa, 1987.

Contains regulations and procedures for registration, management, and renewal of licenses.

17. Several leading cadres in the area have maintained their positions through the Cultural Revolution until presently — for example, the head of the police station (who has earned himself the reputation of being totally unscrupulous).
18. The Party Congress in November 1987 confirmed the legality of private businesses with more than eight employees; the new policy aimed at promoting the good and limiting the bad through improving administraiton (S. Young 1989:74). Zhao Ziyang even stated that the private economy was "still far too small." The theory of the "initial stage of socialism" requires that diverse economic forms coexist. The lack of clearly formulated policies and regulations left the final interpretation to local authorities, which adopted a large variety of practices (ibid.:67). In Chengdu no changes could be registered.
19. Old proverb: *Da er quan, xiao er quan* (Zafanolli 1985:728).
20. Four proverbs: *Wu mian zhi wang; Shen xian da xhang, fan ren zhao yang; Zhi xu zhou guan fang hou, bu xu bai xing dian deng; Bang Liu Wencai.* Liu Wencai was a wealthy landlord outside Chengdu, famous for forcing peasants to work without pay. Now the expression is used toward the "people above."
21. Old proverb: *Da yu chi xiao yu, xiao yu chi xia.*
22. A large number of private shopkeepers were exposed to violence during the Cultural Revolution: dragged through the streets with caps and signs, kicked and beaten up, stabbed with knives, imprisoned, humiliated, and so forth.
23. The policy of the central government is itself ambivalent: While encouraging private businesses, these are subject to unequal competition and legally debarred from raw materials, credit, social services, and so on. In regard to violating the law, central government continually demands measures to be taken against private businesses while tolerating its officials' extracting unlawful fees.
24. Formal language draws on the morality of central authorities. In this respect the Confucian tradition, described as "the doctrine of the exemplary center" (e.g., Geertz 1980:13–15) is continued in the Communist moralizing authorities (e.g., Pye 1988), and thus the state built on moral rather than legal order.

Notes to Chapter Six

1. A dropout problem of alarming proportions was reported already in 1985 (*Renmin ribao*, 3 November 1985). A 1985 World Bank report

estimates that approximately 45 percent of children do not finish primary school (see n. 3), and of those continuing in junior middle school another 40 percent drop out (World Bank 1985:Annex 1; Bakken 1989:150). Youth attitude surveys generally confirm a decline in the students' desire to study and a commensurate interest in making money (e.g., Rosen 1989).

2. Ordinary school-leavers are not assigned state jobs but are supposed to find employment themselves. Only university graduates have until recently been secured state employment. The new vocational schools (*zhiye zhongxue*) and technical schools (*zhuanye xuexiao*), which have been set up at senior middle school level to provide useful nonliterary skills, may have offices to assist their students find employment. However, it goes for all graduates that an increasingly "liberal" job market is rapidly taking over, with the importance of internal *guanxi* in the institution, university, local area, city, and the like shifting to the importance of *guanxi* in society at large.
3. Unemployment in Sichuan: A standard statistical yearbook emphasizes the number of people finding new jobs every year and has no exact figures for unemployment. Among the city population approximately 56 percent of household members have work (*Sichuan jingji nianjian 1988*).
4. *Far Eastern Economic Review*, 6 April and 11 May 1989.
5. The husband was running a small tailor shop before the Liberation; like others, it was incorporated into a collective in the early 1950s. Apart from having all his equipment taken away at this time, he also lost his beautiful wife. According to him, she was "seized" by a Party secretary, who used his authority to enforce their divorce and his subsequent marriage with the woman. In spite of the grudge the husband may have toward the Party, his and his wife's open criticism mark an unprecedented hostility toward local authorities.
6. *Hong yan bing*. The problem is recognized everywhere and frequently discussed in the media and elsewhere. As an example of this see Li 1987: *Hong yan bing chi ren*.
7. *Chengdu wanbao*, 27 February 1989.
8. Stated by Party officials. For instance, expressed in personal discussions with Professor Li Daonan, Sichuan University, and Associate Professor Chen Li, Sichuan University, who were conducting research on the private economy for the Chinese Communist Party Committee in Chengdu. Also see Zhu 1987:106.
9. *Chengdu wanbao*, 13 April 1989.
10. E.g., Shirk 1984:74; Bakken 1989:100ff.
11. The Chinese school system is divided into primary school (*xiaoxue*) stretching over six years, junior middle school (*chuzhong*) lasting

three years, and senior middle school (*gaozhong*), which is also three years. Primary and junior middle school are compulsory, while senior middle school is preparation for university (*daxue*).

12. Again, dropping out of school is an effect of the lack of employment prospects. *Beijing Review*, no. 29 (1989):21 states that the drop-out rate in 1988 was the highest ever in recent years (4.1 percent of all students), and Sichuan is among the provinces with the highest rate of school dropouts, especially in primary school.
13. The national level of alphabetism may actually be dropping because of the scarcity in state employment and the high incomes possible in private business and contract farming, or it may at best stay stable as the older generation with little schooling dies off. In 1985 a World Bank report concluded that unless the drop-out rate decreased, analphabetism will remain at 30 percent (World Bank 1985:Annex 1, p. 7). Since then, the drop-out rate has increased.
14. *Beijing Review*, no. 29 (1989):21.
15. *Shi shi zhongxue jian jie* 1988.
16. While the privatization of values, including a rising contempt for the moralizing national authorities such as the Party, clearly is an effect of the reforms, a strong undercurrent of patriotic sentiment is still found among the young (e.g., Rosen 1989:202).
17. The problem is recognized and much debated in public. A recent very critical book *Zhongguo dangdai shehui wenti* (Problems in contemporary Chinese society) mentions this among the major national problems: "Educated women's cultural level is too high compared to men; they are getting too old when graduating, and there are too few good husbands available to them" (215). The book also addresses the problem of the conditions of life for the young intellegentsia, who have one of the highest mortality rates among the adult population as a result of malnourishment, poor living quarters, and excessive work (51). Other themes include the generational divide, the lack of freedom and security, inflation, gambling, grave robbing, and sex problems, all topics that were discussed in the comparatively free years of approximately 1987–89.
18. Divorce rates in Chengdu have reached a level that probably resembles that of Europe, although no exact figures are available. Staff members of the bureau handling divorces report that they are "extremely busy" (*mang sile*). Mediators in the area of fieldwork admitted that divorces were increasing; apparently there was little difference between "individual" and "ordinary" households in this respect.
19. Martin Whyte (1990) points to the significant impact that formal society's "bureaucratic gatekeepers" may have had in preventing a

modern dating culture from developing among the young. The heavy assaults on the Chinese family institution, especially in 1950–53, 1958–60, and 1966–76 (coinciding with the great socialist constructing surges) were apparently counteracted by deliberate action to prevent a genuine youth autonomy from developing beyond a certain point. In relation to marriage customs Whyte terms this effect "stalled convergence," since the most marked changes had presumably already taken place in the early years of Communist rule.

20. *Xing jiefang yao jinü.*
21. As an ultimate display of force, leading Party secretaries can place criminal charges at random. The four principles of the constitution, and the subjective interpretation they imply, permit, for instance, the category of "counterrevolutionary" to be placed on anyone defying authorities.
22. *Zhongguo Gongchandang wan shui — wo hen si le.*
23. *Xianzai shui you qian, shui jiu shi wang.*

Notes to Chapter Seven

1. For political reasons I did not want to cooperate with any Chinese authorities after June 1989, however innocent institutions like the Sichuan Social Science Academy were. Moreover, my own involvement as chairman of a Danish committee for the support of the Chinese student movement probably debarred me from obtaining a research visa in this period.
2. Numerically the decrease in handicraft businesses was of course less. However, woodworkers, smithies, and tailors particularly had decreased in numbers; of the last category only one of the five businesses interviewed in 1987 had survived.
3. The distribution between traditional and Western medicine in the new clinics is instructive to the orientation of the population; four out of six were set up by units using traditional medicine exclusively: Traditional Medical College (Zhongyi xueyuan), Traditional Herbal Medicine Hospital (Zhongyi zaoyao yiyuan), Chengdu Blind People's Massage Hospital (Chengdu mengren anmo yiyuan), and Chengdu Red Cross Hospital (Chengdu hongshi yiyuan). The remaining two offered both Chinese and Western treatment.
4. *Zhongguo shibao*, 23 October 1989, states that measures must be taken to straighten up tax payments and announces new taxes. *Renmin ribao*, 6 September, however, mentions that the main problem of taxation is not its level, but its administration and collection.
5. The concept has been used in the media with increasing frequency — for instance, on television and in *Renmin ribao* and repeated locally

in *Chengdu wanbao.*

6. An example of taxes and charges as stated by one restaurant owner: industrial and commercial tax (*gong shang shui*), income tax (*suode shui*), city reconstruction charge (*cheng jian fei*), education charge (*jiaoyu fei*), grain fund (city) (*liangshi jijin/shi*), grain fund (province) (*liangshi/sheng*), meat fund (*roushi jijin*), management charge (*guanli fei*), business administration charge (*yingye fei*), revenue stamp (*yin hua*), public order charge (*zhi an fei*), sanitation charge (*qing jie fei*), "putting in order" charge (*paiwu fei*), energy source fund (*nengyuan jijin*), "front-door-three-guarantees" (*menqian san bao*), "self-evaluation-make-up-for-evasion" tax (*zicha bubao*), clean transportation charge (*qingjie yunshu fei*), association membership fee (*hui fei*), employees contract charge (*chengbao fei*), excessive signpost charge (*chao biao fei*). Some variation is found in the charges paid by businesses in different branches.
7. Again in 1989 it was emphasized that tax must be calculated according to accounts; see, for example, *Renmin ribao*, 22 August and 4 September. See also chap. 5, n. 15.
8. Quite recently she had nevertheless read the conclusion of my 1988 report, which had been translated into Chinese and circulated among the association representatives. A surprisingly large number of people were acquainted with its content and argument; most found it "good" but did not want to comment on specific points.
9. An example of the campaigns after June 4 was the one to wipe out pornography (*sao huang yundong*, linking arms dealing to pornography), in which forty thousand private entrepreneurs allegedly were arrested and thirty-seven executed (*Zhengming*, no. 145, 16 October 1989).
10. The 1979 criminal law prescribes capital punishment for a long list of crimes, including a range of counterrevolutionary activities such as harming the state and the people; colluding with foreign states, organizing rebellions, luring state personel; endagering public security by setting fires, causing explosions, sabotaging transportation; stealing property by violence; carrying arms, and so on. Since the 1979 criminal law, the scope of capital punishment has been expanded in 1981, 1982, 1983, 1988, and 1990 to include, for instance, the undermining of the economy and the selling and spreading of pornographic material. For an account of capital offenses see, for instance, *Australian Human Rights Delegation* 1991. For a historical perspective on human rights, see Nathan 1986. For a Chinese discussion of human rights in China in relation to natural law (an implicit attack on legal relativism in China), see He 1990.
11. In the months after the student unrest in May and June 1989, a great

number of young Chinese arrived in Western countries. A large proportion of them were apparently opportunists, since the word had rapidly spread that the Western immigration authorities had no means of confirming their stories.

12. The distinction between *geti hu* and *siying qiye* was again emphasized. Registration within the *siying qiye* business category implies stricter bookkeeping, employment of an accountant and a cashier, and regular inspection by the local ICB. *Siying qiye* are therefore under much stricter control than the *geti hu*, regarded as small and family based.
13. Stipulated to be 5 yuan per month (suggesting a trade-off with the local bureau).

Notes to Chapter Eight

1. For a further discussion on approaches to Chinese studies, see Bruun 1990:140ff or 1991.
2. For the geographical issue see *Journal of Asian Studies* 48.1 (1989). Class, language, and religion are also often mentioned as factors accounting for cultural difference. This position is primarily taken by external observers; few Chinese writers will challenge the cultural integrity of the Chinese empire in historical time and geographical space.
3. The study of Chinese religion at an early stage was influenced by the observation that, as expressed by Lyall (1907:108): "China . . . succeeded centuries ago in bringing her religious doctrines and worships into practical cooperation with her secular organization."
4. See, for example, J. Croll 1989: "Nowhere outside Chinese culture has inclination towards oneness manifested itself with such vigor and turned into such a general and constant tendency" (1). "They [Confucianists] were of the opinion that each region of the Earth produces people of a certain psycho-physical type according to its specific qualities; these regions are heterogeneous which leads to the heterogeneity of the people inhabiting them; therefore Earth divides people. On the contrary, the emperor unites them" (3). Croll concludes that *Universismus* (a term introduced by J. J. M. de Groot) "is still alive, interacting with European concepts in the process of change" (14).
5. The growth of the state is seen in, for instance, the steadily increasing budget, administration, and number of soldiers: in 1898 Sichuan had 27,000 soldiers, in 1911 there were 49,000 at a total cost of 50 percent of all revenue raised in the province; in 1920 there were 110,000, and in 1931, 300,000. Militarization was a powerful trend in

the twentieth century (Adshead 1984:117).

6. Such emancipation also involved fighting the traditional bureaucracy. Thus Mao propagated counterbureaucracy as much as he depended on bureaucracy himself — for instance, by adopting the *baojia* system. The two trends are treated in Whyte 1980.

7. *Public sphere* is here to be understood as relations outside the state's direct control and its organization of *danwei*. Thus the public sphere is perceived as including market relations and, for instance, all relations between state bureaucracy and private business. Similarly, the public sphere concerns relations outside domestic organization and kinship bonds.

8. The notion of the *danwei* as the individual's basic place of belonging is closely tied to the Party organization, which generally is the superior authority within the *danwei*. Björklund (1986:28) present a highly idiosyncratic and passionate view of the *danwei*: "One of the most interesting and powerful features of the *danwei*, at least from the perspective of the outsider, is that the closeness of workplace, residence and social place, all within its walls, creates a cohesive group . . . [T]here is a high level of resident participation in many *danwei*." However, during my fieldwork in Chengdu the *danwei* was rarely referred to in such terms. Rather, the strict social control within the *danwei* is itself becoming a significant reason for going into private employment. Pye (1988:158) notes that the *danwei* "seem in some ways to be reincarnations of comparable traditional institutions, designed to control and meet needs so that no one should have to trouble higher authorities." This is supposedly true for rural life, but in cities like Chengdu no such institutions existed before the Liberation.

9. Closely associated with the marked distinction between the inner and outer spheres is the question of identity. An initial search for the framework in which the individual identifies itself points to the family. The common name, aim, and strategy distinctly given by family authorities appear to be self-perpetuating. However, in this respect profound similarity can be found between the family and the remaining circles centered on the individual. If one compares national, provincial, village, and household identity, some parallel characteristics are obvious. All have in common strong demarcations between the inside and the outside, parted by symbolic as well as actual walls, distinguishable by separate characteristics and defined as oppositions. While national identity in relation to the foreign world has been analyzed in detail (e.g., Bauer 1980), particularist provincial identity has been paid less attention (although it is still a common theme for a great number of provinces; see, for example,

Adshead 1984 and Goodman 1986 for Sichuan). Village identity obviously exists (e.g., Yang 1965), especially when villages coincide with clan or name community. The urban parallel, neighborhood identity, may be less significant, but neighbors still form basic units in terms of mutual trust and assistance. Chinese concepts of common motherland, province, and village are *tongbao*, *tongsheng*, and *tongxiang*. Thus state and family represent the upper and lower levels in a series of demarcations, a series structure that may even encompass the individual as the ultimate level/demarcation.

10. "Birth-ascribed stratification" is used by Potter (1983:465) to describe the belief that rural people are inferior to urban. Hinton (1966:287) calls it a "concept of hereditary social status." "Caste society" is the term used by Pye (1988:18); moreover, "by preventing people from moving freely to find better employment, [Mao Zedong] could not help but increase inequalities by preventing the development of a true labor market." Whatever the term, such assumptions of hereditary social positions are ironic in a Communist society and provide an aspect of the discrepancy between ideals and social practices that I will later examine.
11. The civil society debate originates in the East European transition discourse, which claims that new market activities will develop a more autonomous and politically powerful civil society, gradually weakening the power of the Communist state (e.g., Szelenyi 1988). Its application to the PRC is increasingly criticized on the basis of sociological fieldwork (e.g., David Wank).
12. Especially in rural areas it is a characteristic of successful businesses that they are run by cadres (or former cadres), intellectuals, and demobilized soldiers (e.g., Liew 1989:6).
13. The state nomenclatura system enumerates twenty-four levels of rank for cadres, defining positions from highest central level to smallest local offices, constituting a hierarchy of authority. Party core groups control the highest-ranking positions in practically all significant units (Burns 1987).
14. Class concepts in recent works: S. Young 1989; Xia 1987. In 1989 the Chinese media introduced a new class concept to individual business households; they were singled out as a new "middle class" (*zhongchan jieji*) (*Renmin ribao*, 22 August 1989).
15. Examples of personalized ideals, heroes, and the like include *Yu gong yi shan*, Lei Feng, *Cao yuan ying xiong xiao jie mei*, Huang Jiguang, Dong Cunrui, Wang Jie.
16. As, for instance, expressed in Chinese traditional novels such as *Hong wu meng* (Dream of the red chamber). For oscillations dependent on economic circumstances see, for example, Baker 1979:4.

17. Especially after the reforms the work of women is reported to have increased (e.g., E. Croll 1987:482), but the pattern of unequal distribution of labor is general.
18. The continued conventionalism of the Chinese language expressed in the approximation to traditional patterns has parallels in art and literature. Form is itself expressive of the message.
19. See Gold 1985: *guanxi* is seen as the underlying principle for instrumentalism. The reciprocal practice of *guanxi* is connected to the traditional concept of *bao* — meaning social investments. Gold concludes that friendship and comradeship have been supplanted by instrumentalism and commoditization. Moreover, the situation resembles what is described in classical works: particularism, family and kin solidarity, reciprocity, lack of civil consciousness, hierarchies of sex and age, bureaucratic arrogance and corruption, and so on.

References

Adshead, Samuel A. M. 1984. *Province and Politics in Late Imperial China: Viceregal Government in Szechwan, 1898–1911*. London: Curzon Press.

Arkush, R. David. 1981. *Fei Xiaotong and Sociology in Revolutionary China*. Cambridge, Mass.: Harvard University Press.

Australian Human Rights Delegation to China, Report of the. 1991. Canberra: Parliament House.

Baker, Hugh D. R. 1979. *Chinese Family and Kinship*. London: Macmillan.

Bakken, Borge. 1989. *Kunnskap og Moral. Om utdanningsreformer i dagens Kina*. Rapportserie No. 1. Oslo: Department of Sociology, University of Oslo.

Bauer, Wolfgang. 1980. *China und die Fremden: 3000 Jahre Auseinandersetzung in Krieg und Frieden*. Munchen: C. H. Beck.

Beijing Review. 1989. No. 10. "Interim Regulations on Private Enterprises."

———1989. No. 29. "Facts and Figures: Education in Present-Day China."

Björklund, E. M. 1986. "The Danwei: Socio-spatial Characteristics of Work Units in China's Urban Society." *Economic Geography* 62.1.

Blackburn Chamber of Commerce. 1898. *Report of the Mission to China of the Blackburn Chamber of Commerce 1896–97*. London.

Bloch, Maurice. 1975 *Political Language and Oratory in Traditional Societies*. London: Academic Press.

Bodde, Derk. 1981. "Harmony and Conflict in Chinese Philisophy." In Charles Le Blanc and Dorothy Borei, eds., *Essays on Chinese Civilization*. Princeton, N.J.: Princeton University Press.

Bruun, Ole. 1988. *The Reappearance of the Family as an Economic Unit: A Sample Survey of Individual Households in Workshop Production and Crafts, Chengdu, Sichuan Province, China*. Copenhagen: Center for East and Southeast Asian Studies.

———1990. "Business and Bureaucracy in a Chengdu Street." Ph.D. dissertation. Department of Anthropology, University of Copenhagen.

———1991. "Anthropological Fieldwork and Social Theory." In Ole Bruun, Søren Poulsen, and Hatla Thelle: *Modern China Research: Danish Experiences*. University of Copenhagen: Center for East and Southeast Asian Studies.

———Forthcoming. "The Politics of Entrepreneurship: Private Business Strategies and Urban Bureaucracy in a Chinese Neighborhood." In Andrew Walder, ed., *The Political Consequences of Departures from Central Planning: Economic Reform and Political Change in Communist States*. Berkeley: University of California Press.

Burns, John P. 1987. "China's Nomenclatura System." *Problems of Communism*, September–October.

Chai, Winberg. 1962. "The Development of the Chinese Constitution." *Chinese Culture* 4.2.

Chan, Anita, Richard Madsen, and Jonathan Unger. 1984. *Chen Village: The Recent History of a Peasant Community in Mao's China*. Berkeley: University of California Press.

Chen, Wen-Tsung. 1988. "Marriage Tensions." *Free China Review* (Taipei), December.

Chengdu cheng fang gu li kao. 1986. Sichuan sheng wenshiguan. Chengdu: Sichuan Renmin chubanshe.

Chengdu wanbao. 1988: 12 December. 1989: 27 February, 22 March, 4 and 13 April.

China Daily. 1989. 18 March.

Chu, David S. K. 1983–84. "Sociology and Society in Contemporary China, 1979–83." *Chinese Sociology and Anthropology* 16.1–2 (Fall-Winter).

Comaroff, J. 1975. "Talking Politics: Oratory in a Tswana Chiefdom." See Bloch.

Croll, Elisabeth. 1987 "New Peasant Family Forms in Rural China." *Journal of Peasant Studies* 14.4.

Croll, Juri. 1989. "The Cultural Notion of Oneness and the State in Traditional China." Seminar paper. Modernization and Cultural Change in China, Turku University, June.

Davidson, Robert J., and Isaac Mason. 1905. *Life in West China*. London: Headley Brothers.

Davis, Deborah. 1989. "Chinese Social Welfare: Policies and

Outcomes." *China Quarterly*, no. 119.

Davis, Deborah, and Ezra F. Vogel, eds. 1990. *Chinese Society on the Eve of Tiananmen*. Cambridge, Mass.: Council on East Asian Studies, Harvard University.

Delfs, Robert A. 1986. "China Off the Boil. Sichuan Leads the Way to Economic Slowdown." *Far Eastern Economic Review*. 6 March.

Ebrey, Patricia Buckley, and James L. Watson. 1986. *Kinship Organization in Late Imperial China, 1000–1940*. Berkeley: University of California Press.

Elvin, Mark. 1972. "The High-level Equilibrium Trap." In W. E. Wilmott, ed., *Economic Organization in Chinese Society*. Stanford, Calif.: Stanford University Press.

———1973. *The Pattern of the Chinese Past*. London: Eyre Methuen.

Emerson, John Philip. 1983. "Urban School Leavers and Unemployment in China." *China Quarterly*, no. 93.

Far Eastern Economic Review. 1989. 6 April and 11 May.

Feuchtwang, Stephan. 1992. *The Imperial Metaphor: Popular Religion in China*. London: Routledge.

Fitzgerald, C. P. 1976. *China: A Short Cultural History*. 4th ed., rev. London: Barrie and Jenkins.

Freedman, Maurice. 1979. *The Study of Chinese Society*. Stanford, Calif.: Stanford University Press.

Geertz, Clifford. 1980. *Negara*. Princeton, N.J.: Princeton University Press.

Gernet, Jacques. 1982. *A History of Chinese Civilization*. Cambridge, U.K.: Cambridge University Press.

Gold, Thomas B. 1985. "After Comradeship: Personal Relations in China Since the Cultural Revolution." *China Quarterly*, no. 104.

———1989a. "Guerilla Interviewing among the *Getihu*." See Link, Madsen, and Pickowicz.

———1989b. "Urban Private Business in China." *Studies in Comparative Communism* 22.2–3.

———1990. "Urban Private Business and Social Change." See Davis and Vogel.

Gong, Shiqi. 1988. "Economic Features of Primary Stage of Socialism." *Beijing Review*, no. 31.

Goodman, David S. G. 1986. *Centre and Province in the People's Republic of China: Sichuan and Guizhou, 1955–1965*. Cambridge, U.K.: Cambridge University Press.

Granet, Marcel. [1922] 1976. *The Religion of the Chinese People*. Tr., ed., and with an introduction by Maurice Freedman. Explorations in Interpretative Sociology. Oxford: Blackwell.

Han ying cidian. 1985. Beijing waiguoyu xueyuan yingyu xi. Shangwu yinshuguan.

He, Zhaowu. 1990. "The Concept of Natural Rights and the Cultural Tradition." *Chinese Studies in Philosophy: A Journal of Translations*. Summer.

Hershkovitz, Linda. 1985. "The Fruits of Ambivalence: China's Urban Individual Economy." *Pacific Affairs* 58.3.

Hinton, William. 1966. *Fanshen: A Documentary of Revolution in a Chinese Village*. New York: Monthly Review Press.

Ho, Ping-ti. [1962] 1976. *The Ladder of Success in Imperial China: Aspects of Social Mobility, 1368-1911*. Rp. New York: Da Capo Press.

Hosie, Alexander. 1890. *Three Years in Western China*. London: George Philip and Son.

———1905. "Report by Consul-General Hosie on the Province of Ssuch'uan." British Parliamentary Papers, no. 5.

———1922. *Szechwan, Its Industry, Products and Resources*. Shanghai: Kelly and Walsh.

Hommel, R. P. [1937] 1969. *China at Work*. Rp. Cambridge, Mass.: M.I.T. Press.

Hsu, Francis L. K. 1948. *Under the Ancestors' Shadow: Chinese Culture and Personality*. New York: Columbia University Press.

———1971. "Psychosocial Homeostasis and Jen: Conceptual Tools for Advancing Psychological Anthropology." *American Anthropologist*, no. 73.

Hu, Shi [1933] 1963. *The Chinese Renaissance: The Haskell Lectures*. Rp. New York: Paragon Book Reprint Corp.

Huang, Philip C. C. 1991. "The Paradigmatic Crisis in Chinese Studies: Paradoxes in Social and Economic History." *Modern China* 17.3.

Jin, Qi. 1989. "Why China Will Not Practice Privatization." *Beijing Review*, no. 32.

Judd, Ellen R. 1983–84. "Working Class Intellectuals in China." *Journal of Contemporary Asia* 14.2.

Kraus, Willy. 1991. *Private Business in China: Revival between Ideology and Pragmatic Policy*. Transl. from German by Erich Holz. London: Hurst.

Kuhn, Philip A. 1984. "Chinese Views of Social Classification." See Watson.

Kung, Lydia. 1981. "Perceptions of Work among Factory Women." In Emily Martin Ahern and Hill Gates, eds., *The Anthropology of Taiwanese Society*. Stanford, Calif.: Stanford University Press.

Leong, Y. K., and L. K. Tao. 1915. *Village and Town Life in China*. London: London School of Economics and Political Science.

Levy, Marion J. [1949] 1968. *The Family Revolution in Modern China*. Rp. New York: Atheneum.

Li Xin et al. 1987. *Dangdai getihu — Geti jingying 100 pian*. Beijing: Zhongguo qingnian chubanshe.

Liew, Leong H. 1989. "Chinese Reforms at the Crossroads: Problems and Prospects." Seminar paper: Modernization and Cultural Change in China, Turku University, June.

Link, Perry, Richard Madsen, and Paul G. Pickowicz. 1989. *Unofficial China: Popular Culture and Thought in the People's Republic*. Boulder, Colo.: Westview Press.

Little, Archibald. 1890. "Foreword." See Hosie.

Liu, Yia-ling. 1992. "Reform from Below: The Private Economy and Local Politics in the Rural Industrialization of Wenzhou." *China Quarterly*, no. 130.

Lyall, Arthur Comyn. 1907. "On the Relations between the State and Religion in China." *Asiatic Studies, Religious and Social* (London), vol. 2.

Ma, Jisen. 1988. "A General Survey of the Resurgence of the Private Sector of China's Economy." *Social Sciences in China*, no. 3.

Manoharan, Thiagarajan. 1990. "Basic Party Units and Decentralised Development." *Copenhagen Papers in East and Southeast Asian Studies* 5.

Morse, Hosea Ballou. [1909] 1966. *The Gilds of China*. Rp. Taipei: Ch'eng-Wen Publishing Company.

Mosher, Stephan. 1983. *Broken Earth: The Rural Chinese*. New York: Free Press.

Murphy, Robert F. 1971. *The Dialectics of Social Life: Alarms and Excursions in Anthropological Theory*. New York: Basic Books.

Nathan, Andrew J. 1986. "Sources of Chinese Rights Thinking." In R. Randle Edwards, Louis Henkin, and Andrew J. Nathan, *Human Rights in Contemporary China*. New York: Columbia University Press.

Needham, Joseph. 1969. *The Grand Titration*. London: Allen and Unwin.

———1974. "The Social Position of Scientific Men and Physicians in

Medieval China." *Japanese Studies in the History of Science. Proceedings*, no. 4.

Niehoff, Justin, D. 1987. "The Villager as Industrialist: Ideologies of Household Manufacturing in Rural Taiwan." *Modern China* 13.3 (July).

Odgaard, Ole. 1992. "Entrepreneurs and Elite Formation in Rural China." *Australian Journal of Chinese Affairs*, no. 28.

Paine, Robert. 1981. *Politically Speaking*. Philadelphia: Institute for the Study of Human Issues.

Pan, Lynn. 1987. *The New Chinese Revolution*. London: H. Hamilton.

Parkin, David. 1975. "The Rhetoric of Responsibility: Bureaucratic Communications in a Kenya Farming Area." See Bloch.

———1984. "Political Language." *Annual Review of Anthropology* 13.

Pong, David, and Edmund S. K. Fung. 1985. *Ideal and Reality: Social and Political Change in Modern China, 1860–1949*. Lanham, Md.: University Press of America.

Potter, Sulamith Heins. 1983. "The Position of Peasants in Modern China's Social Order." *Modern China* 9.4 (October).

Pye, Lucien W. 1988. *The Mandarin and the Cadre: China's Political Cultures*. Ann Arbor: University of Michigan.

Renmin ribao. 1985: 30 March and 3 November. 1987: 5 August. 1989: 22 August.

Richthofen, Ferdinand von. 1873. *Baron Richthofen's Letters 1870–1872*. Shanghai: North China Herald Office.

———1982. *Entdeckungsreisen in China, 1868-1872: Die Ersterforschung des Reiches der Mitte*. Herausgegeben von Klaus-Dietrich Petersen. Tübingen: Erdmann.

Rosaldo, M. Z. 1973. "I Have Nothing to Hide: The Language of Ilongot Oratory." *Language in Society* 2.

Rosen, Stanley. 1985. "Prosperity, Privatization, and China's Youth." *Problems of Communism* 34.

———1988. "Dissent and Tolerance in Chinese Society." *Current History*, September.

———1989. "Value Change Among Post-Mao Youth: The Evidence from Survey Data." See Link, Madsen, and Pickowicz.

Rosen, Stanley, ed. 1987–88. "The Private Economy," Parts 1 and 2. *Chinese Economic Studies* 21.1–2.

Schram, Stuart R. 1984. "Classes, Old and New, in Mao Zedong's Thought, 1949–1976." See Watson.

Schurmann, Franz. 1968. *Ideology and Organization in Communist China*.

Berkeley: University of California Press.

Service, John S., ed. 1989. *Golden Inches: The China Memoir of Grace Service*. Berkeley: University of California Press.

Sewell, W. G. 1986. *The Dragon's Backbone*. York: William Sessions.

Shapiro, Sidney. 1981. *Experiment in Sichuan: A Report on Economic Reform*. Beijing: New World Press.

Shi shi zhongxue jian jie. 1988. Chengdu: Shi Shi zhongxue.

Shirk, Susan. 1984. "The Decline of Virtuocracy in China." See Watson.

Sichuan jingji nianjian. 1987, 1988, 1989, and 1990. Chengdu: Sichuan sheng shehui kexueyuan chubanshe.

Sichuan sheng cheng xiang gong shang ye guanli banfa. 1987. Chengdu: Chengdu shi jinniu qu gongshang hang zheng guanli ju.

Solinger, D. J. 1984. *Chinese Business under Socialism*. Berkeley: University of California Press.

———1992. "Urban Entrepreneurs and the State: The Merger of State and Society." In Arthur Lewis Rosenbaum, ed., *State and Society in China: The Consequences of Reform*. Boulder, Colo.: Westview Press.

Szelenyi, Ivan. 1988. *Socialist Entrepreneurs: Embourgeoisement in Rural Hungary*. Madison, Wisc.: University of Wisconsin Press.

Taubman, Wolfgang, and Thomas Heberer. 1988. *Die Stadtische Privatwirtschaft in der VR China — Second Economy zwischen Markt un Plan*. Bremer Beitrage zur Geographie und Raumplanung, Heft 14. Bremen: Universität Bremen.

Taylor, Romeyn. 1989. "Chinese Hierarchy in Comparative Perspective." *Journal of Asian Studies* 48.3.

Tseng, Osman. 1988. "Industrialization Jolts the Family." *Free China Review*, December.

Vale, J. 1906. "The Small Trader of Szchuan." *The West China Missionary News* 8.10 (October).

Watson, James L., ed. 1984. *Class and Social Stratification in Post Revolution China*. Cambridge, U.K.: Cambridge University Press.

Walder, Andrew G. 1983. "Organized Dependency and Cultures of Authority in Chinese Industry." *Journal of Asian Studies* 42.1.

Wank, David. Forthcoming. "Symbiotic Alliance of Entrepreneurs and Officials: The Logics of Private Sector Expansion in a South China City." In Andrew Walder, ed., *The Political Consequences of Departures from Central Planning: Economic Reform and*

Political Change in Communist States. Berkeley: University of California Press.

Weber, Max. [1920] 1951. *The Religion of China, Confucianism and Taoism*. New York: Free Press.

———[1948] 1970. *From Max Weber: Essays in Sociology*. Ed. H. H. Gerth and C. Wright Mills. London: Routledge and Kegan Paul.

Whyte, Martin King. 1980. "Bureaucracy and Antibureaucracy in the People's Republic of China." In Gerald M. Britain and Ronald Cohen, eds., *Hierarchy and Society: Anthropological Perspectives on Bureaucracy*. Philadelphia: Institute for the Study of Human Issues.

———1990. "Changes in Mate Choice in Chengdu." See Davis and Vogel.

Whyte, Martin King, and William L. Parish. 1978. *Village and Family in Contemporary China*. Chicago: University of Chicago Press.

———1984. *Urban Life in Contemporary China*. Chicago: University of Chicago Press.

Wilhelm, Richard. 1930. *Chinesische Wirtschaftspsychologie*. Leipzig: Schriften des Weltwirtschafts-Instituts der Handels-Hochschule Leipzig.

Wilson, Richard W., and Anne Wang Pusey. 1982. "Achievement Motivation and Small-business Relationship Patterns in Chinese Society." In Sidney L. Greenblat, Richard W. Wilson, and Amy Auerbacher Wilson, eds., *Social Interaction in Chinese Society*. New York: Praeger.

Wong, Siu-lun. 1979. *Sociology and Socialism in Contemporary China*. London: Routledge and Kegan Paul.

———1985. "The Chinese Family Firm: A Model." *British Journal of Sociology* 36.1.

World Bank. 1985. *China: Long-Term Development Issues and Options*. World Bank Country Report. Washington, D.C.: World Bank.

Xia, Zhongrui. 1987. "Strengthening Guidance and Management; Expanding Individual Economy." See Rosen, ed.

Yang, C. K. 1961. *Religion in Chinese Society: A Study of Contemporary Social Functions of Religion and Some of Their Historical Factors*. Berkeley: University of California Press.

———1965. *A Chinese Village in Early Communist Transition*. Cambridge, Mass.: M.I.T. Press.

Young, Graham, ed. 1985. *China: Dilemmas of Modernization.* London: Croom Helm.

Young, Susan. 1989. "Policy, Practice, and the Private Sector in China." *Australian Journal of Chinese Affairs* 21 (January).

Yudkin, Marcia. 1986. *Making Good: Private Business in Socialist China.* Beijing: Foreign Languages Press.

Zafanolli, Wojtek. 1985. "A Brief Outline of China's Second Economy." *Asian Survey* 25.7 (July).

Zhengming (Hong Kong). 1989. No. 145 (16 October).

Zhongguo dangdai shehui wenti. 1989. Beijing: Guangming Ribao Chubanshe.

Zhongguo shibao. 1989. 23 October.

Zhou, Qiren, and Du Ying. 1984. "Specialized Households: A Preliminary Study." *Social Sciences in China,* no. 3.

Zhu, Qingfang. 1987. "On the Evolution of Individual Economy and Countermeasures." See Rosen, ed.

INSTITUTE OF EAST ASIAN STUDIES PUBLICATIONS SERIES

CHINA RESEARCH MONOGRAPHS (CRM)

6. David D. Barrett. *Dixie Mission: The United States Army Observer Group in Yenan, 1944,* 1970
17. Frederic Wakeman, Jr., Editor. *Ming and Qing Historical Studies in the People's Republic of China,* 1981
21. James H. Cole. *The People Versus the Taipings: Bao Lisheng's "Righteous Army of Dongan,"* 1981
24. Pao-min Chang. *Beijing, Hanoi, and the Overseas Chinese,* 1982
27. John N. Hart. *The Making of an Army "Old China Hand": A Memoir of Colonel David D. Barrett,* 1985
28. Steven A. Leibo. *Transferring Technology to China: Prosper Giquel and the Self-strengthening Movement,* 1985
29. David Bachman. *Chen Yun and the Chinese Political System,* 1985
30. Maria Hsia Chang. *The Chinese Blue Shirt Society: Fascism and Developmental Nationalism,* 1985
31. Robert Y. Eng. *Economic Imperialism in China: Silk Production and Exports, 1861–1932,* 1986
33. Yue Daiyun. *Intellectuals in Chinese Fiction,* 1988
34. Constance Squires Meaney. *Stability and the Industrial Elite in China and the Soviet Union,* 1988
35. Yitzhak Shichor. *East Wind over Arabia: Origins and Implications of the Sino-Saudi Missile Deal,* 1989
36. Suzanne Pepper. *China's Education Reform in the 1980s: Policies, Issues, and Historical Perspectives,* 1990
37. Joyce K. Kallgren, Editor. *Building a Nation-State: China after Forty Years,* 1990

sp. Phyllis Wang and Donald A. Gibbs, Editors. *Readers' Guide to China's Literary Gazette, 1949–1979,* 1990

38. James C. Shih. *Chinese Rural Society in Transition: A Case Study of the Lake Tai Area, 1368–1800,* 1992
39. Anne Gilks. *The Breakdown of the Sino-Vietnamese Alliance, 1970–1979,* 1992

sp. Theodore Han and John Li. *Tiananmen Square Spring 1989: A Chronology of the Chinese Democracy Movement,* 1992

40. Frederic Wakeman, Jr., and Wen-hsin Yeh, Editors. *Shanghai Sojourners,* 1992
41. Michael Schoenhals. *Doing Things with Words in Chinese Politics: Five Studies,* 1992

sp. Kaidi Zhan. *The Strategies of Politeness in the Chinese Language,* 1992

42. Barry Keenan. *China's Last Classical Academies: Social Change in the Lower Yangzi, 1864–1911,* 1993
43. Ole Bruun. *Business and Bureaucracy in a Chinese City: An Ethnography of Private Business Households in Contemporary China,* 1993

KOREA RESEARCH MONOGRAPHS (KRM)

9. Helen Hardacre. *The Religion of Japan's Korean Minority: The Preservation of Ethnic Identity,* 1985
10. Fred C. Bohm and Robert R. Swartout, Jr., Editors. *Naval Surgeon in Yi Korea: The Journal of George W. Woods,* 1984
13. Vipan Chandra. *Imperialism, Resistance, and Reform in Late Nineteenth-Century Korea: Enlightenment and the Independence Club,* 1988
14. Seok Choong Song. *Explorations in Korean Syntax and Semantics,* 1988
15. Robert A. Scalapino and Dalchoong Kim, Editors. *Asian Communism: Continuity and Transition,* 1988
16. Chong-Sik Lee and Se-Hee Yoo, Editors. *North Korea in Transition,* 1991
17. Nicholas Eberstadt and Judith Banister. *The Population of North Korea,* 1992

By turning this page you agree to join

March 16, 2016

Esteemed Lone Writer,

Every week my writer friends and I try to meet and write together. If we're in town and have time we meet in person, but usually we meet by phone. In the early days just one of us offered a prompt or theme to write about that day. Later, it morphed into each of us offering a prompt so we'd have a choice. Some of us even tried to include all the prompts in our response. Each time we meet we say hello, talk about the weather, then give the prompts, hang up and write. Twenty minutes later we call back and read what we've written to one another. After a year of doing this I realized how much better I liked my writing when I didn't have time to think about it. I found my pieces had more sparkle despite errors in grammar or spelling, despite meandering thoughts or confused ideas. In fact, I think the sparkle was due to those idiosyncrasies. There was always something that surprised me or caused me to think I'd like to write more about whatever had surfaced.

A prompt can be anything. Sometimes it's a poem or part of an essay. Sometimes it's as simple as the words 'Kindergarten' or 'Swimming Lessons.' The feedback we give each other might be I sure want to know more about that! or, I got lost when you said that thing about your uncle. Because we do this almost every week, and because I've grown to love and trust my writing friends, I've learned to enjoy and trust my own writing, too.

Writers often tell me they wish they had a writing group like ours. My hope is that the prompts and stories in this book will inspire you to write as though you have a group. Scribble your thoughts in the margins, fill up extra pages, edit what these writers have written, write the first story that comes to mind when you see the prompt. Don't think too much. Go on tangents. Write without editing. Edits and re-writes come later. And if you can't think of something to write, make something up.

Enjoy yourself. Write what's true.

Bar

How to use this book:

Each prompt is printed at the top of an empty page so you have room to write your response. Limit your self to seven minutes, ten minutes, or twenty at the most. Set a timer and stop when it beeps. After you're done, read my friends' responses. Some are more polished than others. Some wander. Some are literal and some are metaphoric. Some hardly make reference to the prompt. At the end of each of their responses is another prompt, but ignore those if something else is more compelling for you to write. Always write what you're on fire about. If you don't feel like writing something it'll sound like that when you're done. If you're stuck, write about being stuck. If you can't think of anything to write, write about not being able to write. And if you're in the middle of writing and your thoughts take some goofy turn, follow it. Have lots of extra paper on hand.

My only request is that you write for us. I've put our pictures on your empty writing pages to remind you to do that. In other words, see how it feels to write for others VS how it feels to write in your journal. If you're a fiction writer, write from your characters' points of view. Get to know them. Give us all the details you can. What does the kitchen smell like?

What fabric is on the couch? What was your heart really doing when someone you loved left you? Remember that we know nothing about you, your characters or the story you want to tell, so fill us in! Tell us as much as you can. And if you're worried that someone else might not like what you write, or that someone might read what you've written when you're not around to stop them, keep this book with you. Hide it in your glove compartment, put it in your t-shirt drawer. Many of us worry about what others will think. This book is a place to forget all those others (except for us!)

Here's your first prompt:

Draw a picture of yourself and/or your characters

Here's your second prompt:

Kindergarten

we're listening...

Mrs. Fenner said "who has that beautiful voice?" as she strode behind me one of those first warm days when I was five years old and so shy, so very shy.

We were singing this old man with Mrs. Dolan at the piano as our accompanist, banging on the black and white keys, her white short bob following the leaning in and out of her head as she felt the music she played, her black sturdy shoes sliding back and forth between foot pedals, me tugging at my dress, attire I wasn't used to wearing.

As soon as Mrs. Fenner said those encouraging words, I clammed up, couldn't sing, couldn't speak, I hung my head, wanting to disappear, and she seemed to know me, seemed to have a sense of this awkward bird in her classroom, so she placed a hand on the back of my shoulders, lightly, warm, smelling of chalk and faint perfume, her heavy body wrapped in a non-descript dress, her hair in a long single braid that was trussed up over and over around her head, she touched my shoulder, my back, my neck and though I never said or sang another word, my heart was filled with hope.

Which one of your teachers stopped you in your tracks?
(Use extra paper whenever you need to. There's some in the back of the book).

Our kindergarten picture says it all: Walter Burrows, John Walters, Nancy Brown sitting there with the rest of us: Laurie Inglish, Cathy Giles, Victor Williams, me. Integration. We didn't even understand the word. Walter, John, and Nancy were our friends. We didn't play at their houses after school but that's because their houses weren't in our neighborhoods. They took the bus just like we did. It's just that their journey was longer. I hadn't thought of that until just now. It wasn't until after we graduated from college that I went to Nancy's house, and even then, I only stuck my head in the door. By then, I lived down the street. My first apartment was on the same block. Nancy lived with her mom. No dad in sight. I never knew where John or Walter lived. Somewhere in that neighborhood for sure. That's where all the black kids lived. Their houses were small and generally not maintained. Or was it just that they were poor. Now those houses are the houses up-and-comings buy to wiggle their way into suburban Philadelphia life. Nancy lives in Wayne now. She's a single mom too. Loves Jesus and says so regularly on Facebook. John lives in Erie, Pennsylvania. He teaches at a boy's choir school out there. Don't remember the name. He and Nancy and I sang together all through high school. We fashioned ourselves after Lambert, Hendrix and Ross, the famous trio by that name. The original group was one of the first integrated singing groups. One black man (Hendrix) a white woman (Ross) and a white man (Lambert). Scandalous, but I'm not sure we even knew about that when the three of us sang together. We were protected from a lot of things in the early 1960s. The three of us recorded a few Christmas songs together after we graduated from college. It was the second time I'd done a recording session and I felt as though my life was truly beginning; that the whole world was opening up to me. Nancy brought that project to my attention this past winter wondering if I still had a copy of what we sang. I don't and wish I did. I remember making my family sit in my brother's room on Christmas morning that year so that they would listen to the songs. I didn't want to play them while mom was cooking or when everyone else was distracted by presents. I wanted them to hear every word. I'm still like that: I want people to sit and listen the way they would pay attention to a movie or a poem. But people don't feel that way about songs. They'll sit and listen to a symphony or an opera -- the classical forms – but pop songs like mine are meant for background listening. They set a mood while people are doing something else. I wonder how I could change that? I wonder how I could cause people to listen more closely to all the music they love.

What did you do in the talent show? How'd it go?

I don't think that I was particularly sophisticated at five-years-of-age. I wasn't watching Downton Abbey nor was I part of a cocktail circuit that involved mixed drinks. I didn't know about cleavage or high heels. I didn't know about fine food or fast cars. Under the watchful eye of my grandparents living downstairs and my parents living above them upstairs, I was sheltered. Aside from overhearing adults whispering cautions to one another, such as "Little pictures have small ears," I didn't know much outside the confines of home.

And yet I had aspirations. I can't tell you what they were, but like a dog that aspires to run free or a cat that aspires to lie close to the woodstove, I dreamed of bigger things – bigger things than running out in the street to buy fruits and vegetables from the blind man who peddled produce from his wooden wagon drawn by a moth-eaten horse. Or maybe the blind man could see a little – but at five, it was so much more exciting to imagine that he was totally blind.

Given my yearning for life outside the confines of my street and family, you would suppose that I would have looked forward to starting kindergarten. My kindergarten class photo shows me sitting in the front row. I am wearing brown, tie-up Buster Browns, white ankle socks, and a plaid dress with a white, Peter Pan collar. My blond hair is chin-length. My bangs are uneven. I do not look very self-confident or dreamy.

Mom had set a bleak tone. Walking to school that very first day, my mother confided that I had been assigned to the very same teacher whom she had had. The teacher was frightful. So frightful that Mom admitted to being afraid to enter the classroom with me for fear that the teacher would recognize her as a former pupil.

This was not a good beginning.

Twice a week we had music. Rhythm was an important part of the music curriculum. Week after week the teacher game me two, dowel-like sticks.

No drum accompanied the sticks. Was it my bad haircut? Maybe my dress? Maybe my mother? I aspired to play the tambourine. But week after week, the tambourine rotated between the other children.

They say "the sins of the parent are visited on the child." Did I put the teacher off or did the teacher remember my mother?

My next birthday, I'm going to buy a tambourine. It is not too late.

What do you still want for your birthday?

Before we heard the next prompt, Charlotte read the poem "Claim" by Jasey Jueds, about a dog that takes control.
From Keeper *©2013 University of Pittsburgh Press*

Who rescued you?
How were you rescued?

I think of all the dogs who've rescued me in one way or another: Mea,MaGirlMaGirl, Henry the Dog, MaceyG, and Foofoomoo. But Silver, that exquisite Doberman I adopted when I was 22, was my dog. The others came with husbands. Silver was the one who leaned his heavy black butt on my lap whenever I sat on the couch, the one who let me wrap him in a blanket as he fell into the space under my desk, the one who let me use him as a pillow when we lay on the cushy bench in the kitchen. Other people were afraid of him. He was big and boxy, and his tail and ears had been cut to meet the standard of champions; cut before he was old enough to object.

In New York City, when we walked down 8th Avenue to Central Park, passersby would get out of our way, cross the street if they were really afraid. They didn't know his gentleness. After a walk in Central park at dusk one night, he strutted down Broadway with a limb he'd found that was as long as the sidewalk was wide. So proud he was! He strutted like a thoroughbred that's won the Kentucky Derby. Like a king who's won an important victory. On-lookers laughed and smiled as we passed – him on a leash, me, his follower.

We danced together once in the Park. It was early on a Saturday morning in a place where dogs were free to run. No one else was there at first. Our private hill overlooked the lake where later in the day lovers would rent rowboats and move slowly, romantically across the water.

I was a dancer that morning. Who knows what propelled me. I turned, spun, revolved, around and around. Silver was my lover. He didn't bark. He didn't jump around demanding my attention. He too spun and ran in gentle circles on the hill. Both of us offlead. Both of us moving with grace and carelessness. Both of us aware of the photographer taking pictures of us from below. Photos we have never seen, photos that caught it all.

When did you do something that someone else watched and enjoyed?

*

If you are rescued is it the same as being saved? If it's different, why is it different and how do you, the person rescued or saved, actually know?

In the mirror I see dark eyes, more brown than I remember. I see eyebrows arched naturally no plucking maintenance needed. I see a nose wide like my father's, but different from the wide nose of my husband, my daughters. In the mirror, I see the powder falling from my nose resting just above the top of my lip. I see the powder and feel my hand come up to wipe it away, to adhere it to my finger and then swiftly to my tongue before the crystals disintegrate.

I see my life and become aware that I am trapped. Trapped inside the darkness that fills the eyes looking back at me. I see and do not believe.

Beside the mirror is the only door, the only exit from a bathroom almost too small for me and it is moving just a little bit toward me.

"Wait!" I see my lips moving in the mirror.

"Wait" I say again as my lips move in the mirror.

"Mommy!" Her words are urgent. Her dark and almond shaped eyes are likely filling with tears, but my foot is firmly against the door.

"Mommy!" She cries now, reaching the door knob, rattling it to open it.

In the mirror I see dark eyes framed by arched brows. I see my hand wipe away the powder, touch water to my nose, clear the crystals from my lip.

I hear her body slide down outside the door, know the tears fall freely down her face as she begs, "Come out!"

I don't know if I was rescued or saved. I don't know if there's a difference or even if there needs to be. But if I were asked, "Who rescued you?" My answer would always be she did.

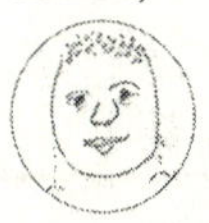

Look in the mirror. What do you see?

Look Out The Window. Describe What You See?

The porch swing hangs empty waiting for the warmth of the rising sun to seep through the Cedars. A farmer's feed pan sits atop an up-ended log. A Crested nuthatch flies to the shag. Hops closer… and closer yet…and finally hops to the edge of the pan to look for bird food. He doesn't stay long. The Pinon jays have beaten him to the bounty. It is slim pickin's.

A rock perimeter surrounds the neglected garden. Two, dead, cedar shags stand sentinel – landing pads for in-coming birds who want to take advantage of the seeds and bird bath. Three, large, variegated green and white agaves grow at the base of the shags. But otherwise, you might say that the garden, devoid of flowers, has gone-to-seed.

At ground level, an in-ground, cement birdbath holds water which is dark olive and opaque glassy white – a trick of shadow. Next to the birdbath and in the shadow of the shag and agave, lies a bronze-colored statue of a young nymph. She lies on her stomach – knees bent, feet in the air, ankles crossed. She has propped herself up on her elbows and in her hands she holds a book.

I love this girl – living in the dirt under a cactus – reading of far off places. Maybe she is reading about walking a forest path or wading in the surf… oh look! A Sandpiper!

A rabbit approaches the garden and tentatively hops six inches and then takes another cautious move – another six inches. It is a slow process. The rabbit stops to listen. He finally makes it to the edge of the sunken birdbath, cocks his head for one more listen and then heedless of danger, dips his head to drink. He drinks thirstily as if he has not drunk in a long time.

A half mile away, the traffic on Highway 50 hums.

Where were you when you saw The Birds? *Haven't seen it yet? How 'bout a movie you saw at the Drive-In?*

*

The courtyard is overgrown. Four pine trees envelope it. They're not yet golden, but many of their leaves are already on the ground. Winter is on its way. I see that Mea pooped out there last night so she must have really had to go despite my having walked her a few minutes earlier. She never poops in the courtyard. I'll clean it up later. Thankfully it's a nice sturdy poop. Easy to pick up. I never planted my flowerpots this year. There didn't seem to be a point. I say I'm going to sit out there each morning and read or write. Michael dreams about late night glasses of wine by the chiminea, but that never happened. The summer has gone by and we haven't enjoyed time at all. We've been racing against the clock for months now. It makes me wonder why we live here if we aren't going to slow down to the tempo of rural life.

The windows were my idea and I insisted. They're bit, well-built and well insulated. They turn out on a 45-degree angle for just enough air
to come through in winter, but not so much that the wind will rip them off in summer. Anderson. I love their windows. I like when I have the good sense to do things right. Before we changed them out, they were short and high on the wall. The room was like a dungeon despite its east-facing wall. This morning the 3-foot long windows are filled with the patchy morning sun coming through the leaves. The cobwebs I swore I wouldn't let build up, have done just that. The screens have dings from the contractor's sloppiness installing them - nothing to complain about, just enough to wish he had been more careful at the time.

Hal and Jamie are leaving this morning. I wonder if they'll ever be back. We're at the age now when you never know if the person you're saying good-bye to will be back. There's no reason to think on of them will go to the heavens any time soon, but we are that age. Maybe it'll be one of us. Who knows? I wish I could live each day as though it were my last like the self-help books suggest. I could only do that when Theo was
sick, and even then it was hard. After all it wasn't me who was dying.

Michael is leaving today too. Maybe while he's gone I *will* sit out in the courtyard. Last week I couldn't wait for the time alone. This week, I'm lonely and he hasn't left yet. I think about his death all the time. All the time.

Was there a time when you bought something big that you couldn't afford? (grab some paper here…)

The First Time I Lived on My Own

For years, in my 20s and 30s, I lived on my own / except when I was living with a man I loved / in a few different places. When I was living on my own, it came from wanting to get away from someone or some living situation that felt restrictive or unhappy or some combination of those.

My first time living on my own happened because I had fallen in love with a man that one of my housemates didn't approve of me seeing. She thought he was too young and spread an aura of judgment to encircle me.

I moved into a tiny cottage to escape her prying.

This cottage was near a lake and it was never constructed to be lived in year 'round – poorly insulated and drafty, pipes that were vulnerable to freezing in the harsh winter temperatures, one propane heater to huddle around when the cold winds rustled the curtains inside the dark living room.

The cottage was just a living room, bedroom, another room, a rectangular kitchen and a bathroom that also served as a closet for the hot water heater. All the rooms were small. Cheap, dark wood paneling. Mildew that crept up the closet walls and ruined several pairs of my shoes and boots before I discovered it. Indoor / outdoor carpeting. Chipping linoleum.

I loved that cottage. It represented freedom to me. The bedroom was sunny. I fixed the place up as best as I could on my own with little income.

My mother gave me the Farberware percolator that had been one of their wedding presents 20-some years before – it was exactly my age – and I still use the same type coffeemaker today because, even now, once in a while, the aroma and sound of percolating coffee on a winter morning takes me back to that tiny cottage and the joy I felt living there.

The young man I loved could come over and we could spend time together without my feeling the weight of my friend's piercing looks.I had small dinner parties and took walks to the lake and felt so independent and grown up.

The kitchen walls were sunny yellow and it was my first of many cozy homes. I think I only lived there about a year – so long ago now, I can't be sure – but I loved that place and that man. So much.

A cabin, a lake, and a hardware store. Ring a bell?

My first apartment was on County Road in Ardmore on the edge of the Black neighborhood. Behind my building were Italians; in front, the Black kids I've only recently figured out were bussed to four different elementary schools when we were all kids in the '60s. Nancy Brown and her mother were four doors down. Both were large, fleshy women; the kind of women you merge with when you hug them. Nancy and I sang together in the choir and later in smaller ensembles with John Burrows who lived two doors down from her. We were the Mod Squad for a while. Now we're friends on Facebook. She's a single mom now too. John's an actor living in Erie, Pennsylvania.

Our apartment stretched the length of the first floor of the narrow single-family home turned multi-dwelling complex. It was a broken down building with a rickety back entrance through an aluminum screen door, and a more substantial but poorly maintained wooden front door. I rented the enclosed front porch from the woman who had the lease. She had the big bedroom at the back. The kitchen had no cabinets, a freestanding old fridge and a brown linoleum floor. The only bathroom was small and grungy, just off the kitchen. Between my 10'x10' porch and the kitchen was a dining room, a sitting area, and my closet. The woman I rented from, whose name I've forgotten, must have had money in her past. Her rugs and furniture were elegant and formal. They didn't belong in this space. I didn't know her. I'd answered an ad in the paper a few months after graduating from college when it was time for me to get my own place. I was money to her. Neither of us was interested in friendship or conversation. We avoided one another as much as possible. She and her boyfriend – probably a married man given their odd and frequent meeting times – had loud and, I thought, too aggressive sex I couldn't avoid overhearing. I worried about her at times but she always seemed pleased when I'd see her in her robe a few hours later. Her cats ate the wires to my stereo speakers. That's when I moved out.

It was not a happy time but it was the first step into my own life, away from the comfy home I'd grown up in.

I loved my little room there. I got my first piano there – an upright that I scraped and re-finished until it looked pretty good and sounded ok, too. It was the room where I set-up my first four-track recorder and removed myself from the world with headphones. I wrote my first real song there: "Friday Night," a quirky song, half spoken half sung, about a shy high school girl going to her first dance in the school gym. That room is where I closed the doors and cried when John Lennon was shot, and it was the room I was in when I fell for Jim, the man who encouraged me to write songs, who taught me about my creativity, and who later wrecked my heart by denying me.

When did an animal wreck something of yours? What were you denied?

Warning Signs

When I Said Too Much

Money as Therapy

Before we got the following prompt, Penny read from Annie Dillard's book The Writing Life, *where the author talks about how a work in progress is feral, wild, and needs to be tamed like a mustang, that this can only done by visiting everyday and reasserting your power over it. The passage was from chapter three.*

When Your Writing is Feral

I was reading in bed when Keith came in. I don't know how her name came up, if I was having lunch with her the next day or if she was coming over to our house so I could give her a Reiki session, but I remember my husband asking, "You know she's in love with you, right?"

Without even looking up from the book, I said, "You always say that, but I think what you're picking up on is my body reacts when I'm around her."

I said it matter-of-factly. I said it without looking up from the page, but when I did, his face told me I had said too much. His eyes were wide, his face troubled. He tightened the belt on his bathrobe. Even though I had said too much he wanted to know more.

"What do you mean your body reacts? You're attracted to her?"

"No, I'm not attracted to her—she's pretty, but that's not what I mean. I mean my body reacts…"

"So you're attracted to her…," he said.

We got tangled up in semantics. What I was trying to say was I didn't want to sleep with her. I didn't want to be with her and not him. But it was undeniable: When she was around, my stomach dipped. I pulsed. I felt awkward and nervous, like a teenager at a school dance. When she was around, I peeked at her cleavage and followed the curve of her muscular arms and back.

We met while I was out walking the dogs, the day before I was to have bunion surgery on my left foot on Halloween 2007. She was driving through our little town in a brand new metallic green Jeep Wrangler that said both "I'm cool" and "I have money." She pulled over, leaned out the window while her boys popped up out of the open top.

"Beautiful dogs," she said. Her long, light brown hair hung below a hip headband. She wore sunglasses.

"Thank you," I said.

"Can we pet them?" the boys pleaded. They were maybe 4 and 8. One was towheaded like my son was at his age; the other skinny with brown hair.

"No, not today," she told them.

"Mom!" they groaned.

"We have to get home for supper," she said.

We swapped a few more pleasantries. When she drove away, I wished I had gotten her name, but it was a small town, so I knew I'd see them again.

Months passed. I had my bunion surgery, which kept me on crunches for three months, and then it was another four months before I really got out and started walking again. I was overweight after lying around for months after my surgery. By the time spring rolled around I was anxious to get back outside and to get the weight off. I had also decided to take Pilates—an exercise that had helped me tighten and firm when I did it years before.

One day while waiting in line at a coffee shop, a business card seemed to call out to me. I took one from a stack and was surprised to see that it was for a Pilates center I had never heard of before. I emailed the woman later that day and she wrote back a very friendly response. We exchanged emails and I tried to figure out how to get $150 for three private sessions.

I was out walking the dogs, plotting how I would drop the weight by my birthday in May, when I saw the green Jeep again. The woman pulled over and the boys popped up again and we continued our conversation from the past fall. This time I was determined to not let her get away without knowing her name.

"By the way, I'm Ann. I live over on Meadow Lane," I said, extending my hand to her.

"Melissa," she said. "Melissa Donovan." Excitement shot through me: She was the woman I had been exchanging emails with about Pilates. It was a sign—I knew it, she knew it.

Somehow I would find the money to work with her. I had to.

When did you find the money you didn't think you had?

None of these prompts work for me today, at least not immediately. I don't feel like writing the obvious for 'Warning Signs': Ben wanting Sarah to be at our wedding, Ben calling Sarah repeatedly on the sly, my catching him repeatedly when I didn't mean to and didn't want to, or Ben sleepless and distracted when Sarah was in danger. I'm tired of them and I'm bored with writing about it.

'Saying Too Much' is a curse I'm blessed and burdened with. I often talk too much, say too much, blurt things out that I think will be funny but aren't. There are hundreds if not thousands of examples – so many that I can't even think of one. Trying to conjure one up to write about makes my eyes cross behind my skull. Yet I write memoir. I encourage myself and others to "go deeper," "tell us more," "give us the juicy bits," not for the shock value but for the value of truth telling. When I read memoir that withholds a detail or a character flaw, I can feel it and I get bored. When a writer insists that her main character is always happy she's not a believable writer. There are probably those who have that view of my writing – or worse: me!

'Money for Therapy' in one of my themes. Less so now than when I was young: I bought things to prop myself up, make myself look good. I think of expensive devices I bought that were more than I needed but had some cache. But like the other prompts, this is a subject I'm bored with. The prompt itself came from a self-help book our therapist suggested called *Money Therapy.* It's lying on the floor at my feet. I read it every so often to knock some sense into myself. On the cover I've put a Post It note that says, "Budgeting does not equal deprivation." Carl, our therapist, wants me to think about my belief that if I make a monthly budget I won't have what I want. I'm not a realist when it comes to money. I've always believed, and it's mostly been true, that everything works out. Bills get paid. Every time I pull my credit card through a keypad I'm pretty much relying on that belief. So boring.

And Annie Dillard? She's in the same category as Bob Dylan for me: I don't get it. Annie's sentences are too formal, too well written, so dense with meaning and self-worthiness that I tune her out then feel smug *and* inferior. Bob Dylan? I know his lyrics are supposed to be brilliant, but I don't understand them. When I hear others sing them it's better, but I always feel like my suburban Philadelphia upbringing has insulated me from feeling the cultural pain that he describes. And I can't tolerate his voice. Generally I love non-singers like him. Singers who, in my view, are the greatest singers: Randy Newman, Tom Waits, Rickie Lee Jones. These people whose voices aren't smooth, they're raspier like speech, they have a need to sing that I can feel. I've never heard that in Dylan's voice. When I hear him sing it's like I'm resisting being shaped by a metal file. Harsh words that feel like sacrilege to write. I can even feel my heart racing and my underarms getting moist knowing I'll have to read this aloud. Someday maybe I'll understand them both.

When did you buy something to make yourself feel better? Did it work?
Who do you dislike that everyone around you seems to love?

It was the look on her face coupled with the sound of her voice, a rising questioning tone that caused me to move to the right lane, slowing in traffic as we headed down the highway. We'd taken a short break from the routine of our lives to sit by the ocean, listening as waves lapped the sand it hugged and the sand surrendered and let go. Sharing that sense of how big and small we are in the world. She couldn't have been more surprised as I chattered on telling stories of my life.

The two-lane road away from one beach town and on the way to another suddenly seemed a metaphor I couldn't quite grasp. I could see the subtext in the lanes, but found I wasn't sure what it all meant. Something I couldn't quite understand just passed by in our conversation.

After a few minutes of dissipating traffic, I chanced a look over for clarification. Breathing out a "What?", my heart beat rapid and strong. Her gaze steady through the windshield felt less passenger-side riding and more driving with determination. There was definitely something.

"I didn't know that." There, she'd said it. Relayed the message clear and with the resilience of high definition radio. The pin dropped and the message rose swiftly to the top and there it was.

Oh shit, I done said too much.

When did you realize it wasn't going to work?

It is hard to imagine Annie Dillard's work becoming feral, but I certainly identify with the intention of the quote. I have hyphenated a-work-in progress because the work is linked to progress and yet…"the work" itself is solid, but the progress is ephemeral – progress is early morning mist on the mountains: the sun warms, and the mist dissipates; progress is storm clouds building on the horizon that fail to deliver; progress is…

Writing of my own work, some work is already written but some thoughts on work are only brief flashes that light the sky and disappear before I can catch them. I find that progress is exceedingly slow. I am so easily distracted by an unwashed dish, an unmade bed, an unwatered garden, an unanswered letter, an unpaid bill. And as I write this, I notice all of my adjectives start with the prefix "un."

And that "un" says it all. "Un is a vacuum – a negative space that begs to be filled. Which leads me back to my lack of self-discipline.

I like to imagine myself in a convent. The windows are narrow slits. The doors are locked. The bed is hard and the covers inadequate. The floor is stone. I am cold. I can't get warm. Visitors are admitted but a grilled separates us. meals would be prepared. Meditation would be required. Silence would reign. Mother Superior would stand ready with a switch. Not that her birch switch would hurt me, but the notion of being switched – not by my own mother, but by another adult would be humiliating. This fear of humiliation would keep me at my desk.

Writing would be my only outlet. I would be inspired and productive. I would make progress.

What have you left undone?

If you're like a lot of people you might need an extra page for this one...

Rules

The Space Between Us

Time you enjoy wasting is not wasted time

This is the world. Beautiful and Terrible Things Will Happen.

Don't be Afraid

You don't call or write anymore. I can feel you pulling away. What did I do to make you want to leave me? I did not ask for this. Are you happy? Content? Do you feel lighter without me? How does it feel to be single again?

Do I really want you back? "What part of you do I miss the most," I ask myself.

I miss the security knowing that I have someone to come home to each evening. I miss hearing about your day. I miss having someone to take care of.

I've got all this time on my hands. Were you really the perfect mate for me? When I look back, I don't think you could fully receive my love. I think we did the best we could with what we knew. We worked extremely hard and built a home together, but we didn't really play. You couldn't let go and just laugh and have a great time.

You found happiness at the beach, on your bike, or on a run. Your world was so insular. You worked a lot. We never took any road trips. I had to arrange all the fun activities. You were only fully relaxed when we left town and went on vacation.

Why do I want you back so badly? Why do I miss you? Do I really miss *you*? What is it that I truly miss? Was I just married in name only? Maybe I crave having a companion, a playmate. I don't know. In the meantime, I miss you. A lot. Now there's just a space between us.

How old were you the first time your heart was broken?

How 'bout the second time?

I'd forgotten about that feeling. Stretching my inner thighs, my outer thighs, my neck, back, and arms. When I first sat down, I thought *here I am in the sun with ten minutes. I could read. I could write. I could knock on the door and go in.* The sun felt warm, warm enough to remove my jacket. Ants crawled across the pavement causing me to rethink the option of lying flat on the driveway. I'm not afraid of ants, I just don't like the feel of them crawling on my skin or up my pants. I thought *well, I could just sit here. Do nothing. I haven't done nothing for a long time. Surely nothing would be a good thing for me to do.* But hard. So I stood, remembering that a few extra minutes is a good time to stretch particularly when the sun is out. Arms to the sky thinking about the vultures in the tree above me who were up there yesterday too. Wings stretched in flight or to dry after a moist morning. Then down, slowly, down to the ground, feeling a slight twinge, reminding me not to push, to breathe, to sigh. Leslie taught me to sigh. In any position when the stretch feels tight, at the very end, sigh. The sound, the act of sighing releases the muscles just a little bit further. That sigh got me in trouble once. Not trouble really, just confusion for my dear, 93-year-old father. I had decided to stretch in the bathroom on the 2nd floor. It's the only room in their house with a door and enough floor space for a person to lie down in private. So I was there on the rug, twisting on my back, pulling my bent knees from side to side, slowly, rhythmically, sighing repeatedly, on the floor for several minutes. My father – in his office right next door, overhearing this rhythm, these sighs, not understanding – finally said, "I think it's time for you to come out of there, Charlotte." *Why?* I thought surprised because I was in the quiet zone. It didn't occur to me until a few minutes later what he'd been thinking. Too late to say "I was stretching, Dad" just so he wouldn't think ill of me. Does he think I would spend so much time in his house enjoying myself in such a way with or without him nearby? I wonder. But it was too late to explain. If I'd tried, he and I both would have had to acknowledge what he was thinking and I couldn't bear that. Wouldn't do that to my dad.

What did you do that your parents misunderstood? Would they understand if you explained it?

The space between us pulsates, vibrates. It pulls us in and confuses us. I'm married. You're not. Still, we won't cross that line. We will leave with our integrity intact. Coming together under the covers isn't necessary because the connection is far deeper than that. I don't need to lie next to you, naked, but oh my, do I want to feel your skin, touch your breasts, kiss you long and deep.

I have to go home, back to him, back to the life I've created in Iowa. But this space between us will not widen. It will gather into itself. It will stitch us together even though we are hundreds of miles apart, even though I am white, a Midwesterner, blonde, blue-eyed—no one you have ever considered for yourself. You're black, a New Yorker who can't fathom how we will ever be more than distant friends.

That space between us doesn't stay intact. It can't. A force we don't comprehend is pulling us together. The space between us disappears through phone calls and emails, G-chats and hotel rooms.

I leave him—not for you, no, but for me. I move farther away from you so that I can be closer to me.

I leave but in the going, I take you along. In my heart. In the space between us.

What did you leave behind?

It is late, and I am on the bus headed north up to Green Lanes. The bus is nearly empty. A young couple furtively gropes one another in the back of the bus. A middle-aged woman with impossible red hair sits up front. A woman with silver, sequined shoes worn with sock sits across the aisle. And that's it. As I said, the bus was nearly empty.

The bus stops, and an elderly man comes on. He swipes his Freedom Pass and starts down the aisle There are lots of empty seats. I'm sitting half way down the bus on the right. The driver steps on the gas, and the elderly man lurches forward.

He wears a Russian-like cap with built in earflaps, a plaid muffler, a greatcoat, and more. I can't see beneath his coat, but it is obvious that he is dressed in layer after layer. Maybe he is wearing everything he owns.

Hanging on to the backs of the seats for balance, he works his way down the aisle, and when he reaches my seat, he stops and falls in beside me. Of all the empty seats, why mine?

He speaks to me in a heavy foreign accent. Who am I? Where am I from? Where am I going? To each question I give a brief answer. Meanwhile, he is moving incrementally closer and closer yet. First we are just joined at the hip. Later at the shoulder.

Like an animal, he burrows in. I am not a woman. He is not a man. I am merely a warm place. I hope our mute communion warms him as much as it warms me.

Have you ever met someone you'd like to meet again?

Your First Favorite Song

A Lie in the Service of Truth

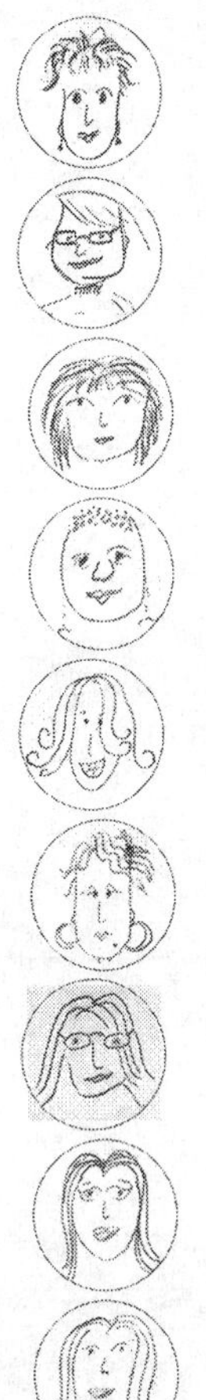

The first song I memorized was "Joy to the World" by Three Dog Night. I thought my sister would think I was cool if I could sing along with them. Not so much.

What did you do to try to impress someone else that didn't work?

Way, way back, what I first remember is the feeling. The feeling of knowing a tune so well it sings itself in my head and taps itself in my footsteps. The words tumble over and over in my mouth. I remember the feeling of a favorite song before I remember the song.

According to the baby book my mother kept for me, the song I loved to sing as a toddler was "The B-I-B-L-E."

The B-I-B-L-E/ Yes! That's the book for me./ I stand alone on the word of God,/the B-I-B-L-E

It has a bouncy little tune, so I can imagine it was fun to sing. But who knows if it actually was my favorite, or if my mom just wanted it to be. Of course, the songs that get stuck in our heads are not always favorite songs. Sometimes they're just stuck. A friend of mine calls this song bondage.

But the first song I remember discovering on my own -- the first song I remember having power over me -- was from the Barbra Streisand movie, *Yentl.* It is the story of a Jewish woman who feels God made her to study the Bible at a time when her tradition only gave this privilege to men.

Something in the combination of story and voice, lyric and melody ignited in my own life. It spoke for something in my 12-year-old experience that nothing else in my world had been able to say. The song was "Piece of Sky."

It all began the day I found/
that from my window I could only see a piece of sky
I stepped outside and looked around/
I never dreamed it was so wide or even half as high!/
The time had come to try my wings/
and even though it seemed at any moment I could fall/
I felt the most amazing things,/
things you can't imagine if you've never flown at all...

The orchestration, Barbra Streisand's powerhouse voice, the look on her face in the movie as she sang. All of this unlocked something achy and hungry in me. Something desperate but also vague. Something I still can't name without diminishing it.

The way I heard them, the final lines of the song stood bravely against the small space of small-minded tradition. They leaned into a divine call toward God's inherent gift of something bigger and vastly more beautiful. All of it wrapped in the rapturous emotion only an adolescent heart can feel.

What's wrong with wanting more?/ If you can fly, then soar.
With all there is, why settle for just a piece of sky?

I begged my mother to buy the record of the soundtrack for me. I played it over and over until I knew it by heart.

Where was the stereo in your house? Who got to use it?

Was it a lie or was it withholding? I don't know if it makes a difference. Either way I didn't do what I was supposed to do. Looking back, I don't know how I could have done things differently, but of course I could have. I could have blurted out the whole beautiful truth and it would have hurt people just as thoroughly. The advantage would have been that I'd know I hadn't lied, hadn't withheld, that I'd done what I needed to do for myself.

I'm talking about falling in love, that wonderful feeling I hadn't felt in over fifteen years. My skin hot and damp to touch, my heart beating hard enough that I could feel it in my chest, and my eyes seemed sparkly and probably were. The world around me was vital again, and more than anything I felt my womanhood stirring and operating again. It was a private and precious time. I didn't want to lose it or diminish it by sharing it with anyone – least of all the man I was married to.

Walks in the woods were my escape. Long, meandering walks alone in the Adirondack Mountains. I'd say to myself *Go! Take off. Find a place you've never been before.* I'd walk for hours a day for what must have been a year. Early on, when the thrill of new love was too strong, I told my husband it was time for us to separate – this time for real. We'd talked about it for years, but the time had come. It only took 28 days of emails and new love for me to realize my marriage was over. 28 days! After 15 years of marriage. I see now that the quickness of it all, plus the lack of argument or resistance from either of us is a testament to how necessary the ending was. We were ready. Not sad. Not regretful or angry. Just fully aware of where we'd gotten to.

Should I have told him then? I wanted to. I needed to, and yet I didn't. I wanted to stay in my fragile, finite bubble of pleasure for as long as I could.

I've written about this so many times, thought about it endlessly, and the conclusion is always the same: I couldn't have and wouldn't have done anything differently. My lie, my withholding, was in service to my self. Joy had been absent for so long and the thrill of attraction was too strong for me to be able to do anything differently.

The soul searching I continue to do has become boring and tedious for me, for you, and for anyone I've leaned on to get me through the whiplash that's followed. Time seems to be the healer. Time has proven the reality of love, and that my lie was in service to that love.

Is there a better reason?

Where did you go when you had nowhere to go?

The Hour I First Believed

We're still here...

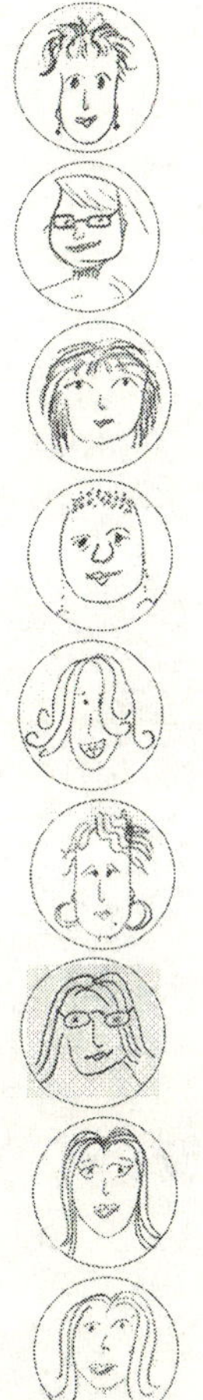

The hour I first believed my mother was dying started with the hospice nurse finding a room for my sister Kari, and I to sit as she pitched the benefits of this hospice program. Hospice Nurse Robin put the royal-blue looseleaf binder on her lap, turning the pages as if she were a kindergarten teacher. I half expected her to pull out a pen and start writing letters upside down too.

In her pronounced southern accent, she said, "Oh hospice is not your grandmother's hospice anymore." She went on to say, "we care for the patient from the moment they enter the program—at home and at the hospice house. We know how important care is at this time of your mother's life. That people can live a long time, in the program, and often do." Nearly an hour has passed since I arrived and I'm having difficulty listening. I find myself drifting down to the pages of the binder and notice they have those adhesive-backed circles used to repair the holes of each page when the page has torn away from the binding clip. How is it I'm sitting here listening to this nurse talk of the advances in palliative care and this process of fixing the holes is still used—still necessary.

Though Robin tries to include me, I know she's really speaking to my sister who told her, deliberately, that she was a cardiac ICU nurse quickly establishing a medical bond between them. With no medical background I'm left to the musing of my brain as it tries to process the term "end stage." Even as they continue working through this new bond, I find thoughts in my mind and follow them in just the way we are told not to do when meditating. Had I known how, I think I would have started present-moment awareness immediately.

Consciously back in the room, once again seeing and hearing Robin as she flips the page and points to the pleasant, almost idyllic building surrounded by spring flowers and carefully-cared for shrubbery. She pulls the leave-behinds, the marketing material from the binder sleeve. I see her business card stapled neatly to the top. I take it from her hands as she and my sister continue to talk using phrases like, the meds didn't seem to 'touch' her, she is 94% occluded, and there shouldn't be any problem getting her approved for hospice at home.

How long did it take for me to believe Robin knew what was happening, understood what was best, was saying not just what I needed to hear, but that she was right about the care my mother would need for the time she had remaining? How long? It was nearly an hour the first part of which was filled with the barking cough of lungs that couldn't quite shake the pneumonia my mother developed. The last part an internal struggle where I found myself back in my mind following the only thought I had left. My mother is dying.

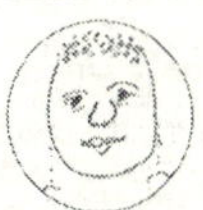

Who was the first person you loved who died? How old were you?
Describe it as though you were that age?
Then try it again from the point of view of where you are now.

Bear Hollow Road is long and steep heading up Mount Marcy. Trees drape over it from both sides, dense and full, colorful in the fall. Walking up is a workout; walking down is a relief. I park my car at the bottom, hide the keys on top of the front tire, then head up. When I lived with Ben, I could walk out our front door, turn right onto a path through the woods that led to a point a little higher than where I park my car now. I used to walk the dogs there a few times a day. When Theo was a baby, I'd say, "this is where God is for me" when we got to a certain curve in the path. There was something about the light that came through the pines, but also a knowing that something more than trees and light was happening there. I felt like I was being watched when I was at that spot. That onlookers were present, interested, but getting on with the life they were leading wherever it was they were. It was comforting. As though I had friends who were paying attention through that stretch.

My walks started getting longer and more rigorous when I met Michael. I needed to work harder. I walked higher and higher, deeper and deeper into the wilderness every day. I wanted to know for sure that if I went off the path I could still find my way home. I needed to know that I could get over my fear of being in an unknown place. More than anything I wanted to be somewhere where no one could find me; where I was truly alone. When I got to the highest, farthest away point on a given day, I'd sit, look up, rest, enjoy the absolute quiet that I found in the woods. I've always been happiest alone.

On a downhill walk months after I'd moved away from that house with Ben, I saw that light again coming through a different set of trees. This was a brighter light that the rose-gold light streaming through the pines years before. It was pure sunlight, nothing particularly holy about it. I'd been filled with angst climbing up. I was tired of loneliness and confusion. Every moment of the previous six months I'd been thinking about what to do about loving Michael. Everything about it was wrong. Lots of people, whole families would be hurt if we came together. But not coming together was impossible. We were already together. We were already a pair despite 2000 miles between us. But when I saw that sun coming through the trees I made a choice. It was instantaneous. I chose to be joyful. I wanted love, and I wanted.

Have you ever been alone in the woods? What did it smell like? What do you want?

Waking. So many sleeps. So many doubts. So many things to awake to, to believe in.

Yesterday, a long-time Christian woman, a woman who has worked at our church and who is now taking seminary classes and coordinating missions trips to Africa -- she looked at me and said, "This summer, in the midst of all this work, I had this thought that scared me: Is God even real?" She practically whispered the question. I know she expected me, as the pastor's wife, to look concerned and offer to pray, to assure her and to chastise her for even thinking such a thing.

Instead, I told her it was a pretty important question to ask. Then she was the one who looked surprised.

The faith tradition I was raised in emphasized a special moment of conversion -- a threshold of belief. And I think what they meant by conversion was something that happened to me about the age of four. But there was no way in the world that something that happened when I was four could be the whole shebang anymore than a first date or even a wedding day is the sum total of a marriage.

So there was the hour I first believed that I was truly, no-kidding, absolutely and at my core -- a sinner (to use the old theological word). I was 28. For while I had prayed the prayer at four and grew up singing the songs and memorizing the Bible, I did not truly believe there was anything wrong with my character. I was an obedient, compliant child. I always did what was asked of me. I was kind and generous. I was forgiving and patient. I was a good student and a good friend.

But at 20, I wondered if the protestant folks I'd grown up with had the best way of doing life. I put some distance between me and the church. I slowly drifted away from the circles of faith, and then I fell in love with a man who was married. It's a longer story than I have time to tell now, but a year after I met him, I was living with him and it had devastated my family. I had disappointed people who thought I would never be the one to step off of the straight and narrow. But their disapproval was not the thing that convinced me I had a deep flaw in my soul that I could not heal. It was not their pressure.

It was me. I was taking a class that summer on film noir -- and had spent the morning sitting in the dark watching Barbara Stanwick turn Fred McMurry from a Disney hero into a cold-blooded murderer. As I stepped out into the hot furnace of the parking lot, I felt like I was on the edge of an abyss. I never, ever thought that I would be the "other woman." Never, in a million years would I have done it. But here I was anyway. And if I could get here, what would keep me, in time, from killing someone?

And if I was capable of that, then grace had a whole new meaning. Than I really, really needed it. And I didn't deserve it. At all.

But there it was, before I even asked for it, I sensed it, I felt it. I was a hot mess. And I was loved anyway. By the maker of love Itself.

Describe God. Be specific.
If you don't believe in God, describe not believing.
(You might need more paper for this one...)

She was old enough to know better

The Next Right Thing

Before the next prompt, Charlotte read Mary Oliver's Poem "Don't Worry" from Felicity *(2015) in which the poet says, "Don't worry," followed by the question, how long do you think it takes a saint to become a saint?*

How do you worry?

Annie chose "She Was Old Enough to Know Better," except all she heard was, "She Was Old."

My mother was old at 60. I am standing behind her, leading her into a private room at a Mexican restaurant, all of her family and friends gathered there to celebrate her 60th. I'm cautious, aware that this surprise may be too much for her. I'm protective, steering her through the crowd to the door of the room, easing her inside, delighting in her delight.

I miss her and yet I feel her everywhere still, even though it's been 12 years since she passed.

I talk to her on my morning walks. I ask her to help me with this and that. A chill runs through my body when I make these requests of her and of others who have gone on to the other side. I smile when it happens, when I feel the cold and know that I am surrounded by beings I cannot see.

My mom loved me. I know that. I wish she had done life differently—and yet. She died at 71, probably 40 years longer than she thought she would. Not a minute too soon or too late. Her body didn't serve her well. She didn't serve her well.

I learned from her example. Learned of self-destruction, of self-preservation, of making different decisions.

She loved me. I loved her. We're still connected even though I'll never again feel her touch—not in the palm of my hand, not on my shoulder. But still I know she's there.

What did you learn from your mom?

Write whatever comes to mind. If you mis-read or mis-hear a prompt, go with it. Some times the most interesting stuff comes from this kind of mistake.

I've been thinking a lot about the evolution of my sexuality, the randomness of the people who were involved. Some of them I didn't know well enough for them to touch me but I let them anyway. There was an adolescent necessity for those experiments.

Earlier, there was a natural evolution from touching Barbie's plastic breasts to playing doctor with Katie and Louise in the McConnell's attic. We touched each other in the dim light and enjoyed first-hand experience. I don't remember talking about it, planning it, or agreeing to it, we just did it. A few years later, Rob Camillino fumbled with my bra. I didn't know him. Hardly said a word to him before we were on someone's couch across from the school. I don't remember enjoying it or not enjoying it, I don't remember feeling guilty or not guilty. It was just something we did. A necessary step

I could go on with my list of boys and later, men. It's not an extra long list but it's long enough for me to wonder why? - not because of its length but because of its quality. There were no bad guys. No one hurt me with violence or aggression. But the list is full of men who were careless, men who had things on their mind that were more important than me. Looking back, I feel responsible for that. Despite every effort on my mother's part, I did not take her advice to respect my body. Each one of the men on my list (except for one, maybe two) was a lazy choice on my part. A choice to stick around rather than act on the fact that I wasn't getting what I needed.

Like Rob Camillino fighting the clasp on my bra, I just stayed at it as if I was obligated to be there, as though I had no choice. Getting to first base didn't require devotion it only required desire and my need to begin sexual exploration with the opposite sex.

I was old enough to know better later in my life, yet I didn't. If a man wanted me and was brave enough to ask, I said yes. And then I'd stick around because I didn't know what else to do; because I didn't know I needed more than a man wanting me in his life. I had to want him too.

If I'd been enjoying myself back then my list would look different to me now.

Where were you the first time you got to second base?
When did you do something you only half-wanted to do?

The Softest Voice

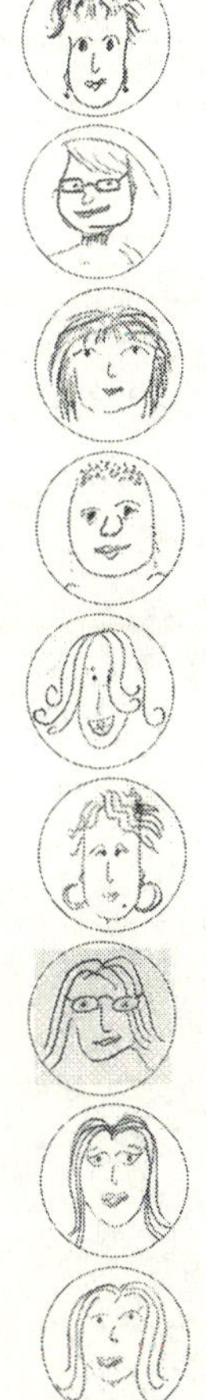

For decades, I've pulled over, removing dead animals from the roadways, whispering prayers for them, to them, settling their lifeless bodies into the grasses and expressing condolences to their friends and families who live in the trees, burrows, caves, but today on this chilly morning, a chestnut colored blur races in from the right side, and as I pump my brakes, swerve, there's a small thud, a very small thud.

With a look in the side mirror, I see a body flip up then down, my heart races, I turn around, go back, put my flashers on, walk to her. I see her right eye, otherwise she's perfect, no blood around her beautiful body, the body with the alternate black and white stripes down the sides of her back, the body with the rust colored tail, cheeks stuffed with nuts.

I pick her up, can hardly believe what' I've done, her body is warm, it's so warm, life was there just a moment ago.

I walk with her tiny body in my hand, and *it's so warm,* I balance on the stones that are slippery and shifting beneath my sneakers and take her to a maple tree, lay her down there, at the base, away from prying eyes, stroke her fur, so soft, so warm.

Nothing I say can take back what I've done, there's nothing to say, yet I do speak to her in the softest voice, I'm so sorry, I'm so sorry. I ask the angels of chipmunks to greet her, to escort her to the other side, to forgive me, to please, please forgive me.

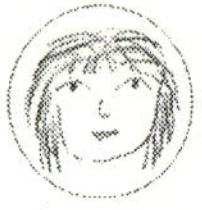

Who have you taken care of? What happened to them?

Apparently, the softest voice is often mine. I was a shy kid. I watched a lot. I listened carefully, everywhere I went. I seldom spoke in the company of strangers.

I used to love sitting with the adults at the dining room table when my parents had friends over. The boys would go run around outside. My sister, who loved to chat, would head up to the dollhouse in our room with her friends. I would stay at the dining room table and listen.

They say children learn through play. That is probably true. But somehow, the world seemed too serious to me to play with toys all the time. Listening to the grown-ups, I could learn all kinds of important things. About the education system (my mom was a teacher and the district Superintendent was a family friend who she'd gone to high school with. His son was my brother's best friend.) About church politics (There were people grousing that the children had used hand motions when they sang a song on Sunday morning. Looked like dancing. It was actually sign language). About all kinds of things that I don't remember specifically but probably shaped what I expected from the world of adults.

I knew to keep quiet in these discussions, or they'd ask me to leave and I'd never hear the stories that held the secrets of survival in the real world.

I kept quiet at school, unless I knew positively that I knew the right answer to the question and then I raised my hand. I got really good at knowing the right answers.

I kept quiet on the playground with other kids. I didn't understand the games they played, the names they called each other, the way to fit in most of the time.

But walking home from school, straggling behind my brothers, I had long imaginary conversations. I was witty and astute. I knew what to say. I was even funny.

The only other time I could be loud was when I sang. I could be loud and confident because I knew the words and had just a good enough ear that I also knew the notes. And when I knew them well enough, it all started to feel spontaneous again.

For a long time as an adult, people have told me I have a soft voice. It always surprises me. I can hear myself. But I have not always wanted to be heard.

What do you want people to hear you say? Why don't you say it?

That Time in the Wilderness

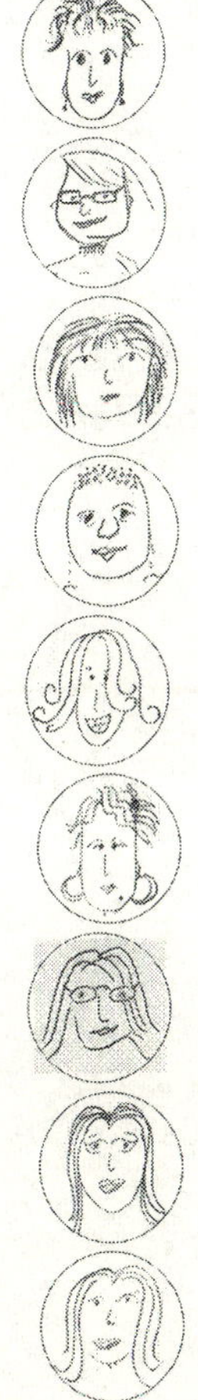

I wake at four in the morning from another bad dream, my heart racing, eyes scanning the dark room. It takes a few moments to remember that I'm safe, to slow my breathing, my pulse.

I can feel the crisp air coming in through the screen and take a deep breath, cleansing my fears. The outdoors is right there, woods, I remind myself, available, safe, but still I lay there for a time unwilling to drift off again in case the dream resumes.

Then, from a short distance away, in the mountain, the contained wilderness, I hear a sound drifting down and through my open window, coyotes, yipping in some cacophonous celebration, greeting one another, teeth flashing, tails low and wagging, so full of wonderful life, that moment of pure silence before the dawn, before the world wakes, before cars and machinery and conversations take over and in that moment, listening to their ancient tongue, I feel safe again.

I'm not alone in the dark anymore.

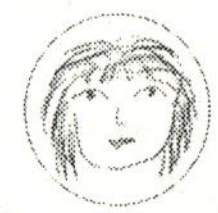

What did you hear at 4 a.m.?

'Wilderness' is relative. Living in London, I came to think of Queen's Wood- an untamed, unmanaged park- as 'wilderness.' Given that Queen's Wood behind our flat was equidistant from three villages (Highgate, Muswell Hill and Crouch End) each within walking distance from one another, I could never get lost. If I had strayed off the path, the sound of bumper to bumper traffic on the Archway, also known since the Roman occupation as the Great North Road, would direct me.

Getting lost was not an option, and yet, the Hansel and Gretel nature of the woods (the wolf... where was the wolf?) was unsettling. The ungroomed nature of the woods juxtaposed with the density of the city was as startling as a hand on the top of a hot woodstove.

The deciduous trees were tall and dense. During the plague years, thousands of bodies were supposedly dumped in this patch. Perhaps the robust trees had fed on the decayed bodies. Leaving a leaf-strewn path, you were on your own.

If you left the Highgate Tube and walked towards Muswell Hill, you would see a gingerbread café on the right. Walking towards the café, you would pick up the path just past the café. If you were to keep walking some distance along the path, you would see a clearing surrounded by 13 ancient oak trees off to the right. Local lore had it, that on a full-moon night, local Druids would gather to invoke the past.

Living just south of Queen's Wood, I would cut through the woods to reach the Tube station. Doing so I would pass an old man who had built a cardboard shelter and was 'sleeping rough."

Again... the juxtaposition of the civilized and wild. Wild and lost.

I used to know the London tube map by heart? What did you know by heart?

*

I climbed and climbed and climbed in those days. Day after day. The end of my marriage, the beginning of a new life I didn't understand or know how to make real. So I climbed and climbed some more. Everyday I went further, higher, further, just to know that I could. Wanting to scare myself and then overcome the fear. I'd climb until the fear of being lost outweighed the longing to overcome my fear. That day in the wilderness, I found an ancient, empty creek that was nearly dry but damp from recent rain. The sun was shining in rays through pine trees. When I got to a place that was as far away as I was willing to go, I took my clothes off. All of them. Adding more fear to my already pumping heart. Wondering if someone would see me. The odds were long. Naked. I lay down on a smooth, damp rock by the empty old stream. I felt the heat and my skin. The sun. The prickers from a nearby bush. I felt alive and brave.

What did you do that surprised and pleased you?

Be bold

What can I do without?

Well-meaning friends would say that I should have washing machine and dryer on the premises. Typically, I do our laundry in our primary residence, our family home in Penrose. We still get our mail there, and picking up the mail necessitates a weekly visit. While I am there, I do laundry. Yes, it would be more convenient to launder clothes in our retirement home, but it has never been an issue.

Nearly every relative and friend sighs and moans about the laundry problem. They go so far to berate Mark for abusing me – denying me... every woman's right to have a washer and dryer close at-hand. Friends shake their heads. They feel sorry for me. Their hearts break for me. What they do not realize is I do not have a washer/dryer issue.

To hear them talk, you would think that I had an old-fashioned washboard in the back yard where my reddened hands and swollen knuckles would scrub the grubby Levis of my husband and the hired man. Listening to my friends' version of events, you would thing that after milking the cows and gathering eggs at dawn, I had to make soap before doing the wash. And then, laundry washed but lacking a real clothes line, I would have to walk about the yard laying the wet clothes over fences and shrubs where all the neighbors could comment on my unimaginative underwear.

Contrary to the opinion of friends who like to make their issues... my issues, I can do without a washing machine at present. I have other things I cannot do without.

I cannot do without coffee. I like it black and strong. Full-flavored with an aroma that hints of South America and Juan Valdez.

Most of all, I would miss my friends who fill me up with love and compassion and forgiveness. These same friends challenge me to be better that I am...introduce me to new ideas...and believe in me more than I believe in myself.

When did you follow the wrong advice?

Last night, PBS broadcast the second of two programs on pre-natal surgery, something I think I'd heard of before but hadn't given much thought to. Babies in the womb who have a condition that's fixable can be operated on to increase their chances of living a normal or better life. One of the children they followed on the show was a little girl named Lily. Her mother was un-married and the father had abandoned her when he heard the baby had a massive tumor growing in her throat that was overflowing from her mouth. The young mother went to Philadelphia's Children's Hospital to see if the doctors there could help her.

I watched as the surgical team removed a mass from Lily's face that was nearly as big as her 6-inch fetal body. Last night we saw her at 4-months with a Joker style smile that was about to be repaired in the second radical surgery of her life. There were other surgeries on the show. Other fetuses, moms and dads in doctor's offices, surgical suites, other anaesthetized children, MRIs, scans, all things I lived through fourteen years ago. I saw things last night I hadn't seen myself but have often imagined, like the clear tape with the width and heft of packing tape that's put over the baby's eyes during surgery to protect them from whatever might spill or splatter while in the OR; or the tattoos that are meticulously placed on the baby's skin to show the surgeon where to cut and how to fold that skin so that everything looks good when the baby has healed; or the tug and the pull of stitches that go deep into the baby's body when they're sewing him back up.

I've imagined these things many times. I made myself imagine them when Theo was going through even more demanding surgeries. His belly was opened wide, his guts removed so that the grapefruit size tumor attached to his liver, his heart, and his gall bladder could be cut away and removed. The day of that surgery, I lived inside my over-sized parka sitting in the waiting room, imagining every step of Theo's day. From the moment he left my arms, already sedated and gone from me, to the moment I saw him again 9 hours later – bloated, bruised, lying on a gurney with nine lines of critical connection to keep him alive, and a doctor hand-pumping air into his body until a ventilator could be re-attached in the ICU across the street. An ambulance was waiting as he flew by me helpless in the lobby of Sloan Kettering. He was alive. It was all I had and it was a lot.

I knew exactly what those parents on TV were feeling. Terror. Shock. Confusion. Disbelief. Love so deep and non-negotiable that all the tests Theo, Ben and I were going through didn't feel like tests, they felt like life. It's what we did.

Sitting in front of the TV, tears streaming down my face, mine had been a time of love more than anything else. I live without that kind of love now.

When did you live without love?

My thirteenth year started with a short sale of the house my family had built in a small town in North Dakota. It was supposed to be our home place for the rest of our lives. But a second mortgage had been taken out to keep my dad's business running. And then the business went bankrupt.

We moved to a working class suburb of Chicago, a place called Addison. A family friend was a pastor of a church on Army Trail Road. He was not using the parsonage next door, so the church let us rent it for a song. Within months of moving in there, my parents divorced after 20 years of marriage.

My dad installed garage doors to support himself and pay child support. My mother could only get work as a substitute teacher. Somehow my mother found another side job, cleaning a Xerox office building after hours five nights a week. My sister and I helped her out, emptying trash cans and cleaning toilets.

Every penny counted. That was the year I learned to look at price tags and curb my own appetites. We had never been wealthy before, but it simply facilitated typical limits on childhood selfishness: I could choose two toys, not five. I could have one treat a weekend, not endless indulgence.

But that thirteenth year, it was entirely different. Peanut butter and cheap bread (past its "sell by" date, so half price), macaroni and tomato paste. My skin was developing its adolescent oiliness, breaking out. But even the cheapest antiseptic cleanser and a bag of cotton balls was outside the budget.

My mother, exhausted as she was, tried to make it fun, tried to turn shopping at garage sales and second hand stores into a treasure hunt. To this day, though, I do hate going to department stores and malls. They seem filled with overpriced excess, and mannequin after mannequin silently declaring that they, who have no voice and no soul, have enough -- and never have to do without.

What did you eat as a kid? Moon Pies? Fried Bologna?

The Corner Store

Habits of Transition

The corner store was a block from my house and at the top of my friend Nancy's street. It was our first corner store, the closest one to our house and situated almost halfway between my two best friends' houses in a safe neighborhood, a small town where everyone knew everyone.

It was the place to go for Wonder Bread and milk and candy. It was a converted gas station – painted white cinder block building, darkened room for the store with only one case/counter – and the room where the car bay had been was closed off. The smell of gasoline and oil lingered. The gas pumps outside were red and I don't think they were operational any more.

A bigger store, the Corner Dairy, was another block away. Family owned and operated, at first it was a wooden building with a couple of aisles. It was our stopping point on the way home from school every day. We'd buy Fresca or Pepsi and Cheetos, Fritos, maybe some candy. They had baseball trading cards and Beatles cards and a rack of magazines like Tiger Beat and Seventeen. Playboy and cigarettes and cigars were kept behind the counter. Mr. C and his wife watched over us kids – not that anyone I knew was a shoplifter but you could feel them, vigilant, when we lingered over the penny candy for too long.

The prices there, my mom and dad said, were too high so we didn't buy much there except our after school snacks, maybe bread and milk. Over the years, the family that owned the store gradually grew it until now it's a full-fledged market with a few long aisles stocked with all the groceries you could need.

My family moved away from that street over 15 years ago so I haven't been back there. I'd be surprised if it's even run by the same family now.

Another fragment – there was another market too – the

meat market – wooden floor boards creaked, darkened room, cases filled with roasts, chicken, fresh cuts, strange pickled things in cloudy jars.

Which did you like better, Oreos or Hydrox?
Wonder Bread or Pepperidge Farm?
Hellman's or Miracle Whip?

In Jamestown, North Dakota, when I was about nine or ten, both my parents sang in the church choir. In the spring that year, the choir director decided to do a big choral "cantata" — a production of sacred music interspersed with dramatic readings of scripture passages and personal testimonies.

It was a big deal for our little church. And the director took his music very seriously. So in addition to the regular Wednesday night choir rehearsals, there was a month of long Sunday afternoon practices. With both my parents in the choir, we kids and the kids of several other families, came and had the run of the church basement.

We really could do anything we wanted, as long as we didn't break anything or interrupt practice. There were massive games of hide-n-seek. Then a complicated, stealthy version of indoor capture-the-flag. We explored all the cupboards in the church kitchen, the janitor's closet, the back row of the balcony, and one week we even discovered that the secret door into the baptismal was unlocked. This was a discovery! And we took turns quietly crawling into the deep bathtub that opened up to the sanctuary from behind a screened window above the organ.

Eventually, we got bored exploring the nooks and crannies of the building. Besides, the weather was warm and fine. The air smelled like damp dirt and things were starting to turn green, so we went out and explored the neighborhood.

Down the street, around the block from the church, on the south end of Main Street where we'd rarely drive, there was a gas station with the little requisite store attached.

I don't remember who said it. Maybe Landon Nitzchke, who was always more courageous than most of us. Or Brenda Benson, who's mom, Shirley, who played the piano for the choir. But someone said, "Let's buy something."

Standing out on the sidewalk, we all dug into our pockets, scoured the curb for dropped pennies, and pooled all the loose change we could find: 65 cents. Then, we walked into the store and searched the candy aisle for what we could afford.

It was the first time I had ever been in a store, let alone a candy store, without parental supervision, limits or finances. We were making our own decision. And no one could tell us what to do!

Finally, we settled on two boxes of candy I'd never had before. Mike and Ike's were pill-shaped, multicolored fruit flavored chews. The other box was a cinnamon flavored version of the same candy, all bright red.

We walked the few blocks back to church, sharing the boxes back and forth as we went, plotting how to collect more loose change by next Sunday. Savoring the sweet, sticky taste of freedom.

What's in your wallet?

I was seven when we moved to Breesport, a small Upstate New York town boasting only of two churches, a school, a post office, the Chemung County Poor House, and Elliott's – a small, two-aisle-wide grocery store.

Although the town was rural and a bit backwoods (every child had lice at least once a school year), I was excited. Finally, after living in the two-bedroom apartment above my grandparent's house and depending on Grandpa or Mon's older brother for transportation, we had our very own large house and our very own maroon-colored Chevy.

Mom was not one to put her foot down, but before we moved in, she insisted on indoor plumbing. I was too young to understand the dynamic, but Daddy was probably regretting that he had been so rash to marry an uppity, college-educated woman with high-falutin' ideas.

And so we had indoor plumbing. It was only a couple of blocks to Main Street and Elliott's store which had just about everything: white bread, milk, flour, canned vegetables and toilet paper. Desires were fewer in 1950.

How honored I felt to be asked to pick up the mail on my way home from school. The heritage, brass boxes were faced with a peephole window a combination dial. Twirling the knob right and then left and then right again, I felt quite full of myself as I pulled out the mail.

Sometimes, Mom asked me to pick up something at the small, two-aisle-wide store. Picking up the requested item, I'd walk to the cash register where I'd lift my chin and say, "Charge it to our account." Doing so, I felt responsible and all-powerful. First, the cashier knew who I was, and second, she knew we would pay our bill at the end of the month.

We were on our way… into the middle class!

Did you ever have lice or some other gross thing that gives you the creeps now? Did it give you the creeps then?

listening...

When Debra saw this prompt she said, "I just *finished a piece called "It's Packed Away in a Box"! Can you use it?" I said, "Sure."*
What's different reading a finished piece
VS a quickly written prompt response?

"It's Packed Away in a Box"

I called my mom on Friday night. I don't call at a regular time but I try to speak with her every week. My sister and her family had just left town for the weekend – Diane usually checks in on them because she lives nearby – so I teased mom, "Are you lonely yet?"

She has an easy laugh, my mom does, though she's got less to feel amused about these days. My dad has Alzheimer's or dementia, we're not sure which because he refused to complete the diagnostic tests a couple of years ago.

Doesn't really matter, I suppose. She calls it "All-timers" and hushes her voice on our phone calls when she wants to share some details of his latest comments or confusions. "He's so forgetful. I try to be patient but it's hard when he asks me the same things over and over and over ..."

A lot of times when we talk now it's about their doctor's appointments, ailments, medications. Maybe news of an occasional outing or visit. But, on Friday night, we somehow bypassed the usual reporting and had a lot of fun, laughing and remembering happier times.

I mentioned to mom that my hair has grown really long again. "It's probably as long, or longer, than when I was in high school," I said.

"I still have your hair, you know. Remember when you got it cut?"

Surprised, I said, "Really? Wow. Where is it?"

She had given me a lot of my childhood and teenage things when they moved 15 or so years ago – *The Better Homes and Gardens* Baby Book

she had filled in with my vital statistics, ink print of my foot from the hospital records and progress (first smile, first word, lost her first tooth), my Girl Scout book, some of my baby clothes and my bronzed baby shoe – but not my hair from when I'd suddenly cut it short.

"In the lock box."

I laughed. "The *lock* box?!"

All I could think about was, 'there's so much stuff in their house already. There's more in there, too?'

It was daunting, all the silk flower arrangements and clothes, not to mention antiques, jewelry, knick knacks, furniture, boxes of photographs … it would take years to figure out what to do with it all when the time came.

"Oh god, what *else* is in there?"

"Oh, I don't know. The deed to the house, our birth certificates, important papers." She paused, "Maybe your hair isn't in there, I don't know. It's here, some place, though."

It was disconcerting, thinking about a long shank of now-faded hair, sitting in a box somewhere, who knows where? Then I remembered that I had saved some hair too.

"Now that we're talking about this, mom, I have one of Diane's curls saved too." It's in a dark green jewelry box – I can see it clearly, a lid that snaps shut, with green velvet lining. It was the box from the gold locket Aunt Charlotte and Uncle Roy gave to me for high school graduation. "It's in a jewelry box, but I'm not sure where it is, exactly. It's here some place …" echoing her. We were both laughing.

My mom liked it, that I had one of sister's curls. When Diane was a toddler, she had a mass of golden brown curls all over her head. And every day, when my mom or I dressed her in one of her cute little outfits, there were yarn bows or ribbons or clips to match what she was wearing.

I was 12 when Diane was born and spent a lot of time playing with her and taking care of her throughout my teenage years, until I went away to college.

And, despite knowing there were so many things saved in every corner and drawer and shelf of our home, I liked knowing my hair was there too. Some day I'd find it, probably when mom and dad were gone, and I'd remember this laughing conversation and how mom and I both knew that we saved too much stuff.

Imagine being on the phone with your mom.
What did she say? How did you respond? Use dialogue.

I love that dress. Still have it. I wore it to a fund raising concert that was given for me after Theo died. It was my maternal grandmother's: black taffeta with painted red and purple flowers all over it. The pedals are outlined in gold. Little black velvet dots meander around the skirt. Underneath, the petticoats pile up, itch, and make a swooshing sound on the floor without the right heels. Mine were just a little too low so I heard myself wherever I went. I would love to have seen Gammy, my grandmother, wearing this dress. She was flamboyant and beautiful. In one picture of her with my grandfather, she's wearing a floppy blue hat with an 8" rim. In the ribbon around her hat, she's planted a big fabric flower that drapes down around her forehead. She's smiling from ear to ear.

When I was little, my father called me Little Gammy. I'm not sure why. I've never been flamboyant. I should ask him what he saw back then. Maybe it was her girlish ways. I certainly had that trait even as I was climbing trees and playing kick the can for hours in the middle of Hill Road. Gammy made this sound with her mouth. She'd pucker her lips, force air through them making a high-pitched "bweeeeeep" whenever she wanted us to laugh. She'd giggle with her whole body then start to laugh, her shoulders shaking all the while. Grandpa was more serious, a Colonel in the Army, fought both wars. He adored her wild spirit and encouraged her to let it out. They had regular parties, scotch and pretzels every afternoon. Restaurants and friends were a big part of their life. His father had died when he was eight He was an only child so he was the man in the family very early on. Gammy game him the childhood he'd missed, I guess. Their first child died when he was two. He was born with Spina Bifida, a spinal imperfection a person can survive these days. My mother was born when he was one. She has no memory of him, of course, but he was always there. Maybe I'm imagining that.

When was a dress more than a dress?

Abigail Thomas sent me one of her new poems the day our group was meeting so I used it as a prompt. Her original title was ***"A Why Bother to Write it Poem"*** *so that was the prompt. Now it's called:*

"Lament"

It's a man and a woman and they've climbed to the top of a mountain and it's evening and from where they stand they can see whole worlds and some tiny bright cities and since he had coaxed her up this high, because he wanted to show her everything, he had his arms around her tightly because she was afraid of falling. And the sun actually did go down on their right at the exact moment the moon rose on their left, and this would have happened anyway, they both knew that, still they were glad to have seen it together. Whether they lay down and made love or did not make love under a billion stars is if no real interest to anyone (there being no small boys present) and who they were, and whether he knew the names for everything and if she loved lavender, if it rained, all these details vanish like everything else, it happens all the time, you know, the sun goes up and comes down it rains, we button and unbutton our clothes and turn on our sides to make love because all warm animals need other warm animals right from the beginning or they go crazy and die so if he had green eyes and she had blue and if they loved or did not love each other for good reasons or bad and if they used the old words and did or did not make promises nobody keeps,
no matter, we'll let it go, no matter.

Sometimes we read something to one another and no prompt is offered. A quiet settles over us and no prompt is necessary.

If you're uncomfortable with silence, describe it...

Zoe and I run out into the early March wind at seven in the morning, we trot down the road, she stopping to pee, looking up and around, running again with her left rear leg still up and peeing, 'come on' she implores, we head to the corner of Swift Hollow, she pulling me, her little body, propelled forward, ears blowing just a bit, making the soft waves of those ears, ripple with the breeze.

I hear the crows at my house, raucously calling to me, reminding me that I hadn't fed them yet, hadn't laid out the unsalted nuts in the shell, the kernels of hard deer corn, leftover cat and dog food, seeds, fruit, whatever looks good and viable.

I glance back toward my house as the road disappears and Zoe propels us forward, 'come on'. I'm not used to leaving the house before feeding the wild but this little one is my charge for the week and so I follow her as she weaves her way through damp leaves, placing her nose in those leaves for any hint of another animal, always moving forward.

I hear a crow overhead, look up, and there's one of my crows who flies directly over us, cawing, perhaps wondering why I'm heading away from the mountain, away from their feeding spot they share with other birds, squirrels, deer, turkeys, chipmunks, and maybe that crow is sending the signal to her friends, 'she's here, I'll try to lead her back'.

On the next foray into the weeds and halfhearted trail that quickly leads to deadfall too dense and vast to scale, Zoe and I turn back, making a game of it, let's head home, I excitedly say to her.

As we wind our way back up, mountain now growing closer again, the crows begin cawing, swooping down lightly, rapid clicks of their bill, and as we turn into the driveway, they fly low past us, leading me to their clearing between the trees.

I open the door and Zoe zips inside the house while I head back outside with pots and bags filled with food, talking with the crows, they responding from the trees, the squirrels now swinging from branches and racing head first down the tree trunks to the ground and I realize, not for the first or second or thousandth time, that no matter where I am in this world, the animals will always fly me home.

Have you ever talked to animals?

I have been reading Mary Oliver and almost every page gives a deep look into the beautiful soul of something nobody ever cares to look at. The things that happen anyway. But still, she is delighted to witness it and then sing a song for us, made up from her ball-of-twine words.

It arrests me. So much happens in any present moment, it's startling.

Last week we sat at breakfast before Andrea left for Austin, and she and her dad named off all the people they know who've died of horrible cancers or sudden accidents in the last year. Then there was the strange sniper shots that have broken car windows and killed a bicyclist along I-25 this summer. The terrorist attacks on tourists, sunning on Middle Eastern beaches. All the things that can break and tear, destroy and kill. And who knows when or where it happens next?

Andrea, the night before, had mentioned how she didn't have insurance in this month between ending one job and starting the next. "Maybe, I should get online now, get some kind of short term coverage. I mean, before I go off and drive 900 miles..." And all the things that can go wrong crowded around the kitchen table in the silent moment when none of us made eye contact.

That's when her dad said that the only way to not go crazy was to stay in the present moment. I nodded, felt my shoulders relax, my heart slow a little. Until I realized that even this — this split second. This paper thin slice of all time is so densely populated with miracles and spectacles.

The citronella ants in the foundation, the doves on the power lines, the seeds already softening in the ground since I planted them this morning, the words taking shape beneath pens, the hundreds of skin cells dying off. The hundreds just coming to be. Oxygen taken into a dog's lungs while she dreams of catching a rabbit on the run.

A hundred million high wire acts happening just now. A hundred million more in the next moment. Why bother to write a poem? Why bother at all since none of it matters?

I cannot help myself. Because the more I see or taste, hear or believe, the more beautiful and real and sweet the nonsense is. I care less and less these days about leaving a mark. More and more, I am willing to be the page on which the lines are written.

Start a paragraph with "I have been thinking."
Start another one with "I've been thinking."

Why bother to write it? You can't, won't read it. Why bother to tell you I meant no harm? Why bother to care that you care?

Why bother to write a poem that would try to explain the unexplainable?

I want you to know I'm happy, really happy, because I know that at some point you would have cared. You would have wanted that for me. But I can't call you up. I could, sure, but I can't. I would open a door I slammed shut. It would say to you that I want something I don't: You.

Why bother to rhyme words? To speak from the heart? To tell you I wasn't lying when I said I'd love you forever? Forever, as it turned out, was much shorter than I could have imagined.

I didn't lie. I didn't pretend to love you. I didn't fake my way through our marriage. I delighted in you. I loved you. I was grateful for you.

But you wanted to keep me and I couldn't be kept.

"I'm not ready to say 'thank you,'" you once said, and then went on to tell me that my leaving invited others—wonderful others—into your existence.

I knew this would happen, but of course it wasn't for me to say. It wasn't for me to ask, "Aren't you better off?" even if I already knew the answer.

I do wish you happiness. I wish you great happiness and contentment. I still cheer you on. I cast well wishes into the Universe, hoping they'll land in your lap.

But I won't beg you to forgive me. It's unnecessary. It's counterproductive. But if I could, I would say to you that you were wonderful. You were perfect.

For that space in time, we were.

Who hurt you when they didn't listen?

It has no weight. No substance. No matter. No real beginning or end. It just is. This love. This madness of attraction. It's unlike the rejection of the past when my body wasn't good enough for him. Wasn't the body he wanted to touch to breathe in, to consume.

I want to understand it all. Why it was so awkward and so good to see Ben again. And yet I was afraid of him. He noticed it, mentioned it even. Said, "you look like you're seeing a monster," and I said, "yes, I am." And we both laughed. Me having just blown a big green bubble of Trident gum as he turned into the gas station and pulled up to the far side of the pump I was using. Me standing there blowing a bubble, him pulling up in a new truck. "Just got it," he says. And all I can think is *lucky you* because he has some money I still think belongs to me and I haven't let go of that fact yet. So I remove the gum and laugh. "This is so tacky, me standing here blowing bubbles when I haven't seen you in four years. It's a crummy habit I've developed." He says, "plenty of people chew gum, ya know, it's ok," but it's not ok with me. I don't want to be chewing gum when I'm talking to the man I married twenty-one years ago; the man I haven't seen for four years, five and a half since we lived together somewhat happy, somewhat empty, wandering and lost because neither of us had the partner we needed. Neither of us had been touched with any tenderness for over ten years, neither of us able to see a future together, both of us honest about the hopelessness of it all.

So I didn't want to be chewing gum. I took it out and looked for a trashcan. There weren't any. They must have been removed because people were leaving their household garbage there. Instead I rolled the green ball between my fingers while we reacquainted ourselves, me and this man I loved all along.

The visit was good. I got to say the things I've needed to say these last four years. Not with vengeance or anger but

with gentleness. "Ya know, Ben, it was really hard to be #2 all those years." I told him that because I knew he'd never understood. His eyes filled with tears. He crinkled up his mouth that way he does and nodded as if to say *I know. You always were #2.* And then I said, "I loved you, ya know." And he crinkled up his mouth again. And I could feel myself wishing he'd say,
"I loved you too" but I knew he wouldn't and I was right. He said, "but we had Theo together and that was really good," and I agreed because it *was* good. We both smiled. We were his parents me and Ben. And if Theo were here, we'd still be a family because neither of us could have broken his heart for anything or anyone.

We hugged. I didn't know if I would ever do that again, if I would want to, or if I would take a step away from him. But we did, twice. He initiated both times and both times he held me tight while I rolled the gum in my free hand.

When did you see someone you never thought you'd see again?
Did you move towards them or away?

Unpacking from the Trip

While I can't remember all the circumstances surrounding the hotel stay last summer, I can remember the exaltation. There was the huge bed, two huge beds, dozens of pillows, a soft brown comforter and blankets of varying shades of oranges and yellows, an enormous television, room service, insulated quiet, privacy.

I opened my suitcase and took out the bare essentials, knowing that I'd only have a few hours to enjoy this array of…what...this dreamy way of living.

The king bed near the window was for the suitcase, the clothes, the other king bed was for me to luxuriate in so I flopped on top of those colorful blankets, spread my arms wide, smiling at the ceiling.

I kept reading the menus of the different cafes and restaurants, imagining what it'd be like to live here for a week, what would I order on Tuesday, Wednesday? Would I have them deliver some scrumptious dessert at ten pm?

There was certainly nothing very interesting outside, a nearby airport, the Colorado heat, and a busy road within feet. No, this was about living inside luxury.

People were walking quietly down the hall in expensive clothing, no doubt living extravagant lives, residing in wealthy communities with manicured lawns, driving Priuses, ringing bells for tea.

Of course, none of that was probably true; most of these people were tourists, on hard earned vacations, indulging in fantasies, like me.

But those several hours, waiting for an early morning flight are etched in me, the scent of the room, the feeling of another way of living, a way of living that I'd never really want, for I'm not easily transfixed by the indoors or luxury, but when my friend, Mary and I meeting the hall at three in the morning to head to the airport and catch the flight back to New York, I tuck a memory into my pocket, a pen while I still have in my desk drawer, it reads 'the Radisson'.

Did you ever stay somewhere that was fancier than you're used to? Why were you there?

Dirty… clean… sort of clean. Hum.m.m.m… clean enough? I bring the shirt to my nose and smell it.

I'm unpacking from a week-long trip to the Gulf Coast. I pack small; regardless, my red carry-on (handwoven by natives in Peru) seems to expand beyond the dimensions of the cloth. The zipper may expand too. I see a small bag, but opening it is like opening a magician's bag of tricks. I open the bag and out fly a dozen doves.

How could so many things come out of something so small? And why did I take so much clothing in the first place? Why did I think I needed the silk blouse? Perhaps the silk blouse fell under the category of 'always be prepared.' I had the silk blouse but I also… please remember that I was going to the Gulf Coast… I also took my LL Bean coat purported to be good to minus 40 degrees.

And I took hiking boots. And black palazzo pants. And a light-weight, hip length blouse to hide my stomach. The blouse features large flowers on a white background. I am not a flower girl. I probably bought the blouse at Goodwill. Perhaps it had a good label. And the price was probably good. I can easily be swept away by a good bargain.

I packed the blouse because it was summer-weight and would cover my stomach. But get this.

When I am home, I don't tuck the blouse in because my stomach *could* be flatter. But my sister's stomach is seriously more Rubenesque than mine/. And so…

At my sister's house (that would be my sister with the larger stomach) I tucked the blouse in.

I tucked the blouse in and as I was doing so, my motivation for doing so slapped me in the face. Sibling rivalry had raised its ugly head.

It was a na.. na…nah…na… na… hah moment. I recognized my motivation. I winced. And still I tucked my blouse in.

It was sort of payback time for all the times my sister beat me at cards. The times her grades were better than mine. The times my mother asked me why I couldn't apply myself to my studies like my sister Christine.

What's the least you need?
What did you wear to cover yourself?

I waited to unpack my bag, hoping that I could somehow slip back to the airport, back into the writing life I left behind in Westcliffe, Colorado. I was here but I wanted to be there. Ken knew he had lost me and so the fight began to keep me. In his asking, "Are we altered?" he already knew the answer.

He picked me up at the airport and we arrived home after 10, both of us fearful, worried about what had happened in my honesty. In sending Ken that essay I had unleashed all that I had kept hidden, even from myself. It wasn't about my sexuality. It was about the truth of me.

I couldn't have know then that I would go back to Westcliffe, alone, months later, but there was part of me that didn't want to unpack the bag. If I unpacked it would mean that part of my life I had unearthed in Westcliffe would be hidden again. By unpacking I would say, "I'm staying" when I didn't want to.

I wanted to be back in Westcliffe, back in the beauty of that place, back in the bubble of creativity that the workshop organizers, teachers and participants had created. I wanted to be with them, all of them—the writers, and of course Michelle.

Oh my God what was that? What happened there? Why there? Why with her? Why with a "her?" What were we to do with the electricity that shot out of us, connecting in some place neither of us could see but we most definitely felt?

God I loved it. I hadn't felt that alive in a long time. Not just across from her at Sangrita's, but in the cocoon of Westcliffe.

Have you ever been somewhere that changed your life? Have you ever been somewhere that felt so good that you wanted to stay?
What did it feel like to feel so good?

*

As Penny gave the prompt this morning I looked for my calendar so I could see into my future but the calendar isn't here. Did I leave it in the suitcase that I stashed on the top shelf in the laundry. I'll need it, so hopefully it's not at my parents' house on the bureau in what we call Dede's Room. My gloves are missing too. Not the gloves that mom gave me seven or eight years ago, which I have proudly not lost yet (or have I?) but the ones I got from Ben's mom when she died eleven years ago.

This most recent trip was the first trip in a long time that TSA hasn't opened my suitcase at some point and checked out its contents. I'm not sure why they look at mine but my guess is that it's the weight (many books inside) or the metal objects they see when they scan it. (Thumb drives, tape recorders, microphones, whatever). They always leave a nice note saying they've been there, and I always wonder if some guy in the sub-basement of whatever airport I've travelled through has checked out my underwear while he's in there. What would he say? *This girl needs an upgrade* or *how does she expect to get laid wearing this shit?*

When I first met Michael, well, even before I met him, I did a full undergarment overhaul. I even went to Victoria's Secret and felt sexy doing so. No matter they had no bras for women like me, no underwear a woman could wear without feeling like the wedgies given by a younger brother many years ago. I did buy a bathrobe, though, and still feel very elegant and feminine wearing it....when I do, which is rarely. I found the underwear I could comfortably wear at Macy's: Jockey's in a nice polyester/fake silk fabric, and bras sized 36A that were still not a little too big for me. What I discovered is that those oversized bras could be worn anyway and make me look like I have more than I do. I didn't want to trick anybody, least of all Michael, but they weren't *that* oversized, and they did make me look more like the woman I thought he was hoping to see. Anyway, the point is, I need yet another overhaul. I'm still wearing those same underpants and banged up bras. They're stretched and stained and generally misshapen but they're what I've got. I take my cue from Michael. His underpants are even older. If he wants me in newer gear, he's gonna have to have some too.

Wait....that's not true and this is memoir: his underwear IS new. I've bought him rather expensive Under Armour underwear every year for Christmas. He loves wearing them and he looks pretty good in them too. Shoot. I've gotta go shopping! It's time. But this time, no bras. I'm getting back to my no-bra days. Undershirts that sort of support are much more comfortable and I no longer care about filling up my shirts a little better, at least not all the time.

The unpacking thing is mostly in my head. When I get back I debate everything: why am I here? What am I doing with my life? How can I make enough money to buy that house I found a mile down the road from my parents? Is it the right house? Could I pull it off? Would Michael be willing? What am I doing here? What am I doing with my life? Over and over again. It takes about a day to run through the questions in the unending way that I do the day I get back. By this morning, I was thinking how nice it is to wake up with deep silence around me, dark skies, two dogs snoring nearby, and a big, hunky fella lying next to me. Michael told me yesterday that everyone he knows is stuck where they are regardless of their finances. For one reason or another they can't just get up and go to some supposedly better place. He's right.

When you were a kid, what did you notice when you got home from being away? What did your house smell like? Where did the light come in? Which lamp was left on?

If this were a spelling Bee what word would knock you out of the competition?

Penny read a snippet from Christian Wiman's book, My Bright Abyss, *in which he suggests that we not only accept but also "come to praise" the fact that we're never going to find a right way that will work for us every time.*

What is it that you must realize?

'Conscience.' That's the word I have to think about it. I remember 'Con-Science' which is how I remember how to spell it. I like how it sounds too: Con-Science. Like there's an art to being a con, which there is. But it's the related words that would knock me out of a spelling bee:

'consciousness' for instance.

That words a killer. I don't even think I've spelled it right here. It never looks right to me. When I write it with a pen the odds of my success are better. Spelling it out loud under pressure would terrify me and guarantee my failure.

Bruce Hornsby wrote a great song about a guy named Tom and his rival who wins the Spelling Bee. The killer word for Tom's nemesus was banana. He spelled it:

B-a-n-a-n-a-n-a

not because he didn't know how to spell it but because he was so nervous he added the extra n-a.

I wonder if you even noticed it was spelled wrong? It's hard to see with a word like 'banana.'

A related word, 'consciousness,' is a word I'm working on on two levels. Trying to spell it is the least of my worries. Learning to be it is another thing all together. I went to bed last night thinking about it as a matter of fact. Not how to spell it but how to have more of it in my life. My mind was busy, busy, busy, like that other kind of bee. I was aware of my busy-ness, so that's good I guess, but what I also saw was that I'm short-tempered and just plain short when my mind is busy. I hurry. I take on too much. I dream about the big, successful finish I'll have when one of a dozen ideas in my head finally takes off. I stop myself: *don't think like that. Don't think big. It always takes you off course, you invest too much. You give away too much, you distract yourself from the quiet work you really need and want to do.* All of this I saw like a mirror that goes on forever. My mind has always worked this way. I'm conscious of that. I'm aware. And I like it this way. Some times. Not all the time, but some times.

What's your wildest dream? How would life change if it came true?

I have a similar problem except
it's the word 'conscientious' that screws me up.

How reassuring to know that there is no right way. I don't know who said this, but if I were to get a tattoo, I'd have the saying inked in black on my left shoulder and I'd always wear sleeveless blouses. I'd be swinging my shoulder toward me so I could read the tattoo in times of self-doubt. Yes, I'd look a bit disabled as I'd hunch my shoulder up and rotate it towards my chest to read it more clearly, the hunched shoulder would be a small price to pay for affirmation: "There is no right way."

I love that! No more mea culpa. No more sorry. No more hung head… no more heavy wooden cross of guilt eating into my shoulder.

How liberating to know that my mis-steps were OK… maybe even acceptable. I am, after all, human. "To err is human; to forgive is Divine."

Those 3 a.m. night terrors… that Goya thing of a sleepless man beset by a leering monster… that cracked celluloid film. The sound has crackles and the picture has faded, but the film is caught in an endless loop warped by time. Round and round it goes as it plays and replays all the mis-steps I have taken.

It's a purgatory thing. I'm in sackcloth, and my feet are blistered from walking on a bed of hot coals. And as I walk, a disembodied voice whispers…

"Remember when you failed your best friend Pam? Remember when you failed your wayward child? Remember when you failed your mother?"

The failures keep coming and only dawn and the smell of coffee brings the light which sends the trolls underground.

Will I come to praise these pin pricks and growing self-awareness? I think I will.

Tomorrow I'm going to get that tattoo.

What do you do over and over again?

we're here, listening...

I was ten years old when I took swimming lessons for the first and last time. I learned to dog paddle and hold my breath underwater. These were big accomplishments for me then, but I've never gone any further with my swimming skills.

I still swim like a 10-year-old who's had just a handful of swimming lessons. Mostly splashing, refusing to open my eyes underwater.

We grew up on a lake, a little reservoir on the James River. We had a speed boat and we all learned to water ski. On hot summer days, we'd find a quiet bay and drop the anchor, swim off the side in our life jackets. I loved those days on the water. But all I know about floating involves a flotation device. I have never gotten the feel for the buoyancy of my own body.

I would like to learn this skill. Or really, from what I understand, it's an unlearning of rigidity, a physical act of trust, a counter-intuitive response to lie back and be held by the vast, terrifying mystery of water -- a medium that makes up more then 90% of my body, but will kill me if it takes up that much of my lungs.

I am afraid to trust the quiver of deep water with the weight of my body.

I would like to learn this lesson before I die. I don't need to know how to snorkle or dive or pull my body through pools, scissor-kicking my legs, opening my eyes to the liquid light below. I simply would love to learn to let go and know with the wisdom of muscle and bone that I will be held.

After Penny read her piece Charlotte offered to take her to the local pool and hold her up until Penny was ready for Charlotte to let her go. ***What would you like help with?***

*

Dana was the best swimmer of the three of us. Her dad used to call her a fish because she was in their pool more than she was out of it in the summer. She and Alice and I used to have tea parties at the bottom of their shallow end. We'd all take a huge breath, puff out our cheeks, and wiggle our way to the bottom, wave to one another, lift our cups to our lips, pinkies extended, then burst to the surface when our lungs couldn't stand it any longer. Then we'd do it again. We were 6, 8, 9, 11, who knows.

I was three when we moved to Merion. Alice and Dana were already on Hill Road, three doors away from one another. We lived around the corner on Cleary Road close enough that Dana and I thought we might be able to send messages to one another at night. We tried to run a pulley from my bedroom to hers using an old ball of cotton yarn my grandmother'd given me. We were going to put our notes in the tissue box we'd hung from the yarn with a paper clip, but the man next door to her wouldn't let us climb his fence to get the yarn across, so we gave up.

Dana was half Japanese. Her grandparents owned a gift shop called Osara's in Berwyn. I loved that store. It was so exotic! They had Japanese sandles, kimono sashes, and chop sticks to push through your hair. Dana's grandmother spoke Japanese, too, which was scary and thrilling at the same time.

Alive was 100% WASP. Her dad was head of Pediatrics at The University of Pennsylvania. He had a dry sense of humor, a long, bulbous nose, and a wide, open grin that makes me smile to think about even now. He'd tease us and tickle us. He even let us listen to our hearts through his stethoscope. Alice's moom was the opposite. She was always reading or lecturing us abot what to do and what not to do. Their house had a stairway that split at the bottom. One side led to the front hall where they had a love seat, the other went down to the den with the '60s leather seats that I thought were cool. When I think of that room, I remember the day Alice's brother Paul got his draft number for Viet Nam. He looked sick as he opened the envelope, but then a smile formed on his face. He didn't have to go. I was 12 with a huge crush on him. He was handsome and nice to me. I didn't understand any of it except his smile.

Dana's mother Jane thought I was a bad influence on Dana. She was the kind of mom who read her daughter's diary as well as any notes passed between Dana and me. I'd used the word 'shit' at some point and that crime followed me for years afterwards.

One summer, during high school, the three of us invited Mick, Teddy and John over for lunch at my house. We made a restaurant in the basement where they could order from a menu and we would serve them. They were neighborhood friends we'd grown up with but now had crushes on. We'd climbed trees together, gone to scout meetings at the same church, and gone ice skating on the lake at the bottom of the hill we lived on. We hung white sheets in the basement to create a small room with a table in the middle. The menu had only one choice: Bacon, Lettuce, and Tomato. Because it was my house, the cooking was left to me.

I'd never made a BLT, nor had I ever seen one made, so I did what I thought was right: I put the raw bacon strips, the lettuce, and the sliced tomato on the bread and threw the sandwiches in the oven. Maybe that's why none of them ever married us!

When was your cooking embarrassing?

I hear a voice or some kind of note in my head, in my ear, 'whales', and I smell the ocean, feel the liquid bracing my body, pushing and pulling, melding and softening, but mostly it's beckoning, imploring, cajoling, whispering, 'whales', there's singing now, moaning, light and dark, and I sink into those voices, those notes in my head, in my ear and I go under and it's beautiful, like swimming into forever, the sun and moon reflecting, so blue, so soft and alive, and I keep sinking down further, feeling the skin of the whales, the breath of eternity, and I'll stay here always and it's oh so lovely.

If you could swim with anyone, who would it be?

I'm not sure if I remember, really, but my fingers gripped the chain link fence and I stood there in my new bathing suit, sobbing, begging, 'please don't make me stay!'

I must have been 4, 5, 6? years old. Young, I know that. And my mom, who was afraid of the water herself and determined not to pass it along to me, had delivered me to swimming lessons at the local pool. She was sitting on the bleachers on the other side of the fence with the other mothers.

She told me this story many times when I was older, so I don't know about the vivid image of my little fingers gripping the chain link fence and my tears part, but I do remember I was scared to put my face in the water and to do the proper breathing. And diving? Oh how I wished I could be one of the kids who stood up straight and sliced into the water, in perfect form, with arms upstretched and a little lift-off bounce on their toes before diving. I tended to bend my knees and plop in, sometimes with a belly splash. And I always wanted to hold my nose too, which really wrecked my form.

Later, at the lake, Daddy gave me a bribe, a promise, one that meant a lot to me. "I'll give you a transistor radio if you learn to swim, if you pass intermediate level."

That summer, on the dock and in the water, splashing with my cousins, I learned enough to swim out to him and after that, we went to buy my coveted radio together.

I've never been a smooth, strong swimmer, but I lost my fear of the water that summer and have since enjoyed being buoyant enough. If I were shipwrecked in strong waves in the middle of an ocean, a doggie paddle, treading water and knowing how to float might – might – save me.

But that transistor ushered in a new era for me for sure. At bedtime, when I was supposed to be sleeping, I kept it under my pillow and at a low volume and I dialed in to the Detroit radio stations across the sound waves of Lake Erie and Ohio. Motown, Top 40, Chi-Lites, Marvin Gaye and Tammy Terrell

… I was swimming in musical pleasure long after lights out every night. I had learned to swim and got all new music as my reward.

When I was in first grade, I traded a bunch of my sister's Barbie Doll clothes for a friend's transistor? What did you trade that wasn't yours to give away?

Black Prince Tomatoes, Black Bread, Basil, and Butter

Longer Nights

Take Care

This house has most of its windows facing south, and being here, I am more aware of the light than any other place I've lived. In the heart of winter, the sun rises directly through the one east window, in the kitchen, then hangs so low in the sky all day, shining in, that the furnace shuts off at 9 a.m. and doesn't come back on until the sun drops behind mountains close to 5 p.m.

In summer, that same sun rises high and the roof shades all but a few direct rays in the early morning and middle evening, when the heat is already cut out of the day here at 8000 feet above sea level.

It is the sun I most follow, taking its progress like a long, rambling story. When it goes down, the night is almost like nodding off while watching a movie. The longer darkness tells a story, too, I suppose, but I only catch it in snatches, disjointed. A plot I cannot entirely piece together.

"I love the dark hours of my being," Rilke wrote in one of his love poems to God. A curious line. Because all the unknowns, the mysteries, lay in the dark hours. The womb. The place of waiting. The slow, creeping growth.

What do you do when you first wake up?
What do you do late at night?

I helped buy the tomato plants but I didn't put them in the pots. Not that time nor did I plant the kale or the cucumbers or the squash. I helped pick the strawberries because I loved them so. Finding them under the green leaves felt like finding a prize. They reminded me of summers in Iowa, picking strawberries with my mother, just the two of us, me following her lead.

"Not the white ones or the pink ones. Only the red. See there? Careful..."

Mom was at peace in the strawberry patch. In my mind it was a giant triangle and she was at the center, stooped, lost in thought, content, not thinking of suicide, not yelling at my father.

If I was good, really good, I could keep that rope off her neck. I could convince her not to drive her car off of the bridge. I could prove to her I was worth staying around for. But I didn't. I couldn't. I quit trying, but I never accepted that I was powerless to change her trajectory.

What was your mother thinking?
How would she answer that question?

Sam Williams had skin as dark and creamy as I'd ever seen. What I remember better, though, was the quiet way he spoke and the low, slow way he walked. Everything about him was slow except his mind. His graceful hands, his gentle eyes – both calm. He had the whitest, shyest smile. He studied Political Science, hoping to go to law school, hoping even more to change the world.

For graduation he gave me an inscribed copy of Chaucer's *Canterbury Tales*. Hardcover. He'd found it an antique store somewhere. Clearly he had more confidence in my literary aptitude than I did. I could never follow, nor was I interested in reading Old English, or any of the classics an English Literature Major was meant to love. What I appreciated was the thought behind the book. No one had ever given me a gift that suggested I had a mind.

But the gift was disturbing too. It was too much, too intimate. Same was not my boyfriend, although the inscription confirmed that he wished otherwise. What he wrote was benig. It was the length and the thoughtfulness. We were young after all. I can still see his handwriting:
careful, even, smooth, with words well considered. I wonder if I broke his heart without knowing.

We were seniors when he asked me to go to his hometown on a Saturday. Manhattan. He was one of the lucky ones who had a car. Driving from Pennsylvania east to the city with my blackest friend was more than a simple car ride. I had never been to New York alone with a friend. I had never left campus in a friend's car to do anything other than get French Fries at MacDonald's down the hill. Even that was rare. This trip was scarier. Farther away. Riskier and dangerous in some brain-washed sort of way - as though a person silly enough to travel into the great city got what they asked for.

Sam's car was big. A sedan. American, of course, with a long front seat and a vast windshield. We left campus in time to watch the sunrise on Route 22 through New Jersey's horse country. I can remember the colors of the sky even now although I'd forgotten we'd left so early in the day. The memory of pinks and oranges as we went east tells me the one thing I wouldn't have remembered otherwise: I spent the whole day with Sam.

Funny how a single detail gives me enough to remember so much more.

Sam took me to Greenwich Village. We walked and walked, ate a meal somewhere. We must have, but what I remember was my constant awareness of his blackness and my whiteness. I could feel other people's eyes on us even when they weren't looking. I remember Stuart's hand reaching for mine at an intersection. Aware, too, of my need to let go of his hand on the other side of the street.

I wasn't his girlfriend. I needed others to know. I couldn't be. I didn't love him in that way. That was part of the struggle.

What gift did you receive that meant more than you were ready for?

As Charlotte read her response to the prompt ***Black Prince Tomatoes, Black Bread, Basil, and Butter*** *she realized her memory must have been wrong. There was no way she and Sam would have left campus early enough to see the sun rise. It must have been the sun setting on their way home that she saw.*

Does it matter?

Have you ever described something incorrectly and decided to let it go rather than correct yourself?

see us?

I applied for the job because it was work I enjoyed, for an organization I believed in and a boss I liked. Also, I needed the paycheck. I had been in Minneapolis for eight months and was surviving hand-to-mouth on freelance jobs. I had applied for anything I could find -- telemarketing, waitressing, dog-walking, tutoring -- and hardly got a call back. In a university town, I was over-qualified.

So when the associate pastor at the church where Jack was working needed a new admin assistant, I was hopeful I might be a good fit. I contacted Tim. He invited me in for an interview. Then he offered me the part time job.

Church staffs are little like sausage factories. They turn out some tasty products, but the process in the back room can be nasty. Church is all about spiritual life in the context of community. And this community had been broken down by some tough stuff, most of which they'd done to each other. Jack had been called in as a specialist interim pastor. And the church staff was part of the puzzle that needed some help.

I had worked on a church staff with Jack before, in Wisconsin. It is where I'd met him. It is where, in fact, I had fallen in love with him. My first marriage was unraveling at that time. His first marriage had been on secret life-support for years. That is a whole story for another time.

But when Jack came to Minneapolis, the congregation knew he was going through a divorce. When I moved to town and started to show up at church, people started to talk.

People started to talk to each other, of course. Only one or two brave souls talked directly to us. Or rather, they talked to Jack. I heard nothing. But I saw everyone. I saw everyone greet me for the first time with that wide open generous midwestern hospitality. I saw bright and articulate church leaders meet me for the first time, have sincere conversations with me, invite me to participate in their community in very specific ways. And then, I could see when the rumor had gotten to them. They stopped making eye contact. They found ways to avoid me. Their conversations would go silent when I walked into a room.

I haven't thought about this painful period for almost two years.

When did you take a job that led you somewhere you didn't think you could go? When have you been talked about behind your back? What did you do to cause it? What didn't you do to cause it?

Selective hearing. Despite the fact that I am making an effort to get out and about… to reintegrate myself in the community, I see everyone and hear nothing.

After walking the Camino de Santiago, I came home… if not transformed… I came home in a bubble of goodwill and serenity. My first act was to resign from the community boards on which I served. I did not want to be tied down, and I did not want to expose myself to toxic conflict.

The five-week pilgrimage across Northern Spain taxed my body, but I thrilled to the spaciousness that comes with walking, reflection, and landscape. Most of all, awash in the friendliness of other pilgrims, each on a quest for inner peace, my heart expanded. Metaphorically I felt a mother's embrace in the warmth of strangers who did not share my language or culture. Politics never came up.

What I have found after my return is that it has been difficult to maintain the Zen-like equanimity I gained. Removing myself from local, state, national and international political dissention has been hard. I try to limit my in-take of national and international news. And yet, lying near a nest of wasps or a hill of ants, you are apprehensive – always waiting to be under attack.

I have also found that my listening skills have deteriorated. I think that I am more and more selective about what I make an effort to remember. I can be in a casual conversation, and I am aware of smiling, nodding, and questioning, but a week later… sometimes days later, I can't remember the details of the conversation.

Obviously, I am not living in-the-moment; rather, I am living in the past. I float in a bubble – afraid that it will break.

Where did you come back from that left you lost in your own life?

Summer Camp

'Summer' is a beautiful word. It conjures up thoughts of vacation, camp, Lake Winnepesaukee, skinny dipping whenever possible, the Moompah – my grandfather's double engine Chris Craft Cruiser that we were allowed to ski behind once a summer, a boat that made a dangerous wake behind it, a wake so big it was thrilling to cross it, jump over it, leap off of it, always with the possibility of a painful fall if I didn't land just right. And sometimes I'd slalom, just like mom. Right leg solidly in the rubber foot cup as I pulled the left foot away from its ski, leaving it near the dock as Moompah zoomed by, everyone on land screaming with enthusiasm, Moompah with his hat, his pipe, his Aqua Velvet, smiling because this was one special day. The left ski fell off as my loose foot slipped into the rubber cup in the back of the right ski. Lean into the back foot, slice the water, watch the wake, gather courage and go – go fast across the hill of water, landing, bent knees, bent elbows to absorb the shock. Crouch. Let the boat pull me across the second wake landing on the far side, the rough water of the harbor to navigate now. Around and around Moompah would drive until we were back at the dock. I'd let go, sink into the lake as the boat turned around to pick up the next eager skier.

Mom could slalom off the dock. Mom can do anything. I didn't think about it then. She was my mom. Whatever mom did was what all mothers did: field hockey into her 50s, slalom skiing until 1985 when they sold the boat, the house, and all the history none of us could afford to hold onto. Tennis still at 86. Voting Chairperson in her town, 16 hours a day at least once a year on election day.

Physics teacher – her decision to start over after 20+ years of professional motherhood.

Mom.

What will life be like without you?

I don't lean on you in every day life. I don't call you with my problems (although you always know when I need you, you hear the quiver in my voice, you always know everything before I do). I don't do things with you – shopping or gardening or driving you to the doctor. I don't go to the grocery store for you or take you to see your friends. You've never needed or wanted any of that. But knowing you're there, knowing I have my mom, that there's you out there, caring, watching, loving me no matter what. I've relied on that. I've needed that. What will happen to me when I don't have that anymore?

for my mom

tell us about your mother

Scrambled Eggs

Midway on Life's Journey

Tell me what you saw

Whenever I see the words 'scrambled eggs' I think of the song "Yesterday." Supposedly the Beatles sang the words "scrambled eggs" instead of "yesterday" until they wrote the final lyric. I also think of my grandparents' kitchen in New Hampshire. Every morning somebody cooked scrambled eggs and bacon. The whole house smelled like breakfast and I remember how happy I was there.

What's the first thing that comes to mind when you think of your grandparents?

I loved my grandmother's scrambled eggs. Mamaw made them in bacon grease. She invited me into them with her Southern accent: "Baby? Ya'll want some breakfast? Some scrambled eggs? Bacon?" I always said 'yes.'

I can still smell Mamaw's house, how when you came in the back door you walked into a laundry room that smelled of Tide laundry detergent. A clothesline strung across it, one end to the other, the room thick with warm air from the dryer and that soapy smell.

I miss my grandmother. She started to go downhill while I was in college. I went to see her with my mother—missing days of class and taking the B instead of the A because it was worth it to see her. She died in 1989, four years after I graduated, just a couple months after my son was born. He wore a little tuxedo sleeper to her funeral. I also bought him an orange sleeper with a jack-o-lantern on the tummy because she was buried around Halloween.

My grandmothers' ankles were as wide as her calves, the tops of her feet swollen and pushing out of her shoes. She always wore dresses and stockings. I loved her little laugh—more of a "tee hee" that floated up than a boisterous laugh that filled the room. She was married to a sad, dark man—my grandfather, who I called "Papaw." When I was little he tickled me inside my panties when my mom and grandmother weren't around. I laughed, but I knew I shouldn't. I was 4, maybe. I'd sit on his lap and he tickled me all over, under my armpits, down my belly, and then his hand slipped into my panties. It's the only time I really saw him smile or heard him laugh. Mostly when we visited he said little and read or talked to my mother.

I always wondered if he molested my mother, if he were the reason she drank. I never told her he tickled me like that. I didn't want to trouble her and I didn't know how to ask if anything like that happened to her when she was a child.

My grandfather loved to read. In his attic were boxes of books about a cartoon character named Pogo. I liked to look at those books, which smelled musty from being up in the attic for so long. I liked that I knew some of the words.

In my grandparents' bathroom, my sisters and I took baths together, two at a time. We loved to look through the glass shower doors, which were opaque and made our eyes look blurry. That made us laugh.

My grandparents' home was tiny and brick and in Memphis, Tennessee. I loved to visit them because spring had already come to their yard and was still a good couple of weeks away in Iowa. We'd load up the station wagon with all of us—eight if Dad went, too. Between the suitcases and kids and pillows and blankets, I don't know how my parents could see to drive.

I loved those trips. I loved my Mamaw and her scrambled eggs.

What did you call your grandma? What did she wear? How 'bout your other grandma? Did they cook anything special for you? Something you didn't like but they made you eat?

Tonight I pulled up an address on Google Maps and I'll tell you what I saw. I saw my old house. The photo was taken in January 2015.

Now I'm trying to recall what I was doing during that time. I look at the picture again and imagine that I might be inside my living room having lunch or maybe I'm in the back working in the office. The living room window is open about six inches and all the other windows are closed so it must be cool outside.

Looking at this picture of my home is like looking at a picture of a family member. My house took care of me and provided safety and shelter for 15 years. I loved coming home. I look at this picture and think of happy memories. Little did I know then that I was about to go through the most turbulent time of my life. At the time, I didn't know that Brian and I would sell that house six months later, that I would leave my hometown and my husband behind.

When I look at that house I see happiness, contentment, joy, laughter, family, friends and comfort. I see all the love we put into the house. I remember the extensive renovations. I remember Brian taking every window out, sanding them down and painting them, and then repairing the ropes on each one so they would go up and down smoothly. I remember designing the front iron gate, picking out the tiles around the door and the paint colors. I remember the care he took in choosing every plant, tree and flower in our yard. From the little brass bell at the front door to the verde green mailbox, to the herringbone pattern in the old Chicago brick walkway, we chose every detail. I miss that house. I miss my life. I would give anything to go back in time and live one more day – as a happy couple – in that house.

That house represents my marriage and the life my husband and I built together, from scratch, and the love we shared with one another.

What happened to that man? Why can't I have him back? Why was he taken from me? Everything was taken from me. Now all I have is a photograph and my memories.

What do you have left?

The sun shining bright and the wind chimes on the front porch moving this way and that with the wind. That same wind that swirled around the house and picked up and dropped off shingle after shingle in the front and back yards. I'll tell you what I saw (and heard) on the road that passes in front of the house—a car, just one, towing a trailer-sized horse carrier only its emptiness rattled around inside and left a hollowness behind, right there on the road.

Did I tell you I saw the effects of silence on my city ears? I didn't feel it though I guess that seems like the way it should have been. I saw it happen over the past two years as the grass grew up. The wind through the blades would tickle my eardrums a little in spring and rise to a thumping sound as the blades seemed to fill out and the wind had to wind around and through. I could see the 'o's' as the wind touched the blades in the full heat of summer and 'ee's' as it thinned in the fall.

I'll tell you what I saw that day, that last day before the neighbor moved in. In the distance, across the pond, I watched the ducks settle within it, saw with my mind's eye the fluttering of their webbed feet holding them atop the water. They floated in rhythm with the pearlescent green algae one just as pretty as the other. There in the pond I saw unison, the way nature sits with itself and finds a peaceful moment.

When do you remember hearing silence?

What I first see is the long, green tunnel of the Appalachian Trail, a tangle of fecund growth. Over growth and under. Dense. Intimate or maybe cloying in a way the wide western landscape is not.

What I saw first, and see next, is distance. Wide, hard space almost impossible to compass with the unaccustomed imagination. Not just the green squares of the midwest, its gently rolling ground marked off by country roads, farm houses, shelter belts of trees and water towers over high school football fields. But something all together bigger.

Rocks catching in clouds. Jagged runs of scree over cliffs. Miles of exposure. Dusty air. Dry ground. A wilderness of oppressive distance instead of a wilderness of suffocating tangle.

What am I midway across? And what do I see from here? It would take a book to tell that, including the landscapes, but also the smaller, ordinary things in front of me, seen clearly, almost fresh.

For instance, all my life I have eaten scrambled eggs, but there is enormous variety in that. My mother's early eggs — dry and crumbly. Then the kind they served at camp — watery and tasteless. But how rich they can be, cooked in too much butter and not over-done. Or the technique, apparently ancient, from culinary France: whisking eggs over a double-boiler with with butter! Hard to believe the tender, custardy result has anything at all to do with summer camp variety I ate at Camp Okaboji.

So here is what I see I'm seeing — here at the midway point to something: that trees have endless moods and big rocks that can kill you just as easily as you can carry a small one in your pocket. That scrambled eggs can make you afraid to swallow. Or they can slip down your throat like pudding.

What I see is that even if the view never changes for the next half of life, there will never be an end to seeing as long as I am willing to look.

What did you see in the distance? What was under your feet?

These pages are for notes, doodles, ideas, overflow, whatever you need. Fill 'em up!

When I respond to prompts, I almost always write in first person. It's personal and memoir-esque. I'm guessing you might respond to prompts that way too. Here are some issues that many memoirists struggle with:

Don't let forgetting the facts keep you from writing the truth. None of us remember verbatim the irritating conversation we had with our mom when we got home late from the prom. The dialogue you re-create is meant to give the reader the essence of your conversation: mom's exasperation the way she would have expressed it, your snippy response the way you would have mumbled it.

Often the truth as we see it is different from the truth as our siblings or parents sees it. This can keep you from writing, too. The word 'memoir' comes from the same Latin root ('*memoria*') as 'memory.' Needless to say, our memories are inherently flawed. If I tell a story about how the family dog ate the couch when we were kids, it's going to be different than my brother's account of the same dog and couch. Both versions are true. Write yours. Let your brother write his.

Recently I had to edit a story I'd written that involved something my husband did many, many years ago and which eventually involved me. I wrestled with how to be sure I didn't trespass on his privacy. I weighed it and weighed it. In the end, I scrapped the story. My sharing it wasn't worth the worry of wondering if I'd trespassed, and I didn't want to give him the power to decide for me. It was a nice story too, painted him in a very good light, but in the end it was his story to tell, not mine. I wrote another story instead. The important thing is to write the story, then decide if you want to share it or not.

If you're thinking about writing a book you're probably asking yourself, *where do I start? How do I end?* The best advice I ever got from another writer was "start in the middle." Our memories aren't chronological so why would our stories have to be? Start somewhere. Start with the story that you feel like writing today. Finish it tomorrow or the next day then write another story that you feel like writing. Worry about how it will all fit together when you don't have any more stories to tell. When you finally put it all together, that'll probably be your first draft. Then get ready for your second, your third, and your fourth. When I was writing *The Present Giver*, I made a list of all the stories I knew I'd eventually want to tell. On a day when I couldn't think of anything to write, I looked at my list and wrote the story that jumped out at me that day. It worked.

Whether you're self-publishing or presenting your work to an agent or publisher, ask trusted readers to take a look before you submit. Don't ask your mom, your spouse, or your best friend. Often these people have too much power over your decision-making. Ask writers you admire who don't know you well, or regular people who read a lot and don't know you well. See what comments they offer. See if multiple readers make the same comments. Be careful, though. They may not be right. But if a number of people say the same thing you might want to reevaluate. Ultimately, though, you're the judge of what's working or not. Trust thyself.

Before you start a project be clear about what you want to write and why. Write it down and remember your reasons as you write. If you're writing to inspire others to climb the Himalayas the way you did, make your stories inspiring. Don't skip the scary parts, or the parts where you doubted yourself. If you're writing the same book for climbers who have already done extreme climbs, maybe you include more technical details, or the special supplies the reader will need. One book is meant to inspire, the other is meant to educate. Different books. Different innards. If you know why you're writing something it'll help you decide what to keep and what to discard.

Find a way to make writing something you look forward to rather that a chore you have to do.

Have fun with it. Love, Bar

Bar Scott leads writing workshops in Colorado and New York.
She also coaches writers and songwriters in person,
by phone, and via skype.
She often prefers the results
when she writes or hums something quickly
and without much time to think.

Published writing includes her memoir,
The Present Giver (ALM Books , 2011),
"Grace" from *Stories of Music, Volume One* (Timbre Press, 2015)
and "Valentine" from *Three Minus One,* (SheWritesPress, 2014)
She has recorded seven albums of original words and music,
and has published over 70 songs.

For more information visit www.barscott.com,
or email her at bar@barscott.com

If your writing group would like multiple copies of this
or any of Bar's other books or CDs,
contact ALM Books for a discount. *Thank you!*

Recommended Reading:
Art and Fear, Ted Orland and David Bayles,
What it Is, Lynda Barry
If You Want to Write, Brenda Ueland,
Thinking About Memoir, Abigail Thomas,
On Writing, Stephen King,
"Place" an essay by Dorothy Allison

The Lone Writer's Writing Club, Volume 1,
Published by ALM Books
POB 576, Westcliffe, CO 81252 USA p:719 371 0228

Bar Scott, Editor and organizer

Cover Design: Erin Papa at The Turning Mill, Palenville, NY.
(With help from someone who always makes me smile, Lucy Swenson)

Photo of Bar ©J.E. Ward

31125580R00097

Made in the USA
Middletown, DE
19 April 2016

Made in the USA
Middletown, DE
19 April 2016